D1550089

William Cook is the author of *Ha Bloody Ha – Comedians Talking*. He has worked for the BBC, and written for the *Mail on Sunday* and the *Guardian*.

The Comedy Store

The Club that Changed British Comedy

WILLIAM COOK

LITTLE, BROWN AND COMPANY

A *Little, Brown* Book

First published in Great Britain by Little, Brown in 2001

Copyright © William Cook, 2001
Foreword © Don Ward, 2001

The moral right of the author has been asserted.

All rights reserved.
No part of this publication may be reproduced, stored in a retrieval system, or
transmitted, in any form or by any means without the prior permission in writing
of the publisher, nor be otherwise circulated in any form of binding or cover other
than that in which it is published and without a similar condition including
this condition being imposed on the subsequent purchaser.

A CIP catalogue record for this book is available from the British Library.

ISBN 0 316 85792 0

Typeset in Berkeley by M Rules
Printed and bound in Great Britain by Butler & Tanner Ltd, Frome and London

Little, Brown and Company (UK)
Brettenham House
Lancaster Place
London WC2E 7EN

'To be anonymous and travelling in an interesting place is an intoxication'

Paul Theroux, **The Kingdom by the Sea**

PEOPLE WHO REGULARLY EXERCISE THEIR FACE MUSCLES CAN EXPECT TO DELAY MIDDLE AGE SAGGING BY TEN YEARS.

Eva Fraser
THE FACIAL WORKOUT STUDIO.

PICCADILLY CIRCUS

A SERIOUS NIGHT OUT

Contents

Who's Who

A guide to some of the people who appear in this book

TERRY ALDERTON Comedian. Former Redcoat and Southend United FC goalkeeper

KEITH ALLEN Actor and comedian

TONY ALLEN Comedian. Founder member of Alternative Cabaret. Probably invented the term Alternative Comedy

CLIVE ANDERSON Comedian and broadcaster. Hosted *Whose Line Is It Anyway?*

MARK ARDEN Actor and comedian. One half of double act The Oblivion Boys with Steve Frost

DAVID BADDIEL Comedian, broadcaster and novelist

ANDREW BAILEY Performance artist. Stage manager at The Gargoyle

BILL BAILEY Comedian, musician and actor. Used to be half of a double act, The Rubber Bishops

ROBIN BANKS Comedian. Played the opening night of The Store

JIM BARCLAY Comedian and actor. Founder member of Alternative Cabaret

ARJ BARKER American comedian. Won Perrier Best Newcomer in 1997

CHRIS BARRIE Comedian, actor, impressionist. Starred in *Red Dwarf* and *The Brittas Empire*

MARK BILLINGHAM Comedian and novelist

RICHARD BLACKWOOD British comedian and musician with his own TV show

SIMON BLIGH Comedian. A regular compere at The Store

ADAM BLOOM Comedian

BOB BOYTON Comedian. A founder member of The Cutting Edge

JO BRAND Comedienne. Used to be a psychiatric nurse

ARNOLD BROWN Scottish accountant turned comedian. Gonged off on the opening night of The Comedy Store. Won the Perrier Award in 1987

ED BYRNE Irish comedian and actor

OTIZ CANNELONI Comic magician

SCOTT CAPURRO American actor and comedian. Won Perrier Best Newcomer in 1994

TIM CLARK Comedian. One of The Comedy Store's top comperes

JULIAN CLARY Comedian. Used to be billed as The Joan Collins Fan Club

SIMON CLAYTON Comedian. Formerly one half of double act The Crisis Twins. Has guested with The Comedy Store Players

DAVE COHEN Comedian and broadcaster. Founder member of The Comedy Store Players

PAT CONDELL Comedian and writer. Brother of Martin Coyote. Founder member of The Cutting Edge

JOHN CONNOR Journalist and producer. Founder of The Cutting Edge

LEE CORNES Actor and comedian. Played the opening night of The Store

PHIL CORNWELL Actor, comedian and impressionist. Appears in *Stella Street*

MARTIN COYOTE Comedian. Brother of Pat Condell. Regular Cutting Edge performer

PHIL DAVEY Australian comedian. Used to be a butler to the British aristocracy

ALAN DAVIES Comedian and actor. Star of *Jonathan Creek*

ALI DAY Former Store stage manager. Married to Kevin Day

KEVIN DAY Comedian. Married to Ali Day

JACK DEE Comedian

ANDY DE LA TOUR Actor and comedian. Founder member of Alternative Cabaret

HUGH DENNIS Actor and comedian. Starred in *The Mary Whitehouse Experience*

FELIX DEXTER The first Black British comedian to perform regularly at The Store

DEBI DURST American comedienne. Has performed with The Comedy Store Players. Married to Will Durst

WILL DURST American comedian. Ran for mayor of San Francisco

JENNY ECLAIR Comedienne and novelist. The only female Perrier Award winner (1995)

ADRIAN EDMONDSON Comedian and actor. Vyvyan in *The Young Ones*. Married to Jennifer Saunders

BEN ELTON Comedian, novelist, playwright and screenwriter

LEE EVANS Comedian and movie star

SIMON EVANS Comedian

Alexei Sayle

Ben Elton

SIMON FANSHAWE Comedian, journalist and broadcaster. Won the Perrier Award in 1989

CRAIG FERGUSON Scottish comedian and actor

CHARLES FLEISCHER American comedian and comic actor. The voice of Roger Rabbit

DAWN FRENCH Comedienne and actress. Star of *The Vicar of Dibley*. Married to Lenny Henry

STEPHEN FROST Actor and comedian. Frequent performer with The Comedy Store Players. One half of double act The Oblivion Boys, with Mark Arden

KEVIN GILDEA Irish comedian. Founder member of Irish sketch troupe Mr Trellis

RONNIE GOLDEN Musician and comedian

BOOTHBY GRAFFOE The only comedian named after a market town in Lincolnshire

JEFF GREEN Comedian

TONY GREEN Comedian

SIMON GRENVILLE Performer and friend of performance artist Andrew Bailey

STEVE GRIBBIN Comic guitarist. Regular performer with The Cutting Edge

RICKY GROVER Actor and comedian. Ex-boxer and hairdresser.

MIKE GUNN Comedian. Used to do his act dressed as an undertaker.

RICH HALL American comedian and writer. Veteran of *Letterman* and *Saturday Night Live*. Won the Perrier Award in 2000

NICK HANCOCK Comedian and broadcaster. Hosts *They Think It's All Over*

KEVIN HAYES Irish comedian

MALCOLM HARDEE Possible inventor of the term Alternative Comedy. Founder member of The Greatest Show On Legs. Runs comedy club Up The Creek

JEREMY HARDY Comedian, broadcaster and journalist. Married to Kit Hollerbach

WENDY HARMER Australian comedienne. The first woman to compere The Store

AINSLEY HARRIOTT Former performer and chef. Now a performing chef

HATTIE HAYRIDGE Comedienne, writer, actress and broadcaster. Starred in *Red Dwarf*

JOHN HEGLEY Comedian and poet

LENNY HENRY Comedian and actor. Married to Dawn French

PHIL HERBERT Actor and variety artiste. Played The Store as Randolph The Remarkable and Hubert Haddock

RAINER HERSCH Musical comedian. Used to be in a double act called The Tebbits.

HARRY HILL Comedian. Used to be a doctor. Won Perrier Best Newcomer in 1992

DOMINIC HOLLAND Comedian. Won Perrier Best Newcomer in 1993

KIT HOLLERBACH American comedienne. Founder member of The Comedy Store Players. Married to Jeremy Hardy

PIERRE HOLLINS Musical comedian

SEAN HUGHES Irish comedian, actor, novelist and poet. Won the Perrier Award in 1990 when he was still in his early twenties

REGINALD D. HUNTER American actor who became a comedian in Britain

LEE HURST Comedian. Used to star in *They Think It's All Over*. Runs The Backyard comedy club

MICKEY HUTTON Comedian. A regular compere at The Store

EDDIE IZZARD Comedian and actor

PAUL JACKSON Produced *The Young Ones*, *Red Dwarf* and *Three Of A Kind*. Subsequent BBC Controller of Entertainment

JANE JANOVIC Actress and comedienne. Phil Herbert's partner in their fish-juggling and fire-eating double act, Hilary & Hubert Haddock

JOCELYN JEE Black British actress and comedienne

DAVE JOHNS Geordie comedian. Former building-site bricklayer.

MILTON JONES Actor and comedian. Won Perrier Best Newcomer in 1996

PHILL JUPITUS Comedian. Team captain on *Never Mind The Buzzcocks*

PETER KAY Comedian and actor. Wrote and starred in *Phoenix Nights*

MARIA KEMPINSKA Founder of the Jongleurs chain of comedy clubs

KIM KINNIE Ex-strip-club choreographer and The Store's erstwhile booker and unofficial artistic director

DANIEL KITSON Comedian

MANDY KNIGHT Actress and comedienne. Appeared in Jo Brand's TV series, *Like It Or Lump It*

MARK LAMARR Comedian and broadcaster. Hosts *Never Mind The Buzzcocks*

BURT LAURENT Producer and co-founder of In The House

JOSIE LAWRENCE Actress and comedienne. Member of The Comedy Store Players

DENIS LEARY American actor and comedian

JENNY LECOAT Comedienne turned scriptwriter

HELEN LEDERER Actress and comedienne. Appeared in *Absolutely Fabulous*

JOHN LENAHAN American comic magician. Regular compere at Leicester Square Store

SEAN LOCK Comedian and writer. Writes for Mark Lamarr

NORMAN LOVETT Comedian. Starred in *Red Dwarf*

CHRIS LYNAM Anarchic clown and street performer

JOHN MANN Comedian and regular Store compere

PATRICK MARBER Comedian turned playwright, director and actor

Richard Blackwood

Nick Hancock

RIK MAYALL Comedian and actor. Rick in *The Young Ones*

SIMON McBURNEY Actor and director. Played the opening night of The Store

KEVIN McCARTHY Comedian, aka The Man With The Beard. Used to be a lorry driver

ALISTAIR McGOWAN Actor, comedian and impressionist.

JOHN McGRATH Stage manager at The Store

OSCAR McLENNAN Performance artist and author. Founder member of Alternative Cabaret

DONNA McPHAIL Comedienne

MIKE McSHANE American actor and comedian. Has performed with The Comedy Store Players, and on *Whose Line Is It Anyway?*

PAULINE MELVILLE Actress and comedienne turned novelist. Founder member of Alternative Cabaret

SEAN MEO Comedian. Former full-time snooker player

PAUL MERTON Comedian and broadcaster. Team captain on *Have I Got News For You*. A founder member of The Comedy Store Players

BOB MILLS Comedian and television presenter. One of the top comperes at the Leicester Square Store

MICKY MILLS Comedian. Played the opening night of The Store

JOHN MOLONEY Comedian

TONY MOREWOOD Comedian

RICHARD MORTON Musical comedian. A founder member of The Cutting Edge

NEIL MULLARKEY Actor and comedian. Founder member of The Comedy Store Players

MIKE MYERS Actor, comedian and movie star, whose films include *Wayne's World* and *Austin Powers*. Founder member of The Comedy Store Players

STAN NELSON Stage manager at The Store

ROBERT NEWMAN Comedian and novelist

OWEN O'NEILL Northern Irish comedian, poet, actor, screenwriter and playwright

BOB PEYTON Helped compere the opening night of The Store

NIGEL PLANER Comedian, actor and writer. Neil in *The Young Ones*

ROGER POMPHREY Film-maker, friend of Keith Allen

MARTIN POTTER Friend and flatmate of Malcolm Hardee. Performed in The Greatest Show On Legs

GREG PROOPS American comedian. Has guested with The Comedy Store Players

STEVE PUNT Comedian, broadcaster, writer. Starred in *The Mary Whitehouse Experience*

Jo Brand

MICHAEL REDMOND Irish comedian

NICK REVELL Comedian, broadcaster, novelist. Founder member of The Cutting Edge

PETER RICHARDSON Comedian, actor, writer and director. Created The Comic Strip

PETER ROSENGARD Life-insurance salesman and co-founder of The Store

ASHLEY ROY Friend of Peter Rosengard. Helped set up The Store

JERRY SADOWITZ Scottish comedian and magician

JENNIFER SAUNDERS Comedienne, actress and writer. Star and creator of *Absolutely Fabulous*. Married to Adrian Edmondson

ALEXEI SAYLE Comedian, columnist and author. The Comedy Store's first compere. Founder member of Alternative Cabaret

JOHN SIMMIT Black British comedian, actor and promoter. Founded black comedy agency Upfront, and plays Dipsy in *Teletubbies*

MARCUS SIMMONS Compere of In The House

LEE SIMPSON Actor and comedian. Member of The Comedy Store Players

MARK SKEETE Bouncer, babysitter and backstage Store superstar

TONY SLATTERY Actor and comedian. Won the first ever Perrier Award with The Cambridge Footlights (1981). Performs with The Comedy Store Players

ANDY SMART Actor and comedian. A frequent performer with The Comedy Store Players

MICHAEL SMILEY Northern Irish comedian

ARTHUR SMITH Comedian, playwright, columnist, broadcaster. One of The Store's top comperes

JO JO SMITH Comedienne. Used to work for pop group Dexy's Midnight Runners

MARTIN SOAN Comedian and performance artist. Co-founder of Malcolm Hardee's sketch troupe, The Greatest Show On Legs

VIVIENNE SOAN Musician. Married to Martin Soan. Performer and punter at all three Stores

JAY SODAGAR Comedian

DAVE SPIKEY Comedian, writer, actor. Writes and performs with Peter Kay in *Phoenix Nights*

MARK STEEL Comedian, broadcaster, journalist and author

STEVE STEEN Actor and comedian. Frequent performer with The Comedy Store Players

JIM SWEENEY Actor and comedian. Member of The Comedy Store Players

JIM TAVARE. Comedian. Does a double act with a double bass

DAVID TENNANT Founded The Gargoyle, the club where The Store began

MARK THOMAS Comedian, writer and broadcaster. Star of investigative comedy show *The Mark Thomas Product*. Writes for *The New Statesman*.

JOHN THOMSON Actor and comedian, as seen in *The Fast Show* and *Cold Feet*.

PAUL THORNE Comedian. Regular member of The Cutting Edge

TOM TICKELL Financial journalist. Played The Store's opening night

SANDI TOKSVIG Actress, comedienne, novelist, broadcaster. Played opening night of The Store

PAUL TONKINSON Comedian. Has presented *The Big Breakfast*

RICHARD VRANCH Actor, writer and comedian. A member of The Comedy Store Players

CURTIS WALKER Comedian and In The House regular

DON WARD Co-founder and producer/managing director of The Comedy Store

RUBY WAX American actress, comedienne and broadcaster

SUKI WEBSTER Actress and comedienne. Frequent performer with The Comedy Store Players

ROBIN WILLIAMS American actor, comedian and movie star. Has made several impromptu appearances at The Store

NICK WILTY Globetrotting comedian. Served in the Falklands

GINA YASHERE Comedienne

PAUL ZENON Comic magician

Foreword

It seems like only yesterday, although one's memories have faded. Reading William Cook's painstakingly researched biography of The Comedy Store has revived them vividly. When I took to the stage to introduce the very first show at midnight on 19 May 1979 while Peter Rosengard looked on quaffing my champagne, I little realised that I was embarking on a journey that would take me from Soho by way of Leicester Square to Piccadilly. Nor did I guess how much The Comedy Store would consume me, heart and soul. 'Good evening everybody and welcome to London's Alternative night out. Before I introduce you to your compere, Alexei Sayle, I have an important announcement to make. Would the owner of the Sinclair C5 parked outside the club please remove it immediately as a rat is trying to drag it into a storm drain.' Thankfully the many jokes that followed over the years drew more laughs than that one! They knew straightaway that I was not 'alternative'. In my youth I had spent ten years as a stand-up on the variety circuit living out of a Ford Escort, wearing a dress suit with flares. My time was up, a new generation was about to explode on to an unsuspecting public.

Reprising the birth of the puking, mewling infant conceived by the unlikely coupling of an insurance salesman and a sometime comic and strip club owner, is a thought-provoking exercise. Discovering the reminiscences of those who were in the delivery room at 69 Dean Street, Soho is a gratifying if sometimes salutary experience. I do not always agree that events transpired as some may recollect. However, pragmatic in the knowledge that everyone sees things differently, I shall not quibble!

When Peter Rosengard and I began nursing our creation, I was not a first time mother, but a seasoned matron in the business of entertainment. Introduced at a weekend garden party in Hampshire, Rosengard and I fell to discussing the comedy scene in America. We had both been knocked out by the incisive and raw humour to be found at a club in L.A. Gritty and entertaining, it had held us both spellbound. There was nothing to compare with it this side of the pond. I told him that I had a club in Soho with a spare room. He said, 'Let's do it'. We would give it six weeks. We put £500 each into a kitty as working capital. If it worked, we would be on to a winner. If not, well not such a great loss and it would be great fun trying. For a couple of years we ran that crazy venue against the odds. Rosengard, used to the fast returns of the world of insurance, wanted it to run before it took its first faltering steps. He was unwilling to invest more. I knew that investment, nurture and devotion would encourage growth and character and balanced books! We parted and I, left holding the baby, was determined not to let it fade away and die. The struggle to raise The Comedy Store to a sturdy adult has been fraught with difficulties. Along with those, however, came the joy and infinite pleasure of discovering the great comic talents of whom you shall read in these pages. I have also made many dear friends for which I am truly grateful.

There is a body of opinion that says that nothing can recapture the excitement of those thrusting and eager exponents of the new alternative comedy scene to be found on stage in the early days. My view is that to repeat that experience one would be obliged to re-live a three-day week, miners' strikes and poll tax riots. You can't go back in time. Evolution is as natural to comedy as any other species. After all, those same struggling young comics, raging against the establishment, are now leading mostly upper middle-class lives, some with several million in the bank. Think Ben Elton, French and Saunders, Rik Mayall, Ade Edmondson *et al*. Still, with New Labour in charge, we're all capitalists now!

However, there will never be a shortage of social injustice to be scathing about and the comics of today will always find meat to chew on and spit out in shards, piercing the pomposity of politicians, the inanities of celebrities and the latest *cause célèbre*. They do it with the same lust to be heard, just in the style of the twenty-first century. They do it every night in Piccadilly and four nights a week in our new venue in Manchester. I am proud to have brought so many talents to the great British public. I am about to shake the comedic tree again in the fashion of the original venue, with the introduction of '…King Gong!' once a month at the Manchester Store and in London in the new year. Once more there will be an opportunity for those who have never set foot on the stage to tread the boards at the Store.

I could not have done it without the loyalty and hard work of my longstanding and able team of lieutenants, led by my dear friend, fellow Tottenham supporter (read, sufferer) and most astute financial advisor, Phil Newton. Kim Kinnie, who, in the early days at Leicester Square, took the reins to the manner born, when I needed to spend time with my growing family. My general managers, Barbara Herbin and Wendy Frediani, whose expertise and stringent administration have helped to make The Comedy Store a total entertainment experience. My wife Sylvie and wonderful children, Nathalie, Sebastien and Charlotte whose love and support have been my rock. A more recent recruit to the team, Charlotte Foley, is skilfully creating another string to my bow, running the fledgling management agency. In Manchester, my young team of Paul Home, Heidi Mavir and Andy Waddington. To all my dedicated staff, both in London and Manchester, I salute you. I must also thank Manchester City Council for their welcome and their confidence in entrusting the city's Millennium New Year entertainment to us. They have also endowed the first Manchester Comedy Festival in the autumn of 2001.

Most of all, of course, I thank those brave, sometimes foolhardy, certainly dogged beings, the comedians. In these pages you will discover their own experiences of the perils and rewards of the live performance. The dejection of failure, the ecstasy of standing in the spotlight in front of a room full of rolling laughter, knowing you have cracked it at the Store and made four hundred people ache with pleasure.

I was asked to write some anecdotes of my own for this foreword, but William Cook and the participants in the rich pageant that is the history of The Comedy Store have done it far more eloquently than I ever could. I hope you will enjoy it as much as I have.

Don Ward
Proprietor/Producer

Introduction

'Good evening and welcome to The Comedy Store. Before introducing your compere for tonight, we would like to point out that whilst witty and constructive heckling has always been a tradition at The Comedy Store – and is still welcome – mindless, rude and abusive remarks disrupt and spoil the show for 99 per cent of the audience who want to be entertained. Anyone indulging in this kind of negative behaviour will be asked to leave. Thank you.'

You won't hear this sanctimonious warning at The Store nowadays, but once upon a time the stage manager was supposed to read it out over the PA before every show. Today, it survives only in a forlorn, handwritten note stuck onto the front cover of a fifteen-year-old desk diary. If anyone tried reading it out tonight, after midnight, they'd probably be shouted down before they began.

This is a book about the club that changed British comedy. How it changed it depends on who you ask. I've asked comics, punters and bouncers and they all have a different answer. There are always several sides to any good story, and I reckon the closest you'll come to the truth about this place is via a murky cocktail of them all. Not even the most dedicated comedy ligger has been here every night, and any collective memory is already out of date. Older comics who no longer play here buff up their recollections with revisionist polish; acts who still play here are honing fresh anecdotes; and younger comedians I've never heard of are already building reputations. Or at least they should be, if The Store has any sort of future. 'You have your time and then the next lot come along,' says Lee Hurst, who was once the new kid on this particular block himself. 'And some of them will be a lot better than us.'

Several comedians told me this book would prise open a can of worms. One comic even likened it to walking a high wire without a safety net. I felt rather flattered by such a melodramatic metaphor, but I reckon he was taking the whole thing a bit too far. It's performers who take real risks, not writers. Writers write books about all sorts of things – the rise and fall of the Roman Empire, the Conservative Party, even Manchester City Football Club. The Store is only a comedy club, after all.

But it's a rather special comedy club, and what makes it so special is the comics. 'Success, Adulation, Power' reads an advert for Caroline's, New York's top comedy club, below mugshots of Tim Allen, Jay Leno and Jerry Seinfeld. 'Not when they worked for us.' The Store could run a similar ad, but it wouldn't quite ring true. Certainly, Britain's comic aristocracy worked here before they were famous. The difference is, many of them still do.

'All the top comedians that have gone on to do their own TV shows, like Jo Brand and Mark Thomas, they all still perform here,' says Australian comic Phil Davey. 'You can't say that about any other club in the country.' Household names like Lee Evans, Phill Jupitus and Alan Davies have all played here in the last few years. And the reason they keep coming back is because they have more fun here than anywhere else. 'I know the happiest days of your life are supposed to be your schooldays,' said Davies, 'but for me they happened here.'[1]

Phil Davey calls The Store a cultural and political centre, a meeting place for comics; I interviewed over 150 for this book, and many of them echoed his point of view. A few comics declined to talk to me. I suspect most of them simply felt they had far better things to do, which is fair enough. Comedians don't strive for success in the hope of spending their free time talking to journalists. And so this book is about jobbing comics as much as chat show superstars, and that's just the way it should be. Smaller stars tend to play The Store far more often, and mop up many more funny stories along the way, while a few of the most famous names that folk drop when they talk about The Store's early days actually only played the place a few times. Every comic needs television to reach a nationwide audience, but even in the digital age, there's only really room for a few comics on peaktime TV, and some of the best comedians simply don't translate to the small screen. Stage and screen comedy are two separate genres, and the live stage is the first and final test of every comedian's career.

So although you may not know some of the names in this book (even if you recognise their faces), at least you'll know they're at the sharp end, right here, right now, performing in front of many more punters than any comedians in the past. In fact, one of the real rewards of watching club comedy is discovering comics you haven't already seen on TV, like Richard Blackwood and Peter Kay, who've both become stars since I interviewed them for this book. But what about all the acts who headlined these shows and have since vanished from public view, their whereabouts now unknown to all but a few friends and former colleagues? And the many more who still work the club circuit, familiar faces to a mere handful of stand-up trainspotters? All the wannabes who never were are just as much a part of this story, and they often have the most fascinating tales to tell.

'Playing here is the equivalent of headlining at The Marquee,' says Jo Jo Smith, who worked for Dexy's Midnight Runners before she became a comedienne. 'When a band played there, they knew they were on their way.' It's the same when a comic plays The Store. 'You're talking to your mate who has a normal job, a day job, and you say, "I'm at The Store this weekend",' says Smith. 'You don't even have to say The Comedy Store.' 'If you're headlining The Store and you storm it, then that's as famous as you need to be,' says comedienne Donna McPhail. 'I can talk about what I like. I can be how I like. I can take whatever risks I like. I am director, make-up artist, writer, performer, everything. When you die, it's humiliating because they hate all of it, but when you storm it, it's all you.'

This is a collection of stories from some of the many people who've worked and played at The Store since it opened, twenty-two years ago. I've tried to remain objective, but it would be daft to try and hide the fact that I'm a fan of modern comedy, and, with a few reservations, a fan of The Comedy Store. Comics aren't historians or statisticians (thankfully), and stand-up is a wonderfully ephemeral art form with a healthy disrespect for former glories. Comics' tales are rarely tied to specific dates. They sometimes have a vague idea about what year a gig took place, but that's normally their natural limit. Often, their stories reveal how The Store reflected changes in the wider world, and occasionally they show how The Store helped to inspire a few changes of its own. Yet most of the stories are here because they're entertaining.

This book isn't a conventional history. It's more of a biography, because the true mark of a first-class comedy club is that it eventually acquires a persona that's utterly its own. That plush Jongleurs flagship, becalmed in affluent Battersea; its chic purpose-built offspring in North London's stylish Camden Lock; Malcolm Hardee's irreverent Up The Creek in South-east London; the local intimacy of The Banana in affable Balham; Downstairs At The King's Head in an unassuming corner of Crouch End; Aberdeen's demure yet welcoming little Lemon Tree; Glasgow's Renfrew Ferry, a disused car deck encased in an enormous greenhouse, a floating crystal on the Clyde; The Empire Laughs Back, a boisterous basement beneath an old Presbyterian chapel on Belfast's lively Golden Mile, where bar staff wear white shirts and black bow ties, like croupiers or cruise-ship waiters. Like football clubs, the best comedy clubs can swap players, be bought and sold, even move to new locations, and still somehow maintain their own unique identity.

The Store is still The Store, in Soho, Leicester Square or Piccadilly Circus, in Manchester's Deansgate or even on Hamburg's Reeperbahn. 'The Comedy Store is a concept, rather than the actual building it's in,' says Store stalwart Kevin Day. And although the steep price of its success is that it's inevitably far more mainstream now, like those historic football clubs that have replaced decrepit terraces with slick all-seater stadia, enough of its old anarchic character still survives. 'Life sucks' reads the graffiti inside a Store toilet cubicle, 'but does it spit or swallow?' In a smarter, more conventional club, that would have been painted over years ago.

This book is an attempt to capture that unruly spirit. Perhaps the personality of any comedy club is a composite of every performance that's happened there, down to the very last laugh – even the last heckle. And that's why this book is dedicated to anyone who's ever been brave enough, or foolish enough, or, in most cases, a bit of both, to stand up in this small, spotlit amphitheatre and try to make a cellar full of perfect strangers laugh like old friends. All the people who've ever played here have made The Store what it is. And in a way, it helped make them.

Part One

From Strip Club
to Superstore

Bouncers opening the doors for the night at the Leicester Square Store

Chapter One

'There's a point when you do stand-up comedy where you just know that suddenly, you've created your own world. It's your world, your point of view, your sense of humour. And then you walk up onstage, and you let people come into it. And you're not doing what you think they think is funny. You're not trying to patronise them. You're not even trying to win them over. You're just so confident in what you're doing that they're going to laugh. And then they accept you on your terms. And once you reach that point, then that's probably the point where you can call yourself a comedian.'

Rich Hall[1]

You get off the tube at Piccadilly Circus and walk up the escalator past the beggars, dogs and buskers, and stumble out into a cacophony of dark noise and a kaleidoscope of shrill neon. '*Blast From The Past*' bellows an illuminated sign, tall above the roaring traffic. 'Ben Elton's latest and greatest novel. Out now.' Two decades have passed since Elton compered London's first and foremost modern comedy club, just around the corner. He's just one of a host of celebs who've graduated from this tiny stand-up pulpit to conquer the wider worlds of theatre, novels, TV and the movies. A decade ago, I went to a comedy club in Manhattan called Catch A Rising Star. That showbiz boast would be far too presumptuous for self-effacing Brits, but in a West End basement a short walk away, it would be equally apt.

These streets are strewn with litter, bursting out of dustbins, cascading down the

subway stairwells. Plastic punks and Continental schoolkids sit on the steps around Eros. American and Japanese tourists wrestle with outsize street maps, holding up the human traffic. Dodging between the black cabs and red double deckers, you hurry eastwards, along Coventry Street, towards Leicester Square. But before you reach the piazza you duck down a quiet side street that slopes reluctantly towards the river. After the lurid spectacle of Piccadilly, there's not a lot to look at.

At first, you assume you must have taken a wrong turn, and you're about to retrace your route back towards the more familiar glare of The Trocadero, The Fashion Café and Planet Hollywood, when you spot two solid bouncers standing guard outside a narrow flight of steps that leads down into the bowels of Theatreland. A queue snakes back around the corner, a noticeboard lists the bills for this week's gigs, and a pale neon sign hangs above the door. You've reached The Comedy Store, London's top comedy club, which accidentally kick-started a mutiny in the populist performing arts. 'You didn't need any qualifications,' says Store veteran Jim Tavare. 'You didn't have to wait for the phone to ring. You just got up, thought of a few things to say that day and then went and tried it out.'

Despite its gradual gentrification from hostess club to tourist attraction, The Store is still the West End show from the wrong side of the tracks. Stand outside with your back to its robust black warehouse doors, and look up into the windows where The Store's new offices are hidden away. 'Lord Delfont of Stepney, 1909–1994' reads a small blue plaque, a discreet tribute to the late great impresario. Maybe Comic Heritage should stick up a similar plate outside The Store. Not here, but where it first started, a few hundred yards north by north-west, beyond Shaftesbury Avenue, into Soho. New comedy's unofficial national theatre may have migrated upmarket, but its original home was really rather more illustrious.

In the discontented summertime of 1979, a few weeks after Margaret Thatcher marched into Downing Street, a brand-new kind of comedy club opened its doors in a rented room in the arse end of Soho. This Dean Street tenement housed The Nell Gwynne, a strip club named after King Charles II's most notorious mistress, who slept here, and much else besides, or so local legend has it. Below this den of pay-per-view vice was a topless bar called The Gargoyle. From the Twenties to the Fifties, the famous and infamous gathered to drink and gossip here: Noël Coward, T.S. Eliot, Dylan Thomas, Bertrand Russell, Francis Bacon, Henri Matisse, Graham Greene, George Orwell, H.G. Wells and Virginia Woolf, not to mention Oswald Mosley, Guy Burgess, Donald Maclean and Kim Philby. By the time this comic cuckoo nested here, The Gargoyle's glory days were long gone, but its famous ghosts lingered on. The way inside was tortuous. Up to the fourth-floor Nell Gwynne in a tiny lift, then back downstairs and into the third-floor Gargoyle. Once inside, there was scarcely room for 100 paying punters, and the weird line-up of acts that filed onto its crowded stage were, at best, undiscovered hopefuls, at worst, hopeless amateurs. Yet pretty soon, this claustrophobic venue became the talk of Soho, and over the next few years The Store sparked a revolt that swept through the Light Ent netherworld like an idiotic inferno. Alternative Comedy was radical, irreverent and, above all, very funny. Everything, in other words, that late Seventies Light Ent wasn't. And The Comedy Store was its HQ.

Comparable clubs soon sprouted up all around, and today the circuit it inspired numbers over 100 clubs in London alone. Yet despite stiff competition from nation-wide chains like Jongleurs, provincial venues like Birmingham's Glee Club and Manchester's Buzz Club, plus smaller local stages dotted around every London suburb, The Store remains new comedy's flagship.

The Store was the first new comedy club in London since the closure of Peter Cook's Establishment Club signalled the end of the Sixties satire boom. Billed as 'London's First Satirical Nightclub', The Establishment cultivated the talents of John Bird and John Fortune, and staged the English debut of Lenny Bruce. What goes around comes around. Bird and Fortune now appear on TV with Rory Bremner, a satirist who cut his teeth at The Store's old rival Jongleurs, while Store veteran Eddie Izzard played Bruce in a play called *Lenny* at The Queen's Theatre, just around the corner from The Establishment and the old Soho Store. Cook's club attracted 10,000 members at two guineas a head before it even opened. The Store was never quite as fashionable, consequently never went out of fashion, and so unlike The Establishment it survived to spawn a legion of imitators.

Now, new comedy is everywhere. Like punk rock, pop's parallel Light Ent putsch, its riotous influence has infected every mainstream art form, from movies to adverts.

The comics who went into The Store included frustrated doctors, accountants, barristers, bouncers, strippers and singing telegrams. They came out as actors, presenters, playwrights and novelists, even political commentators. 'You develop skills which are absolutely applicable to a lot of other careers,' says musical comic Rainer Hersch. 'People find their own route out of it.'

And into virtually everything else. As I write, this week's three main West End openings, Al Murray's Pub Landlord, *Speed The Plow*, with Patrick Marber, and Frank Skinner in *Cooking With Elvis*, all star Store veterans. When I went to see the West End hit *Art*, it starred Tom Courtenay and Albert Finney. It's since featured Skinner (again), Jack Dee, Sean Hughes and Alistair McGowan – Store stars all. Hughes is also now a novelist. So are David Baddiel, Jenny Eclair and Rob Newman. In 1999, the BBC declined to renew Frank Skinner's contract, after deciding his £20 million demand for a four-year deal was 'not just out of the ball park, but out of the country.'[2] Skinner subsequently signed a deal with ITV. The fee was undisclosed, but Skinner was reported to be 'very happy'.[3] It's a far cry from The Store's early days, when comics were paid in drinks vouchers, and future *Red Dwarf* star Norman Lovett would finish his performance by asking if there was anyone in the audience who could give him a lift home.

Comics interviewed in this book include a small-screen chef, an EastEnders scriptwriter and Dipsy from *Teletubbies*. Jeremy Hardy and Mark Steel have both penned prestigious broadsheet columns while countless other wags scrawl softer features for the broadsheet and tabloid press. On Channel 4, Mark Thomas marries practical jokes with investigative journalism, while on BBC1, Jo Brand and Eddie Izzard have both been on *Question Time*, an honour normally reserved for cabinet ministers and captains of industry. 'It is yet another reflection of the political fatigue which has gripped the country,' argued an *Evening Standard* editorial. 'It is a sign of how the entertainment industry drives all before it.'[4]

'There's frankly too much comedy,' agreed Jeremy Hardy. 'I've been asked to go on *Question Time*, but I don't know whether as a humorist or whether they think I'm a serious journalist. I think it's part of the dumbing-down process. They have comedians on *Newsnight* now to do funny little skits. And I think that's hateful. And it's very dangerous.'[5] During the Edinburgh Festival, where the Fringe has been overrun by stand-up, Rob Newman, who advanced from The Store to Wembley Arena, railed against 'the wall-to-wall comedy of our chuckle culture'.[6] Love or loathe it, it started at The Store.

Some comedians do become stars without being Store regulars, but they're often speciality acts, character comics or more surreal, stream of consciousness turns. There are straight stand-ups who reach the top without cracking this place en route, but they're few and far between. 'There weren't as many comics, there weren't as many clubs, so everyone knew each other,' says Mark Lamarr, recalling those halcyon days before stand-up became a middle-class career choice. 'Now every other person you meet is a comic.' But punters still pile into this little club where it all began, because they know that beneath a low ceiling in a smoky basement live comedy lives and breathes in a way it never can onscreen. At The Store, you can say things about the world around you that you could never say on TV.

Over the intervening generation, The Store has moved twice, doubling its modest capacity each time, from 100 in that Soho attic, to 200 in an L-shaped Leicester Square cellar, to 400 in this plush, purpose-built bunker a bottle's throw from Piccadilly Circus. And despite its slick interior, it's retained its intimate atmosphere, which is why it still packs in punters for at least eight shows a week, fifty-two weeks a year. In 1993, the *Evening Standard* even called it the comic equivalent of The Cavern Club. Well, even at the best of times, it isn't quite The Beatles . . . but sometimes it comes a pretty close second.

The photos that line the stairwell give you a good idea of the stars who've played this place on the way up. This montage of agents' mug shots and snatched snapshots is a little Light Ent archive, a daft stand-up identity parade. For punters, it's an enticing appetiser for the treats to follow, but for a young wannabe comic, descending for his first open spot, it's an intimidating overture before the trial to come. 'You think "Oh my god, he's a genius, he's legendary, and I'm nowhere near as good," so you start questioning whether you should be there,' says young rising star Adam Bloom. But perils as well as praise attend an appearance in this ad hoc hall of fame. 'Two people were studying the photos and one said to the other, "Is that Kevin Day?"' recalls Day, now an established Store star. 'The other one says, "I hope he's not on. He's fucking shit."'

Rik Mayall, Nigel Planer and Peter Richardson dwarf the other photos. Planer and Richardson stand side by side, in besuited monochrome, like Dan Aykroyd and John Belushi in *The Blues Brothers*. Sunglasses after dark. Rik Mayall points two fingers to the camera in a parody of punk. Julian Clary smoulders seductively in the chain-store bondage chic of his previous incarnation, The Joan Collins Fan Club, complete with lifelong canine companion and stage sidekick, Fanny The Wonderdog. Clary's cosmetic mask is no surprise, but it's more alarming to see Jack Dee scowling back at you wearing something that looks a lot like eyeliner. Alexei Sayle is clean shaven. Ben Elton wears a beard. Clive Anderson has a full head of flowing locks, as if Elton John had joined The Bee Gees. Tim Clark and Mark Steel both sport tidy moustaches. Jo Brand, billed as The Sea Monster, appears remarkably fresh-faced in a straw hat, with a crab peering over her shoulder. Jenny Eclair looks a lot plumper, as does today's trimmer *They Think It's All Over* host, Nick Hancock. Neither Jennifer Saunders nor Dawn French look a lot different fifteen years later.

The same applies to Paul Merton, although here he's billed as Paul Martin. He'd yet to discover that there was already a Paul Martin in Equity. When he did, he simply followed the same course as Eric Batholomew (aka Morecambe) and George Booth (aka Formby) and borrowed the name of the place he came from. Sean Hughes also looks much the same, though here he's called Sean John Hughes. Playwright Patrick Marber flourishes a prophetic fountain pen. Before *Jonathan Creek* and Abbey National made him a star, a baby-faced Alan Davies, his shaggy mane cropped close, loiters with mischievous intent outside his beloved Arsenal, clutching a crumpled banknote. 'Don't

To Pete + Don at the COMEDY STORE - "Thanks for the break!"
— Robin Williams July '90

give me another break,' stand-up/journalist/producer John Connor has scribbled on his own mugshot. 'The worst set in the world.'

Steve Coogan, Mark Lamarr and Josie Lawrence all jostle for wall space. A fresh-faced Harry Enfield grins down from a great height, in his early incarnation as one half of double act Dusty & Dick. Toilet cleaner turned movie star Lee Evans stares back at you with wide-eyed amazement, as if confronted with a premonition of his future stardom. *Wayne's World* and *Austin Powers* creator Mike Myers stands beside his old pal and double-act partner Neil Mullarkey, still a regular here with resident impro troupe The Comedy Store Players. And Robin Williams, a regular special guest at The Store's previous premises, winks up at you from the foot of this star-studded stairwell. The handwritten note beneath his blown-up snapshot is the only element of artistic licence in this manic montage: 'To Pete and Don, Thanks for the break.' 'I took that picture,' says Peter Rosengard. 'I also wrote that piece underneath. I made it up. And I signed it.'

Peter Rosengard and Don Ward set up The Comedy Store. Rosengard says he had the initial idea. It wasn't an original idea. It wasn't even an original title. He'd visited

The Comedy Store in Los Angeles, and came home with the notion of setting up a similar club in London. He certainly wasn't the first Londoner to visit LA's Comedy Store. And he surely wasn't the first to wonder why there was nothing comparable on this side of the pond. Without Rosengard it probably still would have happened, sooner or later, but in another time, another place, under a very different set of circumstances. Really good ideas are rare, but on their own they don't add up to much. Ward had the economic know-how, and that streetwise savvy which gives some folk the talent to spot the beginning of a good outside bet. He had also been a comic himself, strictly old school, which put him in a better spot than most to see that traditional stand-up was way past its sell-by date. Above all, he had the premises, plus another strip club, The Sunset Strip, just up the road. They couldn't have done it without one another. But the success of their unusual alliance also relied upon a sleeping partnership with Margaret Thatcher.

Thatcherism gave Alternative comics a focal point, a sense of common purpose, and The Comedy Store vented its collective spleen against Thatcherite values in a way that neither Rosengard nor Ward, both successful, fairly conventional careerists, could ever have conceived. Alternative Comedy always claimed to hate Mrs Thatcher, but it would never have happened without her. In London, there were riots in Brixton; in Liverpool and Bristol, Toxteth and Saint Pauls both burnt. But far more significantly for The Store, Thatcher's cronies cut arts subsidies. 'It began to dawn on the Arts Council and the Government that subsidising a lot of theatre companies that weren't necessarily on your side wasn't the wisest way,' says actor turned comic Jim Barclay. Fringe theatre outfits folded, and a generation of radical actors were forced to become stand-up comics instead. 'The reason there were theatre groups in those days was that it was the end of the Labour movement giving out the old grants,' confirms Alternative Comedy's patron sinner, jailbird and prankster Malcolm Hardee. 'When they folded up, the stand-up comedy came about.' Stand-up offered a way to preach a radical message on the cheap. These comic converts stood up for squatters' rights, social security, peppercorn rents and public transport.

Yet although the content was Old Left, the format was New Right. Comics were self-employed, non-unionised and unsubsidised. Instead of scraping by on bursaries, they wrote business plans, and pulled themselves up by their own boot straps. 'I was very privileged to be so self-sufficient,' says Julian Clary, who became a comic after more than a year as an out-of-work actor. 'I negotiated my own fees and I took my own bookings and I could decide how often I worked.' In the get-ahead Eighties, some comedians even signed up for The Enterprise Allowance Scheme, a Thatcherite ruse to transform Maggie's unemployed millions into a new breed of thrusting young entrepreneurs. Well, that was the theory, anyway. Alternative Comedy was arguably the only arena in which it worked.

Don Ward and Peter Rosengard were, in comparison, real entrepreneurs, but that was just about the only thing they had in common. Ward ran a couple of strip clubs, a topless bar and a car wash. Rosengard was a life insurance salesman. Ward's career

was about as alternative as Jim Davidson's. Rosengard's day job was like something out of a sketch by Monty Python. Yet together they would change British comedy forever.

As is almost inevitable in a collaborative creation, Ward and Rosengard tend to differ when pressed to recall the details of their historic, and occasionally histrionic, partnership. They started off together. That much at least they can agree on. They've since gone their separate ways. Indeed, when The Store's twentieth anniversary came around, they even held separate birthday parties. It says something for The Store's status, and the intensity of the bond that founded it, that both these prosperous and busy men found time to telephone me to ask about the attendance at one another's celebrity bun fights, and to tell me why they weren't there. If The Store was just another comedy club, such insatiable curiosity and sporadic indignation wouldn't still be fuelled by fallout from an obscure alliance that ended a generation ago.

But that's enough backstage politics. What about what happens onstage?

Turn the corner, past Robin Williams, the box-room box office, another bouncer, and at last you're inside. The auditorium is part studio theatre, part drinking den, an apt architectural echo of the rival traditions that have informed Alternative Comedy, and the mainstream enterprise it's now become. It feels halfway between a West End stage and an East End nightclub. Add the utterly unfounded suspicion of something slightly unseemly, a nagging, ghostly legacy of The Store's red light roots, shake and stir, and you have a unique cocktail of highbrow, lowbrow and even vaguely illicit fun. No wonder nervous first-time punters still phone up to ask about the dress code. There was no precedent for this sort of entertainment, only the old working men's clubs and end of the pier shows beside the seaside. The answer, then as now, is that you can wear, and say, whatever you want. It's a stately soccer terrace in miniature, pole dancing without the dancers, a showbusiness Speaker's Corner, if you like.

Step onto this sparse podium. It's your last chance to see the sight lines and test the temperature before showtime, but you're also soaking up the history of the place. 'You see it in those photographs down the stairs,' says impressionist Alistair McGowan. 'As soon as you stand on that stage you know that wealth of talent has gone before you.' And now you're stood here, on this bare platform, you can see what he means. There are seats on three sides, and a bear pit beneath. Not so much a performance space, more a sporting arena. The roof feels very close, and up here it's even closer. Staring out from behind the mike stand, you're met by row after row of blood red seats. 'The main thing was to get on, stay on and get off in one piece,' says comedienne Helen Lederer. 'And hopefully be funny.'

In too short a while the doors will open and these empty rows will be filled with a sea of faces, staring back at you, demanding their money's worth. Make me laugh, the whole room seems to shout at you. Once the house lights go down and the stage lights go up, you're on your own. An unpaid open spot. Five minutes. An instant if you're doing well, an eternity if you're dying. And even the best comics died the first few times. Kevin Day wasn't just booed off. He was booed on.

Behind you, to your left, is the twilit sanctuary of the sound and lighting booth, the lair of stage manager Stan Nelson, and beside it the door to your only backstage refuge, more locker room than dressing room. In front of you, to your right, is the bar, hidden behind a black curtain, and behind that, between the kitchen and the cloak-room, is a small windowless office where acts are booked and deals are done. This is where the phone rang when you called up to talk the owner, Don Ward, into giving you this five-minute open spot and the chance to prove to him, and everyone, but most of all to yourself, that you really are as funny as you said you were. Within a few hours, they'll all find out if you were bluffing. And so will you.

It's a big gamble, but if you do pull it off, the potential rewards almost make it worth the risk, which is why there's no shortage of kindred dreamers, be they good, bad or bloody awful. Succeed, and you're past the first and hardest hurdle towards becoming a full-time professional stand-up comic. And even if you fail, you'll still be in very good company. A solid five minutes here may get you another unpaid five in a few months' time, or maybe ten if you're really good or really lucky. If that free ten goes very well, then you may get a proper paid-up twenty. Still a bit too early to give up your day job, if you've got one, but sooner or later a sturdy twenty should get you a fully paid weekend. A Thursday night, two Friday shows and two more on Saturday. Five twenty-minute gigs over three days: a modern stand-up pentathlon. If that goes really well, and your face fits, then you may become a regular, and after that, who knows? Of course, cracking The Store is no guarantee of fleeting fame, let alone lasting fortune. Plenty of comics have played here week in week out and never progressed to national touring or network TV. But most of those who did went this route.

Check your watch. It's nearly half past six. Only ninety minutes to go until show-time. Step offstage and wade through the stalls, still empty, for the next few minutes, at least, until the doors open and the first wave of impatient punters pours down the stairs. Walk past the yellowed press cuttings plastered upon crimson walls, and around the bar, decorated with yet more mug shots: David Baddiel, Eddie Izzard, Frank Skinner. Behind the pillar that bears a framed photo of Tony Allen, the man who invented the term Alternative Comedy, looking remarkably smart in a white jacket with a red hanky sprouting from his breast pocket, is a stuffy little office full of ancient paperwork, with a coffee percolator wheezing faintly in the corner. On show nights like tonight it's usually full of people, but for now it's empty. Danny, the caretaker, must have nipped upstairs for a few minutes. The door is open. Sneak a furtive look over your shoulder. There's nobody around. You'll never have a better chance to pore over two decades of comic history.

Crouched within that airless room, browsing through the battered desk diaries, where all the bookings of these last twenty years are etched in faded Biro, feels a lot like riffling through an intimate memoir, a private record of long-forgotten evenings out, a before-they-were-famous resumé. At the foot of every weekend bill are scrawled a couple of open spots. Most remain as unfamiliar as names plucked at random from a phone directory, one-off hopefuls who endured an endless five minutes stuck in the unforgiving clarity of the spotlight. Yet scattered among these heroic failures are a few future stars. Here and there are mispelt household names doing unpaid try-outs, with blunt one-word assessments scrawled beside them, the home phone numbers of long since abandoned bedsits in the margin. In these beaten-up old year books is the unedited story of The Comedy Store, and to a fair degree, the story of modern comedy.

The first Comedy Store diary begins in 1980, more than six months after The Store's opening night, and the bookings are still mixed up with those of the strip club where it squatted for the first few years. Yet the name that jumps up off the page doesn't belong to a comic or a stripper, but to a dapper, diminutive Scotsman called Kim Kinnie. Over the years, Kinnie evolved from a mere employee into an enigmatic father figure for numerous up-and-coming comics. But here in this diary he's simply billed as the choreographer, the bloke who made sure the strippers took their clothes off in time to the music. Stripping and comedy. It's all in the timing.

Yet hidden amid the lists of strip artistes with sequined handles like Roxy Lee and Monique Starr are the names of comics for whom this spangled stage, complete with glitter ball and slash curtain, would be a springboard to far bigger things than peeling off their underwear for the benefit of Soho's dirty mac brigade. Rik Mayall and Nigel Planer, soon to be immortalised in *The Young Ones*; Ben Elton, who made his reputation writing for that landmark student sitcom, which gave Alternative Comedy a peaktime platform and a mainstream identity; Dawn French and Jennifer Saunders, plus Peter Richardson, who masterminded *The Comic Strip*, which gave French & Saunders their first big TV break.

Other Soho Store pioneers listed in this dog-eared desk diary include stand-up poet laureate John Hegley, future Perrier winners Arnold Brown and Simon Fanshawe, plus Clive Anderson and Paul Merton. Then, in 1983, The Store moved around the corner to Leicester Square. Clive Anderson joined future *Red Dwarf* and *Brittas Empire* star Chris Barrie, plus Ben Elton, Dawn French and Jennifer Saunders on the opening night bill. *Comic Strip* stars Adrian Edmondson, Rik Mayall, Nigel Planer and Peter Richardson were all on the guest list, with the Soho Store's first compere Alexei Sayle, plus new-wave celebs like Time Bandit David Rappaport. This vertically challenged movie star didn't bother to lower the microphone. He simply stood on a chair. And even though 69 Dean Street had acquired a word-of-mouth magic that made it an underground legend, this lopsided cavern underneath 28 Leicester Square was where The Store really came of age.

Despite moving to a different venue, The Store's striptease days weren't entirely over. In 1985, Malcolm Hardee appeared with his anarchic sketch troupe The Greatest Show On Legs, whose finale was a shambolic all-male balloon dance, stark bollock naked, apart from socks and a few strategically placed inflatables. What on earth would Roxy Lee or Monique Starr have made of it?

Sharing the bill with Hardee's wedding tackle was a young American comedienne called Ruby Wax, booked to try out some new material. The following night's compere was her fellow American, actress and comedienne Kit Hollerbach, who introduced Britain to comic impro by starting The Comedy Store Players, still going strong here, twice a week, every week. There's also a listing for Julian Clary, alongside stand-up magician Jerry Sadowitz, the Glaswegian Jewish *enfant terrible* who pricked the soap-box bubble of Alternative Comedy's politically correct pomposity, and showed that new comedy could contain more elemental rage and danger than bog standard anti-Thatcher gags. Unpaid try-outs include Mark Thomas, who went on to dominate The Store for a decade before transferring his political polemic to the small screen.

Future stars fill the diaries' pages. Here's Harry Enfield, whose comic archetypes defined the decade, alongside Felix Dexter, the first black comic to become a regular here, and for far too long the only one, despite The Store's non-racist manifesto. There's post-feminist stand-up Jenny Eclair, nearly a decade before she won the Perrier in 1995. There's The Store's first improvised comedy show, with Kit Hollerbach, Dave Cohen, Paul Merton, Neil Mullarkey and Mike Myers. Although Myers returned to America and became a movie star, Merton and Mullarkey still play here most weeks with The Players. There's some bloke called Jonathan Ross. 'Going to host some Channel 4 show,' reads the diary. 'Wants to practise his material.' A week later, Ross is back, with one word scrawled beside his name: 'Good.'

'I went down surprisingly well,' recalled Ross. 'There was only one fuck off.'[7] Others had a slightly different view. 'I remember him doing an open spot there and never saw him again until he cropped up on telly with *The Last Resort*,' says stand-up double bass virtuoso Jim Tavare. 'He did an open spot and died on his arse.' Tavare certainly died on his arse a few times down here. Today, he has a cult reputation as the comedian who does to classical music what Tommy Cooper once did to magic, but when he first tried out here back in 1986, bereft of his bass, he was acknowledged as one of the worst acts on the circuit.

Here's Charles Fleischer, who was in the UK to dub the voice for the title role in *Who Framed Roger Rabbit?* Fleischer was performing the first of many fine stand-up spots that comics who were lucky enough to see, and unlucky enough to follow, still talk about today. Julian Clary, who later appeared alongside Fleischer in *Carry On Columbus*, was on the same bill. Phil Cornwell, aka David Bowie, Michael Caine, Jimmy Hill, Mick Jagger and Jack Nicholson in the celebs in suburbia spoof *Stella Street*, was also there that month.

Reading these line-ups from fifteen years ago is like scanning tonight's telly listings. In 1987, you could have seen Nick Hancock, *Red Dwarf* stars Craig Charles and Hattie Hayridge, plus TV chef Ainsley Harriott, all in the same show. In 1988, Mark Lamarr shared a bill with Nick Hancock, and Steve Coogan shared a bill with Jack Dee. Today, Coogan is acknowledged as an immaculate character comic, a worthy successor to Peter Sellers, but back then The Store still had to write the word 'impressionist' in brackets after his name in the diary. 'If you had seen his act on the circuit, you would not have even begun to guess what he'd eventually do on television,' says Steve Punt, who played here with Hugh Dennis before teaming up with David Baddiel and Rob Newman in *The Mary Whitehouse Experience*. A week later, Baddiel was on the bill. Rob Newman also played here, and less than five years later, Newman and Baddiel became the first comics to play Wembley. Wembley Arena holds 12,000 people. The Leicester Square Store held 200.

In 1989, even Shane Ritchie, a comic much more readily associated with the trad circuit, did a set. What had started out as an alternative to mainstream comedy was now rapidly replacing it, tempting the most versatile and adventurous trad comics to jump ship. A decade after The Store set up shop, the boundary between Alternative Comedy and Light Ent was becoming increasingly blurred.

In the summer of 1989, The Store celebrated its tenth birthday, and Jo Brand, Jenny Eclair and Donna McPhail were among the acts on a ground-breaking women-only bill. An entire decade after this supposedly non-sexist club opened, men-only shows were still the norm, and it needed an anniversary gala to prompt an all-female line-up. Later that month, Eddie Izzard, one of today's biggest comedy stars, was still only allowed a ten-minute half-spot, that comic no man's land midway between a free try-out and a paid turn, and a nightmare for a comic whose freeform style is impossible to condense. Other talented comics were barely treated better, at first. 'American comic Greg Proops may turn up tonight or Friday and do five to ten minutes unpaid,' records the diary, referring to the star of *Whose Line Is It Anyway?* Yet it didn't take The Store too long to realise that they had a top comic import in their midst. By September, he was on the bill.

The year ended with Caroline Quentin making a guest appearance with The Comedy Store Players. The Store was becoming a crossroads for performers and writers from a wide range of different disciplines. Not just stand-up, or even impro, but acting and writing too. In a country that has always felt safer keeping art and entertainment in separate pigeon holes, The Store was breaking down the barriers between high and low culture. If this club had only ever helped to spawn stand-up stars, it wouldn't have been half so interesting, or influential.

Alan Davies played here in New Year 1990, and by springtime, Eddie Izzard was finally on the bill. It often takes a lot of time and effort to persuade even the best bookers that punters will laugh at anything apart from one-liners. By midsummer, he was hosting, and his biggest battle was already won. That summer, future film actor Denis Leary played the first of several Store sets, while a new topical team show, *The Cutting Edge*, showed The Store hadn't lost its political edge. A season of benefits for The Comedy Store Fund for Sick Children, a charity set up by The Store to train nurses for a children's hospital in Romania, proved that Alternative Comedy hadn't forgotten its campaigning spirit, but a brief note that summer also shows how successfully the club had colonised the mainstream: 'Jack Dee to do five minutes unpaid. He's doing *Wogan* tomorrow.'

'The dilemma used to be, do I want to be on *Wogan*?' said Arnold Brown, when I interviewed him a year later. 'Now the dilemma is, do I want to *be* Wogan?' When Store regular Nick Revell went on the *Des O'Connor Show*, he was accused of selling out. 'I wanted to change people's opinions,' he told his hecklers. 'You changed my opinion,' replied one of them. 'I used to think you were good.' Now, Store stars appear on *Des O'Connor* as a matter of course (alongside prime ministers), and Store punters are more likely to applaud them than heckle.

By the last page of these diaries it's clear that The Store had travelled a long way from its right-on origins. When Kim Kinnie was choreographing strippers on the first page, The Store was the only room where these comedians could learn and ply their new-found trade. Now, it had become a place where they limbered up for the BBC's flagship chat show. But it wouldn't have been anything at all without Don Ward and Peter Rosengard.

Chapter Two

In the summer of 1978, a very successful life insurance salesman in his early thirties went on a well-earned holiday to Los Angeles. It was his first visit to LA, so he asked his hotel porter where to go. 'Have you been to The Comedy Store?' inquired the porter. 'No,' replied Peter Rosengard. 'What is it?' 'It's a club for comedians.'

Rosengard had never been to a comedy club before. The only comedians he'd ever seen were on the ITV series *The Comedians*. 'I couldn't stand those mother-in-law jokes,' says Rosengard. 'I just didn't identify with them.' He didn't even really like classic British sitcoms, like *Hancock's Half Hour* or *Steptoe & Son*. But he loved American humour, especially TV series like *Sergeant Bilko*. 'I used to watch Bilko when I was a kid,' he recalls. 'American comedy was much more of interest to me.' And America's Comedy Store was only five minutes' drive from his Beverly Hills hotel.

Rosengard and his wife went to the Store on Sunset Strip, which just so happened to be the name of one of Don Ward's Soho strip clubs. He literally fell out of his seat laughing. He laughed so much, his wife had to drag him away. 'I'd been going to clubs since I was a teenager in the West End but they were all discotheques,' he says. 'I'd never seen people really having a good time there.' But these comics were young, creative and intelligent, and he loved it.

By comparison, British stand-up was geriatric. 'At that time comedy was the domain of old men,' confirms musical comic Ronnie Golden. 'Guys in their seventies, with no connection to young people at all.' And even the younger British acts, doing old gags for older crowds, looked old before their time. These American comedians seemed so smart and youthful. And unlike most punters who see a good show and go home

Peter Rosengard   **Don Ward**

happy, Rosengard didn't leave it at that. Like every decent entrepreneur, he had spotted a gap in the market. 'Why isn't there something like this in London?' he wondered, on his way out. 'When I come back to London, I'm going to open one.'

However, every holiday romance fades when you get back to Blighty, and after Rosengard returned from LA, he didn't do anything about his plan for several months. It was reading a newspaper interview with Robin Williams that finally spurred him into action. Williams' hit sitcom *Mork & Mindy* had begun transmission. 'I really liked *Mork & Mindy*,' says Rosengard. 'I thought he was a brilliant performer.' Mork got him reading, but it was what Williams said about The Store that really caught his eye. 'He was talking about The Comedy Store. How he started. And how so many other people had started at The Comedy Store.'

Rosengard realised he'd better get his arse into gear, but was never motivated by the prospect of making any money. 'The idea of opening a Comedy Store was purely to do something I loved doing,' he says. 'It would have had to make millions for it to have had a financial impact. It wouldn't have changed my life in any way.'

Peter Rosengard was born in Hammersmith, West London, in 1946. 'We were very liberal Jews,' he says, over breakfast in the Halcyon Hotel in Holland Park. 'Our synagogue was a converted church.' His father, a local doctor in nearby Acton, was a hyperactive Glaswegian Jew, and Rosengard's frenetic childhood was disrupted by financial crises. Yet it sounds happy, all the same. 'I grew up in a house with a lot of laughter,' he says. 'My father was a very charismatic guy. He was a very funny man. He always told lots of jokes and always had a crowd of people around him.' Rosengard went to Latymer School in Hammersmith, alma mater of *Not The Nine O'Clock News* star Mel Smith, as well as actors such as Hugh Grant and Alan Rickman. Rosengard had no desire to act, but he did sneak out at night to sample the clubs and casinos of Soho. He hasn't had a bet since 1971, whereupon his life began again.

He went to London University to study dentistry, but discovered he didn't like teeth, and left after a year. He worked for a bubble bath manufacturer, then volunteered to fight for Israel in the Six Day War. 'If you're going to fight a war,' he says, 'choose a six day one.'[1] He washed dishes and picked peaches on an Israeli kibbutz, came back to Britain, worked in a pram factory, and then went to Sweden, where he worked as a terrible DJ, before his grandfather persuaded him to come home and become a life insurance salesman. On his first day, in 1969, he sold a policy to the cab driver who drove him home. Rosengard is still doing the same job today. In 1992, he sold the world's biggest life insurance policy, worth $100 million, from a cold phone call, and got into the *Guinness Book of Records*, but way back in 1976, he'd already become the first salesman to sell 100 life policies in a month, a feat he's repeated many times since. And by the time he started thinking about opening a comedy club, he was already living in some style. 'I could have done it in my living room,' he says. 'I had a beautiful flat in Cadogan Square.' He also had a Rolls-Royce and an E-Type Jaguar.

Rosengard knew nothing about comedy clubs. He knew virtually nothing about comedy. But his brilliant career as an insurance salesman had given him the most vital attribute for starting this or any other venture: chutzpah. And so he began searching for premises. He wanted a weekend slot in a West End club, but it was at weekends that most West End clubs did most of their business, and vacant slots were hard to find. He saw a few pub function rooms, but none of them felt right, and then a friend of a friend introduced him to Don Ward. 'I'm going to open a comedy club called The Comedy Store,' announced Rosengard. 'Pinched the idea, pinched the name, and I'm looking for a venue.'

Like Rosengard, Ward had also been to LA that year, but to celebrate a divorce. Like Rosengard, he had visited The Store. And like Rosengard, he'd been struck by the contrast between these satirical, cosmopolitan comics and the Jimmy Tarbucks and Lennie Bennetts back in Blighty. 'I found them all so boring,' remembers Ward. 'Nothing changed. It was all the same. Englishmen, Irishmen and Scotsmen, the mother-in-law or derogatory gags against black people.' Ward knew that the younger generation weren't into all that. He'd seen Lenny Bruce at Peter Cook's Establishment Club, and he felt there must be a market for the sort of observational and political material he'd seen in Los Angeles. And like Rosengard, he wondered why nobody had opened a club like The Store in Britain. 'The idea was floating in my mind and the idea was floating in his mind,' he says.

Ward worked as a printer after he left school, before becoming a comic at The Windmill Theatre down the road. The Lord Chamberlain allowed this 'Comics' Dunkirk' to stage nude shows, as long as the models didn't move. 'No one actually came to see the comedians, who existed merely as padding,' explains John Fisher in his trad comedy bible *Funny Way To Be A Hero*. 'However, The Windmill was unique as a training ground. Nowhere else could a young performer experience the accumulative value of doing six shows a day, six days a week.' Michael Bentine, Tommy Cooper, Barry Cryer, Bruce Forsyth, Tony Hancock, Harry Secombe and Peter Sellers all played this place where, as Fisher wrote, 'the young comedian, once he could stifle his sorrows, could at least learn to die with composure and a smile'.

'I'd do my own little spot for an audience that showed total indifference,' says Ward. 'I was never going to get there. I can see that.' Despite supporting Cliff Richard and Marty Wilde, after ten years he knew he was never going to be in the big league, so he moved on to a nearby night spot called The Keyhole Club, where he compered the show and ran the bar and cloakroom. He teamed up with the bloke who did the music at Sunset Strip, and in 1971 bought The Gargoyle and The Nell Gwynne, where he compered by night, introducing trad stars like Jimmy Cricket and Larry Grayson, and ran the business side by day. Seven years later, Peter Rosengard finally came his way. And even though Ward's Nell Gwynne strip show ran throughout the week, crucially, his Gargoyle hostess club was closed at the weekend.

The Store's beginnings are inseparable from the strip club and topless bar where it first started, but before Ward arrived at 69 Dean Street, The Gargoyle was a very different sort of dive. 'You only got in there if you'd been invited,' says Ward, standing outside the club, now a film production office. 'It was like the Groucho's of its day.'

The Gargoyle was founded in 1925 by David Tennant, a spectacularly wealthy and well-bred aristocrat, who spared no expense in converting the early Victorian printing works into London's most celebrated nightclub. The tiny lift that serviced this nocturnal nirvana was barely big enough for four, but once you arrived upstairs, the view was well worth the wait – and the squeeze. Guests were greeted by a flowing fountain, lit by silver stars in a sapphire ceiling, before descending a golden staircase into a beautiful Moorish ballroom, designed by Henri Matisse. The ceiling was 22 carat gold leaf, but the crowning glory was the Matisse mosaic, made of 20,000 fragments cut from two enormous antique mirrors, which scattered guests' reflections into a shattered kaleidoscope around the walls. Francis Bacon said it made people look like birds of paradise.

'It will be a place without the usual rules, where people can express themselves freely,' explained Tennant, when The Gargoyle opened in 1925. 'A chic nightclub for dancing but also an avant garde place open during the day where still struggling writers, painters, poets and musicians will be offered the best food and wine at prices they can afford.'[2] Initial members included Noël Coward, Somerset Maugham and Virginia Woolf. Edward VIII danced The Charleston here. Regulars included Arnold Bennett, Aldous Huxley, Bertrand Russell, Anthony Powell and Evelyn Waugh. During the Second World War The Gargoyle was a haven for De Gaulle's Free French, as well as artistic and literary refugees from Central European countries where the café was the main forum of intellectual life. It was also a haven for a trio of British traitors – Guy

The Gargoyle Club, hosting the first Comedy Store

Barmaid at the Soho Store sporting the comedy-themed T-shirts

Burgess, Donald Maclean and Kim Philby – in the 1950s. For all three spies The Gargoyle's tolerant ambience made it a safe refuge for the love, as well as the ideology, that still did not dare speak its name. Here, both Burgess and Maclean felt free to flaunt their homosexuality, a criminal offence until 1967, and when Maclean, already under investigation by MI5, got drunk and boasted that he worked for Stalin, his fellow Gargoyle guests assumed he was taking the piss.

Not long afterwards, Tennant sold up and went to Spain, where he died in 1968 of a heart attack, hastened by drink. The Gargoyle drifted into a gradual yet steady decline. In 1971, the club was sold to Don Ward.

'I'll go out and find the comedians and promote it,' suggested Rosengard. 'You supply the premises and the staff and the drinks.' And so Ward agreed to give this novel idea a go. 'He was a nice bloke,' recalls Rosengard. 'He seemed like a good bloke.' They each put in £500 for publicity, agreed to split everything fifty-fifty, and shook hands on the spot.

'I don't think Don really realised what was going on at the time,' says comedian Arthur Smith. 'Rosengard was the intellectual inspiration behind it, and Don saw that maybe there was a financial reward to be had, although it took a while before he realised quite how much.' Yet people underestimate Ward at their peril. Rosengard's hare had got off to a flying start, but Ward's tortoise was the eventual winner of this comedy race.

Even at the outset, Ward and Rosengard didn't always see eye to eye. Ward was happy with Rosengard's plan to cover up the topless signs outside the strip club, but he was rather more reluctant to cover up the topless barmaids inside. 'As a self-proclaimed promoter of non-sexist comedy, I was to have a bit of trouble explaining away the topless barmaids to some of the aspiring comedians,'[3] Rosengard admitted later. He insisted the girls wore T-shirts, but Ward took some persuading. 'Talking out arse as usual,' he replied. 'Striptease and comedy go well together. Ever heard of Burlesque?' But Rosengard stood his ground. 'After several heated discussions, Don finally agreed that the contentious boobs could disappear into the new Comedy Store T-shirts . . . but only after midnight, when we opened.'[4] 'Most of the comedians were very disappointed,' says Ward.

Even so, these two incompatible entertainments were bound to overlap. 'If you got there early, the barmaid would be completely topless because she'd still be serving the odd punter that came out from the strip show,' recalls performance artist Andrew Bailey, who stage managed strip shows at The Gargoyle in the early Seventies, almost a decade before he became a performer at The Store.

Ward introduced Rosengard to his choreographer and stage manager, Kim Kinnie, and told Kinnie what they planned to do. 'He thought it was rubbish,' says Rosengard. 'He thought all these people were terrible. He couldn't understand why we were doing this.' Kinnie confirms his early scepticism: 'I thought, "What is all this shit?"' But gradually he changed his mind. After all, it wasn't the first time he'd turned his hand to something new. Before he wound up at The Gargoyle, he'd been an actor and a director and even worked in variety. He'd also done some dancing, which is why he ended up choreographing Ward's strippers. And in this roundabout way, he secured an accidental ringside seat from where he saw comedy come full circle, and return to its music hall roots.

'The first Music Hall Variety started in a pub, because landlords wanted people to drink more,' says Kinnie, who now lives in Glasgow, where he works as a senior TV producer. 'To keep them in a particular place, they put on turns.' As these turns became more popular than the beer, entrepreneurs built music halls, like The Hackney Empire, later revived as a bastion of Alternative Cabaret, where drink was only a secondary source of revenue. The smarter Stoll Moss Variety theatres eventually built an even bigger barrier between drinkers and entertainers, and Variety gradually died. Now, like their Victorian ancestors, The Gargoyle's new comics would be fodder for raucous drinkers, employing a form of humour that wasn't so much revolution as revival. 'You had to prove yourself,' says Kinnie. 'The politeness had been removed.'

By now The Gargoyle was a ghost of its former glory days, and so was Soho. 'It was a khazi,' says Ashley Roy, an old friend of Rosengard's, who helped set up The Store. 'People went out in the West End, but they didn't go to Soho.' Not unless they had something sleazy in mind. 'It was genuinely louche and genuinely threatening,' recalls Alexei Sayle. 'Not pretend threatening, like it is now.' 'You felt a certain air of menace about the place,' agrees comic guitarist Steve Gribbin, who played here, and then both Stores that followed. 'There were more prostitutes on the street. There were more scuzzy-looking characters around. There weren't any media companies.' Today's edit suites and wine bars are yesterday's sex shops and peep-hole parlours.

'The street The Gargoyle was in was a real prostitutes' hang out,' says Gribbin. 'There were girls on the corner.' Prostitutes waited for passing trade on the street outside the club, and hawked their wares from the upstairs windows of the nearby brothel. No wonder the Meard Street entrance was also known as Tart's Alley. 'I remember being propositioned by some woman hanging out of a window,' says impro veteran Steve Steen. 'Do you want anything for three quid?' she shouted down at him. 'What could she possibly have for three quid that's worth having?' wondered Steen.

Coincidentally, it cost punters precisely the same sum to see a comedy show at The Store. 'Would you like to meet after?' girls asked men on their way in. Some who said yes were led into a nearby alleyway where they were robbed. 'You'd see men being led into these doorways and you'd think "Oh dear,"' recalls Phil Herbert, who first played the Soho Store with a fire-eating street act he'd perfected in Covent Garden.

The Store's olde worlde red light ambience was personified by Joe, a seventysomething Jewish doorman in a dickie bow and dinner jacket, who looked like a throwback to an old British B movie. 'He was the most miserable-looking sod you'd ever meet, and you wouldn't believe you was entering a comedy club,' recalls comic magician Otiz Canneloni. The awkward way in, via the old Gargoyle lift, was another accidental asset. 'You only needed the doorman and two people to stand there, and it looked as if there was a queue, so it helped get people in,' says Ashley Roy.

For Patrick Marber, 'London was a much less sophisticated city than it is now, and much less of a late-night city. The Store was one of the few places that was open late at night.' Soho had milliners' workshops and Italian delis, but none of today's sidewalk café culture. When drinkers spilled onto the pavement outside the Soho Brasserie, the police used to order everyone back inside. In 1972, the proprietor of a strip club called The Bus Stop was shot by his business partner who subsequently killed himself. 'The victim staggered along Dean Street as far as the corner, where he died opposite the Golden Lion,' reports my *Passport To Soho*, 'where Dennis Nilsen picked up two of his victims before stuffing them down his drains.' Quentin Crisp complained that you used to be able to get your throat cut in Soho on a really big scale, whereas now it was riddled with dim basements where girls took off their clothes for money.

Ward's club didn't quite fit this description. It wasn't in a basement. Rosengard's friends told him he was nuts. 'Nobody's going to go to a strip joint in Soho at midnight on a Saturday night to see comedy.' But The Gargoyle was small and intimate and Rosengard was smitten.

Soho's seedy squalor was a symptom of a much wider malaise. London was burning, and suddenly, squalor was chic. 'Cash Through Chaos', promised Malcolm McLaren's Sex Pistols in *The Great Rock and Roll Swindle*. They could have been talking about The Comedy Store. 'There was a really good nightclub scene going on in London,' says film maker Roger Pomphrey. 'Whatever your bent was, you could find it, whether it was comedy or reggae or rap.' But while the nightclub scene was booming Britain appeared to be collapsing. 'There was a sourness in the political climate,' says Tom Tickell, a financial journalist who told shaggy dog stories on The Store's opening night. 'All governments were crooked, it was all going to pieces, eat drink and take drugs for tomorrow we die.'

This raw nihilism was a world away from the upbeat observation of the comics Ward and Rosengard had enjoyed so much on Sunset Boulevard, but like all brilliant ideas, their ersatz Store soon acquired a momentum of its own. A nation teetering on the brink of a collective nervous breakdown was the perfect focus for a new generation of comedians. 'There was a generation that didn't have mothers-in-law, there was a generation that weren't racist, there was a generation that had grown up with a whole different perspective,' says Alternative Comedy guru Tony Allen. 'It was the baby boom generation that was not part of straight society and also not part of the straight left.'

And for these baby boomers, London life was still relatively cheap. They didn't fork out half a million quid for a terraced house in some humdrum suburb; they squatted rent free in Central London locations: Cambridge Circus, Tottenham Court Road, even Covent Garden. 'It was the birth of Gay Pride and Rock Against Racism,' says Martin Potter, who lived with Alternative Comedy pioneers Malcolm Hardee and Martin Soan, and became the third member of The Greatest Show On Legs. 'We used to go on marches and demonstrations and we squatted. No one had any money. The equivalent generation today has got much more concerned with money. In those days, money wasn't really an issue. It was just having a good time.' 'Going out and getting pissed and having a right old fucking giggle,' confirms Roger Pomphrey. 'That was the order of the day.' But while pop music had acquired a campaigning conscience more than a decade earlier, comedy still hadn't composed any protest songs of its own. All that was about to change.

'It became apparent that there was another universe of things to make jokes about, and of course there was the supreme irony that it was taking place in some rather grubby strip club,' says Arthur Smith. In February 1979, Rosengard and Ward held a press conference, and announced this new club would open in April. And so the strange stage was set for Alternative Comedy's accidental advent. Premises, drinks and staff were all sorted. There was even a new logo, a big red grinning mouth, which was commissioned by Rosengard and Ward for a nominal fee from a freelance designer. It's still The Store's trademark today. There was only one thing missing: comedians. But where to find them?

They placed a perfunctory small ad in the *Evening Standard*, the *Evening News*, *Punch*, *Private Eye*, *The Stage* and the *Jewish Chronicle*. They wanted to find a Woody Allen or a Lenny Bruce and they thought they were probably going to be Jewish. 'Comedians wanted for new comedy and improvisation club opening W1,' read the classified one-liner. 'Call Peter Rose.' They also dreamt up a poster: 'Question. What's the difference between Sky Diving and doing five minutes on stage at The Comedy Store? Answer. With Sky Diving, you can only lose your life. Wanted. 1. Comics. 2. Would-Be Comics. 3. Frustrated Dentists.'

Ward anticipated only a few responses but there were hundreds. Rather than accept all applicants unseen, they were able to hold auditions. However, as these auditions revealed, the problem wasn't quantity but quality. 'It rapidly became apparent as the months slipped by and I was sitting there in this empty strip club, downstairs at The Gargoyle, that the people were terrible,' says Rosengard. Apart from Woody Allen or Lenny Bruce, he didn't quite know what he wanted, but he knew what he didn't want, and these auditions confirmed his worst fears. *The Stage* advert attracted hordes of resting holiday camp turns, while the *Evening News* solicited a host of hopeless amateurs. A sixtysomething housewife sang 'I'm Only A Bird In A Gilded Cage' with a birdcage on her head, and 'Any Old Iron' in a dress decorated with scrap metal. There was even a saxophonist who played 'I'm Forever Blowing Bubbles' in a glass tank full of water, but he never made the audition. His tank was too big to fit inside The Gargoyle's tiny lift. Mind you, Rosengard was an absolute beginner himself. 'I'd never auditioned anybody in my life,' he says. 'I used to clap.' It was only when he saw some auditions in a movie that he realised it wasn't the done thing to applaud.

'The opening night party was looming,' remembered Rosengard, a decade later. 'I'd invited every TV head of Light Entertainment and comedy in the country, dozens of producers and directors, scores of journalists, photographers, TV camera crews, all to witness the brilliant new comedians that I'd discovered. The only problem was that I hadn't discovered any.'[5] There were chauffeurs, builders, bank clerks, Butlins Redcoats, advertising copywriters, accountants, even a policeman, but no comedians. At least, none who made Ward and Rosengard laugh.

The first comic who actually made them laugh was a Birmingham University student called Lee Cornes, who called Rosengard after seeing his advert in the *Standard*, and auditioned in a sales training room at Rosengard's Abbey Life offices, off Oxford Street. Cornes did two sketches, one about a surgeon removing every organ save the right one, and another about a man delivering a lecture on rabies, the tabloid terror plague of the age, unaware that he was suffering from the disease himself. 'I was amazed that it was actually in his office,' recalls Cornes, twenty years on. 'He was doing it all rather surreptitiously. He didn't want to disturb the people around him.' Fat chance. In the rabies sketch, Cornes barked like a dog, and ended up literally frothing at the mouth, a finale interrupted by the arrival of Rosengard's boss. 'This is Lee,' said Rosengard. 'He's thinking of joining us.' Life insurance's loss was Alternative Comedy's gain. Cornes became the first act to ever play The Store.

But Ward and Rosengard's biggest break by far was the appearance of a stocky Scouser in his late twenties. 'I saw this bloke standing there, chewing gum, in a leather jacket,' remembers Rosengard. 'Tough-looking bloke.' This burly Liverpudlian watched all the other auditions with an appropriate expression of contempt then performed a strange, inspired monologue about a fierce altercation in a cake shop. His name was Alexei Sayle. 'He did a couple of monologues which I could probably quote by heart ten years later and have done many times,' says Rosengard. 'Don't go anywhere,' he told Sayle. 'You're our compere. You're the one who gets a fiver.' The rest of the acts, they'd decided, would be performing for free. 'He's saved our lives,' thought Rosengard. Well, The Store's life, anyway.

Sayle's wife had seen the advert in *Private Eye*. It's a measure of the sort of place Soho was then that she feared this 'new comedy and improvisation club' might merely be a novel variation on an old Soho theme. 'My wife thought it might be some strange scam to get you to buy a bottle of champagne for £100,' says Sayle, 'so when Peter Rosengard offered me a drink, I said no.' Mrs Sayle needn't have worried. Rosengard needed her husband far too much to try and fleece him with fake clip joint bubbly. 'He was a lot better than anybody else,' says Rosengard. 'Without Alexei, we wouldn't have had a Comedy Store.'

Sayle wasn't only a lot better than anyone else Rosengard had seen, he was also

Alexei Sayle, the first compere of The Comedy Store. He was to prove Peter Rosengard and Don Ward's salvation

completely different from the competent but conventional trad comics Ward had worked with in the past. 'I'd been sitting there for three months and I'd never seen anything like it,' says Rosengard. 'I was aware I'd found a brilliant comedian. I didn't know how much material he had, but the intellectual thug was a fantastic character.' 'It was so refreshing,' agrees Ward. 'His routine possessed nothing sexist or racist.'

Sayle saw a palpable sense of relief spread across both their faces. 'It can't have been more than a month before we opened,' says Rosengard. 'We were getting pretty desperate because of all these terrible bloody acts. I had a whole list of people who wanted to appear, but nobody was funny.' But by the end of Sayle's short set, they were both doubled up with laughter. 'We thought we were going to end up with nobody,' they told him. 'We still might not have a show.' Yet now they knew that however awful the other acts were, Sayle would hold the gig together. 'We needed an anchor,' says Ward. 'He was our anchor.' And with Sayle onboard, they even felt bold enough to abandon the auditions. 'People aren't going to audition to tables and chairs,' said Ward. 'They'll audition to the public. That'll be our show.'

Ward's bravado was well founded. Sayle anchored The Store, and gave it a fresh persona that survives today. 'The act baffled his early audiences,' confirms comedy writer

Mark Lewisohn. 'This type of full-frontal comedy attack, while common in the USA, was virtually unheard of in Britain.'[6]

But there was far more to Sayle's act than novelty value. 'To talk directly to the audience was unheard of unless you were in a suit and a big bow tie and talking about your mother-in-law,' says Sayle. 'It was the first time that anybody had used honesty in show business. I'd build up an act and if they bombed, I'd say, "Well, they were shit, weren't they?" Nobody had ever done that before, because the whole ethos of show business had been to lie.' Nowadays, caustic comics are commonplace, but back then, despite several years of punk and new wave, any comic who worked without a fourth wall was expected to be obsequious and sycophantic. Not Sayle. 'I've never been somebody with some love of strangers,' he says. 'Most comedians have a terrible desire to be liked, which I never gave a fuck about, really. I wanted them to find me funny. But to like me? Who cares?' Rosengard was delighted. 'I wanted somebody to say, "That was a bunch of crap, you were fucking terrible, get off,"' he says. 'I loved the idea of a compere who told the audience to fuck off.'

'He was running with the hare and the hounds,' says Tom Tickell. 'As a technique, it was brilliant, because he clearly couldn't lose.' And though it wasn't Tickell's comedic cuppa, he could see Sayle suited the spirit of the age. 'I recognised Alexei was different, but it wasn't a difference I liked,' he explains. 'He had a kind of toughness you probably need to be a good comedian. A lot of the rest of us were too full of self-doubt, but there was a certain belligerence and self-confidence which I do remember thinking was going to stand him in good stead.'

But Sayle wasn't just a shock jock. 'Alexei had attitude, and attitude like that hadn't existed in British stand-up for a long time,' says Arthur Smith. 'He didn't care if he alienated people. He had a view of the world and he was going to tell you. And if you didn't want it then fuck you. He didn't attempt to make you love him. He swore. He was rude. He was the absolute opposite of all the showbiz you'd seen on TV. He was the complete antithesis of the standard light entertainer.'

Attitude is a product of experience, and Sayle's experience was unique. Unlike most left-leaning comics who became famous at the Soho Store, his roots were resolutely working class. French and Saunders both came from RAF families, Rik Mayall's father ran the drama department at a teacher training college, and Ben Elton's pater was a Professor at Surrey University; indeed, his uncle was Regius Professor Emeritus of Modern History at Cambridge University, and a knight of the realm. Conversely, Sayle's dad was a railway guard, his mum was a football pools clerk, and both of them were members of the Communist Party. Hence little Alexei didn't spend his Cold War childhood holidays on the Costa del Sol, but on free family train trips behind the Iron Curtain.

It was this cocktail of Marxist rhetoric and proletarian toil that gave his extraordinary act its alluring blend of highbrow material and lowbrow delivery. 'He was the first comedian to articulate that working-class people weren't the lumpen proletariat,' says first-night veteran Arnold Brown. 'His opening routine was about going to an art gallery and combining being a thug with an interest in art.' No Labour lackey, Sayle didn't only attack the arrogance of the New Right; Brown recalls a gag that mocked the dependency culture of the Old Left. 'I damaged my trousers last week,' recites Brown. 'The council still haven't been round to repair them.' The Tories were in the ascendant nationwide, but London was still a GLC ghetto. 'Thatcher got in with only a very small majority the first time around,' says Sayle. 'My stuff was often more about satirising the Left.'

But whether they lacerated Left or Right, what made his barbs hit home was Sayle's mesmeric stage presence. 'He looked funny before he opened his mouth,' says Brown. Squeezed into a skintight suit that harnessed his burly torso like a bespoke straight jacket, Sayle ranted and raged, but his anger was always entertaining. 'It's hard to laugh at a gag when you've heard it a few times,' says Steve Steen, 'but I used to go back and watch him and just laugh and laugh and laugh.' And you laughed with Sayle, not at him. 'You heckled Alexei at your peril,' explains Ward. 'Woe betide you if you got in the way.' His crowd control was so self-assured that even when it wasn't clear what he was talking about, it scarcely mattered. 'Often I wasn't quite sure what he was saying, but I wasn't going to argue with him,' recalls Soho Store punter turned performer Otiz Canneloni. 'He'd come across with such aggression and confidence.' 'Now, he's a rather amiable, avuncular kind of person,' says Clive Anderson. 'He probably always was.' Yet without his inventive, energetic genius, The Store might never have taken off, and Anderson speaks for countless comics when he says, 'You couldn't have had The Comedy Store without Alexei.'

Sayle's Liverpudlian wit wasn't the nostalgic whimsy of The Beatles in their cheeky but adorable mop top phase. His bilious Scouse recalled the bleak realism of Alan Bleasdale's *Boys From The Black Stuff*. Like the post-industrial everymen of Bleasdale's bitter drama, Sayle had drifted in and out of a string of dead-end day jobs two of which – DHSS clerk and labourer on London Underground's new Jubilee Line – are such icons of their times, you wouldn't dare to invent them.

'In Liverpool there's a great tradition of loquacious philosophising mixed with violence,' said Sayle. 'You could imagine people having a fight in a pub over the meaning of the word anthropomorphic. In London, they'd be fighting over a coat or a dodgy deal. In Liverpool it would be Carthusian dualism. The first bit of material I ever wrote was about a bloke coming down to London and getting into a fight about futurist art.'[7] Hence his stage persona. 'He's very different from me. Put in prison for GBH at the height of the Mod era, and got twenty-three A levels and a degree in sociology when he was inside.'[8]

Sayle was the right person, in the right place, at the right time. Expelled from the sixth form of his grammar school, he spent five years at art schools in Southport and Chelsea, and became 'one of London's bottom ten' freelance illustrators, before an old Communist Party school friend called Cliff Cocker, who'd been in a school play with Sayle, asked him to join his Brechtian cabaret troupe, Threepenny Theatre. Sayle thought it was a terrible title, but he joined up all the same. At first, Sayle played

Brecht himself (quite an uncanny resemblance), but he soon graduated to far more anarchic and amusing stunts, like playing bingo with dozens of identical bingo cards. 'Alternative bingo. You don't shout House, you shout Squat.' When everyone in the audience won at once, Sayle would haul them all up onstage and humiliate them. 'Out of the first five gigs, one ended in a riot and several ended in fighting,' recalled Sayle. 'One of them ended with me throttling somebody on stage, with several hundred punks and skinheads just howling with anger.'[9]

The angry act that evolved out of these absurdist bingo games was the act Sayle took to The Store. No wonder Ward and Rosengard had never seen anything like it. Yet the two men were as much of a culture shock for Sayle as he was for them. 'I lived in a tower block. All my friends were teachers or worked on the buses. My wife had some sort of office job and I was washing dishes.' The night before The Store opened, Rosengard gave Sayle a lift in his Rolls-Royce. Sayle didn't even know anyone who had a car. Rosengard drove him to a restaurant, where Sayle was amazed to hear him address the waitresses by their first names. And until some idiot forgot to lock The Store fridge, and the comics all helped themselves to the house bubbly, he'd never even tasted champagne. 'I remember having a long chat with Tony Allen about whether we'd accept a limo,' says Sayle. 'Tony thought it was politically OK to have a chauffeur, if you sat in the front.' Such discussions proved a trifle premature. Sayle tasted his first champagne and rode in his first Roller, but throughout his time at The Store, he still cycled into Soho, chained his bike up outside, and cycled back home to his Fulham tower block after every gig.

Compared to most comics, Sayle was radical, even revolutionary, but by the anarchic standards of punk rock, it was really nothing new. 'Things that we were talking about were going on in the pop music business for years,' he says. 'The big thing we did was to take that pop music ethos, and transfer it into Light Entertainment.' Sayle's heroes weren't comics, but acts like Ian Dury and John Cooper Clarke, who bridged the gap between performance poetry and new wave music. There were a few comic precedents for his stand-up style, however. 'The early models I had were people like Jasper Carrott and Billy Connolly.' Their material was very different ('they were ex-folkies – their stuff was less political, more anecdotal'), but like these two established comedians, Sayle also rooted his act in reality.

To anyone from outside Merseyside, or maybe Clydeside or Tyneside, however, his anecdotes seemed far too grotesque to pass for observational comedy. 'Some of it was kind of burgled from the Pythons,' he admits, 'but what I added to it was a kind of violence.' Monty Python didn't intimidate their audience, and Sayle's raw aggression attracted a very different crowd from undergraduate Python fans. 'There was an audience out there that wasn't being served.' This audience wanted to hear jokes about radical politics and recreational drug abuse, not Englishmen, Scotsmen and Irishmen, or even dead parrots. And this was the place where they could hear it. Sayle's full-scale assaults often failed elsewhere. 'I can remember me and Rik and Ade doing a private party for CBS Records and girls crying because we'd frightened them so much,' says

Sayle. 'We'd ruined their Christmas because they were locked in this little room with a madman shouting at them.' 'I'm going to get fired,' said the bloke who'd booked them. 'Here's your money. Now fuck off.' However, the same confrontational delivery that reduced nice CBS girls to tears was an essential survival skill amid the drunken rough and tumble of The Store.

Clive Anderson

Nevertheless, not every future superstar who played the first night was as aggressive as Alexei. Clive Anderson appeared at this premier, and even though he scarcely shone, he did go on to build a solid reputation as a competent Store stand-up, with a quiet yet self-assured act that poked subtle, self-deprecating fun at his conventional appearance and liberal credentials.

Anderson had heard about The Store from 'media giant' Jimmy Mulville. With Rory McGrath, Mulville founded Hat Trick, which, alongside Griff Rhys Jones and Mel Smith's Talkback, is one of Britain's top independent comedy producers, with TV hits like *Father Ted*, *Drop The Dead Donkey*, *Whose Line Is It Anyway?* and *Have I Got News For You?* Back then, Mulville was a radio producer who also did a live show with Anderson, McGrath and Jones called *An Evening Without*. Mulville was invited to audition at Ward's Gargoyle, so Anderson went along too.

'All auditions for comedy are rather pointless things because it's something you deliver to a room full of people,' says Anderson. 'It's not quite so good to two stony faced people who've been sitting all day listening to people telling jokes.' Unlike many of the other auditionees, who had no previous comic experience, Anderson, like McGrath, Mulville and Jones, was a Footlights veteran who'd performed in revues at university, and on tour around the country. He was invited back for the opening night.

However, these subsequent household names were the exception rather than the rule, and with only a handful of decent turns onboard, Ward and Rosengard opted for quantity over quality, padding out the gaps between the promising acts like Cornes, Sayle and Anderson with about twenty eccentric amateurs.

One of these amiable cameos was Tom Tickell. Despite his splendidly comedic surname, Tickell actually works as a financial journalist for the *Guardian*. One of the nicest things about The Store is that most of the folk who've played there still have fond memories of the place; not only those famous comics for whom it was a first step to nationwide or even international stardom, but also the anonymous also-rans, who could quite easily be forgiven for preferring to forget their fleeting and unsuccessful spell in the spotlight. Fame is far more likely to rob a performer of their sense of fun than anonymity, and Tickell retains enough good humour to relish the memory of his brief flirtation with show business and laugh at the shortcomings that prevented him from advancing any further.

'I knew it would fail. It was the second great financial prediction I'd made. The other was telling Andrew Lloyd Webber that *Jesus Christ Superstar* would never succeed.' Tickell knew Peter Rosengard through work. At a party, Rosengard had heard him tell comic stories in different accents. But apart from a teenage appearance on Radio 4, Tickell had only ever done a bit of after-dinner speaking, plus a few parodic turns at Speaker's Corner, where Alternative Cabaret pioneer Tony Allen also performed. Yet with an enthusiasm that Tickell likens to a pneumatic drill, Rosengard persuaded him to repeat these stories at the opening of The Store. 'He was rather desperate to get people on the first night,' says Tickell. 'I suspect he was also looking for a piece in the *Guardian* about my experiences, which he got. So I was useful to him in a sense, and that enthusiasm just carried me along.'

As an illustration of Rosengard's persuasive powers, Tickell tells a tale of his friend selling life insurance by motoring around the West End in a chauffeured Rolls-Royce. 'When he saw a likely looking punter he'd stop the car and offer them a glass of champagne.' Rosengard would then give them a lift to their office. 'Have you ever wondered why you aren't in a Rolls-Royce?' Rosengard would ask them. 'He'd give them the sales pitch all the bloody way from wherever they were to their offices.' Factual or apocryphal, it's a neat illustration of Rosengard's reputation for high-flying salesmanship. No wonder Tickell was powerless to resist such hard-sell charm. 'This will be Britain's first ever stage where unknown, aspiring comedians can see if they have what it takes,' Rosengard told Tickell. 'It's a brilliant idea, a smash hit. We want humour that's new, fresh and different. Alternative Comedy. The idea's taken the American west coast by storm.' But would it create the same sort of storm in south-east England?

Remarkably, the club opened only a month behind schedule. They had assembled dozens of acts, and Ward agreed to provide free champagne for all the guests. However, on the afternoon of the first night, Rosengard suddenly realised he'd completely forgotten one crucial ingredient. American comedy clubs used a red light to tell the comics when to get off. He didn't have one. In a panic, he asked his pal Ashley Roy, aka Billy The Kid, to rush out before the shops shut and hire one for the night. He arrived back just before the first guests, clutching an ornamental dinner gong. 'What's that?' asked Rosengard. 'They didn't have a spotlight, so I got this,' said Roy. 'We can just tap it gently and then they'll know it's time to go.' 'You couldn't tap this thing gently,' said Rosengard. 'You'd hear it in bloody Westminster.' But he had no choice. They were out of time. And so the gong was born.

'I went to the BBC props centre and I got this gong,' recalls Roy. 'I don't think it's ever been paid for. I should think there's probably about four thousand pounds' worth of rent on it.' But even on the first night, Roy made sure he got his money's worth. 'I was on the stage gonging people off it seemed like every minute.'

Roy was working as a fashion photographer in nearby Wardour Street when Rosengard told him about The Store. He spread the word around neighbouring night-clubs, and even found time to watch one of the teatime auditions at The Gargoyle, featuring never discovered stars like Brian The Nun, a civil servant who told shaggy dog stories, and a pianist who promised to tell some jokes but never quite got around to it. Not very promising, but the best business ideas are often based on hunches, and Ward and Rosengard were right to trust their gut instincts. Even so, it was the best part of a decade before The Store went full time; meanwhile, striptease provided a far steadier income. 'Don wasn't prepared to let the strip go,' says comic Jim Barclay. 'It was his bread and butter at the time.'

However, although neither Rosengard nor Ward knew it at the time, their club would supply a demand that hadn't been met since the demise of Music Hall. Out of this vacuum evolved a performance style whose emphasis was on interaction between stage and stalls. 'It's a class issue,' says another first-night performer, Simon McBurney. 'Working-class theatre died because it became subsumed into television.' The theatre that survived grew increasingly remote and intellectual, while TV drama lacked the live frisson that makes the audience part of the creative process. 'People have a need for live performance,' he says. 'People want to associate with other live human beings.'

The Gargoyle was built to hold about 100 people, but Rosengard had been told most folk he asked wouldn't come to the opening night, so he sent out 500 invitations. 'I didn't know anybody in television,' he says. 'I invited everybody from the managing director of the BBC downwards.' Several hundred turned up, and by showtime, the place was as packed as a rush-hour tube train, with thirsty, talkative media liggers knocking back Ward's free champagne. Some were even swigging his bubbly from the bottle. 'They were all drinking and it was packed and hot and people were wondering when the show was going to start,' says Rosengard, of an atmosphere more reminiscent of an am dram last night than a professional world premier. 'Here we go, win or lose, let's have some fun,' Ward told Rosengard as they shook hands before the show.

'Ladies and gentlemen,' announced Ward, above the drunken din. 'Welcome to Britain's newest form of entertainment.'

'You would have thought it was the opening of the Palladium,' says Kim Kinnie. But Rosengard felt a lot less bullish, and Tickell wasn't even listening. He was far too worried about his own impending turn. He sat in a corner, muttering to himself, going through his lines, like a monk repeating a mantra.

'I'd lined up thirty comedians,' recalled Rosengard. 'At least twenty-five of them were diabolical.'[10] Actually, there were twenty-eight. Four of them are now established show business figures, and four more are household names. Lee Cornes is an actor,

Golden. 'They'd learned their skills.' And the Alternative comedians learned from them. 'It was very slick, it all flowed and they got a lot of laughter,' says Tony Allen. 'You learned your version of that.' Although they didn't admit it at the time.

'The audience very quickly became the people who decided what they wanted to hear and didn't want to hear, which is best,' says Rosengard. But this audience wasn't bothered about being politically correct. As Ronnie Golden puts it, 'they couldn't give a fuck.' 'Some acts would deliberately put in a sexist gag and do a few mother-in-law jibes as a joke, and people would tut and wag their finger,' explains Variety artiste Phil Herbert, aka Randolph The Remarkable. 'Your punter doesn't know anything about being PC,' says Jane Janovic, Herbert's partner in his fire eating and fish juggling double act. 'He laughs at what's funny, and that was normally the way at The Store. When Philip used to come on doing Randolph, people regularly used to go, "Get off, you fat bastard," and of course when I used to come on, people used to shout out, "Show us your tits."' Once she did, but only by accident, when her boob tube slipped down during a fish dancing routine.

One Northern club comic was booed off for cracking racist jokes, and comic turned novelist Nick Revell once pulled off an open spot who asked if there were any schwarzers in. 'I remember Julian Clary getting heckled off by some homophobic Americans and I really tore into them.' Revell told them to fuck off out of Lebanon and fuck off out of here, which got a resounding cheer. But Revell's routine about police brutality was met with heckles of 'Fuck off, you red,' and for every punter who was offended, there were several more who weren't outraged by the old one-liners, just bored. 'It wasn't so much that it wasn't PC,' argues Malcolm Hardee of the more traditional comedy. 'It was just that it was an old-fashioned joke.'

It was Rik Mayall who told Malcolm Hardee about The Store. 'There were all these naked girls in there, which was great, because all the barmaids were topless,' said Mayall, recalling his first visit. 'Alexei came on and held a gun to my head,' he added. 'I shat myself. It was fantastic. I'd never seen anything like it and that's when we decided we wanted to be on there.'[2] Hardee was performing with Mayall, Adrian Edmondson and Martin Soan in a sketch troupe called The New Fundation at the Woolwich Tramshed, a pioneering comedy venue in South-east London (the original Fundation included two PE teachers called Gareth Hale and Norman Pace, who became household names a decade later as The Two Rons). 'We did this place last week,' Mayall told Hardee. 'It was the opening week of The Comedy Store. You want to give that a go.' Hardee and Soan went along the second week, and liked what they saw. 'If you survived three shows without getting gonged off, you were on the payroll,'[3] wrote Hardee, but the pay packet wasn't much to write home about. The compere was paid fifteen quid, solo turns got eight; Hardee and Soan shared a tenner between them. 'We weren't accepted as being artistic,' says Hardee. 'We were more like the rough old herberts.' Mayall and Edmondson's manic knockabout wasn't terribly different from Soan and Hardee's but Mayall and Edmondson had both done drama degrees at Manchester University. Soan's higher education consisted of three weeks at art school, while Hardee took his A Levels in prison. Hardee ended up doing benefit gigs as part of his community service, but he had a few stormers at The Store. 'My best memory was following Harry Enfield. He'd died a complete death. They were a horrible rowdy Friday night audience. I went on and stormed it and did about forty-five minutes.'[4]

Soan and Hardee's Greatest Show On Legs might actually have made it along to the first night, had it not been for Hardee's intimate relationship with the Old Bill. He and Soan were on their way into the West End to audition, having seen an advert in *The Stage*, when they were pulled over by the police. 'Why did the police stop you?' I ask Soan. 'Because I was with Malcolm,' he replies. 'Malcolm cracked a joke in the police station, they kept us in for bloody hours and we missed our audition.' It's a pity The Greatest Show On Legs didn't play the opening night, since Soan and Hardee claim to have coined the phrase Alternative Comedy. 'There's a very good-natured dispute between us and Tony Allen about the phrase Alternative Comedy,' says Soan. 'He says that he coined it, and Malcolm and I insist that we coined it with the help of a landlord in Salcombe.' When they played a pub in this seaside town, The Greatest Show On Legs discovered the Salcombe Yacht Club was staging a cabaret nearby, so they called their show Alternative Cabaret to distinguish it from the tamer event at the yacht club. My money's on Allen's comedy cooperative of the same name, but it's a nice story all the same.

The Store was building an underground reputation, but although audiences were beginning to get the joke, the press were slow to catch on. 'We want a photo of you banging the gong, with Don Ward and all these barmaids, all with very tight T-shirts with The Comedy Store logo,' a photographer from the *Sun* told Jim Barclay. Barclay refused. 'I don't know if you saw my act,' he told them, 'but I usually start by saying, "My name's Jim Barclay and I tell jokes which precipitate the downfall of capitalism and bring an end to tyranny and injustice wherever it rears its ugly head." It doesn't really sit that well surrounded by a bevvy of T-shirted talent.' Worse was to follow. The first night Dawn French and Jennifer Saunders played The Store, the act before them, Andy de la Tour, was interrupted by a racist heckle. 'Before you knew, chairs and bottles were flying,' recalled French.[5] The police arrived and dealt with the trouble-makers, but next time they encountered an unruly audience, the troublemakers were policemen on a stag night. 'I'm not going to stand for this,' said French, still every inch a teacher. 'You are just going to shut up and we are going to get on and finish this sketch.' 'Show us your tits,' bellowed the boys in blue. 'Why don't you show us your knob, sir?' retorted French.[6]

Yet French and Saunders were never militant feminists, even under such sustained chauvinistic provocation. 'They were actually more powerful and influential in the feminist movement for being funny women,' says Steve Frost.

Non-racism and non-sexism eventually became common consent among the comics, although Sayle still poked fun at his political convictions. 'I'm an Alternative comic, which means I'm not funny,' he'd say. 'I'm a non-sexist non-racist, so if you don't laugh at me, you're a fucking Nazi shit bag.' However, a lot of Sayle's fans weren't squatters and activists, but squaddies and policemen. 'It's the shaven head,' he says. 'I'd point out to them that I was a Jewish Marxist, but they didn't care.'

Other comics were better at the PC theory than the practice. 'A lot of the guys used to sneak in the back and watch the strippers,' recalls Lee Cornes. But only if it was free. 'We wouldn't go and watch the strip if we had to pay,' says Jim Barclay. 'We used to nip in the back and watch it and then we'd deny having been to see it. I'm like everybody else. I'm interested in women taking their clothes off. I can see that it's wrong, but I'm still going to go and watch it.' 'Sometimes we couldn't find any comics because they'd come in early and all gone to The Nell Gwynne,' says Ward. The radical spirit was willing but the reactionary flesh was weak. Yet even feminist comediennes weren't always affronted. 'That was all part of the glamour as far as I was concerned,' says Jenny Lecoat, who came here from the folk circuit. 'I'd never been anywhere near a strip club and it just added to the whole mythology of the place.' But comics who were offended didn't have a lot of choice. 'There was no stand-up anywhere in the country,' says Peter Rosengard. 'This was the first stand-up comedy club.'

The strip show at The Nell Gwynne usually finished before eleven, but the comedy show in The Gargoyle didn't start until midnight. Ward and Rosengard didn't want comedy punters getting mixed up with the dirty raincoat brigade, yet despite their best efforts, these two incompatible audiences inevitably overlapped. 'There used to be punters passing each other on the way in,' explains Jane Janovic. 'The exotic punters would be coming down and Comedy Store punters would be going up.' And when rising audiences persuaded Ward to introduce a second stand-up show, at eight o'clock, the same time as the strip show down below, it was a recipe for further chaos. Comedy punters provoked an outcry among the strippers by sneaking into the strip show without paying, while strip show punters would wander into the comedy by mistake. Sometimes, they still saw striptease. 'Japanese tourists used to come into The Comedy Store thinking they were going to see a strip show,' remembered Malcolm Hardee.[7] 'They did see one when The Greatest Show On Legs were performing.' The finale of this anarchic sketch show was a fan dance performed by a few flabby blokes in socks, juggling strategically placed balloons, hardly the sort of striptease these tourists had in mind. 'It didn't really matter,' says Hardee.

'Because the Japanese character is quite sort of subservient, they'd just sit there and stare at you.'

'One night, a girl who was stripping downstairs came up and did a stand-up act upstairs,' says Jim Barclay. But not all her colleagues stuck to straight stand-up. 'There was one mad girl who, when she wasn't getting any laughs, would get her tits out,' recalls Lee Cornes. 'We were trying to encourage as many women as possible and they were the ones who were closest to hand,' says Tony Allen. 'Don would actually stop them going on.'

'For a shy twenty-four-year-old, it was a bit of an eye opener,' remembered Paul Merton. 'There was a stripper doing an exotic act in the lounge area and I thought to myself, "At last, I know I'm in show business." It was either The Comedy Store or becoming a Redcoat at Butlin's, smiling inanely at pensioners. For my first open spot, I did a monologue about a policeman on an acid trip, got paid in beer tokens and walked all the way home to my bedsit in Streatham on a tremendous high.'[8] But nothing lasts forever. Laughter, to paraphrase Raymond Chandler, is a lot like alcohol. 'The first kiss is magic, the second is intimate, the third is routine. After that you take the girl's clothes off.'[9] Merton got fed up with doing stand-up at the young Store, although he now regularly performs with the Comedy Store Players. 'The audience would always be so pissed, and you have to do joke, joke, joke, hammer, hammer, here comes the punchline and you won't miss it no matter how drunk you are. Then you'd come off and someone would say, "Great show," but I'd find no enjoyment in it.'[10] Yet it was good while it lasted. And for Merton, it lasted a good few years. 'I will never again be as scared as that. I felt as though my heart rate had trebled and that I was the only three-dimensional person in a roomful of cut outs.'[11] Sometimes, real life can seem a poor second.

The Eighties polarised political opinion. Britain, never One Nation under Labour or the Tories, split into two separate political camps. 'There was no sense of the consensus you feel now, where roughly everybody probably wants pretty much the same things,' says Jenny Lecoat. 'In those days, you were either one of us or one of them. It was us or the enemy. Us meant you were a socialist, a feminist, you were into alternative lifestyles, you violently hated the Tories, you probably took drugs.'

What's more, these new comedians were a generation younger than the trad comics they'd usurped. Trad comics paid their dues on the working men's club circuit. These new comedians shunned conventional stand-up apprenticeships and took the short cut to the top. Most were in their twenties, and felt they owed nothing to anyone. Only a few were in their thirties. Arnold Brown, in his early forties, was the oldest by far. And twentysomething comics are bound to be more radical than their fortysomething counterparts.

However, politics wasn't the only track in the mix. 'They'd talk about the GLC, but they'd talk about the pop charts,' explains Paul Jackson. 'They'd talk about television. They'd talk about being in love. They'd talk about sex. They'd talk about

Clive Anderson performing at the Soho Store. Rick Mayall watches in the audience (second from left)

beer. They'd talk about anything, but politics was such a part of our lives at that time that it was an automatic thing to talk about that, too.' Clive Anderson, one of The Store's first fledgling stars, was scarcely the kind of comic you'd associate with class war. 'A shy barrister called Clive Anderson exudes a benignly patrician air: the only anxiety is whether he'll summon up the courage actually to tell jokes,' reported the *Observer* in 1980. 'His act – it is more a self-effaced ramble – begins slowly. Gradually, he warms up. "I am nervous," he admits privately. "I can't see the point in disguising it." Searching for words which won't come, he tells the audience, "I can't remember gags. My memory's not what it was. At least, I don't think it is." It turns out he's brilliant.'

Despite this rave review, Anderson never believed his chaotic weekend hobby would eventually become his career, even though both his jobs required quick wits. 'You have to think on your feet,' he says. 'It's called not having enough material.' Alexei Sayle's gong was a bit like a judge's gavel, but legal comparisons only stretch so far. Generally, jurors don't bay for blood and briefs rarely respond in kind. 'It was very raucous, very noisy, very aggressive,' confirms Anderson. Football hooligans used to chant from one side of the room to the other, but it was the collision of incompatible punters that made this audience so volatile. 'There was this rather macabre drunken Saturday night crowd of lads who'd come from the football,' says Jim Barclay. 'There was a lefty show-biz crowd and the establishment crowd, who were just intrigued.' The variety in the audience more than matched the variety onstage. 'The audience were very bohemian,' agrees Martin Potter, 'but they were all there for the same reason. To have a good time and heckle off the acts.'

And unlike impro or panto, this was audience participation on the audience's own terms. 'A bond has been established between myself and you the audience,' Arnold Brown would tell these punters. 'We can sum it up in the one word. Resentment.' These stand-up pioneers didn't simply recycle their best material, pandering to the safer tastes of critics, agents or producers. They couldn't stick to tried and tested routines because they were too busy trying to control the chaos around the room. 'People used to be disgustingly rude to the comedian,' recalls Ashley Roy. 'If someone had a glass eye, they'd say, "You one-eyed bastard."'

Plenty of these early performers were future stars, but the acts who went nowhere fast were an equally big attraction. 'Maybe they were rubbish, maybe they were good but couldn't be bothered, maybe they were having disasters, but that made for an interesting evening,' says Anderson. 'It was so hostile and anarchic,' recalls Jim Barclay. 'You were watching loads of other people, and you learnt as much from the bad people as you did from the good ones.' There was a macabre element in the audience's fascination with bad acts, like that grotesque night when a harmless turn whose entire act consisted of opening a music stand wasn't gonged out of his misery, but goaded with ironic applause. At times like these, stand-up stops being performance art and becomes a blood sport.

Yet Barclay still felt like he was a part of something big. 'We were all onto something new and there wasn't that backbiting that there was in the acting profession,' he says. 'People were all very supportive.' They even ventured out of London. 'Tony Allen and Andy de la Tour and Ben Elton and I all got in my tiny little Citroën and went off to Totnes to do a festival, and it poured with rain all weekend. There was mud everywhere. We were in this tent in this field and we performed the same material to the same audience all weekend.' Being a comic in 1979 felt a lot like being a student in 1968. 'I played the CND Hyde Park demo to a quarter of a million people,' he recalls. 'Then, in the evening, I went off to do the Balham folk club and there were twelve people in the audience.'

For the first few months, at least, The Store's future was far from certain. 'There were no acts,' says Robin Banks. 'The whole night was open spots.' Even getting punters was a problem, since Soho wasn't the all-night funfair it is today. 'It was quiet at night,' says Ashley Roy. 'At one o'clock in the morning there was no fucker there.' Sundays were even worse. 'Soho died on a Sunday,' says Don Ward. And so did his Sunday shows. One Sunday night Ward phoned Alexei Sayle at The Store. 'How's it all going?' he asked Sayle. 'Well, I'm on the bill,' replied Sayle. 'French & Saunders are on the bill.

Rik and Ade are on the bill. Peter Richardson and Nigel Planer are on. Andy de la Tour is on. Tony Allen is on. And we've got nine customers.'

'There were more comedians than audience,' confirms Rosengard. 'I used to say to the comedians, "Come out of the dressing room and sit in the audience, because we have no audience." There were times when we thought, "Bugger it, this is not working,"' he admits. And when someone stole the microphones, Ward also wondered if it was worth going on. To add musical insult to financial injury, during his Dangerous Brothers double act with Rik Mayall, Adrian Edmondson used to dismantle Ward's piano. 'Every week I had a row with Ade,' says Ward. 'Do you have to take the piano apart?' he'd ask Edmondson. 'Every week it's costing me money to put it back together again on Monday morning.' At least it got a few laughs, which was more than some future stars often managed. 'French & Saunders used to get regularly booed off,' remembers Ward.

Punters who did turn up came to bury the comics, not to praise them. 'These people were there to take the piss out of you,' says Otiz Canneloni. 'It was a battle of wills, and the comedy came second.' The atmosphere was one of confrontation, not communion. 'People would come on and say, "Good evening, ladies and gentlemen," and they'd get gonged off,' recalls Phil Herbert. 'No matter how good they were, people weren't getting a go, because the audience realised their power,' confirms Kim Kinnie. 'A lot of them then came along for that reason, so they could destroy whatever was going on onstage.' Even Alexei Sayle ended up asking the audience to give the acts a chance, often to no avail. 'We didn't have enough acts to fill the bloody night, because they were being gonged off,' says Kinnie. 'They controlled it. We didn't.'

Inevitably, even the most thick-skinned comics became sick and tired of turning up to be abused. 'You wouldn't accept that in the street,' says Lee Cornes. 'Why accept it onstage?' Most comedians were cannon fodder, so The Store needed at least a dozen every night. 'Have we got any comedians coming tonight?' Peter Rosengard would fret before every show. 'Are they going to turn up?' Sometimes, he had to go and fetch them in his Rolls-Royce.

The Store soon ran so short of acts that Rosengard even got up and had a go himself. Not that he needed much encouragement. 'His heart was in it,' says Norman Lovett. 'He wanted to be a comedian himself.' And in The Store he'd created a playground where he could live his dream. 'He was terribly innocent,' says Lee Cornes. 'He went down appallingly, but it didn't stop him from jumping up and doing it again.' Not everybody was so indulgent. 'I've got a frustrated comic on my hands,' thought Ward. Yet Rosengard's comedic frustration was a help, as well as a hindrance. 'If Peter couldn't have had a chance to tell a joke and get in the newspapers, The Comedy Store would have folded,' says Ashley Roy. 'His ego is what made it go.'

Rosengard was often more amusing offstage, like the time he turned up with a Sony Walkman when they were still a newfangled novelty in Britain. 'I remember him putting it on, trying to impress everybody,' says Martin Soan, 'but there wasn't anybody else with a Walkman, so he didn't realise the fatal mistake of talking when you've got a Walkman on.'

Mind you, Rosengard had the last laugh. He never cut it as a stand-up comic, but today he's a prolific speaker on the international sales convention circuit. A few years ago, in Tokyo, he earned £10,000 for a thirty-minute speech before an audience of 10,000; a lot more money than today's comics earn for twenty minutes at The Store, and in front of a lot more punters, too. Until those try-outs at the old Soho, Rosengard had never performed in public before. Maybe it did him some good, after all.

'I think he may have a hankering to be doing almost anything except what he is doing,' said Alexei Sayle, of this thick-skinned yet simultaneously sensitive salesman. 'He probably wishes he was a stand-up comic.'[12] But Sayle's assessment of Rosengard's stand-up is typically blunt: 'He stinks.'[13] 'I heckled him off,' recalls punter turned stand-up Ian Stone. 'I think that's why I get booked here so regularly, because Don really appreciates me. He was terrible, though. God he was terrible, and I think he tried it once and realised he was better off doing insurance.'

Rosengard got The Store off the ground, Ward kept it up and running, but Kim Kinnie was the biggest influence on the comics themselves. For performers brimming over with fresh ideas but often woefully bereft of conventional stagecraft, his traditional show business background was a godsend.

'Here's a comic I can relate to,' thought Kinnie, the first time he saw Paul Merton perform. And when Kinnie could relate to a comic, his dedication knew no bounds. He'd spend hours talking to up-and-coming comics like John Hegley, discussing how to hone their acts. Yet there were other nights when stand-up was the last thing on his mind. 'It was like a Wild West saloon,' he says, remembering one of the nights he had to call the police. 'Having been brought up in Glasgow, one of the things I've always known, if you're in the middle of a fight, don't move. If you move, you get hit. If you stand still, on the whole, you're all right.'

One night, fellow Glaswegian Arnold Brown walked onstage to do his set, took one look at the audience and walked straight off again. Other comics responded in kind. 'They'd tell the audience to fuck off,' says Rosengard, 'and the audience told them to fuck off.'

'It really was a murderous place,' remembered yet another Glaswegian, the performance artist Oscar McLennan. 'I had this pint in ma hands and I looked down at this table in front of me and it just looked like a nest of young chicks waiting to be fed, mouths opening and closing away. I didn't really think about it. I just poured this pint all over their faces. And this guy picked up his pint and threw it back, so I picked up the table and up-ended it. This broke out all over the front row, and I picked up the table and threw it at the audience.'[14] Another night, McLennan was provoked by a party of dental students. 'I just lost it,' he admits. 'I just leapt over the stage trying to get at this guy's throat.' A year later, McLennan ended up in a dental hospital, for treatment under general anaesthetic. 'Do you ever perform at The

Comedy Store?' asked the dentist, as McLennan was about to go under. 'No,' lied McLennan, before he passed out, 'you've got the wrong man.' But a few years after that, he was on his way out of The Store when he met a punter coming in. 'Do you remember me?' asked the punter. 'No,' said McLennan. 'I'm the dental student you attacked that night,' said the punter. 'That was a brilliant night, wasn't it? Let me buy you a pint.'

McLennan had heard about The Store from Tony Allen, whom he met at Speaker's Corner while busking in Marble Arch. McLennan had been a labourer, bookies' boardmarker and London Transport station foreman, and had spent a year bumming around Europe, begging, stealing and selling bent watches. But even this streetwise Scot found The Store intimidating. 'It was just a bear pit,' he says. 'It was just horrible. People weren't coming there to listen. They were just coming there to act like arseholes.' His debut was a disaster. 'I had to get out of my head to do it,' he says. 'It was the only way I could face getting on there. It was the most terrifying thing I've ever done in my life.' He barely lasted a minute. However, his second gig went well, and this brief flicker of success kept him going during the bleak months that followed. 'It was a year of failure, but it took over my life,' he says. 'You'd get gonged off after two minutes and you'd spend the next two or three days curled up in a foetal position, and then get another idea and this would see you through the rest of the week and then you'd go back down again.'

Wannabes were welcome to come back and get gonged off as often as they wanted, and McLennan was tough enough to keep returning, and learning from his frequent failures. And if you could bear the drunken abuse, The Store was a place where anyone could learn for free. 'Anybody can get up and do it, which was the whole ethos of punk.'

'It wasn't a job, and no one thought it would be a career,' agrees Martin Potter. 'Beer was the form of currency in those days. We were all doing it just for fun.' 'If you were going to perform, you got somebody else in for free, and you got three free drinks, so we started as a solo act and then moved to a double act, so we could get four people in and six free drinks,' explains Otiz Canneloni of The Legendary Canneloni Brothers, the double act he formed with his brother-in-law, Martin Coyote. 'We used to say if we could make one hundred pounds a week we'd be laughing. We were making nothing then. Absolutely nothing.'

These eccentric turns certainly made The Store more colourful, but in those precarious early days, it was Alexei Sayle and Keith Allen who kept the club together. 'Alexei had the intellectual energy and Keith had the danger,' explains Arnold Brown. 'They were the fuel of The Store.' Aptly, these two stand-up firestarters had met in yet another strip club. 'I did some extra work in this Italian film which was being shot in a strip club with this woman giving a blow job to two guys, and Keith was there playing a barman,' recalls Sayle. 'You're the host of The Comedy Store,' said Allen. 'I must come down there.' And he did.

Keith Allen had played a comedian in a play called *Radio Beelzebub*. In that play,

Keith Allen at The Store

the comic turns on his audience. At The Store, Allen did much the same thing. His malevolent contempt mesmerised crowd and comics alike. 'You never knew what he'd do,' says Arnold Brown. 'You never knew what he'd say.' Brown can still recall his favourite Allen one-liner. 'When he went to the country,' he recites, with relish, 'it was the first time he'd seen horses without a policeman on top.' 'An incredibly gifted man,' agrees anarchic clown Chris Lynam. 'He could just go off at any tangent.'

'Keith was just mind blowing,' concurs Paul Jackson. 'It's one of the sadnesses of it all, a) that Keith chose not to follow that in a more fulsome way than he ever did, and b) that as a result, there's very little material of what he did, and he denies it now. I've tried to talk to Keith about it. I've tried to get him to revive some of the routines he did and he claims not to remember them.' Jackson sums up Allen's appeal as 'This is what we do and if you don't like it fuck off.' It was a far cry from the ingratiating etiquette of the Light Ent showcases Jackson was used to. 'The comedy was incredibly clever, carefully woven out of nothing,' says Jackson. 'He was sexy. He was charismatic.' And he loved making his right-on spectators squirm. 'Keith understands the power of comedy,' says Jackson. 'The place just didn't know what to do.

'"You come to see me bust my balls up here, and saying what you want",' Jackson recalls Allen telling his gobsmacked audience. '"And then I say something fucking risky and you've all gone fucking wimpy on me."'

Another ball-busting turn was Allen's treatment of a journalist who'd just given him a good review. 'It wasn't the first he'd got,' says Jackson. 'He was picked out as the hot tip pretty early on.' Yet this journalist made the mistake of returning, with a friend, and taking a table right in front of the stage. 'Keith then turned on this guy and let forth with a load of vitriolic abuse,' recalls Don Ward. 'He picked up the champagne bucket, full of iced water, took out the bottle, and poured the whole lot over his head. He left him sat there with the champagne bucket on top of his head and the audience hooting with laughter.' 'It sounds so arrogant, but it wasn't,' says Jackson. 'It was absolutely what rock and roll had been to a different generation. It's ours. It's our culture. You don't fucking understand. We don't want you coming down here, writing good reviews.' And anyway, Allen's antics were much better publicity than any arts page write-up. 'Is the guy that throws iced water over us going to be on tonight?' eager punters asked Ward the next week.

'He'd relish hecklers because he'd destroy them,' says Roger Pomphrey, a regular punter at the Soho Store. 'He could speak louder, faster and sharper than anybody. If you ever analysed what he said after the event, it was often probably very ruthless, very rude and maybe even wildly inaccurate.' But more often than not, he was spot on. 'He didn't mind telling people home truths. He'd say, "You're not a funny fucker at all. You're a middle-class twat who's only just come down from university."'

This insult also applied to a fair few Store performers, who were equally intimidated by Allen's remorseless wit. 'He terrified them,' says Pomphrey. 'They were all genuinely really frightened of him.' And with good cause. 'Keith went on the stage behind this comedian, and he didn't know he was on, and Keith got his dick out and started to urinate through this bloke's legs,' recalls Pomphrey. 'When the bloke realised that the inside of his trousers were all wet, not of his doing, he turned around and noticed Keith and left the stage.' Practical jokes are always cruel, but laughter is amoral. '"I'm really sorry, I just can't do it tonight, the thing is my father's just died",' Oscar McLennan recalls Allen telling the audience. 'He must have gone on for about fifteen minutes about his father,' says McLennan. 'He literally had people in tears.' 'The funeral will be on Thursday,' said Allen. 'I'll be there with the disco.'

Clive Anderson also fell foul of Allen's irreverent attitude to his fellow performers. One night, Anderson was onstage and his old friend from the Cambridge Footlights, John Lloyd, creator of *Not The Nine O'Clock News*, was in the audience. Anderson wrote for *Not The Nine O'Clock News*, so he thought it would be fun to point Lloyd out and make him the target of some mock deferential wit. 'Just a way of jollying up my material.' It was the only time his act ever went wrong at The Store. With its prime-time BBC2 slot, opposite BBC1's *Nine O'Clock News*, a dream team of Rowan Atkinson, Mel Smith, Pamela Stephenson and Griff Rhys Jones, who replaced Chris Langham after the first series, plus up-and-coming comedy writers like Richard Curtis, Andy Hamilton, Guy Jenkin, Andrew Marshall, David Renwick and Ruby Wax, *Not The Nine O'Clock News* was the most talked about sketch show since *Monty Python's Flying Circus*. But its nationwide success gave it a mainstream status that inevitably set it some way apart from this spit and sawdust club, and Ashley Roy recalls Griff Rhys Jones and Pamela Stephenson both getting gonged off at The Store.

Unfortunately for Anderson, Keith Allen was also there that night, and took Anderson's introduction as his cue to lambast *Not The Nine O'Clock News* as middle-class rubbish, and to berate Lloyd, and Anderson too. 'He might have had a drink or two,' says Anderson, who had to finish up and get off, his act ruined. 'I was rather annoyed about that,' he adds, although he doesn't sound at all cross today. Yet when so popular and forceful a performer starts to tear into a punter, there's not a lot you can do about it. Allen and Lloyd's lively debate about the show's merits outlived

Anderson's hastily contracted set. 'It involved some long, heated conversation in the lift.'

Despite Keith Allen's starring role in Anderson's worst Store set, Anderson is still full of admiration for Allen's anarchic free spirit. 'I can remember one fantastic stunt that he did where he came on with a ventriloquist's dummy,' says Anderson. 'He was naked. The dummy was dressed up.' Clearly, this was not the normal gottle of geer routine. 'Every so often, he'd just slightly readjust his willy.' Anderson can still recall the rough gist of what Allen said. '"You will notice that I'm using one of the ancient techniques of ventriloquism, because the thing about ventriloquism is it's quite hard to stop your lips moving, so the technique is to distract the viewer's eye away from your mouth while you're doing it. And I can guarantee that while I'm standing onstage naked playing with my willy, that you haven't been looking at my lips."'

Allen's act wasn't overtly political, but his education was a template for Alternative Comedy's classless appeal. From comprehensive school, he won a scholarship to a public school, got expelled, returned to his old comp, got expelled again, and graduated to a detention centre and Borstal. He went to a further education college and then Cardiff's Welsh College of Music and Drama, worked as a stage manager at London's ICA, and decided against being an actor after appearing in an all-male production of *Macbeth*. Instead, he started a rock band, and then disbanded it after it attracted an unsolicited National Front following. Allen was the star of The Store for several months, even though nobody was ever entirely sure if he would show up. Above all, he was madly funny, despite having virtually no jokes. Performance artist Andrew Bailey recalls him coming on with a huge pile of plates, and smashing them, one after another, on his head.

'He did an act once when he didn't even come on stage,' says Ashley Roy. 'He had the microphone, and he was sitting in the dressing room. He said, "I am so funny and so famous I don't even need to appear onstage."' For five minutes or more, the audience sat and watched an empty stage. One night, he left a tape recorder centre stage, playing the first five minutes of his act, before his eventual entrance. It was a surreal stunt worthy of the best absurdist theatre. 'I liked people like Keith,' says Peter Rosengard. 'I liked people who were on the very edge.' 'He was the best, but I had to stop booking him in the end,' says Don Ward. 'He was too unreliable.'

Alexei Sayle's stand-up was more concrete and controlled, but like Allen, his humour was an immaculate revenge against an over-educated elite. Ever since *That Was The Week That Was*, the smarter sort of TV show, from *Monty Python* via *The Goodies* to *Not The Nine O'Clock News*, had been top heavy with Oxbridge talent. 'Alexei hated that privilege,' says Arnold Brown, 'because he's a working-class man. He thought he was as talented as they were, but they all went to Cambridge. It was a kind of Mafia, an Oxbridge Mafia.' Sayle's sense of fun was just as literate and eloquent as any Oxford or Cambridge University revue, but it felt far closer to Brecht than Beyond The Fringe.

Plenty of Oxbridge comics still played The Store. Clive Anderson, Nick Hancock,

Neil Mullarkey, Tony Slattery, Sandi Toksvig, Richard Vranch, Punt & Dennis and Newman & Baddiel all came from The Cambridge Footlights, a varsity club started back in 1883 to play a cricket match at a lunatic asylum. However, once The Store's influence began to spread, such well-read wags learned to keep their Oxbridge CVs quiet.

Brown, a greengrocer's son who was raised in a Glasgow tenement, admits he camped up his working-class background. Brown's roots weren't remotely privileged by the standards of today. 'We had no money,' he says. 'We used to go to public baths.' But his humour was about the culture clash between these working-class beginnings and his bourgeois adulthood. His adopted Hampstead home, which he dubbed 'NW Twee', was a world away from his Glaswegian origins, and the gulf informed some of his finest and funniest gags, like the one about the two-year waiting list in Glasgow for people who want to vandalise phone boxes, or the people in Hampstead who live in council houses and have second council houses in the country.

Brown wasn't the only Store comedian in this sushi socialist postcode. Back then, Ben Elton also lived in Hampstead, class war's biggest target in their Bash The Rich offensive. 'It didn't hurt that his professor father and teacher mother were able to give him the use of a Hampstead flat while he was earning £15 per week at The Comedy Store,' reported the *Evening Standard* in 1984. 'I sometimes think the flat was my biggest break ever,' Elton told the *Standard*. 'But I'm big-headed enough to think I'd have made it anyway.'

It was the sudden collision of these two worlds that gave The Store its dramatic tension. Alternative Comedy had hijacked a Light Ent vehicle which seemed so intrinsically conservative that before comics like Sayle played The Store, the very idea of left-wing stand-up was virtually inconceivable. Comic and academic Oliver Double cites a book called *Make Em Laugh* by Eric Midwinter which claimed: 'it would be difficult to conceive of, for instance, a Marxist comedian treading the boards of one of the private theatre circuits, not just because the management would object, but because the audience would feel uncomfortable.' *Make Em Laugh* was published in 1979, the year The Store opened.

A few writers were far more prescient than Midwinter. In 1975, Richard Eyre directed the premiere of a remarkably prophetic play by Trevor Griffiths, whose work had been produced by 7-84, a radical theatre troupe whose actors included Store comic Jim Barclay. (The name referred to the statistic that 7 per cent of the population hogged 84 per cent of the wealth, not that 7 per cent of the theatre companies hogged 84 per cent of the Arts Council grants.) *Comedians* was about a bunch of night-school comics who try out at a local working men's club in a bid to impress an influential talent scout. The anti-hero of this seminal drama anticipated Alternative Comedy's confrontational class anger, and although Jonathan Pryce made the part his own, onstage and then on TV, the role could have been written for Keith Allen. Yet even though Griffiths foresaw a new kind of comedy, he didn't foresee The Store, and the problem for the frustrated genius of this piece is that he has nowhere to play. 'You have

Tony Allen, the man who probably invented the term 'Alternative Comedy'

a certain talent maybe as a mime,' the talent scout tells him. 'Music hall maybe, but there is no music hall. You want to be a comedian, you'd better start somewhere else. There's no way you'll get started with what you've got.' Before The Store, comics like Allen shared precisely the same problem. 'If you want to get on, lad, you'd better sort a few problems out first,' says the scout. 'Don't give us your hang-ups straight. Too hot to handle.'

Far less famous than Keith Allen, yet even more influential, was Tony Allen. They weren't brothers, although even Roger Pomphrey, who lived with Keith's real brother Kevin, made the same mistake at first. 'Tony Allen was always making political points,' explains Otiz Canneloni. 'Some of them were humorous, but he'd be very calm and collected. Alexei was more of a piece of dynamite, waiting to go off.'

In an era when radical comics wore normal clothes onstage, Allen dressed flamboyantly, but his hand-me-down Dickensian chic was the least remarkable aspect of his act. Ladbroke Grove's best-dressed squatter tackled challenging topics like bisexuality, and the format his humour followed was often as radical as its content. 'I don't want you to clap,' he told the audience, at the end of one of his sets. 'It was a very weird atmosphere,' says Arthur Smith, the compere that night, who had to come back on afterwards and tell the audience to have a clap, to restore some semblance of normality. 'Tony was never actually all that funny, but he was thoughtful, and his influence was great,' says Smith. 'He challenged Ben Elton to go onstage and not get laughs, which was a ridiculous thing for a comedian. You're supposed to get laughs. But it was an interesting idea, to be a comedian who could get laughs but chooses not to.'

When a comic uses laughter as a means to an end, the laughs often end up getting in the way. And yet Allen could write sidesplitting one-liners when he wanted to, street-smart parodies of trad one-liners that simultaneously mocked the straight establishment and his own anarchic counter culture. 'This drunk homosexual Pakistani squatter trade unionist takes my mother-in-law to an Irish restaurant,' ran one such gag. 'Says to the West Indian waiter, "Waiter, waiter, there's a racial stereotype in my soup."' 'You never quite knew what you were going to get,' says Nick Revell. 'When he was at his best you always knew he would be able to deal with complicated ideas and keep getting the laughs.'

However, Allen also wrestled with taboos that even Alternative comics feared to face. 'Tony did an amazing routine about rape,' remembered Simon Fanshawe. 'I'd never seen anyone do anything as dangerous and as exciting.'[15] Fanshawe was similarly brave. A few years later, he became the first comedian to tackle AIDS on TV, not just breaking new comic ground, but maybe even saving a few lives, too.

The best comics refuse to compromise, but their resolve can come at a steep price. 'He'd never pander in the slightest,' explains Arnold Brown. 'Alexei never pandered, but he had a sense of theatricality. Tony was more interested in putting across his own point of view. Audiences turn away from being told what to think. That was his Achilles' heel. He wanted to be commercially successful, but on his own terms, and that's impossible. You can't do what he does and be acceptable.' Every comedian must persuade his punters to share his viewpoint, and as Don Ward built a more mainstream audience at The Store, Allen's views became more isolated. 'He was the right man at the right time,' says John Hegley. 'An anarchist in Thatcher's Britain.' Trouble is, times change, as Tony Allen and Margaret Thatcher both discovered.

'It's been a mystery to a lot of people why Tony didn't take off and find television fame and success like the rest of them,' says Martin Soan. 'A lot of the younger comics know who he is but they just find him a laughing stock.' They don't share Soan's surprise and disappointment that Allen, like most innovators, never had his fair share of recognition. But if commercial success is your only yardstick, innovation counts for nothing. 'None of the new acts know,' says Arthur Smith. 'They just think he's a stupid old git.'

'At his best, he was a fucking master,' says Kim Kinnie. 'I've seen Tony do a Friday night you'd die for, one of the best stand-up nights I've ever seen. Saturday night, I'd watch him just die on his arse.' Inconsistency is the price you pay for trying something new, but as The Store became slicker, consistency became crucial. 'Talent isn't the ability to be brilliant,' explains Alexei Sayle. 'It's the ability to be brilliant night after night after night, and that's what a lot of performers don't have.'

Allen's immense influence can be seen in the work of comics like Mark Thomas, and if TV had been sufficiently versatile to create a format like Channel 4's *Mark Thomas Product* when Allen's star was still in the ascendant, maybe he would have found the platform that his talent deserved. Allen's enduring gift to The Store was his social conscience, and against all odds, some of that non-conformist vibe still survives. As Auden said of Yeats, Allen's eventual epitaph will be that he became his admirers.

One act that really epitomised the young Store's experimental flavour was a performance artist called Andrew Bailey. Bailey was playing fairs and festivals with a troupe called Theatre Of Lies when he first heard about The Store. 'I went and checked it out and I loved it,' he says. 'God, I loved it.' But when he returned to do a turn, he went back with his friend and fellow performer Simon Grenville. Grenville went onstage first and got gonged off. Then Alexei Sayle introduced Bailey as Grenville's friend, which didn't help. Bailey got gonged off too. 'It was a pretty humiliating experience,' says Bailey, 'but I still loved it. I loved the energy and the buzz, and this idea that you could just do it yourself.'

Bailey had worked as a stage manager at The Gargoyle way back in the early Seventies, almost a decade before The Store began. He even stage managed the strip show at Raymond's Revuebar, picking up g-strings at the Boulevard Theatre, where The Comic Strip started out. He worked backstage on an Australian *Jesus Christ Superstar*, and as a dresser at the National Theatre, and it was only after he answered an advert in *Time Out* for a children's puppet show that Bailey drifted into comedy. 'I should have stayed in Australia, really,' he says. 'I never thought I was a comedian, and then one thing led to another, and I'm a clown.' But what a clown.

When Bailey returned for a second try, he had to follow Keith Allen. Allen did three-quarters of an hour. 'Some poor fucker's got to follow this,' announced Alexei Sayle, bringing on Bailey. But this time around, Bailey had transformed his appearance, and his act. Dressed in dark glasses, leather jacket, striped pants and red clogs, he strode across the tables and jumped up onstage. 'Give me a G!' said Bailey. 'G!' screamed the audience. 'Give me an O!' he said. 'O!' repeated his punters. 'Give me an N!' 'N!' 'Give me a G!' 'G!' 'Put it together!' bellowed Bailey. 'What have you got?' 'Gong!' And with that, bang on cue, he went.

'That was fantastic!' Peter Rosengard told him afterwards. 'You really fooled the audience!' agreed Jim Barclay. Like some stand-up kamikaze pilot, Bailey had turned the tables on the crowd. And from then on, he became a regular turn at The Store.

One of Bailey's contemporaries at The Store in the early Eighties was a young unknown rookie called Ben Elton. At the outset, Elton was a lot less confident than either Keith or Tony Allen, yet unlike either of them, he quickly found an effective small screen forum for his humour.

'He was very, very insecure,' says Peter Rosengard. 'He'd always ask me after every act, "How was I?" I'd always say, "You were brilliant, Ben. You were brilliant.' And he was. 'Ben obviously was a tremendously talented guy and he and I became good mates,' says Rosengard. 'If I really liked them, I used to sell them insurance.'

'He used to be so unsure about what he had done that night,' says Arnold Brown, of the conversations they shared on their way back home to Hampstead. But Elton needn't have worried. After *The Young Ones* made him Alternative Comedy's hidden voice, *Saturday Live* made him its most visible face. 'The reason why Ben's on BBC1 and Alexei's on BBC2, is that Ben tells people what they know already, but he does it in a wonderful way,' explains Brown. 'Alexei creates his own world. It's a harder world to assimilate, but purer.'

Yet Sayle's televisual world was a pale imitation of his stage shows. For Rosengard, seeing Sayle live was like the time a band called The New Yardbirds played the Swedish nightclub where he worked as a DJ. This band later changed their name to Led

Zeppelin. 'Nothing I've ever heard Alexei do on television has ever captured that excitement,' says Rosengard. Unlike Sayle, Elton mastered the small screen, but he was a lot less bullish than Sayle about The Store.

'It was horrible,' said Elton, recalling his Store debut. 'I felt ill all day. I remember leaving the tube station, sort of eleven o'clock or so, with The Jam, "Down In The Tube Station At Midnight", ringing in my ears.'[16] It was here that Elton developed his motormouth delivery, rattling off his gags so rapidly that no heckler could get a word in edgeways. 'He's not a spontaneous comic,' says Ward, 'so he developed that style so no one got in his way.' But whatever Elton lacked in spontaneity, he more than made up for with hard graft. 'He was always writing,' adds Ward. 'Each week there'd be new material coming in. He was so hungry.' Lots of comics have the talent to succeed, but Ben Elton also had the dedication.

'I think I would have calmed down by now if it hadn't been for The Comedy Store,' said Elton, in 1983. 'It has done many good things. It's given performance opportunities to a lot of talented people out there – and an enormous number of completely

Ben Elton in 1983

crap people as well – but the bad side is that the gong was abused, which has left a lot of comics scarred, and I think me most of all. Having become compere of The Store for a few months in the summer of '81, I really got a battle instinct with audiences. I don't think that's good and I don't approve of it but I still can't shake the idea of taking on an audience. That was what The Store did to you.'[17] Like the night he had to call the police. 'I went offstage and asked for the police to be called. I went back to the microphone and informed the rowdies that the police were on their way and they could either wait or leave now. As Tony Allen said, "If you can't deal with one bunch of thugs, the only real thing you can do is call another bunch of thugs," which I thought was a bit uncharitable at the time. But it was a good joke.'[18]

During the early Eighties, Elton toured with Andy de la Tour, another key player at the Soho Store. For two years, de la Tour was an actor with a radical theatre company called Belt & Braces. When the company took a rock show on tour, since de la Tour didn't sing or play any instruments, he started cracking jokes and telling stories instead. He quickly acquired a taste for it, and after the tour ended, he read about The Store in *Time Out*.

'Andy de la Tour was terrific,' says Arnold Brown. 'He was incredibly political. That was the first time I'd seen something so overtly political anywhere.' De la Tour's Northern Irish observations certainly pulled no punches. He even did a routine about Tory MP Airey Neave, Margaret Thatcher's Shadow Secretary of State for Northern Ireland, who made the first British 'home run' from Colditz, disguised as a German officer, in 1942, and was murdered by an INLA car bomb in the House of Commons car park in 1979. 'People were howling for him to get off,' says Sayle. 'I left him on.' De la Tour's Irish material was guaranteed to divide the room. 'A strong Irish contingent were cheering Andy de la Tour's routine but there was also a bunch of squaddies in the audience and it got heavy and that felt like there was ground being broken,' says Tony Allen, who came to The Store from another radical theatre company, Rough Theatre. 'This is what it's all about. Getting through to people about political issues.'

At The Store, you were never only preaching to the converted, but such polemical diatribes still had a fairly finite appeal. 'Comedy is about pointing out the gap between people's expectations and reality,' says Brown, 'but it's a bit purist for lots of audiences if you're too left wing.' Most Store comics were merely ideological by omission. 'Rik never did anything political,' says Lee Cornes. 'Nigel Planer and Pete Richardson weren't political. A lot of Alexei's stuff isn't really very political. His early stuff was surreal.' At a time when racist and sexist gags were still mainstream entertainment, even neutrality was some sort of statement, but it's surely not just a coincidence that two of the most political Store pioneers, Tony Allen and Jim Barclay, are among the least famous today, while two of the least political acts, Rik Mayall and Adrian Edmondson, are among the most well known. 'They were all big grown-ups, being really cool and very dangerous and telling jokes about Mrs Thatcher,' remembered Mayall. 'We were the ones saying, "Hello. We're arseholes."'[19]

'I could see that Rik was a star immediately,' says Peter Rosengard. 'He had tremendous charisma.' 'Rik Mayall was incredible,' agrees Nick Revell. 'Rather than going out there and trying to grab them, he let them come to him, and you really knew you were in the presence of somebody who had a great deal of comic ability and composure.'

'I kind of hated them really, because they weren't doing stuff about Northern Ireland or Thatcher,' admitted Sayle. 'It was obvious that they were stars right away.'[20] But before they could even get onstage, these rising stars had to fight their way into the building. 'All the acts would jump the queue for the lift, but this caused great resentment because the audience would queue for two hours to get in,' recalled Ben Elton. 'I used to hate having to say, "Excuse me. I'm a comedian. Can I use the lift?" People would shout out, "If you're a comedian I'd better see you onstage, or else you're in trouble." I didn't mind that, but much more worrying was when they shouted, "You had better be bloody funny or else you're for it!"'[21]

'I remember you from last week,' hecklers would tell stand-up poet John Hegley, as he rode upstairs in that tiny lift, eyeball to eyeball with several punters. 'I'm going to give you a hard time this week as well.' But there was nothing namby pamby about

Hegley's brand of blank verse. 'You came in a bit too soon there, mate,' Hegley would tell his hecklers. 'Probably the story of your life.' And Hegley's crowd control wasn't confined to pre-prepared put downs. 'Hegley used to play with the hecklers and enjoy the interruptions,' says musical comic Pierre Hollins. 'Take what they're saying onboard. Turn that into a joke. Don't just stamp on it, because every heckle is an opportunity for another laugh.'

But this audience had a weapon that even the best put down couldn't counter: the gong. 'Without the gong we wouldn't have had a Comedy Store,' explains Peter Rosengard. 'It wouldn't have lasted. We'd have just had Alexei. People came to watch people get gonged off. It was the place where you could shout, "Fuck off."'

Remarkably, most acts took this ritual abuse in their stride. 'We wanted to get gonged quite quickly because you still got your money whether you got gonged or not,' recalled Dawn French.[22] 'Occasionally, the unruly minority got their way, but it wasn't off the cuff,' says John Hegley. 'The consensus ruled.'

Once the club started to attract more accomplished entertainers, this gladiatorial gimmick began to do more harm than good. 'If you give a gun to somebody who's not used to using a gun, it's not a good idea,' says Andrew Bailey. 'That's what the gong was. It was a gun. Feel free to press the trigger any time you want. You gave a licence to a fucking lunatic.' And Bailey wasn't the only act who felt that way. 'It got too anarchistic because it attracted the wrong element,' agrees Arnold Brown. 'People just came along to gong.' Often, the only defence was to laugh about it. 'Last week I was so bad,' Brown would tell the audience, 'I was gonged off in the lift.'

'The idea of the gong was so that we kept control of the room,' says Don Ward. It had the opposite effect. 'When there was anybody doing anything of interest, the audience would shout out for the gong,' says Tony Allen. 'Shut the fuck up,' he'd tell them. 'Carry on,' he'd tell the acts. But not every compere was so supportive, and the audience ran riot. 'They found it rather clever to gong off some of our established people,' says Ward. 'They didn't deserve to be gonged off.' Sometimes, even Alexei Sayle struggled. 'There were bad nights when I thought my career was over and I'd died and I was never going to work again,' he explains. 'When I had a couple of weeks off as a compere, I went there drunk and got gonged off. I was terribly upset.'

The gong created a frantic, frenetic house style which still survives at The Store today. So it's ironic that the comic who brought about its removal was probably the most profoundly influenced by it. 'Ben really didn't want the gong there,' says John Hegley. 'Ben really hated it.' Most comedians sided with Elton, but although the quality of the shows improved, The Store was never quite so equal ever again. Elton didn't miss it. 'Sometimes in my worst nightmares I'm back as compere of the Gong Show trying to decide whether to gong some act off because the comic's got a soft voice and the hecklers are giving him a bad time.'[23] But other comics weren't so sure. As Sayle says, 'It certainly made the comics sharpen up their act.' And ten years later, the gong still had some fans in unlikely places. 'If you were lying, or a hypocrite, you got gonged,' said Rik Mayall. 'When they took the gong away it was a terrible mistake.'[24]

Despite its removal, this Alternative Comedy clapometer had shifted the balance of power between act and audience, from stage to stalls. And twenty years later, it still hasn't quite shifted back again. 'Since Music Hall days, it was the first time you could go to a show and heckle,' says Martin Potter. 'I don't think anyone there had been privy to that before. Most people went there because they wanted to heckle, so the acts had to be really good to survive. The interaction between the audience and performers was a new thing. That was an integral part of the evening.' 'Heckling was new,' says John Hegley. 'It was a new way of communicating.'

With or without the gong, this Soho Store was already quite different from its Los Angeles namesake. 'There was a sense of danger that you didn't have in LA,' says Rosengard. 'There was no heckling in LA.' And as the word spread, entertainers of every kind flocked to see this brand-new spectator sport. Stood on that small stage, blinded by the spotlight, acts knew anybody could be lurking in the darkness beyond. One night, Keith Allen subjected a punter to a stream of particularly rude put-downs. The punter turned out to be Frank Zappa.

Mainstream comics soon became natural bogeymen at The Store, but at first, a few of them actually came along to see what all the fuss was about. 'Les Dawson turned up one night and did fifteen minutes and was brilliant,' recalls Jim Barclay. 'I don't think he gave a fuck,' adds Ashley Roy. 'He could deal with any audience.' 'Some of the material is bad,' said Dawson, after his very well-received set, 'and there's one or two on here who'd get murdered up north. But it's useful, because it's a place to fail, and no matter what type of comedian you want to be, you need the experience of failure.'

Other visitors from the trad circuit were equally diplomatic. 'Des O'Connor was actually pretty easy going,' recalls Alexei Sayle. 'He was very genial, and people took the piss out of him.' But other old-time turns weren't so suave, or successful. 'Lenny Bennett was the famous one, who went up, full of confidence, and died on his arse,' recalls Sayle, who gonged off Bennett after he was heckled by Tony Allen. 'He said, "Well, you're going home on the bus. I'm going home in a Rolls-Royce."' Rather like Peter Rosengard.

Rosengard tried to encourage established comics to try out new material at The Store, but most agents weren't enthusiastic. 'Jasper Carrott and Billy Connolly never came down. Rowan Atkinson promised to, but got lost and went into a sauna massage parlour by accident, asked if it was The Comedy Store, got punched in the stomach, was sick and went home.'[25] Young unknowns had a great deal to gain here and not a lot to lose, but for comics who were already famous, it was the other way around.

Alternative Comedy's anti-establishment spleen was eventually satiated by its conquest of the establishment, and alternative and mainstream have now virtually swapped places, ousting to the seaside margins those older, more traditional turns whose success and status Alternative comics once despised. However, the anger these adultescent renegades harboured towards their more conformist elders was originally very real. Keith Allen admitted he was 'obsessed with Max Bygraves because he was symbolic of everything I didn't like about entertainment.'[26] Allen was fired from his job as a stagehand at the Victoria Palace for walking onstage naked during a Bygraves performance. Allen's band subsequently performed a song called 'Max Bygraves Killed My Mother'.

He wasn't the only Alternative infected by this paradoxical but potent mix of envy and contempt. Alexei Sayle thought that 'all conventional comedians stank,' including Les Dawson. 'I hated them, all of them,' said Sayle. 'They were crap.'[27] Not every Store comic was so outspoken, but it soon became clear that trad stand-up wasn't welcome here. Much of it was simply trite and tired one-liners about blokes walking into pubs, but although some mainstream gags were misogynistic and xenophobic, most were simply the last pathetic wails of a generation of entertainers fast being left behind.

'It's impossible to overstate how sad and lonely and tragic those old guys are,' said Sayle, who subsequently created a comic character called Billy Chariot, a parody of a trad warm-up man. 'They can't touch people at all. All they can do is gags.'[28]

'It was inherently obvious you weren't going to be making jokes that poked fun at people simply because of their racial origin,' says Clive Anderson. 'Did we really laugh at jokes that just said aren't poofs funny, aren't women weird and aren't these black people rather odd?' Yes, we really did. And despite The Store's far-reaching influence, some still do. In 1987, Granada removed all the racist gags from a revisionist repeat of *The Comedians*, but on the trad club circuit, racial jokes are still common. 'What d'you do for a living?' popular trad stand-up Jimmy Jones asks a black punter, in a 1992 video of his live show. 'Don't work? What a surprise!' This former greengrocer then offers him some fruit from his onstage stall. 'D'you want an orange, or would you rather have a banana?'

Yet the real revolution was one of authorship, not ethics. Trad comics shared a common reservoir of material. 'We were all doing each other's jokes,' says Robin Banks. 'All I was doing was bits and pieces of Jimmy Jones, Bernard Manning and Charlie Williams.'

Like Buddy Holly or The Beatles, Alternative comics wrote their own material. 'You never nicked another comic's jokes,' explains Jim Tavare. 'When I did a few working men's clubs up north, I noticed the blatant robbery of material, and everyone doing the same act. The new comics had a genuine artistic bent that didn't exist up north and that's why it took over.' Not just by them, but about them, these new jokes defined who these new comics really were. At best, they were so particular to the stage persona of their authors that they simply wouldn't work performed by any other comic. 'The jokes become so much a part of them that it's impossible for anyone else to do them,' confirms Arthur Smith, who was depicted on the BBC's *History Of Alternative Comedy* putting his fist through a photo of Jim Davidson. 'No one can do Harry Hill's material. To nick Harry Hill's jokes would be absurd.'

At the 1987 Edinburgh Festival, Paul Merton tripped over his trousers while playing football, broke his leg in three places, developed a blood clot that nearly killed him, and caught Hepatitis A from the hospital food. Merton's fellow comics did a benefit at The Store, and decided it would be a fitting tribute to each crack a few of Merton's jokes. 'It was terrible,' says Smith. 'As soon as you tried doing someone else's material it just didn't click at all.' In these early days, it was invention and originality more than politics that brought the punters flocking into The Store.

'My day job CV was terrible because I just cocked up everything, because I always had this bee in my bonnet about trying to be an actor,' confesses *Red Dwarf* star Chris Barrie, over a curry in an Indian restaurant around the corner from The Store. As well as playing Arnold Rimmer in *Red Dwarf*, he also created Gordon Brittas in *The Brittas Empire*, a sitcom archetype who's been likened to Alf Garnett, Basil Fawlty and Victor Meldrew.

When he first went to The Store, Barrie was working as a clerk and a van driver. However, he had a special skill that most Store comics could only dream about: Barrie was a gifted impressionist. Good mimics are always rare, and back then they were even rarer. Mike Yarwood had already had his heyday and Rory Bremner was still a teenager. Until Bremner revolutionised the genre a decade later, many stand-ups thought of impressions as an intrinsically trad or mainstream turn, like conjuring or ventriloquism. 'I'm not sure whether this is the sort of stuff we should be doing down here,' Jim Barclay told Barrie. 'Do you do any alternative impressions, like a pigeon flying back from the library?' 'No,' said Barrie, 'I'd rather do the conventional ones.'

Tony Allen, always a comic visionary, could see the huge potential of impressions, but he was frustrated by Barrie's relatively conservative approach. 'You could do so much more,' Allen told Barrie. 'If I could do those voices, I'd be bringing the government down.' Barrie impersonated Labour leader Michael Foot, but he also impersonated Arsenal manager Terry Neill, and audiences were happy to take his impressions at face value. For Barrie, The Store became an oasis amid the frightening underworld of Soho, and the big city beyond. 'You felt quite safe there,' he says. 'You were in this little deep hole of joy and creativity, and hopefully laughter, away from the pressures of the outside world.'

In 1982, he chucked in his day job and went on the dole, but it wasn't long before the outside world came banging on his door. He was hired by *Spitting Image*, and from then on The Store ceased to be the centre of his universe. Yet now, after all his TV success, he's surprised to find those late nights in that hostess club still mean something to him. 'It's only the further you get away from it that you realise how important and interesting it really was,' he says. 'Nothing has ever quite matched the atmosphere of that Dean Street Comedy Store for me. And nothing ever will.'

When fellow *Red Dwarf* star Norman Lovett first went to The Store, he was working as an invigilator at the Whitechapel Art Gallery in London's East End. He met a few artists, and even got a book signed by Gilbert & George, but the actual work was deadly dull. 'You sit there, bored out of your skull and you're not even supposed to read a book, because you're supposed to keep an eye on all the art, but the hours went so slowly,' he says, at the new Piccadilly Circus Store, twenty years on. But Lovett was leading a double life. By night, he supported punk bands like The Clash and 999, and eventually, he heard about The Store. Lovett decided to pay a visit. After all, what did he have to lose?

Lovett arrived early and was shocked to be served a drink by a topless barmaid. 'It felt very strange asking for a beer from someone who hadn't got any clothes on,' he says. Onstage, it was even stranger. 'I was scared,' he says. 'The gong frightened me. Everything frightened me.' He sang some songs and played the guitar. 'It was terrible,' he says. Lovett wasn't the only one who thought so. Adrian Edmondson thought it was awful too, and told him so. But Lovett stuck at it. He'd drink three pints before he went on, and when he finally plucked up the courage to put down his guitar, he went down well. For the first time, he actually got paid. Only a fiver, but he was thrilled.

And it got better. One night, after the show, he went on to The Zanzibar, a popular post-Store haunt, and Wayne Sleep sent over a bottle of champagne. He got a spot on *The Young Ones*, and a regular part on *Don't Miss Wax* with Ruby Wax. Then he landed the lead role of Holly the Computer in *Red Dwarf*. For an unlikely star who didn't start performing until his early thirties, it certainly beat sitting on a stool in an East End art gallery, telling punters not to touch the pictures.

'We'd have people creeping up the fire exit and getting in through the back door,' explains Don Ward, during a nostalgic stroll down Dean Street. 'People were taking their life in their hands to get into The Store. When I found people climbing up the drainpipes to get in, I knew we had something special.'

Chris Barrie

After a few wobbly months, The Store had become a cult. The Gargoyle was hip again. 'On a Saturday night, at twelve o'clock, if you were anybody, you'd better be at The Store,' says Jim Barclay. 'You knew you were at the centre of what was happening, the most significant thing that was happening artistically in the country,' says Sayle. 'We were at the best party in town.'

'People would often join the queue without knowing quite what they were queuing for,' says Phil Herbert. Foreign tourists waited in line, thinking they'd found the hottest floor show in town. And in a way, they had. Even celebrity punters were happy to queue up. 'It didn't matter who you were, you had to queue like everybody else to get in,' says Peter Rosengard. 'David Bowie came down one night, and Eric Idle brought Robin Williams, but they had to queue like everybody.' That lift only held four people, however famous they were.

Soon, the comedy was selling so well that Ward abandoned Saturday striptease altogether, much to the disappointment of some comedians, who'd become accustomed to arriving early for a free sneak preview. 'Unless you had people fucking onstage you couldn't really compete with what was going on on the video circuit in Soho, where you could go and sit in a basement and watch a live sex video,' says Tony Allen, recalling Ward's explanation of why his brand of exotic dancing had passed its sell-by date. A few years before The Store began, there were some twenty strip joints in Soho. A few years later, there were only three, two of which were owned by Ward. 'Striptease became very old hat,' says Ward. 'Lap dancing seems to have taken over. It's the same meat, different gravy.' He kept up his Sunset Strip around the corner, but it was stand-up, not lap dancing, that became the new karaoke.

Ward and Rosengard could have been forgiven for thinking they'd finally hit on a winning formula, and that all they had to do now was sit back and wait for the money to pour in. Yet revolutionaries have a nasty habit of revolting against one another, and as soon as The Store became a cult success, it started to unravel.

Peter Rosengard's Anglo-Jewish chutzpah had sparked this stand-up revolt, much as Brian Epstein and Malcolm McLaren made stars of The Beatles and The Sex Pistols. Yet like Epstein and McLaren, and a lot of other creative catalysts, Rosengard's relationship with The Store's key players was often volatile. 'I dragged Peter Rosengard into the kitchen one day,' confesses Sayle, 'got him by the neck, throttled him, banged his head on the wall and quit.' Sayle felt confident his departure would herald the end of The Store. 'When I left, I genuinely believed it would fold without me,' he admits, a generation later. Sayle's prediction proved premature when his role as The Store's resident compere was filled by a wannabe wag called Ben Elton, but the chief problem for Sayle's fellow future stars wasn't backstage or onstage, but front of house. 'They kept saying, "We've got to control the audience,"' says Kim Kinnie. However, in the end, it proved far easier to find a different audience, in a different auditorium.

Peter Richardson left to set up a rival comedy club, The Comic Strip, at The Boulevard Theatre, beside Paul Raymond's Revuebar. Like The Nell Gwynne,

Raymond's Revuebar was a strip club, a fact reflected in The Comic Strip's double-edged title. But that was about all these two clubs had in common. The Revuebar was only a short walk away from The Gargoyle, but it was on the southern edge of Soho, further from the red light district, and nearer the tourist traps of London's West End. Unlike The Gargoyle, The Boulevard was a smart studio theatre, which wouldn't have looked too out of place on nearby Shaftesbury Avenue.

'It was a slicker, more professional, theatre-based revue show,' says Lee Cornes. 'They weren't under the same pressure.' There was a lot less heckling, and instead of The Store's open door policy, star turns were booked for proper runs, while lesser lights were turned away. 'We turned up a couple of nights and they wouldn't put us on,' says Martin Soan. 'That's when things started moving commercially.'

No wonder Richardson was able to cherry pick The Store's top turns: not just Sayle, but Nigel Planer, Richardson's partner in their double act, The Outer Limits, plus Arnold Brown, who'd become one of the best stand-ups at The Store. They were joined by two of The Store's most promising comic duos, Rik Mayall and Adrian Edmondson, and Dawn French and Jennifer Saunders. Even Ben Elton's arrival at The Store couldn't compensate for the posse of talent who followed Richardson away from Soho's red lights, towards the brighter lights of Theatreland. 'This was just a platform to move into television,' says Oscar McLennan. 'That's all The Comic Strip was ever about.'

But who could blame them? Sayle called The Store a circus, and even John McVicar likened it to a Roman Arena. 'The good ones decided that they wanted to be more than part of a gong show, a freak show,' says Kim Kinnie. 'They felt they were being exploited. We were using them as fodder, which is why the rest of them moved away, because they wanted to progress with their comedy, to be allowed to develop.' And although Sayle's dramatic exit wasn't quite enough to finish off The Store, nobody would have been at all surprised if the mass exodus that followed had brought down the shabby big top they'd forsaken.

Yet despite these plusher premises, or maybe even because of them, something was missing from The Comic Strip. It just didn't have the same magic as The Store. Partly, it was the theatrical layout. 'You lost all that excitement,' explains Rosengard. 'The stage was up there and the audience was down here and there was a big gap between them.' But something more intangible had also been mislaid en route. 'The Comic Strip was actually a much less inventive club,' says Sayle.

It also attracted a very different class of punter, even if Sayle did his heroic best to deter them, as future comedienne Jo Jo Smith discovered at The Strip's opening night. 'Are there any Lenny Bruce fans in the audience?' asked Sayle. 'Yes,' said the old boy sat beside Smith. 'Larry Adler,' said Sayle. 'He's fucking dead, so fuck off.' Adler picked up his coat and left. It was all a bit lost on Smith. At the time, she didn't even know who Lenny Bruce was, never mind Larry Adler. Yet despite Sayle's best efforts, even bigger celebs like Bianca Jagger soon pitched up, attracting column inches to match. An article entitled 'Four Letter Night Out For Bianca' called Rik Mayall a 'four-letter gag

Peter Richardson, who lead the exodus from The Store to The Comic Strip

merchant'. Mayall was so pleased with this job description, he put it on his passport.

It was just the sort of publicity Richardson's new club required. Sure enough, all the core Comic Strip team soon became small screen stars, apart from Arnold Brown, who was jettisoned, like a comedic Pete Best, just before their big trip Down Under, to the Adelaide Comedy Festival. 'He should have been a huge star by now,' says Peter Rosengard. 'He didn't fit the image. He was too old.' 'They were the Sex Pistols of comedy and I was more like George Burns,' said Brown. 'Or is it Robert Burns?'[29] But there aren't too many amusing jokes about becoming a super-star, and failure is far funnier than success. 'I'm a comedian with a cult following,' quipped Brown. 'The cult at the moment is the Hare Krishna move-ment.'

Don Ward was magnanimous in defeat. 'They were writing their own material and they needed a format that let them present it in their own way,' he conceded graciously, only a few years later. 'The Comedy Store is essentially a factory, a conveyor belt. They'd developed to a stage where they could-n't fit in with that.' Yet for a while, it must have felt as if anyone left behind at The Store had missed the boat. Even Ben Elton, The Store's new rising star, sounded pessimistic about his future. 'I can remember Ben saying to me one evening, "I've come into this business too late,"' recalls Ward. 'I said, "What are you talking about?" He said, "The Comic Strip's formed, and I'm not part of it." I said, "This is only the beginning. I think you'll be bigger than any of them. But I wonder if you'll remem-ber The Store when you are."'

For a while, it looked like there might not be a Store to remember. Not only had Ward and Rosengard lost most of their top acts, but their brittle partnership had reached its inevitable breaking point. 'I could see a future for comedy over the whole week and he wasn't so sure,' says Ward. 'He was happy with the weekend arrange-ment.' 'If we don't do it,' Ward told Rosengard, 'someone else will.' Ward offered to sell Rosengard half his business, including the striptease and the topless bar, for £25k. Rosengard didn't come up with the money, so Ward returned Rosengard's initial invest-ment of £500, and dissolved their partnership. Well, that's Ward's version. Rosengard's is slightly different.

'I really think we've got something huge here,' Rosengard told Ward. 'These guys want to perform five nights a week.' The way Rosengard remembers it, Ward agreed to go ahead, but said he wanted £40k for half the lease, plus stock, fixtures and fittings. Rosengard got some advice from a friendly West End agent, who told him Ward's lease was about to end, the rent was about to go sky high, that Ward would have to move out, and that Rosengard's money would end up in Ward's pocket. Rosengard tried to negotiate a lower figure, but it eventually became clear to Ward that Rosengard wasn't going to give him any money. 'We'd never had any rows or disagreements,' says Rosengard. 'He'd been a good friend to me. I used to talk about all kinds of things to Don in his little office. I liked Don. I trusted him. And then suddenly, I got this letter one day in the post from a solicitor.' The letter dissolved their partnership. Rosengard wasn't allowed onto the premises. 'I was pretty upset about that, naturally, because as far as I was concerned, I was The Comedy Store. We were the co-founders.'

Rosengard consulted his solicitors, and what had begun as a fun, funny hobby became a boring business wrangle. 'All the comedians will go on strike because they're all my mates,' he thought, but he soon realised these socialist comics weren't quite so militant about industrial action when it came to their own careers. 'These kids wanted to perform,' he says. 'They didn't want to get involved.' But he didn't bear a grudge. 'That's the reality of life. People have got to look after their own.' There was no stand-up picket line outside The Store.

Rosengard quickly started another comedy club, The Last Laugh, in a restaurant in Baker Street. Ben Elton, Alexei Sayle, Rik Mayall and Adrian Edmondson all played the opening night, in front of a packed house. However, while The Store was central, intimate and open every weekend, The Last Laugh was too far north, far too big, and only available for comedy on Wednesdays. After a few months, Rosengard decided to close. Luckily, despite The Store's success, he never gave up his day job. 'I'm still selling insurance,' says the man from Abbey Life in the Aston Martin Virage Volante, who spends £200 a week on breakfast at Claridges, and £300 a week on Havana cigars. 'I've made a fortune selling insurance.' But he never made a fortune from The Store. 'I don't believe in looking back,' he explains. 'It wasn't my career, and I'm very proud that I did it. Somebody had to have the idea. I had the idea. It wasn't an original idea. I saw it in America. I never had an original idea in my life. I just nicked it, brought it over, and did it there and it was wonderful.'

Rosengard later managed pop group Curiosity Killed The Cat, who became fashionable, albeit briefly, in the late Eighties. In 1999, his Last Laugh production company completed a £250k pilot with Planet 24 of *Cloud Cuckoo Land*, an animated sitcom, with voiceovers by Clive Anderson, Arnold Brown and Alexei Sayle. Rosengard reckons it will become a British *Simpsons*. 'I have these kind of creative ideas once every ten years,' he says. However, he's never opened another comedy club. 'I've never really wanted to do it again,' he says. 'I'm not into being a club owner. That wasn't what it was about.'

Twenty years after the end of their brief but fruitful alliance, these former business partners still aren't speaking. And after staging rival twentieth anniversary parties, in different venues, on successive nights – Alexei Sayle, Clive Anderson, Nigel Planer and Peter Richardson went to Rosengard's bash; David Baddiel, Alan Davies and Lee Evans were at Ward's; Jim Barclay and Ronnie Golden were among the few comics who went to both – The Store's estranged odd couple look set to stay that way. Since they went their separate ways, Ward has built up The Store from an after-hours gong show into a multi-million pound business.

'Don's done a fantastic job in developing it and keeping it going all these years,' says Rosengard. Yet for most of the comics who were around at the beginning, Rosengard remains the infuriating but adorable bloke who together with Don Ward started The Comedy Store, if not Alternative Comedy. 'He was out of order sometimes, but I loved him,' says Andrew Bailey. 'He is the one man that brought us here.'

Ward's new-found autonomy didn't last long. In 1982, The Gargoyle's owners sold the freehold. 'It was offered to me at three hundred thousand pounds, but then you might as well have said three million,' says Ward. 'There was no way I could afford three hundred thousand pounds so they sold it on to someone else.' The new owners more than tripled his rent, from under £18,000 a year to almost £60,000. 'There's no way I can make a profit on this so I'll be returning the keys to you,' he told them. 'Of course they didn't believe me,' he says. But Ward wasn't bluffing. At the end of the next quarter, he shut up shop for the last time. 'There you are,' he told them. 'That's it. It's all yours now.' But Ward had the last laugh. When he gave back the keys, he also surrendered the drinks licence.

Ward kept The Sunset Strip, which he still runs as a strip club today. 'A variety of women in various costumes will take them off sequentially to recorded music,' reports my *Passport To Soho*. 'Continuous shows, so in theory you could stay until they threw you out, but after a while it's not a lot of fun, so most of the audience shuffle home to take it out on the wife.'

The original Store closed on 23 December 1982, and Rik Mayall topped this last-night bill. The first series of *The Young Ones* had finished transmission only a fortnight earlier, making him a household name, but in stark contrast to today's starstruck punters, his new-found fame turned this anarchic audience against him. Mayall was heckled off, but this rebellious crowd might as well have saved their breath. Even in this final show, normally a lame excuse for syrupy votes of thanks in traditional show-biz circles, the comedians were happy to heckle one another. 'Keith was in one of his particularly vicious moods,' says Roger Pomphrey. 'He could be very vicious. He'd stand on the side of the stage or at the front of the audience at the bar and shout.' That night, he was shouting at Tony Allen. 'Keith, I've got one question for you,' replied Tony from the stage. 'Why are you such a mean motherfucker?' It was the only question worth asking, and the only one without an answer.

And so the curtain came down on this riotous club with a very public spat between two of its most radical leading lights. It was a fitting farewell. Even in its death throes, there were no crocodile tears of phoney camaraderie. Right to the end, The Store's irreverence prevailed.

The aftermath of this fraught final show was similarly chaotic. 'We were very drunk and a few of us went on a nicking spree,' says Pomphrey. His personal haul included an ancient review of a show performed there some eighty years before, and the holy grail of Alternative Comedy, The Comedy Store gong. 'It was one of those drunken nights, and we all just ended up piling out of the club with our coats stuffed full of glasses,' says Pomphrey. 'We were drunk and we didn't give a shit.' Today, this sacred comic relic is gathering rust in his back garden. 'I imagine there are some other people who would put a greater romantic attachment on it than I do, so if anybody wants it, I'll auction it for charity. But if they don't want to pay for it, no one's getting it back.'

The Soho Store had begun with a bubbly bang, but it ended with a flat wimper. For rising stars like Mayall, *The Comic Strip* and *The Young Ones* had already provided a fast track into television, and later even feature films, while those who couldn't or wouldn't hitch a ride with them went their separate ways. For all but the brightest stars, it felt like a door was closing, not opening. Even though the circuit eventually recovered, it was never quite so insane again. 'When the first Store died, that whole era died with it,' says Martin Soan.

Some of the comics who'd seemed most at home at the Soho Store never really found another time and place they could inhabit so completely. Most of them eventually found a home from home on London's gradually emerging comedy club circuit, and their indignant bile, previously reserved for trad stand-up, became more evenly distributed. 'Ben Elton himself became the target of abuse for his perceived political correctness by the Glaswegian nihilist stand-up, the fiery Jerry Sadowitz, who burst on to The Comedy Store stage in the mid 1980s,' recalled Arnold Brown.[30] But that was on a very different stage, at a very different Comedy Store.

Mark Thomas at the Leicester Square Store

Chapter Five

'The Subway has closed its doors after two years of sweaty nights,' wrote Derek Jarman in his diary. 'Neither the Metropolitan Police, nor the iron guards of the Moral Majority, nor yet the semi-detached minds of *Gay News* (that sister to the *Daily Star*) will shed a tear. London has lost quite the best gay bar that I remember. It had some of the best music in London, showed the latest videos in rooms quiet enough to have a conversation in, and had the Capital's first back rooms. Back-room sex can be the sweetest and most transient. The imagination runs riot. Earthbound minds suddenly take on angelic bodies, and the anonymity is a treasure.'[1] It was this sweet back-room sex that lost the Subway its license. Andrew Bailey used to see moustachioed, leather-clad men coming in and out of this clandestine cellar during the small hours, as he walked across Leicester Square, on his way home from the Soho Store. When The Subway moved out and The Store moved in Bailey realised that the clubs shared the same underground address.

Well, sort of. Ward actually restarted The Comedy Store in March 1983, a month after Maria Kempinska opened her Jongleurs comedy club in a South London restaurant turned roller-skating rink above a bar near Clapham Junction. At first, The Store only ran on Saturday nights, upstairs, with a disco during the week on the two floors below. When the owners lost their lease, Ward moved downstairs, where the rent was lower.

'During that period, Don was tireless,' says Kim Kinnie. Finding The Store's second home was one thing; securing it was quite another. Despite Ward's endeavours, The Store didn't settle into the old Subway until July 1985. During those two fallow years,

The Comic Strip team had become small screen superstars, and for a while it looked like Kempinska's Jongleurs, rather than Ward's Store, would reap the rewards of the stand-up boom that The Store had started. It certainly wouldn't have been the first time a movement's initial innovators were left empty handed. If Jarman's beloved Subway had survived, maybe this book would be about Jongleurs, rather than The Store.

Andrew Bailey never doubted The Store would reopen, sooner or later. 'Don was onto a winner,' he says. 'He's a very astute businessman.' Which is why he was so surprised The Store stayed dark for so long. 'It seemed like a really bad move,' he says. 'Clubs were flourishing everywhere.' And while The Store was dark, these new clubs matched the standards The Store had set, and sometimes even surpassed them.

When Ward eventually reopened, he had a bit of catching up to do. Jongleurs was always a business, but back then The Store was a stand-up speakeasy, and the acts reflected this more informal house style. 'These guys had enormous personalities, which you don't see today, but they weren't high-profile people,' says Jim Tavare. 'Jongleurs had people like Rory Bremner and Fry & Laurie. The Store attracted more conversational acts.' And inevitably, the bigger names at Jongleurs lured some punters away from The Store. 'You can't talk about The Store without talking about Jongleurs because it had such a huge effect on it,' says Bob Mills, who became a comic at the Leicester Square Store. 'It wasn't a better club, but it was a very different club from The Store. It ran on a different ethos. It was much more professional. A lot of the more serious comedy goers started to drift towards Jongleurs. They could be just as rowdy, but they were much more middle class.'

To many comics, this Battersea club soon became synonymous with those twenty-something Thatcherites called Yuppies. 'Jongleurs, by virtue of its position, was a junior stockbroker club,' says Hugh Dennis, who played there with his double act partner Steve Punt. 'They're all City types who've got their own flats in Battersea, and Mum and Dad paid the deposit,' Donna McPhail told me, in 1993. 'I was doing a joke about my bank manager, and I said something about an overdraft, and some guy said, "What's an overdraft?" And the whole room laughed.' McPhail said, 'I have nothing to say to you people,' and left. It was the only time she'd ever walked off. Yet most comics didn't feel so strongly, and as the more affluent punters drifted South, some Store acts inevitably started to follow them.

Competition from Jongleurs helped to clarify The Store's house style. As befitted its title, Jongleurs billed speciality acts such as juggler Steve Rawlings. 'Jongleurs was still a cabaret venue,' says Steve Punt. 'They'd have jugglers on, and music and magicians.' With its smaller stage and lower ceiling, the Leicester Square Store was far too confined for physical comedy, so Ward made the new club a leaner, meaner alternative to Jongleurs' variety, and a stark contrast to the old Soho Store. 'We're going to be the hardnosed edge of stand-up,' decided Kinnie. 'We're going to go for the unsayable.'

'Kim didn't really like too many costumes or props,' confirms Arthur Smith. 'A small stage, a low ceiling, no jugglers, none of that. He was always very resolute about never booking what he called circus acts. It was what he called hard stand-up. One man, one woman, one microphone. That's it. Even double acts didn't always do that well.' Don Ward agreed. 'Don is not too keen on prop acts,' says Jim Tavare. 'If he had any artistic thing to say at all, it was, "Don't use props". He started this fashion of just a guy with a mike.' And the crowds followed suit. 'They weren't bothered about seeing jugglers or bands,' says Steve Punt. 'They were there for comedy.'

As comedians realised slicker sets meant more money, the eccentric amateurs began to fade away. 'It needed those bizarre acts to make it what it was,' says Martin Potter, recalling a magician who handcuffed punters together, and a juggler who knocked himself out with a cannon-ball. These acts had given the old Soho Store its magic, but with each passing year, there was less room for them under Leicester Square.

There wasn't just more room onstage at Jongleurs, there was far more room for the audience, too. The big tables attracted group bookings, and Jongleurs became a popular choice for parties. 'The comics were almost secondary,' explains Eddie Izzard. 'They were the entertainment.' At The Store, the ambience was just as exciting, but more intense, like a crucial sporting fixture rather than the carnival atmosphere at Jongleurs. 'It was quite different from Jongleurs,' says Nick Hancock. 'People came to see comedy, as opposed to comedy being a diversion from the rest of the night out.'

Fifteen years later, this is still The Store's defining ethos. 'It's stand-up comedy,' says Don Ward. 'It's not cabaret. I've got nothing against gay comics but I don't want drag acts. I'm not into too much visual comedy.' Comic conjurers like Otiz Canneloni and Paul Zenon both play here, yet most character comics get short shrift.

But first, Ward needed a new licence. Like The Gargoyle, The Subway only had a club licence. Ward wanted a public licence, so punters could stroll in off the street without signing in or joining up. And this meant an audience with a Justice of the Peace. 'I carried a bit of baggage with me from the old days,' admits Ward, 'but fortunately we'd taken along press cuttings from *The Times* and the *Telegraph*.' The Store, explained Ward's lawyer, was a theatrical enterprise which had discovered stars like Alexei Sayle. 'Alexei Sayle?' asked the JP. 'I've heard of him.' 'Yes,' said Ward's lawyer. 'He has his own series on television.' 'Very entertaining young man,' enthused the JP. 'Very entertaining.' Ward got his licence, but he was still skint. 'I was broke,' he says. 'I'd come out of The Gargoyle owing thirty thousand pounds. I wasn't a limited company. I couldn't file for bankruptcy and start all over again. I owed people money. I had to sweetheart the bank. I had to sweetheart the brewery. I crossed my fingers and everybody got put into promise land.'

Renovation took another nine months, and with the stakes so high, it was no wonder that on the opening night, Kim Kinnie was worried nobody would turn up. He couldn't have been more wrong. 'The place was jammed,' he recalls. 'People kissing in the corner, people throwing up.' Not all that different, in fact, from the first night at The Gargoyle a few years before. The antics onstage were equally anarchic. 'We were pretty pissed and thought it'd be a great idea to get our cocks out,' recalls Lee Cornes. Yet despite such stag night pranks, unlike The Gargoyle, these new premises felt like

a professional comedy club. 'It was a really significant night for a lot of people,' says Dave Cohen, a founder member of the Comedy Store Players. 'We all thought, "Something's happened here. Something's moved on. We've moved on from being a bunch of friendly amateurs."'

Yet even in the mid-Eighties, the comedy circuit was still underground. The press didn't pay it much attention, and most Soho Store acts who'd become small screen stars had moved away from stand-up into more theatrical formats. Comedy clubs still relied mainly on word of mouth, so at first, Ward only staged comedy on Saturday nights. During the rest of the week, he put on music, including a rap night called The Language Lab and a funk night called The Cat In The Hat, whose punters included future Store favourite Bill Bailey. 'We had a lot of security,' says Ward. 'We had problems with people who were trying to get in with drugs.'

Despite these problems, the music nights proved very successful, and who knows whether Ward might have moved away from stand-up entirely, if he hadn't had a phone call at three o'clock one Saturday morning. There'd been a knife fight between two punters. Both men were now in hospital. Ward went straight to Leicester Square.

'They had the white ribbons round the place,' he says. 'You couldn't get in.' Eventually, he found his way into the foyer. 'It was as though somebody had painted it red. There was blood everywhere. It made me sick to the bottom of my stomach. If one of them had died, I could have been in very serious trouble because I was the licensee and owner.' Thankfully, both men survived, but Ward was badly shaken. 'I wanted to be out of the club business completely,' he says. 'I wanted to get out of it there and then.' In the end, he decided to stop Friday's music night. From then on, Friday had its own comedy bill.

Kinnie tried to persuade performers from the old Soho Store to return, reassuring them that this new Leicester Square Store wouldn't be a bear pit. They even played a recorded announcement by Ward, warning punters against overzealous heckling, but that sounded too much like finger wagging so they stopped it. Putting bouncers on the door helped, but fine comics like Norman Lovett still proved too subtle to flourish in this rough house atmosphere. 'There's no room for wimps at The Store,' says Jeff Green. 'It's a very macho gig.' Paid-up turns had about thirty seconds to prove them-selves, and open spots had about ten. 'I used to go to Leicester Square with my stomach knotted, not knowing what was going to happen,' says Kinnie (and he wasn't even performing). 'It was horrendous. I'm amazed we all came out of it alive.' If he had too much red wine inside him, he'd yell at the audience to shut up. If they wouldn't, he had to throw them out himself. Several punters even threatened to wait for him out-side, and as he says, 'I ain't exactly the biggest, butchest thing in the world.'

Audience facilities were pretty spartan, but for the entertainers, they were virtually non-existent. There was no backstage lavatory, so comics had to run the gauntlet of drunken punters queuing to use the public toilets, or, far more frequently, piss in the dressing room sink. 'Women used to complain,' says Arthur Smith. 'It's quite hard for a woman to piss in a sink, much harder than a man, so it became a bit of a badge of honour.' Not even every man could manage it. 'I've got too much of a shy bladder to piss in the sink,' says David Baddiel. 'It's odd to think that one of the great moments in my life has been pissing in a sink that Jo Brand has pissed in,' says Phill Jupitus. Not that she ever relieved herself in front of him. 'I used to get the most trustworthy one to hold the door shut,' she says.

Not every comedienne was quite so bold, but pissing with the audience required as much bravery as pissing with the acts. 'One of the worst things for the women was that you had to queue to go to the toilet with the punters,' says Donna McPhail, who was far too middle class to relieve herself backstage. 'I was queuing for the ladies toilet and I heard this woman say, "There's a woman on next," and another woman says, "Women just aren't funny, are they?"' McPhail did a storming set, just to prove them wrong.

For Pierre Hollins, this ad hoc urinal became so familiar that one night, he returned home at four in the morning and went to take a piss in his own sink out of sheer force of habit. This improvised communal pissoir was especially hard on Julian Clary. 'I was the only one who needed to use the dressing room to do my make-up,' he recalled. 'I'd be sitting there with someone pissing in the sink, inches from my face.'[2]

But even backstage at the Leicester Square Store, there were limits. 'I never saw anyone shit in the sink,' says Bob Boyton. 'For comedians, it's really important to have a shit.' Especially before a show. 'The great thing about comedy is that it always cures any kind of constipation,' says Alistair McGowan. 'The whole day before I did The Store I was on and off the toilet. I'd known nothing like it in my life.' 'You never ever meet a constipated comedian,' confirms Hugh Dennis. 'I certainly wasn't during those days.' And for this essential function, even the most versatile piss artistes had to venture out into the auditorium. 'All I can remember is the fear,' says Dennis. 'Desperately wanting to go to the loo again, and wondering how long you'd got before you went on because you had to time it right.'

But the absence of backstage toilet facilities wasn't the biggest handicap. Even worse, there wasn't a stage door. This meant the only way out was through the audience, which was especially humiliating when you'd died, as even the best comics often did. 'There was no easy exit,' explains Jenny Eclair. 'There was no way out. You had to walk through them.' Jack Dee was luckier than most. He drove a motorbike. 'I used to go onstage and absolutely die a death, and go back in the dressing room and put all my motorbike gear on, including my helmet, and walk through the audience, so no one would recognise me,' recalled Dee.[3] 'If they looked at me I'd just go "pizza delivery", and get out of the building as quickly as I could.'

Getting in was almost as much of a problem. 'I used to hate going down the stairs,' says Dominic Holland. 'You'd walk past the audience and some people would say, "Who are you? What are you doing, mate?" You'd be pushing in, and I was waiting for someone to say, "He's shit. I've seen him." And I would have died if that had happened. That would have crushed me.'

If you'd been booed off, there certainly wasn't much incentive to stick around, since the facilities were downright dreadful. 'It was a nightmare of a room,' agrees Kim Kinnie. 'If you wanted to design a worse room, you couldn't.' The sightlines were awful. Virtually every seat had a restricted view. The best seats were behind pillars. The worst ones were in a cramped corridor that stretched back to the public bar, at right angles to the stage, finishing up in the so-called Sheep Dip, which sank below stage level, where the floorboards had been removed due to rot. This building had once housed the famous 400 Club, home from home for London's 400 most fashionable clubbers, but that was sixty years ago. Now the walls were chipped, the lino was scratched and the fake gilt and velvet chairs were pitted with cigarette burns. *Time Out* called it London's most famous underground car park, but there wasn't enough room to even park one car in here. 'It was diabolical,' admitted Ward, after he finally moved out, a decade later. 'I don't know how I got away with it for so long.'[4]

'It was long and thin and you were in the middle of it, with nothing on your left, and a huge long row of people going back into the darkness on your right,' recalls Jo Brand. 'I always felt sorry for the people sat up there,' says Arthur Smith, a regular compere here. 'You could play to them, but you'd get a stiff neck.' However, not many comics felt so sympathetic, since this twilit corner was where hecklers congregated. These latecomers were usually the most pissed, and if just one of them became bored, their discontent spread like wildfire. 'If you get a heckler at the front, you can actually eye-ball them and give them as good as you get,' says Phil Herbert. But once you were up onstage, these hecklers were invisible. 'You couldn't see them, but they could see you.'

Yet even when the punters could see the performers, there usually wasn't a lot to look at, since the actual playing space was tiny. 'There was no room on the stage whatsoever,' says Andy Smart, whose double act, The Vicious Boys, had to perform its slapstick sketches on the spot. 'It was like playing a tube station.' Some comics played their set-ups straight out front, and their punchlines down the corridor. Others delivered their entire set to the corner inbetween. Either way, the consequences of this lopsided layout were often quite surreal. A comic could be storming one end of the room and stiffing at the other. 'The room dictated the kind of act that worked,' says Kim Kinnie. 'Visual acts tended not to work because the buggers couldn't see you from the Sheep Dip.' And even if they could see you, there usually wasn't a lot to see. 'There wasn't physically enough room to chuck flaming torches around or get anything other than a single guitar onto the stage,' says Steve Punt, who used to perform back to back with double act partner Hugh Dennis, like Custer's Last Stand. Improvisation was even worse. The Comedy Store Players would squeeze half a dozen bodies onstage, for what Mike McShane called hieroglyphic impro.

Physical comics struggled to be seen or heard, but stand-ups flourished as these handicaps only added to this basement's anarchic ambience. 'It shouldn't have worked, but it did,' says Dominic Holland, who first came here as a starstruck punter. Others like him would queue for hours, even in the pouring rain, just for an outside chance to squeeze inside. 'It was the Wembley Stadium of Alternative Comedy,' says Patrick Marber, and although it may seem bizarre to liken a sporting arena that holds the best part of 100,00 people with a stand-up cellar that barely held 200, in the late Eighties, it was the closest comedy came to its own twin towers.

'It was a filthy hole,' says Bob Mills. 'It was dirty and it smelled and the dressing rooms were horrible.' And he loved it. 'All your history at The Store was on that stage. Everyone you admired. Everyone who'd influenced you. Everyone you looked up to. Everyone who was part of the history of your movement had stood where you stood. They weren't figures from the past. They'd been there. The stuff you did onstage was about fifty per cent of it. The rest of it was sitting and talking, and hearing people like Paul Merton.' 'As you opened the dressing room door, he would be exactly facing you at the end of the room, almost like he was holding court,' recalls comedian Simon Clayton. 'Paul Merton was like the godfather,' agrees Jim Tavare. 'He'd be the one with the stories.'

'My favourite comic in the dressing room was Paul Merton,' concurs American comic magician John Lenahan. 'He just has the best wit of anybody I know.' 'Once Paul Merton is on a roll and he's holding court, it's absolutely hilarious,' says Phil Herbert. 'Some of the funniest nights at The Store were spent in the dressing room with acts off duty, not performing for an audience but performing for each other.' But the dressing room was much too small for big get-togethers. 'Sometimes it would drive you mad,' says Lenahan. 'By the end of Saturday night there'd be twenty comics in this dressing room.' And if you were the one comic who was still waiting to go on, it was hard to get your act together. 'It was very long and thin,' says Steve Gribbin. 'It was like being in a railway carriage, and then the door opened, and you were virtually onstage.' And so most comics spent their time in Derek Jarman's old back room, scene of so many unbuttoned Levis.

Paul Merton with Josie Lawrence at The Store

In theory, this back bar was open to paying punters, but in practice, it was out of bounds to anyone apart from comedians; anybody else who wandered in was made to feel very unwelcome. 'The public hardly ever seemed to be in there,' says David Baddiel. 'There must have been a sort of unspoken force field to that room.' And almost all the comics in there weren't even on the bill. Most other comedy gigs were in pubs that kicked out at closing time, so comics who had played elsewhere would come on to The Store for the midnight show, where they could drink until three. By the end of the late show, there'd be comics from out of town gigs as far afield as Leeds. 'Everybody who was working everywhere ended up at The Store,' says John Lenahan. 'It was our nightclub.'

Acts who were too full of themselves were cold shoulderd, but for acts who fitted in, it was like being a member of a secret fraternity. 'It was always full of people you knew,' says Bob Mills. 'It was a hotbed of gossip and everyone who came would have a story.' 'People would walk in from other gigs with really long faces and you knew they'd died horribly somewhere,' says comic guitarist Richard Morton, 'or people would walk in and lie about their gigs, and then another comic who'd been on the same bill would tell you what actually happened.' But dying at The Store was the most public humiliation. 'You'd do a college gig in Norfolk or Cornwall and nobody got to hear of it,' says comedienne Jenny Eclair. 'You failed at The Store and it was round London like a rash.'

Between the stage and the back bar was a convenient porthole, which must also have come in handy during Jarman's back-room days. Comics would peer through to see what was happening onstage, but an act had to be doing very well, or, far more frequently, pretty badly, to tempt them back out again. There's remarkable backstage solidarity among comics, but out front, *schadenfreude* takes over. Steve Gribbin likens it to sharks smelling blood in the water. 'A guy dying on his arse would be guaranteed to clear the changing room,' says Lee Cornes, recalling a naked bloke in a transparent plastic suit and a man with a brown paper bag over his head. 'A terrible act is a sight

to behold because it becomes amusing for entirely the wrong reasons.' And in those days, open spots still went on at the end of the late show. 'There is something that people enjoy sadistically about someone dying on their arse,' says Jo Brand. 'Comics like watching other comics die.'

Yet at least when you died, the other comics came out to watch. If you didn't, they usually stayed in the back bar and carried on with the party. And as comics often laughed louder than the audience, usually at something completely different from what was happening onstage, it sometimes felt as if there were two shows going on in tandem, a good show out front, but an even better one just out of sight. 'I used to feel sorry for the people onstage,' says *Red Dwarf* star Hattie Hayridge. 'The other comics would go down there like a social club, and the ones onstage could hear all this chattering.' And if you weren't generating enough laughter to cover up the noise from the back bar, you knew you were doing badly.

But for some comics, being in the back bar was almost as important as the show itself. 'Having to actually do the gig was a pain in the arse,' says Jo Brand, who likens the back bar to a works canteen. 'I just liked being in there and having a laugh and getting pissed and talking to people. I could have quite easily gone without actually doing my twenty minutes at the end of the night.' No wonder Nick Hancock called it a low-rent Groucho Club. The Leicester Square Store was as much of a club for comics as a comedy club. 'I was single, so I'd go and hang out there all the time,' says Jim Tavare, who eventually met his wife down here. 'You'd usually go down there and get a gig out of it. Kim would put you on if someone hadn't turned up. We may as well have lived there. It was like a comedy factory.' Hanging around here, he picked up everything from film and TV work to weddings.

'That's where you made all the contacts,' agrees Ainsley Harriott. 'That's where all the parties happened afterwards, and often when the club closed down you'd be there until god knows when, just sitting down there drinking.' One night, Arthur Smith and Paul Merton got locked in by mistake, and passed the time with a drinking marathon until the cleaner let them out the next morning. Another night, Phill Jupitus and Tim Clark stayed there entirely of their own volition, drinking until six in the morning, and then went straight out to breakfast.

This informal atmosphere attracted some chic outsiders. Craig Ferguson brought Fiona Fullerton, Denis Leary brought Matt Dillon, and old Soho Store stars would still drop in for old time's sake. 'You could still wander in the back bar and see Peter Richardson and Rik Mayall and Ade Edmondson,' says Bob Mills. 'They'd still pop down and have a drink.' Another night, Australian comic Phil Davey spotted Ben Elton lurking behind a pillar, watching the show. Most other comics were too cool to say hello, but Davey strolled over and congratulated him on *Stark*, his first novel. 'I detected he was kind of nervous,' says Davey. 'He was almost shaking. He was sensing real fear. I think he was about to go on tour and he was really worried about it.' 'I don't know how you guys can do this,' said Elton, who'd done it so many times himself. 'Once you're up there it's easy,' said Davey, trying to calm his nerves. 'But what if you die?' asked Elton. 'I couldn't handle it.' 'It's no problem,' said Davey, and went on and died the worst death of his life. 'The whole crowd became so uncontrollable, everybody was heckling me,' he says. 'It was a nightmare.' When he got offstage, he looked around for Elton. He was nowhere to be seen.

'When Ben Elton turned up to the tenth anniversary of The Comedy Store in 1989, I asked him why he never went to the comedy clubs anymore,' recalled John Connor. 'He replied, "Because they all take the piss out of me." He was referring to the other comics.'[5] Yet Elton also saw some good gigs here, too. The day after Arthur Smith stormed The Store, he got a phone call from Elton. 'I just want to say I thought you were great,' said Elton, who'd been there with Rik Mayall. 'He's very generous like that,' says Smith. 'I've heard he's done this to other people as well.' 'He was very kind and encouraging to other people,' confirms comedienne Helen Lederer.

But although Elton's kind words were a welcome bonus, the ultimate arbiter between success and failure was how you went down in front of 200 paying punters. Before you could claim your place in the back bar, you had to please this baying mob. 'If you couldn't hack it down The Store, you probably weren't welcome,' says Jeff Green. 'If you weren't playing down there, people would look down their nose at you.' And the man who decided who played here and who didn't was a dapper, diminutive Scot whom Green and Patrick Marber both call The Godfather.

Kevin Day with Mark Thomas in the back bar at the Leicester Square Store. Kim Kinnie looks on

In Soho, Kim Kinnie's role had been choreographing the strip shows. In Leicester Square, he became a kind of unofficial artistic director. 'He'd always tell you to piss off as soon as you walked in the building,' says Jim Tavare, but like virtually every other comic who ever played here, Tavare was still desperate to impress him. 'If you did a good gig, he'd say, "Bring your diary in next week, Tavare." That was a huge accolade. You'd definitely arrived. I haven't had a bigger high since then.'

'There are very few moments in a life where you feel that sort of elation of accept-ance, and for me, when Kim phoned me up and gave me a booking was one,' agrees Patrick Marber, for whom Kinnie felt like a charismatic uncle. 'He just seemed like a wise old bird who'd seen it all, done it all, knew it all, and you just wanted him to give you the nod.' Most bookers simply book comics who do well and don't book those who don't, but Kinnie helped his comics hone their acts. 'Take it slower,' he'd tell Tavare. 'You were crap tonight.' 'Don't look at the floor,' he'd tell Phill Jupitus. 'Look at the audience.' 'He'd bitch at you,' says Jupitus. 'He'd tell you you'd done wrong, and that was terrible.' But these comics took it, because they could tell that this tough but tender-hearted Scotsman knew what he was talking about. 'We did a guest spot every six months, depending on the memory of Kim Kinnie,' explains musical comic Rainer Hersch, who cut his comic teeth at The Store, as one half of a double act called The Tebbits. 'If you died, then you had to wait slightly longer before he forgot who you were.'

'I've seen him be a right bastard,' says the comedian Simon Bligh, but Kinnie's blunt wit could never quite conceal his love of comedy and comedians. His Glaswegian candour was a form of bravery. He could be cruel to be kind, breaking the bad news to self-deluded comics who'd almost died, and still thought they'd done a stormer. He knew which comedians would never make it, and he wasn't afraid to let them know. He always told them straight away. However, Kinnie also knew which comics were special, and he knew how to woo them. 'The minute we walked in, the very first time, he made us feel at home, like we'd always been there,' says American comedienne Debi Durst, recalling her first visit to The Store, with her husband and fellow comic Will Durst.

'My job was to care about them,' says Kinnie. 'That's all I did.' But he did a whole lot more besides. 'Kim was so much more than the guy who did the bookings,' says Nick Hancock. 'He was a bit of a guru.' 'He knew how to help the performer,' says Ainsley Harriott. 'He made them believe in themselves.' And he did it without crossing that fine line between advisor and performer. 'He never told you how to do jokes,' says Hancock, but he helped countless comics learn how to find their own style.

Kinnie had a rare, refreshing blend of enthusiasm and cynicism, and because he came from a theatrical background, he understood dramatic basics, and helped comics understand them too. 'The comic's approach is very different to the actor's, but ultimately you're doing the same thing,' says Nick Revell. 'Whether it's very close to your own character or not, it's still a performance, and there are still certain fundamental constants that apply.' 'It coalesced everything I'd ever done before, and maybe not done very successfully,' reflects Kinnie. 'Suddenly, through The Store, I was able to use all that knowledge.'

'He decided whether you played there or not, and if he took agin you, you didn't play there,' says Bob Mills. 'It was as simple as that.' But he was open to persuasion. 'There was a lot of acts that he'd say, "I don't like them very much, but everyone else seems to, so let's give them a go," and he was very willing to say, "Yes, I was wrong. They're good. Let them play." There are very few comics who at some point in their lives haven't been influenced and helped along by Kim. He would be the one who would say sometimes in a quiet corner, "Why are you being so aggressive? Just go on the back foot a bit and you'll see. They'll relax as well." He knew the game. He had tremendous vision.' Like the time a mainstream comic stormed The Store. 'What did you think of that?' the comedian asked Kinnie afterwards. 'That was good,' replied Kinnie, 'but come back when you're doing your own stuff.'

'He could see something in comics nobody else could see, and he would bring it through, even if you died a death,' says Mickey Hutton, a regular store compere. Even

Kim Kinnie, 'The Godfather', who booked the acts and helped develop a whole new generation of comics

on the worst nights, Kinnie would stand by the acts he rated. 'Me and Kevin Day were opening the first half and we were both off within six minutes. It was a nightmare,' recalls Hutton. But Kinnie didn't mind. 'It's not you,' he told them. 'It's them.' In some ways, he was even more devoted than the comics themselves. 'Kim watched every single act. He never came in the back for a drink. He always watched the acts from the sound booth, and he was always coming in and shouting at us for being too noisy.'

'This little camp, intense choreographer had an instinctive eye for what works as comedy,' says Kevin Day, who made Kinnie the godfather of his first child. 'If somebody was ostensibly popular or the flavour of the month, Kim could see beyond that.'

Part producer, part promoter and part creative consultant, Kinnie's role was difficult to define, but he made a big difference. 'He had very little to do with the punters or the public or indeed the administrative day to day wrangles, but in terms of spotting and encouraging talent he was fantastic,' says Day. 'Kim saw things in Jack Dee that maybe Dee didn't even see in himself. But when he tried to manage acts he was spectacularly shit, in fact so shit that one of his acts couldn't even get a booking at The Store.' However, there were plenty of decent managers. There was only one Kim Kinnie. And his mainstream roots gave these new comics a unique ally. 'Most people from his background looked upon us with a certain sense of bitterness and anger,' says Day. 'They didn't think we should be taking up their breathing space, let alone their TV screens. Even though we thought what we were doing was valid and important and different, at the time the press didn't share that idea. People were very sniffy about so-called Alternative Comedy.' Not Kinnie. He made these comics feel like proper comedians, rather than upstarts with chips on their shoulders. 'He'd seen a lot of mainstream comics, and he was fantastic at telling us that there was a tradition of subversive comedy that went a long way back, and that we were part of that. He told us we were as good as people we'd read about in books.'

'Kim loved the company of comics,' says Dave Cohen. Yet long after he'd graduated from strippers to stand-ups, his Soho background still came in useful. Who else could have taught Julian Clary how to flounce with a feather boa? 'He wasn't just there to make money out of you,' says Clary. Uniquely, Kinnie cared. 'He wasn't in it for the money,' confirms Donna McPhail. 'He helped The Store evolve. He wasn't a frustrated performer, which a lot of these promoters and bookers are, so it wasn't personal. He just delighted in other people's skills.'

This new Store eventually ushered in a new intake of comedians, but there was also an initial overlap with the old one. One such survivor was the first act on at the old Soho Store, Lee Cornes. 'Lee was very loose,' says Simon Bligh. 'He'd be quite pissed a lot of the time and once I remember he did the same thing twice. He did a routine about fish and chips in the first half, and he did it in the second half, because he was pissed, and it was really hilarious.'

But this apparent incompetence was actually an elaborate joke at his audience's expense. 'He'd compere the first half, and then go on in the second half and do exactly the same material,' explains Jo Brand. 'He was really performing for other performers, not for the audience.' Sure enough, punters would bellow, 'You're shit!' But the other comics were delighted. 'I remember a couple of times him saying to us all, "I'm going to go on and deliberately die,"' says Nick Hancock. 'He'd get halfway through a piece of material that was going really well, and then he'd deliberately alienate the audience by going, "I can't remember where I put my car."' It was a joy to watch, as long as you were in on the joke. 'The comedians were doubled up at the back,' recalls comedian Sean Lock. 'He was just dying and there were eight comics at the back creased up laughing.'

For years, Lock thought the point of playing The Store was to entertain the other comics. And in a way, it was. 'Lee Cornes was my favourite,' says Mark Lamarr. 'He was The Store for me. I saw him one night where he didn't do any of the punchlines. He just did all the set-ups and then changed the punchlines, for no point at all. It was just me and Steve Frost at the back, pissing ourselves, but everyone else was baffled.' 'Everyone loved Lee,' says Arthur Smith, 'because he didn't give a fuck.'

But being a comic's comic can be a bit of a mixed blessing. Comedians have to sit through one another's sets ad infinitum, so they're bound to prefer acts who try something new. Most punters are watching a comic for the first time, so the most successful are often those who keep honing and polishing the same twenty-minute set. 'All the comedians remember me fondly,' says Cornes, 'but the audience probably wouldn't.'

'Lee Cornes was one of the staple comperes when I was stage managing here,' says Ali Day, who met her husband, Kevin Day, while working backstage at The Store. 'One way he'd compere was to pretend each time he went onstage he was more drunk because he'd had another two pints in the dressing room. The audience used to really go for it.' Then, one night in the early Nineties, something changed. 'He was doing his drunk act and the audience weren't laughing.'

Cornes doesn't play here anymore. And yet he can still cut it, given half a chance. The last time he played here was as a special guest at Mark Lamarr's one-man show. He didn't want to do it. He was feeling bored. He had a bad back. He said no. 'I'll pay you one hundred pounds for ten minutes,' offered the promoter. 'All right,' said Cornes. He

Arthur Smith, looking uncharacteristically smart

went on dressed as a pantomime cow. Twenty minutes later, he was still onstage, and he was still going strong.

Costumes of any kind were a rarity in the Eighties. The fashion was for dressing down, not up. This casual dress code was symbolic as well as practical. It implied the comic and the crowd were the same sort of people. 'It was almost a badge of honour to come on scruffily dressed, the opposite of what a classic comedian wears,' says Arthur Smith, who personified this indifferent naturalism. Smith once did a gig in a pair of tracksuit bottoms, but his laid back style wasn't confined to his wardrobe. The same immaculate indifference permeated every aspect of his act. As Smith once said, 'My life is dedicated to the notion that I shouldn't have to be awake before ten o'clock.'[6]

Smith's stage persona was so informal, and his relationship with the audience so spontaneous, it scarcely felt as if he was performing at all. He seemed more like a regular punter who'd left his pint at the bar and got up to have a go, even though a real punter would never seem so relaxed. 'It's extraordinary how ordinary he is,' says Donna McPhail. Yet despite his deceptive nonchalance, it wasn't always so easy, even for him. 'I died on my arse,' he says, recalling his debut at the old Soho Store. 'I was petrified.' He arrived at 8pm, only to find he wasn't due onstage until 2am. 'When you're the open spot and you're mingling with the acts, you feel rather humble and pathetic, and I drank more and more and got more nervous,' he says, in the deserted front stalls of the new Store one afternoon. 'It was so traumatic, I didn't do it again for six months.' Yet even though his own performance was a shambles, he was still inspired by the other performers. 'I've never seen anything like this,' he thought. 'I want to be part of it.' Smith never played the Soho Store again, but he was suitably inspired to try out elsewhere on the circuit, and by the time he made his debut at the Leicester Square Store, he'd graduated from open spot to compere.

Smith was already in his late twenties, relatively old for a Store rookie. He'd been in a band and in revue, but as he stepped out onto that tiny stage, blinded by the lights, in front of 200 drunken punters, he felt as though this was what he'd been building up to for all those years. It felt like coming home. 'I can do this,' he thought. 'I belong here.' It was a role he made his own. 'You know you're promoted from the second division to the first division once you've played The Store,' he says. 'You never quite know if you're a comedian, even when you're beginning to get paid, but there comes a time when you think, "I'm a comedian," and it's largely liable to coincide with playing The Comedy Store.'

Smith's inspiration was Alexei Sayle. For Smith, Sayle was the comic equivalent of punk. When Smith saw Sayle's autobiographical stand-up, unblemished by daft props or silly costumes, talking about the real world rather than make-believe, the mild literary parodies Smith had been doing suddenly felt old fashioned and out of date. 'Your template for a stand-up then was Jimmy Tarbuck or someone with a frilly shirt doing formulaic jokes about going to pubs, and Alexei, and Tony Allen, blew that apart.'

The fact that these acts were often at loggerheads with their audience only added to the appeal. A lot of this difference was due to the location. 'You've got a more conservative audience here. You've got blokes from the City. In a pub in Hackney you're going to have a more sympathetic liberal atmosphere.' The friction between stage and stalls was often more fun than the consensus that comedians encountered elsewhere. When Smith caught a punter reading the *Sun* during his set, he ripped it up in a frenzy of right-on origami. The punter insisted Smith refund him the price of the paper. 'We were martyrs,' quips Smith, 'bringing a left-wing sensibility to a bunch of pissed-up right-wing businessmen.' Yet this tipsy business ethic soon spread from stalls to stage. 'For years, my whole house was full of cash. It was wonderful. I never went to the bank for years. You'd open your drawer. There's another fucking envelope from The Store.'

Like Sayle, Smith shunned those eulogies that are the stock in trade of trad comperes. However, other comics didn't always appreciate his less than sycophantic style. 'This is such bullshit, isn't it?' said Smith, midway through a conventionally gushing intro for fellow Store stalwart John Moloney. 'Frankly, I hate the fucker and he's shit.' Smith didn't mean it, and Moloney did just fine, but every joke has a victim, and if Smith's gag hadn't run the risk of upsetting someone, it wouldn't have been so funny. 'He's only just forgiven me,' says Smith. 'He didn't talk to me for two years.'

If there weren't enough open spots, Smith simply plucked them out of the audience. 'Who wants to come up and tell a joke?' he'd ask, at the end of a late show. And by then, the audience were usually all so pissed, he actually found plenty of volunteers. 'It was like watching a car accident,' says stand-up and novelist Mark Billingham. 'It scared the hell out of me.' A few of Smith's conscripts, like Felix Dexter, went on to become professional comics, but most froze in the spotlight. 'Often, you'd get up the drunk one who'd been heckling all night,' says Smith. 'They were amateurs. They didn't know what the fuck they were doing.'

Yet these instant recruits were often saner than the proper try outs who booked ahead, like the bloke who told the tale of Little Red Riding Hood, dressed as Myra Hindley. 'It didn't matter that they were dying or that the audience were screaming at them,' says Billingham. 'It was half performance art and half therapy.' Another open spot died on his arse doing impressions of ancient celebs like James Cagney. 'Maybe you should try doing somebody who's still alive,' suggested Smith. He came back the next week and did impressions of Arnold Brown, John Hegley and Alexei Sayle, with gags lifted wholesale from their acts. 'It actually didn't go too bad, because he had quite funny material.' Another open spot actually got his end away in the dressing room, even though he didn't have much of an act. 'He didn't go that well,' thought Smith. 'How did he manage that?' He wasn't the only one. Tony Allen also had sex backstage, while the comic Tony Morewood was onstage.

'At the midnight show, someone always had to go down the pan,' says Julian Clary, recalling this netherworld of spilled drinks, broken glasses and overflowing toilets. 'If they'd gone really badly, you'd probably go quite well, and the other way around.' Backstage there was gladiatorial camaraderie. 'All of us were people who didn't fit in anywhere else.' But onstage, it was dog eat dog. 'I never felt very safe there, because of the layout of the place,' he says, amid the calm comfort of his elegant yet understated North London home. 'You had to go through the audience to get to the stage and there was nowhere to run to.' Once he'd put on his make-up, he was stranded backstage, with no monitor, so he had to listen through the dressing room door to hear how the other acts were doing, and once you were on that stage, your back was literally against the wall.

Yet this rough and tumble bearpit actually provided the perfect foil for Clary's languid stage persona, helping him to create the caustic interplay with his audience which became the mainstay of his set. 'They were right on top of you, which was a good thing for my act,' he says. 'That's where I started picking on them, before they picked on me.' His best form of defence was all-out attack, and he even invited hecklers to join him onstage. 'Sometimes they'd try and grab the microphone, and once you give a drunk man the microphone, you can't get it back without some loss of dignity.' No wonder he seemed so cool on his game show, *Sticky Moments*. Relatively anarchic by televisual standards, it must have felt positively staid by comparison. 'They're definitely a crowd, they're not an audience,' he says. 'They'd chosen to come and see comedy. They hadn't chosen to come and see you.'

And the world outside wasn't any kinder. Clary lived on the notorious Brook estate, in the suburban hinterland of Kidbrooke. At forty quid a gig, he could scarcely afford a taxi, and the last train left Charing Cross at half past ten, so if he did the late show, he had to walk to Trafalgar Square afterwards and catch the night bus back to Eltham. 'It was a really rough estate,' he says. 'I lived in this horrible little council studio dump, but it seemed all right at the time.' For unlike other comics, Clary had a canine ally who was far more loyal than any straight man. 'Fanny The Wonderdog, a six-year-old mongrel from Battersea Dogs Home, blessed with a deadpan expression that's weirdly reminiscent of Buster Keaton, watches the proceedings with a kind of withering stare that would freeze a Gielgud or an Olivier in mid-flow,' reported *Time Out*. 'If anyone did heckle,' says Clary, 'she'd shut them up with a look.' Hounds are far harder to heckle than humans, but sometimes the bedlam was even too much for this man's best mate, and she'd flee to the sanctuary of the dressing room. Yet her impressions were well worth waiting for: the Pope, the Queen Mum, The Duchess of York, Edwina Currie, Wayne Sleep, and her *pièce de résistance*, Tower Bridge.

Fanny's showbiz career began completely by accident. 'Fanny and I went everywhere together,' said Clary, in 1986. 'She would wait in the dressing room for me. But some clubs didn't have dressing rooms, so I used to bring her onstage. At first she'd just sit on a stool. Then I discovered her talent for impressions and there was no stopping her.'[7] At first, Fanny would appear onstage to riotous applause. But after she was knocked down by a car, on tour in Newcastle, she became scared of the sound of clapping, and Clary had to tell audiences not to applaud. Thereafter Fanny came on to absolute silence, and like forbidden laughter in the classroom, the tension was electric, as audiences teetered on the edge of applause. But her showbiz days were numbered. Fanny announced her official retirement in 1988, at London's Hackney Empire. After a decade of secluded bliss *chez* Clary, her arthritic hips could no longer handle his stairs, so she spent her final few years with Clary's parents. Clary had always said she'd see him reach forty, and sure enough, she died, blind, deaf and incontinent, but happy, a few days after his fortieth birthday.

'It is with great sadness that we have to report the death of Julian Clary's Fanny,' ran the *Guardian*'s obituary. 'The whippet that brought a touch of class to Clary's early stand-up act, The Joan Collins Fan Club, has passed away aged nineteen.' 'I shall miss her terribly,' said Clary, recalling the faithful hound he saved from four months solitary in a rabbit hutch, 'but her spirit will live on.'

TV had plundered the top talent at the old Soho Store, but after The Comic Strip decamped to Raymond's Revuebar, and The Gargoyle closed down, the media more or less lost interest. Now the Leicester Square Store was finding its feet at last, and TV was finally waking up to the fresh possibilities of straight stand-up. 'People who'd been working round the clubs were now suddenly getting an awful lot of slots on television,' recalls Simon Clayton. And the main motor of this small-screen boom was Channel 4's *Saturday Live*. This mid-Eighties variety flagship, masterminded by Paul Jackson, made stars of two Store turns, Ben Elton and Harry Enfield, and really put modern stand-up on the map. With its West End location, and its reputation as the club where The Comic Strip and The Young Ones cut their comic milk teeth, The Store was the club where telly people went to trawl for comic talent.

Saturday Live host Ben Elton's political stand-up became synonymous with 'right on' Alternative Comedy and the era from the Falklands War to the Gulf War was the heyday of political comedy at The Store. 'It was a larger appetite than we had back in the States,' says West Coast wit Will Durst, who once ran for mayor of San Francisco. 'If you weren't part of the solution, you were part of the problem.' 'People really cared about being non-racist and non-sexist,' adds Durst's fellow American John Lenahan.

'There was a lot of comics who genuinely thought at the time that nobody should have to pay money to see comedy, and there was always a kind of unease with lots of the political comics about the fact that they were being paid good money to go onstage and talk about social injustice,' says Kevin Day. 'There was a lot of unease about the fact that this place had lights and a sound system and doormen, and it was paid for by somebody who had more business sense than we did.'

Both Lenahan and Day were at The Store during the Poll Tax demonstration. 'I was in town for the march,' Day says. 'I turned up at The Store and none of the acts were there, but Lenny Henry had turned up because he was about to go on tour and wanted to try out ten minutes.' The audience had all arrived, so Kinnie asked Day to go on. It felt like the evacuation of Saigon. 'None of the acts have showed,' Day told the audience, over the sound of police sirens from the streets above, 'but we've got a geezer out of the audience who said he'd try and keep you entertained.' On came Henry and the room erupted. 'I remember going to The Comedy Store and realising that I didn't have to rely on impersonations so much and that I could be funnier being myself,' said Henry.

These comedians were sincere, but there was also an element of vested interest about political sympathies at The Store. 'A lot of people on the circuit did work for the GLC,' says Phil Herbert. 'It was a terrible thing when the GLC went, as far as people getting funds to put shows on.' Local government-funded comedy scarcely fitted the concept of the comic as a fearless maverick, kicking against the establishment pricks. Don Ward's upfront capitalist Store seemed refreshingly scrupulous by comparison.

During its first decade, Alternative Comedy had fashioned a fresh set of ideological restrictions of its own. Yet the radical values that freed comedy from reactionary atrophy ten years before now threatened to stifle it with a different set of prejudices, not nearly so pernicious as those they ousted, but equally monotonous nonetheless. Policemen and Ulster Protestants replaced Black and Irish labourers as right-on bogeymen, and Thatcher became a politically correct mother-in-law. Cracking jokes about prime ministers is the proper job of stand-up comedy, but this Comedy Store Aunt Sally was condemned with bilious savagery conspicuously absent from equivalent quips about her male ministers, using terms like bitch or cow that often degenerated into blatant misogyny.

These targets were strong majorities, rather than weak minorities, but any knee-jerk joke, good or bad, grows predictable if repeated ad infinitum. And although these comedians poured their bile over robust public figureheads rather than helpless private individuals, as their trad predecessors often did, bigotry is still bigotry, whether it dresses to the left or to the right. 'Therein lies one of the Left's great perversions,' concluded Siŏn Simon in the *Daily Telegraph*. 'We are tragically prone to smug, complacent, self-congratulatory, self-reinforcing insularity.' Even Marxist Leninist comic Jim Barclay said there was nothing more pompous than the Labour movement.

'Alternative Comedy has its own taboos,'[8] observed Arnold Brown during the Eighties, and by The Store's tenth anniversary year, Thatcher's last full year in office, Alternative Comedy's blacklist had spread way beyond its initial anti-racist boundaries to colonise an entire set of leftist preconceptions. The word cunt had always been verboten. 'The whole room went dead,' says Steve Frost, recalling the time he said the word onstage. 'I had a big lecture from Tony Allen about which words you can and cannot use.' But by now, there were plenty of topics outside this narrow remit that younger, less radical comics simply didn't feel free to discuss. 'Talking about women was out,' says Jeff Green. 'You couldn't talk about your girlfriend.' Even the word was frowned upon. Green tried doing political gags, but his heart wasn't in it. 'Everybody ended up talking about their childhood, because it was inoffensive, and it wasn't going to piss off any of the comedy police,' says Green. 'That's what happens with censorship. Everything becomes bland. The left were very censorious. They'd cast a beady eye, and because you're new, you don't want to be blacked, so you tended not to say what you actually wanted, because people with more clout could bad mouth you, and that was it. You were out.'

Some pragmatic comics paid lip service to the PC police, topping and tailing their sets with right-on rhetoric. 'As long as you started and finished with something deeply political and militant they all loved you,' says Phill Jupitus. 'As long as you started and finished by saying the government are evil, you got an encore.' 'You felt like you had to fulfil this brief,' says Sean Lock, who started out with a set peppered with a few token political gags, because he thought it was what was required of him, until Lee Cornes asked him what he was doing. Even Alternative Cabaret veterans like Oscar McLennan sensed the endemic impotence of anti-Thatcher tirades. 'You were preaching to the converted,' he says. 'The vast majority of Alternative Cabaret audiences already hated Thatcher.' Like Orwell's *Animal Farm* set in a comedy club, The Store had become a Light Ent metaphor for how every revolution eventually atrophies, into conservatism, corruption, and decay.

'Performer and audience begin with the premise that badness means the police/Norman Tebbit/the *Sun* newspaper/God (or any similar authority)/the Nolan Sisters/cruise missiles/Saatchi's/heroin,' claimed the *Guardian* in 1987. 'Goodness means whales/*Socialist Worker*/guilt/Diane Abbott/UB40s/benefit concerts/cocaine.' The *Guardian* was right about the performers, but the audience was another matter. As early as the Falklands War, there was a discernible gap between these left-wing comics and their more right-wing punters. 'It was a given that you were against it, even though the majority of people in the country were all for it,' says Arthur Smith, recalling how the war drove a wedge between the crowd and the comics. 'A lot of the audience would be for what was going on in the Falklands, but nevertheless you had to go on and say you hated it.'

Playing to punters with the same opinions was a soft option for right-on acts. 'Anybody who was doing observational stuff was mentioning fucking Thatcher every minute and a half, and you could be guaranteed that even if you didn't get a big laugh, you'd get "Yeah, you're right",' recalls trad circuit refugee Paul Zenon. However, plenty of comedy clubs were more politically strident than The Store. 'What are your political beliefs?' asked a promoter at a Camden club, when Zenon asked him for an open spot. 'We just book acts on that basis.' 'Doesn't it matter if I'm funny or not?' asked Zenon. 'That's a bonus,' he replied.

For a few years, PC threatened to stifle the movement The Store had started. 'Acts would be booed for saying girlfriend or boyfriend,' says Mark Billingham. 'I'd see perfectly good acts get heckled offstage and then much less talented acts be accepted because they were from a perceived minority. And then Jerry Sadowitz came along and blew it all out of the water by walking onstage and going, "Nelson Mandela. What a cunt."'

'The whole PC thing got incredibly out of hand,' says Richard Morton. 'When Phill Jupitus and Lee Hurst came down to The Store, they brought in a sort of laddish comedy. They did very laddish gags, but because you knew they were intelligent blokes, you knew they didn't mean it in an evil, wicked, nasty way. You could make jokes about the battle of the sexes again, things that were deemed sexist before. It opened up new avenues of comedy again, and also it was more honest. What was the point in people going to the pub talking like they do, thinking like they do, then coming to The Store and pretending? That isn't the real world.' Any more than the old mythology these stereotypes replaced. 'Mother Teresa's retired,' quipped Morton. 'Lazy cow.' The Soho Store echoed the anarchy of punk. Now the Leicester Square Store mimicked the shift from Militant Chic to Ecstatic Bohemia. Again, this small stage led the way. 'Everybody was stifled with political correctness,' says Donna McPhail. 'Thank God those days are over.'

By the Nineties, the anti-racism war had been largely won and the anti-sexist battle largely lost, but the audiences remained a volatile yet representative mix of right-on and unreconstructed minds. 'Two guys and a girl started heckling me for being homophobic,' says Sean Lock, recalling a Store gig which showed that crowds can laugh in all the right places for all the wrong reasons. 'I did this piece to them about why I wasn't homophobic and it went down really well.' The next night, back at The Store, Lock was collared by a huge rugby player. 'I saw you last night, I brought my mates down to see you because you were brilliant,' he told Lock. 'The way you dealt with them poofs.'

Even though the acts and audiences had both become less left wing, Thatcher's resignation in 1990 still sparked a mass celebration beneath Leicester Square. By that evening, The Cutting Edge, The Store's topical team show, had written heaps of fresh jokes to accompany the party atmosphere. The Store had opened in the same month that Thatcher had moved into Downing Street. Now she was moving out, but The Store was still going strong. However, for Don Ward, her departure provided a welcome break from a string of gags that had long since passed their sell-by date. 'We can't keep saying Maggie Thatcher's a cunt, Maggie Thatcher's a cow, Maggie Thatcher's a warmonger or Maggie Thatcher's got no feelings for the poor,' he thought. 'We know that. Give us something else.' And freed from her overbearing presence, The Cutting Edge rose to this new challenge. John Major's victory as the new Tory leader was announced only a few hours before The Store opened that night, yet like news hounds on a satirical evening paper, Cutting Edge comics are at their best reacting to breaking news, and by showtime, they had plenty of new material about Britain's new prime minister. 'John Major says he's working class,' declared comedian Bob Boyton, brandishing his gilt necklace. 'Where's his gold chain?'

Yet after Major replaced Thatcher, radical acts like Boyton became scarce, replaced by younger, more ambitious comics, less bothered about social injustice, and more interested in number one. And many punters felt much the same. Since 1986, when Channel 4 started screening *Saturday Live*, starring Store stars like Rik Mayall and Adrian Edmondson as The Dangerous Brothers, and Mark Arden and Steve Frost as The Oblivion Boys, political stand-up had become mainstream entertainment, thanks mainly to the prolific talents of the show's host, Ben Elton. 'We needed Ben,' says Helen Lederer, but although Elton's influence was immense, the sheer success of his anti-Thatcherite rants transformed political stand-up into a ubiquitous cliché, and it became increasingly difficult to crack jokes about politics in the clubs without sinking into sub-Eltonesque self-parody.

Steve Punt and Hugh Dennis played The Store the night after the 1987 General Election. 'We'd been up all night, watching the election, getting more and more pissed as the third successive landslide rolled in,' says Punt. Despite his stinking hangover, he arrived at The Store with plenty of political material, but the punters had passed the point of satire. 'It was beyond a joke. The audience didn't want jokes about five more years, no matter how agit prop they were. They wanted to be transported somewhere else.'

Punt wrote political comedy for *Weekending* on the radio, and for Rory Bremner and *Spitting Image* on television, but when he used the same topical gags in the clubs, they didn't work. He preferred performing apolitical routines with Dennis. 'There was always a bit of a division between the people who thought the purpose of The Store was to bring down the government, and those of us who were just having a bit of a laugh,' explains Dennis, who kept up his white collar career as a brand manager at Unilever for his first six years as a comic.

Now, at the turn of the Nineties, this bit of a laugh brigade was in the ascendant, as relatively conventional comics who'd been ignored by TV during the Eighties finally found the small screen slots their talent had always warranted, and the press attention that went with it. At last, comics who'd scraped by during the last decade were pocketing decent fees, and stand-up's shifting status was echoed underneath Leicester Square. There was fast money to be made. Around about the same time that the Tories finally dumped Thatcher, Alternative Comedy finally discovered Thatcherism.

However, after the comic dream of Thatcher's resignation came true, Major's shock victory in the 1992 General Election was a very rude awakening. Lots of comics expected a Labour win, especially after Red Wednesday, when three polls gave Labour seven, six and four per cent leads, only a week before polling day. But given the results of his own Store straw poll, Lee Hurst shouldn't have been surprised. During the run-up to the election, Hurst asked Tory punters at The Store for a show of hands. Very few hands went up, and naïvely, he assumed that the Tories were done for. Yet whenever he hauled an outed Tory up onstage, he'd play with them, without malice, then say, 'Let's be honest now,' and more hands would go up than before. Conservative Central Office should have saved their money. Hurst's own private poll pointed the same way as their own.

Nevertheless, at the start of their Election Night show, the Cutting Edge comics had all felt confident. 'It started off with the assumption that Labour were going to win the election, which, for the most part, all the performers were pleased about,' recalls Kevin Day, 'but we underestimated how many people in the audience didn't want Labour to win.' As the results came in, the Labour punters became more subdued and Tory punters grew more vocal. 'It was the Basildon result that finally made everyone realise,' says Day. 'Pockets of the audience were going mad.' These True Blue cheers weren't reciprocated onstage. 'You see shots of a last-minute goal going in at Wembley and you see players falling to their knees. That's what the performers were like. But then about two minutes later, somebody said, "Well, actually this isn't a bad result because it gives us five more years of taking the piss," which is probably an argument for how shallow and facile comics can be, because the rest of the country can go stuff themselves.'

'Everyone expected Labour to win,' says Richard Morton, who was also on the bill. Now, Morton sees Neil Kinnock's triumphalist Sheffield rally and the *Sun*'s 'turn out the lights' election day front page as twin turning points, but back then, he was naïve enough to assume the Conservatives would lose. 'The whole tone of the show was "It's the end of the Tories",' he says. Morton reckons more than three-quarters of the crowd were anti-Conservative, if not pro-Labour, but it was the Tory minority which created such dramatic conflict around the room. 'These guys have got some courage shouting out for the Tories,' thought Morton. 'Don't you know it's all over?' But they didn't. And it wasn't. 'As the show progressed, and we were relaying the results to the audience, it was becoming more and more evident that Labour had lost it,' he says. 'It was suddenly dawning on us that the Tories were going to get back in.' Yet he didn't begrudge his Tory punters the last laugh. 'They were great for the show,' he says. 'I'm glad they were there.'

Not all Morton's fellow performers felt so magnanimous in defeat. 'You fucking scum,' thought Hurst, amid the Tory cheers. 'If you want to be a Conservative, if you want to vote for these pieces of shit, that's your choice, but have the fucking balls to admit that you do it. Stand up for your convictions.' It affected his performance. 'There was no smiling in the material anymore,' he says. 'There was no happiness there at all. You were spitting stuff out.' Even the backstage staff were infected by the rancour around the room. Stage manager Stan Nelson had to pull one comic away from a punter, nearly lost it with another, and then had to stay behind until five in the morning, derigging the set. 'It was going to be a celebration,' says Nelson. 'It just turned into an awful wake.'

'I always felt bitter that I wasn't invited to do it, although I think I would have given up being funny,' says Bob Boyton, one of the original Cutting Edge team, whose conspicuous absence from that night's line-up showed even the comedians had migrated towards the middle ground. 'There was a big group of dentists in that night,' he says. 'The better it looked for the Tories, the more cheerful these dentists were. That's just what you expect from those bastards.' Boyton has false teeth.

'It was a really strange atmosphere,' says Morton. 'Everyone had enjoyed a very funny show and we'd all done well, but by the end of it, everyone was stunned because Labour hadn't got in. Also, our material then was looking almost kind of fraudulent, because it was all based on Kinnock winning, and it was all wrong. We'd got it completely and utterly wrong.' Morton was gutted. 'When I used to do me little jokes about the Tories and Thatcher, I was hoping in my naïvete that it was making some small contribution to getting them out.' Not anymore. 'No one's taking any notice of what you say when you're onstage,' he realised. 'You have no bearing on current events.' The next day, still cursing the English electorate, Morton flew to Ireland to do a gig. 'This is what you deserve,' he thought, as he boarded a plane to Dublin. 'You can keep it.' But when he returned home after his weekend away, it hit him even harder. He realised he'd misjudged the mood of the population at large. Morton wasn't the only one. 'The comics who did their political satires suddenly had to take a good look at themselves, and wonder if they were making any headway into public opinion.' Most decided they weren't, and made way for those who weren't bothered either way. It was the end of an era.

Less than two years after Major's triumphant return to 10 Downing Street, The Store went the same way as New Labour, moving into more upmarket premises, and attracting a more broad-based clientele. In an unwitting metaphor for these changing times, Ward swapped his former gay nightclub for a former burger bar. 'It was the dying embers of the ethos of Alternative Comedy,' says Bob Mills. 'Anyone who was there and played that place is now part of history, and anyone who's doing it now can only look back at that history. They can never go there and be a part of it.'

'I grew up in that room,' says John Lenahan. 'Some places are funny, some rooms are funny and this was a funny room. People were funny in that room.' 'I loved that old place,' says Richard Morton, 'even though it was a hard room to play.' The last performance was by The Comedy Store Players. Fitting, since the foundation of this impro troupe was one of the most lasting and influential achievements of the Leicester Square Store. And the last joke ever cracked on this tiny stage was by Paul Merton. Doubly fitting, since of all the stand-up and impro jokers who found their comedic feet down here, Merton was about the only one with a foot in both camps. As the crowd shuffled out for the last time, Nat King Cole's 'Unforgettable' echoed around the tiny auditorium. 'You know that feeling when you think there must be something else somewhere else that's better than this?' said Arthur Smith, when the club closed. 'Well, if you went onstage at midnight in The Comedy Store, you didn't think that. You thought, "This is the place to be."'[9]

Chapter Six

Like the move from Soho to Leicester Square, the move from Leicester Square to Piccadilly Circus was mainly about money. Even selling out every weekend, and most weekdays, Don Ward was only making about £20,000 per year profit. He was already paying over £60,000 in rent, and the next rent review was only two years away. At that time, in that part of town, rents were doubling. It was time to move on. He'd heard about an empty basement on the other side of Leicester Square, which had been shared between Taco Bell and Burger King, until they sold out to TGI Friday. TGI Friday was owned by Whitbread. Whitbread supplied beer to The Store. Ward made a phone call. TGI wanted the upstairs room. They weren't interested in what went on below, so Ward took a stroll across Leicester Square and paid a visit.

'It was a shell,' says Ward, in his smart new suite of offices above The Prince Of Wales Theatre, over the road from The Store. 'It was stripped out to the bare concrete.' Yet all Ward could see was a state-of-the-art comedy club. 'I must have this room,' he thought, as soon as he walked in. 'This is going to be my room.' It would cost him three quarters of a million to make it happen, but he was undeterred. 'As soon as I walked in the door, I knew where the stage and bar would be.' He got a late dance licence, sold his lease on the Leicester Square Store as a disco, and by the end of 1993, he was ready to move in. This time, there would be no music, and definitely no strippers. 'No dancing, no top-less girls,' Ward told *The Stage*. 'Just the spoken word.' 'This place has been built just for telling jokes,' confirms Phill Jupitus. 'That's all it's there for.'

The Piccadilly Circus Store was the final realisation of Don Ward's dream. Here, at last, was a proper purpose-built comedy club, a 400-seat auditorium, with its own

Queues outside the Piccadilly Store

state-of-the-art sound booth and a decent dressing room. And the acoustics are wonderful, especially that rush of laughter that hits you when you're up onstage. 'They all felt it was a great space to play,' says Kim Kinnie, 'especially when it was packed.' Arthur Smith cemented the move by carrying that dressing-room sink to its new home on the other side of Leicester Square. 'Don's kept the sink,' says impro comic Richard Vranch. 'It should be in a glass cabinet.' Its new role is merely ceremonial, for the dressing room actually has its own ensuite lavatory and shower. 'The comedians have got their own toilet, which is a kindness to the public rather than the comedians,' says Jack Dee. It was the surest sign of all that The Store had finally arrived. 'This is brilliant,' thought Donna McPhail, the first time she set eyes on the new Store. 'It's been built for us.'

At last, Alternative Comedy had created a venue that could compare with that Los Angeles comedy club of the same name. In many ways, it's even better. 'America invented stand-up comedy clubs,' argued comedian Boothby Graffoe. 'Now they should take a look at The Comedy Store to find out how to run them.'[1] No two drink minimum. No waiters pestering you to fork out for a refill. If you want a beer or a burger, you have to queue up with everyone else. The bar and diner are out of sight, if not entirely out of sound, of both stage and stalls. No tables to break up the bank of seating. You put your plate on your lap, and your drink between your feet. 'The Comedy Store doesn't compromise the comedy,' says Lee Hurst. 'Nothing is allowed to get in your way. No waitress service. No death by cutlery.' The club Rosengard dreamt of and Ward built up was made for comedy, not food and drink.

And the mood backstage is often better too. 'American comedy is really competitive,' says John Lenahan, who's made his home in London and became one of the main comperes at the Leicester Square Store. 'American comics would come into the dressing room and they'd pace around and they'd give you their CV and they'd have to prove their worth, and we'd all just be sitting around saying, "Relax, take it easy, have a piss in the sink," and they couldn't get their heads around it. They couldn't understand how we could all be so laid back about it all.' And even with a proper toilet to piss in, that laid-back attitude still endures.

There are other decent purpose-built comedy clubs in Britain. But at The Store, comedy is the only reason to be there. When a comic steps out onto that small stage, and into the brutal scrutiny of the spotlight, at least they know their audience is there for one thing, and one thing only. Not the refreshments during the show. Not the disco afterwards. Just comedy. Jongleurs is a party. The Store is a habit. With its West End location, The Store attracts more than its fair share of tourists. But down here, they're not visitors or even customers, just punters. Comedy works best in basements, with low ceilings and tight crowds. The first Soho Store felt that way, even though it was actually several storeys high, the Leicester Square Store was that way, and most comics agree that this new Store retained almost all of that old atmosphere, with mod cons attached. 'It's much better being able to retreat from the stage to the dressing room,' says Julian Clary.

'It was an appalling room from a punter's point of view,' says John Mann, a regular compere at the new Store, recalling the lousy sightlines underneath Leicester Square, where even the comics had a restricted view. Here, unlike Leicester Square, there's nowhere for hecklers to hide. 'It was a very difficult room to control,' adds Mann. 'Here you can actually work out where people are. I don't think there's a spot in this room you can't control.'

'Laughter is like electricity,' says Simon Evans, another stand-up who's made his name at this new Store. 'It needs to conduct, and if you start breaking people up it doesn't conduct so well. There's no other club in England that I know of where so many people are so tightly packed in, all facing the stage, no distractions. They've got a beer in their hand, maybe, but they've got no table in front of them, dinner and menus and all the rest of it, and if you make a significant number of them laugh it'll spread. It's just like a huge wave. If you're used to paddling off Weston Super Mare and then you hit Big Sur for the first time, it really is that different. It's a fantastic feeling. Once you get that laughter underneath you, it lifts you right up and then you're free.'

Some of the mod cons can be a mixed blessing. 'It's now much harder to get free drinks out of the bar staff,' says Kevin Day, 'because they've put close circuit cameras in.' And the monitor, which allows comics to watch the show on a small screen backstage, has had mixed reviews. It's handy for comperes, but it can induce a certain degree of paranoia among the acts. 'When you're onstage you're always thinking, "I wonder what them bastards are saying,"' says Geordie comic Dave Johns. 'Whether they're going, "Not this old shite again."' Yet even though this auditorium is far smarter than in Leicester Square, compared to Jongleurs, The Store still retains its old speakeasy feel. 'You get met at the door by somebody who shakes your hand and shows you through and makes sure your hotel room is sorted out,' says Simon Evans, of the five-star treatment he gets at Jongleurs regional gigs. It's more down to earth at The Store. 'You push your way through the crowds to get to this quite grotty little back room. There's a few bottles of water in the fridge and some percolated coffee which has probably been there since the week before.'

Yet some Leicester Square veterans believe this new Store has lost its radical spark. 'It belongs to the Jongleurs ethic,' says Bob Mills. 'Punters paying big money to come in and wanting safe results.' Mills played this new Store over fifty times, but for him, it never felt like anything other than another clean, bright comedy club. 'Artistically, it was a disaster,' he claims. 'It was like an out of town arts centre gig and it never ever

Comics including Rhona Cameron, Dominic Holland and Owen O'Neill backstage at the Piccadilly Store

recaptured the thrill of the old place.' 'It hasn't got the same nooks and crannies,' concurs Hattie Hayridge.

'This place has got atmosphere,' says doorman Mark Skeete, 'but it hasn't got the sort of atmosphere that little club used to hold.' Most of all, the back bar has bitten the dust. 'The huge problem, I always felt, was that it never had the back bar,' says Kinnie. 'Comics still swing by to socialise,' says comedian Simon Clayton, 'but not like they used to, because there isn't that open space away from the show.'

Most comics accept the move was inevitable. 'It's like the house I lived in when I went to college,' says John Lenahan. 'Much as I loved that house, I wouldn't want to live in it now.' For a new generation of stand-ups and punters, this is the place that thrills them, even if you no longer have to claw through a scrum of pissed up punters to reach the bog or bar. And any backstage quibbles are small beer beside the bonuses of the wide open space out front. 'The stage is big enough to run round,' says Eddie Izzard. 'It's better than the one they had before.' And compared to Leicester Square, the sightlines are superb. 'The further you were away from the stage, the lousier the view,' says Simon Clayton. 'Now it doesn't matter where you are. You get a great view. Right at the back is probably more interesting because you get a better panoramic perspective of the whole gig. Not just what the comic is doing onstage, but how the audience are reacting to it in front of you.' From the front few rows, punters still look right up the stand-up's nostrils. It may be double the size, but somehow, that old intimacy between stage and stalls prevails. 'Compared to Jongleurs, it's still quite bohemian,' says Bob Boyton. 'Once you get inside, it's got that jazz feel.'

'The old Store was a lot more intimate, with a smaller stage,' says stage manager John McGrath. 'It's still a small stage, but the auditorium's so big, we were worried it was going to lose that intimacy. I don't think it has. I think it's a very warm room.' Any larger, and waves of laughter would begin to break up before they hit the back wall, but 400 seats is small enough for companionship, yet big enough to be a crowd. 'It used to be more of a clubby atmosphere,' says fellow stage manager Stan Nelson, but like McGrath, he believes the pros outweigh the cons. 'The comics love playing here,' says Stan. 'They say it's like no other gig there is. It's laid out perfectly for stand-up, because they are the most important thing in the room at that moment in time.'

McGrath and Nelson stayed up for two days, bringing down the farewell show at the old Store and lugging all the lights to the new Store, across Leicester Square. 'All of a sudden we've got a new venue to set up, and we'd got twenty-four hours before the show starts all over again,' remembers McGrath. 'You're racing against time.' But when they finally pulled it off, it was the best feeling in the world.

That opening night was a great gig, featuring Soho survivors like Tony Allen, Arnold Brown, Lee Cornes and John Hegley, plus Leicester Square favourites such as Jo Brand, Jack Dee, Eddie Izzard and Paul Merton. However, many Store veterans had to fight for laughs that came a lot easier underneath Leicester Square. 'The old acts actually struggled,' says Keith Dover, who started at the Leicester Square Store back in the late Eighties, but belongs to that new breed of classless apolitical stand-up at the Piccadilly Circus Store. 'Nick Revell was the only one who held his own that night. The other acts found it really difficult, and the new acts that had been playing were the ones that done the business. Comedy had moved on.' Stand-up is competitive sport, not performance art, and past form counts for nothing.

But apart from Revell, there was another veteran who bucked this trend. Julian Clary had created a front page furore the night before at the British Comedy Awards, by cracking an outrageous, hilarious joke about fisting Norman Lamont. 'This is great news for comedy clubs,' wrote Malcolm Hay in *Time Out*, after LWT apologised, and warned everyone to behave themselves on live televised shows. 'They'll be where you go to hear what comics really think.' The Store's opening night didn't disappoint. And nor did Clary, despite his brief encounter with Lamont. 'He didn't do any material about him, but he came onstage wearing one marigold glove,' recalls McGrath. 'That was enough. That endeared him to me forever. That was probably one of the funniest things I've ever seen. Nothing needed to be said. The audience got it instantly, and we were up and running. We were away.'

However, after the move to Piccadilly Circus, Clary only ever returned for the odd gig, and plenty of other stars followed suit. Despite Kim Kinnie's preference for spartan political stand-up, there were still plenty of quirky acts at the Leicester Square Store, and few of these eccentrics survived the move upmarket. But then Kinnie returned to his native Glasgow, to become a TV producer for STV, and Don Ward resumed the bookings. Ward's populism further streamlined The Store's appeal. 'Don likes gags,' says Dave Johns. 'Good gag tellers and good jokes.' 'There were two theories,' explains Oscar McLennan. 'If you can play The Store, you can play anywhere, and if you can play The Store, you can't play anywhere else.' And paradoxically, there's some truth in both of them.

Even some conventional comics lost out when Ward took over from Kinnie. Comedy is the most subjective of art forms, and inevitably, Ward had his own ideas about what was funny. 'I don't know what Kim saw in me, but he gave me lots of gigs,' says Australian stand-up Phil Davey. 'When he left, my gigs decreased enormously, because Don had only seen me once.' In the set Ward saw, Davey attempted to pacify his rowdy punters by chucking chocolates at them. 'Don thought it was a pile of shit. He thought I couldn't possibly be a comedian and didn't book me for ages. Eventually, I won him around and I gigged here, but I used to gig here more when Kim was here.' Davey was one of the lucky ones. Many smaller acts never gigged here again, while other bigger acts moved on of their own accord. 'Mark Thomas used to be the king down here,' says Davey. 'Now he doesn't play here at all. Mark Steel. Where's he? Where's Jeremy Hardy?' These three comics have all found far bigger fish to fry, but is it just a coincidence that they're all left-leaning political stand-ups, the sort of comic Kinnie adored?

'The comedians that work down here are mainly sex based,' explains Davey. The Conservatives had been on top for so long that party political comedy had become emasculated. Last time the Tories were in opposition, The Store hadn't even opened, and to paraphrase Arnold Brown, most Store punters were too young to have had sex under a Labour administration. So it was scarcely surprising that by the time the Conservatives were eventually defeated, eighteen years to the month after The Store first set up shop in the premises at 69 Dean Street, the heyday of political stand-up at The Store had already come and gone. On the night of the 1997 General Election, The Cutting Edge performed a special show, just like they did in 1992. Yet this Piccadilly Circus show was very different from the one five years before in Leicester Square. In 1992, a shock Conservative victory scuppered The Store's pre-mature celebrations onstage, although not around the room. In 1997, the result surpassed even the most extravagant New Labour expectations. For a club founded a few weeks after Thatcher moved into Number Ten, this show felt like a special watershed. And unlike the 1992 election show, The Comedy Store still has the tape.

'You're all pissed, aren't you?' Martin Coyote asks his election night audience, opening The Cutting Edge show at eleven o'clock that evening. He gauges the vocal allegiances of the room. There are loud cheers for Labour, and far quieter ones for the Tories.

'Turkeys voting for Christmas,' says Coyote. 'Why are you voting Tory?' he asks a woman in the front row. It turns out she's got eleven to one with William Hill on a Conservative victory. It's a clever comeback, but she'll regret her bet, and her backchat, before the evening's out.

Despite the upbeat atmosphere, Coyote confesses he's suspicious of Tony Blair. 'How can you trust any bloke who, when he was a student, was lead singer in his own band and claimed he never experimented with drugs,' he says. 'That band must have been shit.'

Coyote announces several early results. There's an 11 per cent swing to Labour, giving them an estimated majority of 100. There are loud cheers around the room, but this bold prediction will actually prove to be an underestimate. 'National Health,' yells a punter, apropos of nothing. 'It's not good enough to just shout out all the words you know,' says Sean Meo. 'This is not basket weaving. You're in the wrong room.'

'The way things are going, one man in particular could lose his seat,' predicts Steve Gribbin. 'This might be the last time I can ever do this song.' Well, for a few years, at least. 'I never thought I'd be singing it on a night like this,' he adds, midway through his abusive ballad about Michael Portillo. John Moloney leads a chorus of 'Labour's Coming Home', to the tune of 'Three Lions' by Baddiel & Skinner and The Lightning Seeds, but compared with the rampant euphoria onstage, the audience response is surprisingly muted. As the stage lights go down and the house lights come up, 'Celebration' by Kool & The Gang swamps the auditorium, but this crowd are merely celebrating the end of something old and stale, rather than a brand new beginning. At least they're spared yet another rendition of 'Things Can Only Get Better'.

After the show ended, the bar remained open, and punters and performers stayed on to watch the results come in on the big screen. 'Suddenly, Portillo's face was up on screen,' recalls Martin Coyote. Labour Gain, read the caption. 'The place went mental. People were up on their feet, hugging one another.' It was like someone had scored the winning goal in a cup final. Some happy punters even bought Phil Davey champagne. Coyote finally went home around half past three, but Stan Nelson walked down to Downing Street, and on to Smith Square, to heckle Major and Portillo as they returned to Tory Party HQ. By breakfast time, Nelson was with 1,000 other party people, greeting John Prescott on the South Bank. 'I couldn't get in but I saw all the celebrities come out and they were all cheering,' says Phil Davey, who followed Nelson to Downing Street and on to the South Bank after the show. 'Eddie Izzard came out, which I thought was hilarious, because obviously he's a huge celebrity now, but at the time I just thought, "What's this comedian in high heels doing at a political rally?"'

Not every comedian was so ecstatic. At the election night show in 1992, Lee Hurst had felt out of step with the celebrations around the room. Yet now, in 1997, after a Labour landslide, he felt out of step once more. When Portillo was defeated, he felt a small semblance of joy that these politicians were reaping what they'd sown. Yet as they sat in The Store after the show and watched the Labour gains flood in, Steve

Gribbin could sense Hurst wasn't in tune with the party atmosphere. 'Come on, cheer up,' said Gribbin. 'Steve, all I'm prepared to concede is things will be different – they won't be any better,' replied Hurst. 'With the Tories, you know what you'd got,' he said, 'but these people, they're pretending to be something they're not.'

But at least the result would force comics to employ more sophisticated political humour. 'It was very easy to go up there and go, "Mrs Thatcher isn't really a nice person," and get a big cheer,' Hurst says. 'They just don't buy it any more.' Today's broader audience doesn't emasculate radical comics, it empowers them. 'You've not converted people, but you've made people who probably don't agree with you react in a way you want them to, which means they've listened,' he explains. 'Back then it was very much preaching to the converted.'

'There was a peculiar atmosphere of euphoria tinged with anxiety at the first post-election Cutting Edge,' reported the *Big Issue*. 'If Labour are just as bad as the last lot, will anyone stand up and say so?'

Another night, another audience. The show is over. The house lights go up, suddenly, revealing the pale faces and bleary eyes of commuters who've hurried here straight from work, and drunk too much and laughed too loud, and now have to navigate their respective 400 journeys home. The pounding pop resumes its assault, driving punters from their seats. They smooth the creases from their crumpled suits and skirts, and flood out, up the stairs, even more swiftly than they arrived, a few hours before. Restless twentysomethings in search of nightclubs, a costly late night drink or the consolation of fast food. Older, careworn parents hoping merely for buses, tubes or mini cabs, homeward bound, before the babysitter switches to double time. The bar staff are already sweeping up, gathering greasy plates and spent glasses, in preparation for tomorrow night's double bill.

But despite this departing hubbub, there's also a quiet commotion among the gaggle of tipsy stragglers around the bar. Peter Mandelson's Notting Hill mortgage resignation is headline news, and Charlie Whelan, Gordon Brown's press secretary, is huddled alongside Mark Steel at a corner table. They sit beneath an old snapshot montage of Keith Allen, kitted out in charity shop student chic, barrister Clive Anderson, looking every inch an amiable Open University Social Studies lecturer, and explosive Alexei Sayle, clean shaven, with a full head of hair, on the tiny strip club stage of the old Soho Store. In another photo, Rik Mayall sups from a Seventies dimpled pint pot. Whelan was the sympathetic subject of Steel's weekly leader page column in yesterday's *Guardian*. He's also an old friend of Store compere Tim Clark, and this trip Up West comes amid the Robinson home loan revelations that have stripped away yet another layer of gloss from Tony Blair's shiny smart New Labour government. The Comedy Store used to be a club where obscure comics lambasted a remote, oblivious government. Now it's a club where government figures go to unwind.

Part Two

Nights Out at The Store

The original Cutting Edge team (from left to right): Bob Boyton, Richard Morton, Mark Thomas and Nick Revell. The vendor is Bob Boyton's daughter

The Cutting Edge

So how much difference did all that political comedy actually make? As Paul Daniels might have put it, not a lot. Throughout the Thatcherite Eighties, the Tories seemed invincible, kidnapping satirical caricatures like Harry Enfield's Loadsamoney, and adopting them as triumphalist icons, even heroes, of their own. Direct attacks on Mrs Thatcher herself proved spectacularly impotent. *Spitting Image*, fronted by Fluck & Law's excellent latex lookalikes, and voiced by Store stars such as Chris Barrie, Steve Coogan, Hugh Dennis, Harry Enfield and Alistair McGowan, reinforced the stereotype of strong leadership peddled by the Tories themselves, while the depiction of Thatcher as more of a man than her male cabinet ministers merely bolstered her own myth.

In a way, each side benefited from the other. The happy synergy of The Store's salad days and Thatcher's Prime Ministerial honeymoon gave an early leg up to The Store in particular and Alternative Comedy in general. 'It was the biggest piece of luck I ever had,' says Don Ward. 'She was a tough old boot, and this gave the comics loads of material.'

Thatcher politicised stand-up, and nowhere was her unintentional gift more startling than at The Store. After she resigned, I asked several Store regulars about her effect on Alternative Comedy. 'Margaret Thatcher was the epitome of everything we disliked about society, but she was big and vivid, and that's what comedy is about,' said Arnold Brown. 'In a recession, comedy is the only growth industry. It is cathartic relief for the impotence of the Left.' 'Margaret Thatcher is totally responsible for Alternative Comedy,' said Jerry Sadowitz. 'If Thatcher created a riot, Alternative Comedians were the looters. She made the boundaries much clearer.' 'Alternative

Comedy helped to mythologise Mrs Thatcher,' said David Baddiel. 'All her enemies went along with her mythology. Her strength, her endurance, even her masculinity. We won't subvert our leaders until we ignore imposed assumptions about what they're really like.'

Alternative comics attacked the Tories, but the topics they tackled were chosen for them by the Tory tabloid press. 'The values of new comedy were very closely related to new capitalism,' said Jeremy Hardy. 'Style became more important than content.' As Julian Clary concluded, 'Alternative Comedy was one of the few successful small businesses of the Thatcher years.'[1]

But while Thatcher helped to define and focus modern stand-up, it was under John Major that political comedy finally found its teeth. This elusive leader inspired subtler, funnier, and ultimately far more effective forms of protest. By 1997, the Tories had become a laughing stock. It was the comics who cracked the jokes, and some of the best gags came from a topical team show created by a journalist called John Connor.

'Connor was a young sketch writer, stand-up and freelance journalist,' wrote Connor, of himself. 'Crap at all three, he decided while compering a show and watching a performer crack jokes with a paper bag over his head that comedy might be very silly but as nobody else was going to write about it, he would.'[2] Connor started the cabaret section in the London listings magazine City Limits, which helped put new comedy on the metropolitan map. Poacher turned gamekeeper, he eventually completed a very unlikely career change from comedy hack to comedy producer. City Limits folded years ago, but Connor still produces that stand-up impro hybrid at The Store every week.

I hadn't seen The Cutting Edge for several years, and I was surprised how much tighter – and lighter – it had become. In the early Nineties, it was an erratic yet resolutely angry show. Even in the mid-Nineties, it was indignant, though more polished. Now it scarcely even sounds strident. The comics still rip the piss out of people in the news, but the tone is far more flippant, almost amiable. There's just as much to laugh about, but a lot less to be upset about. When The Cutting Edge began, in Leicester Square, there was a feeling that things were bad and getting worse. Now it feels like things aren't going to get any better, but nobody seems to mind. 'It started off with a very political ethos,' explains Cutting Edge regular Ian Stone. 'Now it's just six guys having a laugh and playing around with the audience.'

The Cutting Edge play The Store every Tuesday, and every Tuesday John Connor is at The Store. He chairs the seven o'clock conferences, where the comics sketch a rough outline for the format and content of that night's eight o'clock show. 'He used to have this game plan for the whole show, and he used to write it all out on this little clipboard,' recalls Richard Morton, one of the original Cutting Edge team. 'Audiences couldn't give a toss about game plans.' And from the first heckle, the comics were often forced to do something completely different anyway. 'Poor John Connor used to be sitting at the side, pulling his hair out.' Connor has ditched the clipboard, but he still watches each unique performance unfold from the relative safety of the sound booth, stalks the dressing room during those frantic intervals, as comics write fresh material for the second half, and unwinds afterwards with the cast in the Comedy Bar down the road.

Connor first went to The Store in the early Eighties, when he was still a student. 'That's the only night I've ever paid,' he says. 'The next week I came back and did an act.' He died on his proverbial arse, but watching comics heckle one another planted the seed of an idea that eventually became The Cutting Edge. 'Why don't we get the comics onstage together heckling each other?' he wondered. And it's this competitive, jousting quality that forms the basis of this show. When Lee Hurst first played The Cutting Edge, he forgot the punchline of his first joke, and the rest of the team turned his forgetfulness into a running gag that lasted the entire evening. However, comic partnerships still require co-operation to even survive, let alone thrive. 'Building a stage relationship with another performer isn't instant,' says Connor. 'Stand-ups are all lone gun fighters.'

Nevertheless, there are stand-ups who are brave and versatile enough to break out of their solo straitjackets, and for them, The Cutting Edge is a prestigious and relatively lucrative gig. Today's core performers have been together for several years, and there's no shortage of competent replacements waiting in the wings. Compared with the raw, untutored talent at the Soho Store, Connor believes today's Cutting Edge crew is streets ahead. Back then, only trad comics could handle rowdy audiences. 'They had all the old comedy put-downs, and everything else that goes with that, and the stage time to learn their craft. These boys had to learn their craft from scratch. The level of skills then was nowhere near the level of skills now. A good comic's been onstage for five years before they really know what they're doing.'

Today's Cutting Edge comics would have stormed the old Soho Store, but without the Soho Store, there wouldn't be a Cutting Edge. 'Unless you've got the spaces to work, nothing can happen,' says Connor. Before The Store, BBC Radio decided who was funny and who wasn't, and their say-so was a self-fulfilling prophecy. 'There was no learning ground,' he adds. 'Without The Store, without that moment in time, maybe without punk as well, that wouldn't have happened.'

But by the end of the Eighties, club comedy had become more standardised, and Connor was bored. After the anarchic variety of the Soho years, The Store swiftly set a familiar pattern for the entire circuit: a compere, four comics, four twenty-minute sets. Connor wanted more varied delivery, more topical material. He wanted something with more balls.

Like all good ideas, the concept was so simple, it was a wonder nobody had ever tried it before – half a dozen comics discuss the week's news in a blend of pre-prepared stand-up and off the cuff impro, prompted by audience suggestions. It was built around Mark Thomas and Kevin Day, two of The Store's more political stand-ups. Yet although Thomas and Day always went down well, by 1990, when The Cutting Edge began, political stand-up was already swimming against a turning comic tide, and an increasingly apolitical crowd favoured surreal, character and observational comedy.

The Cutting Edge was more of a reactionary revival than an avant garde revolt. 'We wanted to remind people there was a reason for Alternative Comedy, there was a reason why it was different to what had gone before, and what was starting to come back again,' says Day. 'We all shared the same ambition – to say straight stand-up is as good as, if not better than, any other form of comedy. This is what you can talk about with straight stand-up. You can deal with issues. You can deal with ideas.'

To this central partnership, Connor added Bob Boyton's politically motivated street-wise wit, plus Pat Condell, whose brother Martin Coyote is now a Cutting Edge regular. He also recruited Nick Revell. Revell is political, but he has a softer style, a warmer stage persona and is also a prolific writer. Yet Connor reckons the match winner was Richard Morton. 'He was the key to why the show was successful.' Morton's contagious Geordie bonhomie can warm up the coldest room. Connor liked the way this cheeky comic played the clown, but the main reason for his success was music. Morton started out as a musician, and only became a stand-up after playing in a comic guitar duo called The Panic Brothers. Though his satirical songs always amuse, he can carry an audience on sheer musicianship alone.

Connor had seen comperes struggle to avoid an anti-climactic finish after the last act raised the roof. His solution revived an old vaudeville convention. 'I wanted a song to finish the show because I wanted them all onstage together.' Persuading stand-ups to sing was a nightmare, but then another comic guitarist, Dave Cohen, introduced an improvised twelve-bar blues which is still the show's curtain call.

The first night was packed. 'It was scary,' says Morton, 'because I barely had any gags.' But then, as now, off-the-cuff humour was most effective. When one of Nick Revell's jokes fell flat, Bob Boyton plucked the E string on Morton's guitar. 'What was that?' asked Revell. 'That was the sound of you dying,' said Boyton.

Yet after the opening night, the audiences dropped off, and the team sometimes played to only two dozen punters, and went home with door splits as small as twenty quid each. Now it's one of the club circuit's best paid gigs, but it didn't turn around overnight. 'It was horrendously hard to get it to work for the first few years,' says Connor. 'It took me a long time to loosen the show up. Now the show can be really political and very heavy when it needs to be. It can also be completely tongue in cheek.' This unique blend of teamwork, topical humour, new material, improvisation and audience participation makes it far more risky for performers than straight stand-up. 'You're taking some punches,' says Lee Hurst, 'because you're trying new stuff.' Sean Meo once asked for a topical suggestion. A heckler told him to fuck off. 'That's not topical,' retorted Meo. 'Fuck off now,' replied the heckler.

Like The Store itself, The Cutting Edge is basically a boys' club. Jo Brand and Donna McPhail have done it a few times, but generally this six-strong team is exclusively male. Connor did call Hattie Hayridge when the show began, but unfortunately he phoned her at ten o'clock in the morning, the crack of dawn for comics. Hayridge was still in bed and all she wanted to think about was getting back to sleep. Yet she has no regrets. 'I like it as a laddy thing,' she says. 'Blokes don't mind insulting each other.

They get self-conscious if there's a woman there.' But sometimes they get self-conscious if there isn't. 'A couple of times the boys wrote jokes so foul and sexist, they said, "Would you do my joke because if I did it I'd get a boo, but if you did it, you'd get away with it,"' recalls Donna McPhail. 'Sean Meo did one. It was when they had the earthquake in San Francisco, and it was something like a man having sex with his wife and the earthquake starts and he goes "Oh my god, it's the big one," and she went "All right, come all over my tits," and Sean said, "Do it for me, Donna, do it."' So she did it. 'There was this horrible silence,' she recalls, 'and then everyone pissed themselves.' She enjoyed the teamwork. 'It wasn't the money,' she says. 'Some weeks you got bog all.' But in the end, like all the other women, she left. 'I was the only woman in the team,' she says. 'There was too much pressure.'

'The Cutting Edge isn't about politics,' claims Jo Brand. 'It's about knob jokes, and that's why I did it.' She wasn't bad at it, but she didn't really enjoy it. 'Very good political satire is really hard to do because you need to know an awful lot about politics, which most comics don't. Mark Steel does, and he's very good. He's managed to hit the mark, as has Jeremy Hardy. Most other comics haven't got a bloody clue. They'll mention Tony Blair and that's the politics out of the way, and then they'll make a joke about his hair.' And maybe that's just as well. 'If you did a truly political show and talked about Marxist sociology and employment law and economics, people would be bored shitless.' And some news stories, like the Kosovo conflict, simply prove to be bereft of laughter. 'People don't want to hear about war,' says Cutting Edge comic John Fothergill. 'You can't tell jokes about bloody genocide for christ's sake, not unless they're really funny.' 'I was reading the paper this morning,' said Martin Coyote, in a Cutting Edge show during the Kosovan war, 'and just for a bit of light relief, I stabbed myself in the leg with a fork.'

'We try and make it topical because that's how we generate material,' says Cutting Edge regular Paul Thorne. 'But shows during the Christmas period, when there are a lot of office parties in, they just want sex and knob gags and jokes about drinking, and if that's what they keep paying for, that's what you've got to give them.' As he says, it's no use saying, 'I know you want jokes about condoms, but here's a really good one about General Pinochet.' Punters are the best barometer, and there are limits to the average spectator's news sense. 'You get some people who never read the bloody papers.'

Thorne says political comedy became harder to do when John Major replaced Margaret Thatcher, but New Labour's first year in office also posed transitional problems for The Cutting Edge. 'You were riding on this wave of euphoria for about a year and we were scuppered,' says Thorne. 'We were desperately fishing in our heads for stuff that we'd done before the election.' Thorne needn't have worried. Normal service was resumed soon enough.

A big breaking news story always gives the show a special edge. 'There were times when we were literally able to break the news to an audience about something that had only happened a few hours earlier,' recalled Mark Thomas. 'One prime example was when Maxwell died.'[3] The Cutting Edge did a special show called Maxwell Ahoy, even though the news of Robert Maxwell's death at sea only broke a few hours before showtime. When Rajiv Ghandi was assassinated, just half an hour before a show, the audience thought they were making it up.

Steve Gribbin's Ron Davies song was a perfect example of the rapid response stand-up that The Cutting Edge does best. 'That story broke on the Tuesday,' explains John Fothergill. 'Stevie did that on the Tuesday night, and "Do Ron Ron" was the headline in the *Sun* on Wednesday morning. He was thrilled to bits that he got there three or four hours before the press.'

The Gulf War, the Russian coup of 1991 and the last two elections were other highlights, however the biggest event of all wasn't a political crisis, but the death of Diana, Princess of Wales. 'I was actually doing the late show at The Store the weekend when she died,' recalls Martin Coyote. 'There's a fair chance I was actually on stage when she crashed. I had a whole routine in my act about the land mines. How she couldn't kill herself if she tried.' This was always a popular routine, and that night it took the roof off. He had a few pints and caught a cab home. The cabbie turned on the radio. Diana had been in a car crash. Next morning Coyote woke up to find a

message on his answering machine from Sean Meo. 'You think we had a bad night last night,' said Meo. 'Turn on Ceefax.' Coyote did as he was told. Diana was dead. He phoned Meo. 'What are we going to do about it?' asked Meo. 'We've got to do Diana gags because if we don't we're not Cutting Edge,' replied Coyote. 'This is a real benchmark of whether we're at the cutting edge or not.' 'You're right,' said Meo. And so they started writing new material. On Monday, Connor phoned Coyote. 'There's some sort of discussion as to whether we should deal with the subject or not,' said Connor. 'Maybe we should not deal with it.' 'Of course I'm going to deal with it,' replied Coyote.

On Tuesday night, there was tension in the dressing room. 'All of us were nervous,' recalls Steve Gribbin. But Don Ward was adamant. 'Tonight of all nights we've got to do it,' said Ward. However, the comics were having doubts. 'Are these people going to go for this?' wondered Coyote beforehand.

But Ward was right. 'We had an audience in there cheering the roof off,' says Connor. 'A few people left, but we went for it.' 'We only had three walk-outs and they were all Americans,' says Gribbin. 'They thought it was vile.' Yet not every detractor voted with their feet. 'We did have heckles,' admits Gribbin. 'People were going "shame, disgusting", but that made it highly charged.' And although a significant minority did object, a substantial majority were hungry for dissent they couldn't hear anywhere else. As Ward said, 'They'd come along because they wanted to hear another voice.' The target wasn't Diana's actual death, but the hysterical reaction to it. 'It was an absolute joy to be able to say, "No, this is bollocks," and do it in a comic way and take the roof off,' says Connor. 'The only people that did anything about it were *Private Eye* and us.'

The next Saturday, after the funeral, Stan Nelson, the stage manager, went into the dressing room and told the compere to mention Diana straight away. 'I want it mentioned straight off,' he said. 'They know someone's going to mention it, and they're just waiting.' But in other venues, they waited in vain. 'All comics were told: "No reference at all. No reference whatsoever. You cannot refer to it. It's not to be referred to onstage."' After Boothby Graffoe claimed Diana had been assassinated by florists, some punters wrote to The Store to complain. And a full month after the funeral, feelings were still running high. 'John Moloney got threatened,' says Gribbin. 'Some blokes waited for him outside The Store and said, "You're a bit of a cunt and you think you're quite clever, you fucker. We know where you live."'

Even The Comedy Store Players ran into trouble. Their first game on the night after Di's death was an audience participation number in which punters are invited to shout out 'Die.' In the end, they used another word. Conversely, The Cutting Edge had made waves about Diana even before she died. 'Three young Sloanes stormed out in noisy protest at what Kevin Day was saying about Princess Di,' reported *Time Out*. 'All he did was question the adulation she'd received for her courage in picking up a baby which had AIDS. And suggest she was running very little risk at the time of finding herself on the wrong end of an unprotected fuck.' More recently, Paul Thorne divided the room with a gag about the Royal wedding of Prince Edward and Sophie. 'She's going to wear something her predecessors didn't,' says Thorne. 'A seat belt.' And even today, Diana gags still split this audience straight down the middle. 'At least he's managed to achieve something,' quipped Coyote, after Prince Charles turned fifty. 'Princess Diana never managed fifty years.' Some punters found it fantastically funny. Others booed. 'It still divides the nation,' says Coyote. But all the best gags do.

'Who's been here on a Tuesday night?' asks Martin Coyote, kicking off another weekly Cutting Edge show. The whole house cheers. 'How many haven't?' The whole house cheers again. 'How many will shout out whatever I say?' The whole house cheers once more. The rest of tonight's team joins Coyote onstage, and do a few gags, by way of introduction. Paul Thorne talks about visiting the Monet retrospective at London's Royal Academy. He got a very good view of the backs of tourists heads. Steve Gribbin bills himself as the secret love child of Barney Rubble. It's a remarkably accurate description. 'Very nice to be back in London,' says Sean Meo, 'where smiling is a sign

of weakness.' Junior Simpson congratulates a bloke in the front row who is celebrating his twenty-first birthday. 'Happy birthday. You can now take it up the arse.' Last up is Lee Hurst, a famous face from his appearances on *They Think It's All Over*. There's always a special buzz around the room when a big star plays The Store, but once you've become a household name, viewers feel they know you, and in the live arena that casual recognition can work both ways.

The first game, Joke Challenge, begins. The audience members shout out subjects, the comics provide instant gags, and the audience then shouts live or die until there's only one comic left alive. Hurst steps up to the microphone. 'Die!' yells a heckler, before Hurst has even opened his mouth. 'I wish you would,' retorts Hurst. The flurry of famous monickers that follows is a succinct cross section of millennial celebrity: Jerry Springer, Jimmy Hill, Leonardo di Caprio, Mike Tyson, Michael Jackson, Monica Lewinsky, Jonathan Aitken, Chris Eubank and Rupert Murdoch. Other topics include Viagra, Ecstasy and artificial insemination. That was the year that was. At the end, Hurst is the winner.

Even when a routine doesn't work, Hurst turns defeat into victory. 'Call the Comedy AA – that joke broke down,' he says, during a stand-up duet with Sean Meo. 'Trouble with knob gags – you can't get the parts nowadays.'

Next on is Steve Gribbin, with a string of gags and satirical songs about the week's events. There's a ballad about junior doctors, and another about Pinochet. 'All that fuss over a little wooden boy.' Paul Thorne joins him for a number about New Labourite middle-class pretensions, in which disgusted residents of Tunbridge Wells invade the inner cities, and posh thugs ask people al fresco. Then the entire team elicit topical suggestions from the audience, about which they'll write new material during the interval, in a large padded dressing room complete with Jacuzzi and a Malaysian lady-boy called Nigel. At least, that's how Thorne describes The Store's backstage bunker to the audience. Thorne rejects any subjects that aren't topical. 'Puberty? That may be topical for you, mate,' he tells one punter. 'Gay sex at sixteen?' he tells another. 'Are you suggesting a subject or just shouting out your CV?'

'Someone's just found their clitoris,' says Thorne, as a soprano squeal heralds his second-half entrance. Thorne needs a punter to judge which Cutting Edge comics have written the best material during the interval. He chooses Dean, the butt of numerous first-half jokes. Thorne hands him a two-sided black disc bearing the legends Hit and Miss. 'It's not very politically correct,' says Thorne. 'It should be Ms, but we've been using its since the Seventies.' 'Give him a hit, Dean!' yells a female heckler. Luckily for Thorne, Dean desists. 'You're kind of cute,' Junior Simpson tells Dean. 'You ought to form a boy band called No Pubes Yet.'

'Strap in for a few genocide gags,' says Martin Coyote, whose subject is Serbian Aggression. 'That's a top gag in the dressing room,' he says, when one such joke falls flat. 'I'm not going to say anything against the social services,' says Steve Gribbin, whose topic is child abduction. 'I've got two kids and I want to keep them.' But the winner is Junior Simpson with a routine about the National Health Service. Paul Thorne finds the spectator who suggested the NHS, and brings him up onstage to collect his prize. 'You've won two tickets to any show in the West End, down here, next week,' says Thorne, 'where you'll hear me do the same joke again and again and again.'

Bob Boyton

'I was absolutely pissed the night before,' says Bob Boyton, recalling his Store debut. 'I was still hung over.' We're sitting in a spartan basement around the corner from the old Soho Store, where he works rehousing homeless men. Boyton may not be a working comic anymore, but he still has that ageless aura that's common to so many stand-ups. Onstage, his harsh Estuary English accent and narrow, knowing eyes made him intimidating, almost scary, but offstage, he couldn't be more welcoming. Thankfully, he's got his false teeth in, but in a way, I wish he'd whip them out again for old times' sake. Boyton's presence at the Leicester Square Store and his absence from the Piccadilly Circus Store show how The Store has changed during the last decade.

'Bob wouldn't be able to do ten minutes here now, and I don't think he'd mind me saying that,' says Store regular Kevin Day. 'I don't think he'd want to,' says his wife, former Store stage manager Ali Day. 'Audiences almost expect a suit and tie now,' explains Kevin. 'They expect people to make an effort. They're not happy anymore with taking your teeth out. And calling the Queen Mother a whore isn't done anymore.'

'The big gig, the gig that could have made my career and I couldn't do it,' Boyton says, without the slightest suspicion of self-pity. 'They looked in my eyes and heard my voice and saw that lack of self-belief.' Boyton's modesty makes a welcome change, but he's being a bit hard on himself. Although his routines could be hit and miss, he had many more good gigs than bad ones, and for several years he was one of the comics who gave The Store its character, not just onstage, but in the back bar and the dressing room. 'There were nastier audiences; The Tunnel, by the end, was much nastier,' he says, of the riotous forerunner to Malcolm Hardee's Up The Creek. 'There was a neo-fascist element there which you never got at The Store. I never felt under any physical threat. Those blokes on the door did their job really well.'

Boyton's career highlight was an Amnesty benefit with The Cutting Edge at the Duke of York's Theatre during the Gulf War. 'If it hadn't been for The Cutting Edge I never would have been on the West End stage, and that was one of the best nights of my life, and if it meant that loads of people came to The Store and made Don even richer, that don't worry me,' he says. 'The audience were to the left of The Store audience, and I was just what they wanted, and I gave it to them.'

And there was no better feeling than stepping out into Leicester Square, into the small hours of Sunday morning, still giddy from the afterglow of a storming end to a Store weekend, or drinking the night dry in a back alley tapas bar, after a roof-lifting Cutting Edge gig, with the rest of the team, plus all the resting comics who'd come to see the show. 'I must have said farewell to a bit of good liver,' says Boyton, without a trace of regret. 'It's all part of being in the movie of your life.'

Jack Dee

Jack Dee

In the Nineties, Alternative Comedy followed the Labour Party from the hard left of political opinion towards its softer centre, and The Store led comedy's gradual migration into this more classless middle ground. One comic epitomised this steady moderation and modernisation: Jack Dee.

Dee's fellow waiters kept telling him he should become a comedian. 'You're funny,' insisted all the staff in the restaurant where he worked. 'You should go onstage.' But Dee had never seen himself as one of those fat blokes in a frilly shirt and sequined dinner jacket, cracking hand-me-down jokes about his mother-in-law. He knew nothing about modern comedy, but he had heard about a club in Leicester Square called The Comedy Store. And so, with his workmates' plaudits still ringing in his ears, he finally went along to see what all the fuss was about. It felt seedy and industrial, a lot of people trapped underground in a small, black metallic box, but Dee instantly felt at home. These people spoke his language. 'This is exactly what I do, except I'm not doing it yet,' he thought, in wonder, as he watched his first ever live stand-up show. 'This is where I'm meant to be. They've started without me.' Dee knew he had that same spark. And that was when he decided to become a player, instead of a spectator.

A week later, he went back and did an open spot, and it hit him like a thunderbolt. 'I feel at home onstage,' says Dee, at the smart Soho headquarters of his TV production company, Open Mike. 'There's a part of me which doesn't live until I'm onstage, and that only lives when I'm onstage, and if you have that in you, it's quite a difficult thing to reconcile with a normal life, because you're constantly driven by this need to be onstage. This is why actors and comedians put up with the most appalling hardships and difficulties and adversity when they're starting out, and sometimes throughout their career, because they're driven by something more important than the things that are driving them away.'

'I was called to the stage at 2am,' recalled Dee of his first night. 'I was blinded by the lights and deafened by the volume of my voice going through the mike. But I did get a laugh and I was hooked.'[1] Paul Merton had been on, but most of the audience had already left. Dee thought it was a disaster, but he did a lot better than the other open spots that night. 'How long have you been doing this?' Ward asked him afterwards. 'I haven't done it before,' said Dee. 'Keep coming back,' said Ward, 'and I'll keep putting you on.' Ward kept putting him on, but that wasn't the only reason Dee kept returning. Back then, The Store was the only comedy club he'd heard of.

'What other clubs are you doing?' asked Bob Mills, after a few months. 'What do you mean?' asked Dee. 'What other clubs are there?' 'Look in *Time Out*,' said Mills. Dee saw there were lots of smaller clubs around London, where he could hone his act, so he left The Store well alone for a year and didn't return until he'd acquired the equipment to crack it. 'My sole ambition was to get my name on the blackboard outside,' he says, of his first two years on the circuit, when he was still working behind a bar during the day. 'That's all I ever considered. I never even thought about making money or being thought of as professional. That was beyond my dreams at the time.'

Television had been quick to exploit the sketch-centred talents of Soho Store stars like Rik Mayall, Adrian Edmondson and French & Saunders, but it was slower to find suitable vehicles for the more spartan stand-up skills of the Leicester Square Store stars. However, just as Dee had honed his act for a year in the relative privacy of smaller comedy clubs, outside The Store's spotlight, now The Store gave him several years to refine his humour even further, outside the even brighter spotlight of TV. This enforced gestation period paid off, not just for Dee but for plenty of his colleagues. At the 1990 Edinburgh Festival, Sean Hughes won the Perrier Award. In 1991 Frank Skinner won the same prize (Dee was nominated). In 1992 the winner was Steve Coogan. In 1993, it was Lee Evans. All advanced to TV stardom almost immediately but until then, they were comparatively anonymous in TV terms, even though they'd already become star turns at The Store. These weren't wasted years, but an apprenticeship well spent. 'I've seen comedians who've gone into television too soon, before they could cope with it,' says Dee, 'and it's not been good for them.'

For several years, The Store was Dee's home from home, backstage as well as out front. 'Having never belonged to any sort of group before in my life, I felt more at home with these people than anyone else.' He never found such backstage camaraderie again, and even on Britain's biggest stages, he's never experienced the same excitement as storming The Store. 'The front row are practically touching your knees, and although that is potentially a very intimidating situation for a performer, when it works, the energy you get from the audience and what that does to your performance is absolutely extraordinary.'

It was during this time that Dee discovered his proper stage persona. And he only found this cartoon version of himself after he got so fed up that he stopped trying. 'I really didn't care anymore,' he says. 'I'd lost interest.' He decided to give up, but he wanted to honour the last few bookings in his diary, and it was at these gigs that he located his true comic voice. 'I'd left all of that stuff backstage of trying to be upbeat, trying to fool the audience into thinking I was this dynamic, energetic guy,' he says. 'Not wanting to be liked is very important.' But it took a truly dreadful evening to force him to be himself. 'It was one fucking awful gig that Rob Newman had set up, and he didn't turn up, so I had to put the chairs out, so I was very pissed off.' The other stand-up on the bill was Mickey Hutton, an indefatigably jolly Geordie. Dee knew he couldn't compete with Hutton's indestructible *joie de vivre*, and it was then that something clicked. 'There was no looking back.'

'Jack Dee started with a cheeky chappy approach,' confirms Don Ward. 'It didn't work, he got disillusioned by it all and that came across in his act. That chuckaway style began to work.' 'I remember coming down and someone saying, "Jack Dee's on," and I said, "Who's Jack Dee?"' recalls Alistair McGowan, who honed his impressions down here. 'They said, "He's been around for a while but he's brilliant now." And I remember watching Jack in his sharp suit and the sharp haircut and the sharp manner, and it was just astonishing. You did think straight away, within six months that man should and probably will be a major star.'

'A suit is surprisingly neutral,' Dee told me, a few years later in an interview for *FHM*. 'You're not making a statement either way.' Dee's tailor is Eddie Kerr in Soho, who makes suits for stars as diverse as Lee Evans, Harry Hill and the PG Tips Chimps. Charity shop chic was out; the old showbiz uniform was back in fashion, and so were the values that went with it.

Thatcher's sudden departure freed the smartest comics from her shadow. And nobody personified this liberation better than Jack Dee. 'Everyone was going on and on and on about Margaret Thatcher,' he told me. 'I could see audiences being bored and wanting something different.' Dee was neither misogynistic nor remotely racist. He wrote all his own material. His humour was provocative but thoughtful. His routines weren't politically apathetic, but his instinctive cynicism stretched way beyond those safe and predictable Tory hate figures to include anyone who told him what to think or how to vote. His bugbears were social and economic rather than party political, and in a brave new world where deregulated big business could bully or even bypass Parliament, Dee's finger was far closer to the political pulse than those right-on wags who shared election platforms with Kinnock & Co.

'There's no political party that will put this country in any better condition than it's already in,' Dee told me. 'I don't believe in any political system. That's not to say that I haven't put the boot in. I've said some fantastically vicious things about various political figures, Conservative, Labour and Liberal, but to me, they're all in the same basket. I don't differentiate.' Unlike ersatz squat or bedsit comics, Dee's material was unashamedly bourgeois. 'I take great pride in the fact that I'm middle class, that I've got a wife and a car and a mortgage, because these are the things I share with my audience,' he told me. 'Audiences relate to me. I'm going through what they're going through.'

Increasingly wealthy, punters' interests and concerns were less purely parliamentary. When David Tennant founded The Gargoyle Club in 1925, he envisaged an unlikely alliance between rich patrons and deserving artistic poor. Over half a century later, a few blocks away at the second Store in Leicester Square, Dee bridged this gap between rich and poor. His dad was an executive. His housewife mum was raised in a theatrical household which was more famine than feast. When the money ran out, Dee went from private prep school to rough and tumble local comp. He worked as a waiter. In a Britain whose class boundaries were becoming increasingly blurred, Dee was a comic everyman. When I saw him entertain several thousand punters of every conceivable age and social status at that resolutely middle of the road Mecca, The Hammersmith Apollo, comedy's two rival crowds, previously divided into fringe theatre and mainstream musical audiences, started to come together again, maybe for the first time since the demise of Music Hall. Shabby students, smart casual lads and ladettes, dowdy middle-aged professionals, even pensioners in their Sunday best.

Dee became typecast as deadpan, but his bulldog on Valium persona was a foil for some groundbreaking wit. For the previous decade, virtually every modern stand-up had at least paid lip service to the received values of student socialism. Dee's bitterness and anger went deeper than these usual suspects. His humour wasn't just resolutely apolitical. It was unapologetically aspirational. And at The Store in the late Eighties, that was about as revolutionary as a comic could be. 'I was desperately trying to climb up the social ladder and make something of myself,' he says. 'It would never occur to me that there were people who didn't want to do that.' And so he moved onwards, and upwards, before his happy Store nights could turn sour. As he says, 'You can either go out on the road and learn to be a real comic, or you can go down The Comedy Store and be a hero every weekend.'

The Comedy
Store Players

Despite The Store's tough-talking, wisecracking reputation, stand-up isn't the only kind of comedy you can see here. The Leicester Square Store also launched a troupe whose comic style was more influential than that of The Cutting Edge. This troupe was called The Comedy Store Players and you can still see them twice a week, every week, at the London Store, and once a week at the new Store in Manchester, too.

'Who's seen The Comedy Store Players before?' asks Richard Vranch, the only comedian with a doctorate in nuclear physics from Cambridge University. A few hands go up. 'Who's never seen The Players before?' A few more hands. 'Who's never been here before?' A few more. Unlike stand-up punters, our job isn't just to laugh, or even heckle. We will provide the impetus for every sketch, and the quality of our suggestions can make the difference between a bad show and a good one. Vranch asks for an interesting location. 'Milton Keynes,' yells a punter. 'I said interesting,' says Vranch. He asks for a household object you wouldn't normally find in a kitchen. 'A husband,' shouts a woman, but Vranch is distracted by a commotion at the rear of the room. 'Is that Steve?' he asks, squinting into the lights, as a latecomer saunters down the aisle. 'Yes,' booms a deep voice in the darkness. But this is no tardy punter. This is a missing member of the cast. 'Where the fuck have you been?' asks Vranch, as Steve Frost joins the rest of the team onstage. 'As you can see, we're all very professional,' Vranch

The Comedy Store Players in action: (left to right) Paul Merton, Richard Vranch, Josie Lawrence, Jim Sweeney

tells the audience. 'Is this an improvisation night?' asks Frost. 'Oh fuck.' The room is already awash with laughter, and The Players haven't even begun.

'That's the end of that game, thanks to your destructive instincts,' Neil Mullarkey tells us at the close of their usual icebreaker, a romp called Die, in which punters gong off unsuccessful performers, just like in the old Soho Store days. Mullarkey outlines the next game. 'It sounds rather dull, but highly humorous in the hands of seasoned professionals such as ourselves.' And with a little help from his friends, he fast forwards through a flurry of contrasting dramatic styles, provided by the crowd. A Bertolt Brecht ballad about the oppressed proletariat, a school Nativity play, featuring a suitably inept rendition of 'Silent Night' on descant recorder, Steven Berkoff and Shakespeare. 'You will now recite the opening scene from *Henry the Fifth*,' Frost tells Mullarkey. 'Hello,' replies Mullarkey, without missing a beat, 'I'm Henry the Fifth.' It's a delicate balance between competition and co-operation. Watching Players trying to trip one another up is one of the show's pleasures. They're always happy to drop each other in the shit, as long as it keeps the show out of it. 'If you really want to dump the crap on somebody, just turn them into an inanimate object,' says sometime Player Steve Steen. 'You wander on and there'll be somebody there waiting, probably got a million great ideas, and you say, "Come on, darling, we'll sit on this bench," and turn somebody into a seat.'

The second half begins with an instant musical. Tonight's *meisterwerk* is set in South America. 'A condor flew above the Andes, thousands of feet high,' says Vranch, as Andy Smart flies past. 'The condor fucked off,' he adds, as Smart metamorphoses from condor to bride. Tony Hawks plays the husband. 'It was their wedding night,' says Vranch. 'They had never made love.' All-male arranged marriages are a familiar pattern for The Players. 'I've snogged more men onstage at The Comedy Store than I have in my life,' confesses Lee Simpson. 'Well, actually, a lot more.' But this consummation is rudely interrupted by Frost and Mullarkey, as two bandits who reckon Smart is the reincarnation of an Inca princess. 'That was a true story,' says Frost, as the cast take a bow.

Smart asks us for a workplace. 'Condom factory,' shouts someone. 'We get that quite a lot,' says Smart, wearily. Bog brush is another bugbear. 'There are so many times you get stuff about toilets,' Steve Steen told me later. 'Maybe there's something about sitting in a darkened room and being able to call out stuff without necessarily being seen.' Whenever they ask for an occupation, you can bet someone will shout out 'gynaecologist.' Eventually, they settle for a see-saw factory.

As a finale, Frost and Hawks join Smart in a trio of experts speaking with a single voice. We have to suggest a suitably unusual area of expertise. 'Stamp collecting,' yells a woman. 'That's not that unusual,' says Smart. 'Chicken wrestling,' bellows a bloke, and this three-headed expert launches into a nonsensical treatise on this non-existent sport, even breaking off in mid-flow to berate a woman for sneaking off to the toilet. It's unique and unrepeatable, yet within a few hours, it'll all be forgotten.

'You can't actually save the material and flog it as a writer,' says Steve Steen. 'In all the years I've been doing it, I've only ever managed to sell a one liner, so you're never going to get rich on it.' Players themselves usually can't recall what they've said or done within just a few hours. 'I saw you at The Store the other night and really liked your sketch,' punters tell Steen when they spot him in the street. 'I'm sorry,' he replies. 'I cannot remember.' 'You might think "There were fifteen fucking brilliant jokes you could write up into a brilliant television sketch there," but no one can remember them,' says Richard Vranch. 'You do get a cult following, people who come along again and again, and the reason they like it is because you can't go and buy it on CD. You have to be there.' Like good actors, good improvisers live only in the moment, and once that moment is over, it's as if it never happened. 'It's like Amaretto paper,' says Arthur Smith. 'You light it and it's gone.'

If you like comic impro, thank Kit Hollerbach, Mike Myers and Franklin D. Roosevelt. Over half a century ago, FDR's government started a scheme to teach communication skills to immigrant children, and hired a drama teacher called Viola Spolen to make up some improvised drama games. Viola's son went to Chicago University, where he taught her games to his college friends, and when they graduated they founded their own impro troupe, Second City. This Chicago company helped launch comic stars like Alan Alda, Dan Aykroyd, John Candy, Bill Murray, Joan Rivers, James and John Belushi, George Wendt (Norm in *Cheers*) and Dan Castellaneta (the voice of Homer Simpson), but above all, it established the fundamental rules of comic impro. 'No matter what the other person says, you support it,' explains Rich Hall, one of many American comics who's since guested with The Players. 'That was started by Second City.'

Second City proved so popular, it even spawned an outpost in Toronto. Mike Myers joined this Canadian troupe three hours after leaving high school, and when he left Toronto to perform in London, he brought his memories of these impro games with him. He sought out a show at the Gate Theatre in Notting Hill, by a bunch of former Footlighters, one of whom was Neil Mullarkey. Back then, not many British comics had heard of this famous Chicago troupe, but Mullarkey was one of the few who had, and Myers and Mullarkey formed a double act.

They did their first open spot at a comedy club in Chiswick, compered by Alternative Comedy pioneer Tony Green, but they didn't have five minutes of material, so they finished off with a few minutes of improvisation. 'Mike was brilliant at it,' says Mullarkey, backstage at The Store, a few hours before a Players show. 'I'd never done it before.' Mullarkey's brain was swimming. He felt as if he'd been kicked in the head, but he can't have done too badly, because they got a booking out of it. Mullarkey made a stencil and sprayed Mullarkey & Myers on an old curtain, and they started playing the circuit.

Myers was an ocean away from home, but he had no trouble fitting in. 'His parents were British and he'd always liked British humour,' says Mullarkey. 'That's the reason he came to live in this country, because he liked Monty Python and Peter Sellers.'

Meanwhile, American comedienne Kit Hollerbach had also pitched up in Blighty, bringing her own memories of these games from the Californian impro troupe she'd worked with: The Comedy Store Players from The Comedy Store in LA. Hollerbach soon became a familiar stand-up in London comedy clubs like The Store, and in 1985, she booked a spot at the Edinburgh Festival, alongside Dave Cohen and Paul Merton. They just so happened to book into McNally's, the same venue as Mullarkey & Myers.

McNally's was run by Karen Koren, a Scandinavian Scot who now runs one of Edinburgh's biggest comedy venues, The Gilded Balloon. McNally's was much smaller and anyone working there was bound to meet up. All five comics got talking, and Myers and Hollerbach discovered they'd both done impro on the other side of the Atlantic. 'Mike had loads of interesting things to say about improv,' recalls Cohen. 'Paul and Neil and I didn't have a clue about any of it.' However Hollerbach persuaded them to try several ad hoc impro shows in Edinburgh that summer, and although they often only performed to single figures, they all enjoyed it so much that when they returned to London, they asked Kim Kinnie if they could do some impro at The Store. Kinnie asked Don Ward. 'What the hell's impro?' asked Ward. Kinnie told him. 'OK,' said Ward. 'Let's give it a try.' Ward gave them a graveyard slot on Sunday, a night when

The founders of The Comedy Store Players: (left to right) Mike Myers, Paul Merton, Kit Hollerbach, Neil Mullarkey

most West End theatres are dark, but only the second half was improvised. 'We decided to give them half an evening,' says Kinnie. 'We did half a show of stand-up, and half a show of improv, to see how it went.'

'I was absolutely terrified,' admitted Neil Mullarkey, recalling that first Players show.[1] In the first half, Cohen and Hollerbach did stand-up, and Mullarkey & Myers did sketches, and in the second half, they all did impro. It wasn't a great success. 'At first, we were, frankly, not very good,' confessed Mullarkey. 'Going to see a show where the performers didn't know what they were going to say was not terribly attractive.'[2] Yet at least he was in the cast, unlike Paul Merton. Merton went along anyway, and afterwards Hollerbach made a backstage speech saying how much she wanted him on the team. Merton wasn't an overnight sensation, but eventually he proved Hollerbach right. 'It took Paul a while to warm to it,' says Cohen, 'but Kit really pushed for him to do it.' And unlike Cohen, Hollerbach or Myers, he's still a regular today.

Yet the main problem wasn't the cast, but the format. Stand-up and impro was a confusing combination. 'The two didn't mix,' explains Ward. 'They're not the same audience.' Kinnie reckoned the improv was now strong enough for an entire evening, so Ward ditched the stand-up and the show improved straight away. 'The impro team is still showing its rough edges,' wrote *City Limits* in 1986. 'Only the experienced North Americans Kit Hollerbach and Mike Myers shine, though Dave Cohen's on-the-spot songs are excellent. But it's definitely on the way to becoming a very good act.' 'Improvisational comedy is the ultimate test,' Kit Hollerbach told *Time Out* later that year. 'You have to break away from your material and go out on a limb. The funniest things aren't always the ones that are scripted or planned. Comedy is elusive. You can't bottle it up and keep it. Sure, stand-ups can make a fair job of packaging it so they know the same product will sell time and time again. But what's best is always those brilliantly funny fleeting moments, on stage or in life, which you'll never be able to reproduce in the same way again.'

Although the show improved, the box office didn't. Clearly, Ward wasn't the only one who hadn't heard of impro. 'Unless you were in the business, and had done a bit of improvisation, the word didn't mean anything to anybody,' says occasional Player Phil Herbert. 'Unless you'd done it at drama college, you didn't really know what the games were about.' And not enough punters were willing to pay a fiver to find out. Audiences rarely reached three figures, and after eighteen months, Ward was sick of subsidising this strange show. 'It still wasn't pulling the punters,' says Kinnie. 'We were going to dump it.' As a last resort, Ward offered The Players a door split rather than their regular £30 a week, a traditional vote of no confidence that's usually the kiss of death for a comedy show. 'We thought that was it,' says Neil Mullarkey. 'We thought it was going to the wall.' The Players accepted Ward's last rites. They didn't have much choice. It was either that or nothing.

It was the best business decision they ever made. 'The week after we went on the split, it turned the corner,' remembers Kinnie. 'The numbers doubled.' Suddenly, punters were waiting outside, hours early, to grab the best seats. 'They got a regular following,' says Herbert. 'You'd see the same faces in the audience every week, coming up with different suggestions.' After almost two years, The Players had finally found an audience, and after subbing the show for so long, Ward had given away a big slice of his investment. He's never tried to change the terms of this untimely deal, however, which makes this one of the most lucrative comedy gigs on the club circuit, for performers, if not promoters.

Hollerbach also started impro workshops, which, in the early days, were just as important as the actual shows. In these classes, she taught English entertainers to make this American artform their own. 'Kit's contribution can't be overestimated,' declares Dave Cohen. 'She made it accessible. She understood where English people were coming from, so rather than trying to force an American version of it, she gave people the space to develop it in a way they were comfortable with, so a very English version of improv developed.'

In the late Eighties, guest Players included impressionist Rory Bremner and actress Caroline Quentin, who worked with her sometime husband Paul Merton in the show.

Richard Vranch at the piano, with Jim Sweeney

Stand-ups like Arnold Brown, Julian Clary, Jeremy Hardy, Nick Revell and Mark Steel all mucked in, but the next regular recruit wasn't a stand-up comic, but a doctor of nuclear physics.

Neil Mullarkey had met Doctor Richard Vranch at Cambridge University, where they'd both been members of Footlights. Following his doctorate, Vranch had become a Fellow. 'I'd been engaged in research on the way that nuclear bombs destroy computers,' Vranch told *Time Out*, who called him the Dudley Moore of his generation. 'Top secret stuff. Rather scary. I wasn't feeling too happy about the work.' Vranch resigned his fellowship and joined a theatre group called The Millies. At first, he was only invited to play the piano in the interval, but he'd also been in a double act with Tony Slattery and worked with top improviser Jim Sweeney, so he was soon playing music throughout the show, and also acting in all the games, becoming a pivotal member of the cast. 'All really good improv is always dictated by the piano player,' says Rich Hall. 'So many times, it's the piano player who saves those sketches.'

'I can't read music,' reveals Richard Vranch, in the dressing room of The Store. 'I'm not a musician and I hate being accused of being a musician.' You never would have guessed after seeing him playing the piano on TV's *Whose Line Is It Anyway?* Greg Proops says Vranch is probably the best musician he's played with. However, here at The Store, with The Players, he's not just the piano player, but a fully fledged member of the impro team. And even though his impromptu musical numbers tend to attract most plaudits, Vranch finds performing off-the-cuff music no more difficult than a spontaneous verbal scene. 'It's exactly the same,' he says, 'except one of the voices in it is a musical instrument.'

Vranch met Tony Slattery at Cambridge, and they formed a double act. When they started out on the club circuit, the Soho Store had already closed and the Leicester Square Store hadn't opened, so they never played The Store together, but they did play Jongleurs, alongside acts like Rory Bremner, Arnold Brown and actress and singer Josie Lawrence.

Lawrence proved to be the perfect foil for Vranch's musical talents. Vranch can play an improvised song in any style. Lawrence can sing it, instantly, with words that scan and rhyme. She's done folk, funk, soul, gospel, opera, calypso, heavy metal, music hall and country and western. She's even done Russian reggae, whatever that is. Only one suggestion ever defeated her: male voice choir.

Lawrence had done some angst-ridden improvisation at drama school, but she didn't encounter any of the funny stuff until 1986, when she played a manically depressed Glaswegian housewife in a play at London's Donmar Warehouse. The Donmar did late-night cabaret, and one turn was an improvising duo called The Rupert Pupkin Collective, aka Jim Sweeney and Steve Steen. Lawrence had never seen anything like it. She loved it and she asked them if she could join in. She'd never been more nervous, but the adrenalin buzz more than made up for it, and when Paul Merton caught a filthy cold in Edinburgh that summer, The Players asked her to fill in for him. The thing that made her most nervous was that she was wearing a dress. 'I don't like improvising in a dress,' she said. 'When you're rolling about, you don't want your bits hanging out.'[3] But even without her improvisational trousers on, she still held her own. 'Fine debut,' said Mike Myers, afterwards.

The current core team: Paul Merton in the middle and then clockwise: Neil Mullarkey, Josie Lawrence, Richard Vranch, Andy Smart, Jim Sweeney, Lee Simpson

'If you think just before you go on, "We're going to do a two-hour show now, and we don't know what we're going to do," then you get nervous,' explained Lawrence. 'If you just have a glass of beer and a chat about what you've done that week, and then I just go on, making sure my lipstick's all right, then that's fine.' But she still gets nervous. 'The only difference is that I don't get the runs like I used to.'[4]

It was only after Myers returned to Toronto in September 1986 that the show acquired its distinctive British character, as The Players, who'd relied on Myers to carry them in the early days, were now forced to make the show their own. 'It started to become much more English, much more personality led,' says Lee Simpson, of a show that began to include more cultural references, and a particularly English brand of irony.

The Player who contributed most to the troupe's English accent was Paul Merton. 'Once Mike left, the entire success of The Players was down to Paul,' says Cohen. 'It would have been a good show without Paul, but it would have developed along much more American lines.' Merton's first taste of impro wasn't at The Store, but at Wimbledon College with an English teacher with the regal name of Windsor. Every Friday Mr Windsor split his class into groups and made them all take turns performing spontaneous playlets. Merton's classmates never called this improvisation, or even ad lib, but that was precisely what it was.

Merton's impro style was the opposite of Hollerbach's support and co-operation ideal. 'Paul completely broke all the rules that Kit suggested,' says Cohen. 'You must always give. You must always say yes. You must always get involved.' Instead of agreeing and adding, Merton stood upstage, folded his arms, and watched the scene unfold. But then just as it began to dip, he'd embark on one of the brilliant monologues that became his calling card on *Have I Got News For You?* The Players gave Merton the freedom to develop his flair for spontaneous flights of fancy that he never would have had in a normal stand-up show. 'He's always slightly at odds with the situation,' says Clive Anderson. And although he eventually became more involved in the actual games, the unique quality of his impro is that it remains one step removed. 'Paul Merton is superb,' says Phil Herbert. 'He's very good at not saying anything and letting you garble on in an attempt to be humorous, and then he'll do a line after you've stopped speaking and get the laugh. He's excellent at that. A very good improviser, completely surreal and bizarre, he'll take the game into great unexpected fantasies. He's an expert.'

And so despite American imports, from Hollerbach and Myers to Greg Proops and Mike McShane, The Players has become very different from its Chicago prototype. 'Americans seem to be better physically and Brits seem to be better verbally,' says Mike McShane. 'Americans try to think of funny characters who use their whole body to be funny,' agrees Neil Mullarkey. 'We're not so keen to throw ourselves into a character.' Americans pride themselves on morphing instantly into whatever the scene demands, but Brits like Paul Merton and Julian Clary often get bigger laughs by sticking to the same stage persona, whatever part they're playing. 'We know each other so well, the show is almost a sitcom, in that we have these characters who are ourselves onstage, and onto that we then add any character we play,' says Mullarkey.

Like all the best team shows, each member brings something different to the group. 'Merton's good for surrealist stuff,' says Simon Clayton, who's guested with The Players in the past. 'Mullarkey will do posh. Jim Sweeney's an everyman. He'll fit in, punch the story along.' And rather like compering, that's an elusive and usually thankless skill. So often, Sweeney will rescue a flagging sketch and get it back on track, only to step aside and tee up the punchline for someone else. 'He's the best improviser I've ever seen on every level,' says Mike McShane. 'People would be really ham strung if he wasn't around, because he sets up so brilliantly.'

The Players never stop looking like they're having fun, or laughing at themselves. However not every entertainer has such fond memories of working with them. 'They talk a lot about being supportive and helpful and how important it is in improvisation to back up other people, but I found them to be the most obstructive and unhelpful group of people I've ever met in my life,' claimed Nick Hancock. 'I firmly believe that my three outings with The Comedy Store Players put my career back ten years.'[5] Yet whatever went on in the wings, by the end of the Eighties, The Players were really beginning to hit their stride. Indeed, for many punters, impro, not stand-up, was their introduction to The Store.

Josie Lawrence and Paul Merton had not yet become household names, but they didn't have too long to wait. In 1988, Mark Leveson and Dan Patterson, who'd already devised *Whose Line Is It Anyway?*, came to see the show, and gave them a nationwide platform for their improvisation. Patterson made them do an audition, which must have rankled, since they'd already proved that they could cut it at The Store. 'They've never forgiven us,' quipped Patterson. 'They blew everyone else off the stage.'[6] And no wonder. 'It was an endless line of straight men,' said Merton. 'You couldn't go wrong.'[7] Leveson and Patterson also recruited Richard Vranch as their pianist. Chaired by Clive Anderson, the series became a national and international hit, and a bigger, broader audience flocked to The Store to see Lawrence and Merton in the flesh. '*Whose Line* was an enormous boost to us because it put the form in the public domain,' says Neil Mullarkey. 'It put us on the map.' Only a year after it started on Channel 4, The Players were selling so well on Sundays, they started doing impro on Wednesdays too. 'We came down expecting no one to be there,' says Richard Vranch. 'It was packed.'

But *Whose Line* fans who came to The Store to see The Players discovered live impro was very different from the version on TV. 'Our way of presenting improv is the best way, yet it doesn't work on TV,' says Ward. 'It's too stylised the way they do it. There's more variety in what we're putting on.'

Live impro is more versatile. 'You could build up a theme,' says Mike McShane. 'A weak-assed joke, over the course of twenty minutes, could become hilarious.' Players can develop characters and situations, and even make comic capital from their cock-ups. Impro looks more shambolic on TV, and if things look messy, people change channels. 'They expect it to be slick and sharp and confident,' explains Steve Steen. 'The emphasis is on short, sharp, punchy scenes. As many laughs in the fewest minutes possible.' Audiences weaned on edited TV impro can arrive at The Store with unrealistic expectations, but Debi Durst, another American veteran of both formats, also far prefers the relative freedom of live impro, especially at The Store. 'The audience goes with you and if it doesn't work, it doesn't work,' she says. 'It's no big deal. As long as you looked as if you knew what you were doing onstage, and never let them see you sweat.'

'It's like a night in the pub with your mates, except you get paid for it,' says Arthur Smith. 'You go out, you have two hours in the company of your friends onstage, go off and have a pint and a curry afterwards.'

Paul Merton summed up the Players' appeal on *The South Bank Show* a few years ago: 'You sit in a room trying to convince a commissioning editor that a joke's a funny joke and he can't get it. And then you go to The Comedy Store and you think of something off the top of your head and you do it and the audience roar with laughter. It doesn't have to go through a committee. There's no budget considerations. "I've thought of something funny. I've said it. It's funny. Great. We'll move on."'

Back at The Store, the evening has turned surreal. Lee Simpson is playing an Afghan soap-opera and sheep-shearing specialist, with a simultaneous translation by Richard Vranch. Steen asks for a workplace. 'A prison shower,' yells one punter. Sweeney asks for a style of drama. 'Tarantino,' yells a second punter. 'Pantomime,' yells a third. This show feels like a mad mixture of both.

The Oblivion Boys

For a few years, Steve Frost had one of the most famous faces in the land. If you saw him on his own, maybe you couldn't quite place him. But if you saw him alongside Mark Arden, you'd have no trouble. Frost and Arden are the blokes from those lager ads who used to say, 'I bet he drinks Carling Black Label.' And whatever Carling paid them, they were worth every penny; for a while, that slogan became a byword for anything even vaguely remarkable in virtually every field.

Frost and Arden were a comic item long before the admen came along. They met at drama school in the Seventies, but they'd been 'resting' for the best part of a year when they went to see The Comic Strip at The Boulevard Theatre in the early Eighties. It looked like much more fun than sitting around and waiting for the phone to ring, or trekking along to auditions, so they decided to give it a go.

They started off in Newsrevue, where they met Lee Cornes, who got Frost and Arden a gig. They called themselves The Oblivion Boys. 'We were hopeless,' says Frost, but they got a good reaction, and Peter Rosengard told them to come back again.

Rosengard's hunch was right – The Oblivion Boys soon found their form, and the club became their showcase. They landed roles in *The Young Ones*, a regular slot on *Saturday Live*, and even the title roles in a West End production of Tom Stoppard's *Rosencrantz & Guildenstern Are Dead*. 'We loved it,' says Frost. 'We were getting paid money, and people were laughing at our stuff. It was fantastic. It was a bit of a dream world.' They did a TV show in the foyer of the Royal Festival Hall and a live gig at The Royal Albert Hall. They also played the college circuit, including a gig at Sheffield University, organised by an accounting and financial management student called Eddie Izzard.

The Oblivion Boys didn't just play The Store, they besieged it, storming the auditorium and taking the audience hostage. 'It was pertinent because there were lots of sieges going on,' says Arden. 'We used to scream and shout and rant and race on from different parts of the theatre.' They'd ask for a round of applause for a couple of Falklands veterans in the audience. The punchline was, these veterans were Argentinians. Then Arden would reveal that his family had just been injured in an awful car crash, including a broken-fingered piano-playing brother and a broken-legged ballet-dancing sister. Arden would cry real tears as the crowd wondered whether it was a wind-up. 'You're joking?' Frost would ask him, poker faced. 'Of course I'm fucking joking,' Arden would reply. 'They died instantly.'

Like trad double acts, they feigned disagreements between themselves, but their fierce quarrels were nothing like those amicable tiffs between Cannon & Ball or Little & Large. Sketches often ended with one of them storming offstage, leaving the other to finish alone. These arguments seemed so authentic that even Cornes had to check they hadn't fallen out for real. And unlike most double acts, they never had a funny man and a straight feed, which made their onstage spats even more realistic. 'You never quite knew where the joke would come from,' says Arden. 'People used to like us because it was like listening in on a conversation in a bar.' Even the bouncer on the door was taken in. He didn't believe they were comics, and wouldn't let them in. It was only their daft props that persuaded him. 'Why the fuck would I be coming into London with all these things in my pockets?' asked Arden.

The Oblivion Boys were so busy putting each other down that most hecklers couldn't get a look in. Those that did were simply incorporated into the act. Sometimes, Frost sat in the audience and heckled Arden, or vice versa. If one of them wanted a pint or a piss, they'd go, and leave the other one alone onstage. One night, Arden was boozing after another show in Hampstead, when they were asked to do a small hours show at The Store that evening. Arden arrived rather the worse for wear, lay down onstage to stop the room spinning, and nodded off mid-routine. However, Frost had trouble persuading the audience that his impromptu nap wasn't part of the show. 'That's all we can do, because Mr Mark Arden has fallen asleep,' announced Frost, walking away, leaving Arden asleep onstage. He was only awoken by the applause.

Some of their finest performances were in front of the rowdiest crowds, like the time they tamed a gang of drunken dental students at two in the morning. 'They were causing havoc, and people were getting booed off and we just didn't want to go on,' says Frost. 'For some reason we hit their funny bone.' They had only a half-hour set, and that night they tried to play it as short as possible. They were on for forty-five minutes. They'd had fifteen minutes of solid laughter, and the students were applauding when they left.

After the improvisational style of The Oblivion Boys, Frost was a natural choice as a regular guest with The Comedy Store Players. He'd done all the games at drama school, where he'd always shone. Comic impro came even easier. Improvisers are supposed to support each other, but at The Store, different rules apply. 'I'm a naughty boy and so as soon as someone tells me not to do something, I do it,' he says. '"Have you got any fish?" "No, we've only got carrots." Wrong, because you've stopped the scene, but the audience laughs. You've messed the fish guy up. He says, "I came in for fish." "Well, we've got carrots the shape of fish." All of a sudden, you're off on something else. You don't have to stick to the basic rules. You just trip each other up.' And even after all these years, doing a good gig still feels fantastic. 'You just feel like a god,' says Frost. 'You just float.' And Frost always knows when he's gone down really well. 'You come off with a big grin on your face and you leave the building without getting your money.'

Eddie Izzard leaving The Store

Eddie Izzard

There's an extraordinary buzz at The Store tonight. Eddie Izzard is doing a guest spot with The Comedy Store Players. It's not the first time he's done it, and it probably won't be the last, but tonight is extra special. Right now, Izzard is the hottest comic in the country. He's just become the first solo comedian to play Wembley Arena, and a few days after entertaining an audience of 12,000 in an aircraft hangar built to house the world's biggest bands, he's playing a basement club that barely seats 400. No wonder there's a palpable sense of excitement in the air. The house lights go down, and the stage is still shrouded in darkness, but as Izzard takes his seat, you can almost taste the adrenalin in the air.

Such great expectations can be a mixed blessing in a small space, which is why only the best and bravest comics return to clubland once they've acquired enough commercial clout to sell out bigger halls. If Izzard was doing a solo stand-up spot, he could easily harness this frenetic energy, but this is a team show, and unless all The Players are on their toes, his star status could destabilise the entire evening. Most midweek crowds need cranking up, but this one needs calming down, which may be why Jim Sweeney's introduction seems deliberately downbeat.

'This is a show which is all improvised so heckling is not allowed,' warns Sweeney. 'If you really want to heckle, you can go outside and heckle the pigeons.' Sweeney's warning does the trick. Improvisation requires a good degree of concentration from its audience, and even though these punters remain frisky, at least now there's a fair chance they'll stop whooping long enough to listen to what's being said.

Sweeney sets up the first round, that rapid-fire word game in which the audience strikes out hesitating contestants by shouting 'Die!' Even Izzard isn't immune. Despite the hysterical reception, he proves himself to be a good team player. If anything, his contributions are a bit too restrained. However, the audience's verdict isn't always final. 'Stay where you are,' Sweeney tells Suki Webster, when the audience round on her without due cause.

The next game is a bizarre blend of mime and tag wrestling. Sweeney asks for an unusual job. 'The example we always give is the person who draws the white lines round dead bodies for the police, or the person who puts the little holes in the side of the Bic Biro,' he says. 'The guy who perms Michael Bolton's hair,' suggests one punter, but the team opts for 'the person who puts the chips in the lavender woodchip wallpaper that was bought by Michael Owen to be put up in Hampton Court.' Suki Webster has to guess this job from the clues contained within the ensuing scene. Eventually, she cracks the code, but most of the laughs come from her mishaps along the way.

Stephen Frost asks for a location where two people might work. 'My mum's brothel,' shouts a punter, but Frost opts for a banana plantation. Neil Mullarkey asks for styles of film and theatre, and Frost and Izzard's banana plantation shifts from *The Godfather* via school play, kung fu and Shakespeare to a bizarre James Bond musical. By the time the interval arrives, the audience is treating Izzard like just another member of the team.

Richard Vranch starts the second half, narrating a make-it-up musical entitled – thanks to the fertile imagination of this audience – Revenge Of The Killer Kumquats. Suki Webster plays Professor Jenkins, creator of a mutant kumquat with a mind of its own, and Eddie Izzard plays an evil genius called Jeff, who's done something similar to bananas. 'Professor Jenkins secretly loved him,' narrates Vranch. 'She wanted to rip her clothes off and show him everything she had. But we haven't got the licence for that.' Well, not anymore. After several songs, they settle their scientific differences over a huge fruit salad. The final game is a cod Shakespearean play, and again, the title is a gift. 'The Taming Of The Shrew Part Two,' shouts another punter. 'The Bitch Is Back.'

'You have to stop thinking,' says Izzard of impro, in an Italian restaurant a short walk away from The Store. 'If you think, "I know where this is going to go," someone will come on and take it somewhere else.' He's starring in *Lenny*, Julian Barry's play about iconoclastic comedian Lenny Bruce. The director is Sir Peter Hall. Not bad for a bloke who didn't even complete his accounting and financial management course at Sheffield University. He's a lot more thick set than Bruce, but he's dyed his blond hair black for the role, and his face looks pale and gaunt beneath the dark quiff that's replaced his normal sandy mop top. He still doesn't look like Lenny Bruce, but he doesn't look like Eddie Izzard, either. He's an actor, not an impressionist, after all.

Acting and impro have heaps in common, but stand-up and impro are poles apart. And although Izzard's stand-up style is improvisational, it's a completely different sort of improvisation from the games The Players play. In fact, Izzard reckons his spontaneous stand-up makes it even harder for him to adapt. 'It takes a certain amount of unlearning,' he says, over a mid-afternoon glass of champagne. 'You have to unlearn some stand-up, especially if you're improvising stand-up.'

Izzard's spectacular success must taste especially sweet, since for a long time his showbiz career seemed to be going nowhere. 'Three years of Edinburgh shows – nothing happened,' he recalls. 'Four years of street performing – nothing happened.' After seven years, even Izzard's self-belief was dented. 'I don't think I can do any of this shit,' he thought. 'I thought I could do it, but nothing's happening.' Only when he decided to get to the top slowly did he finally start to succeed.

Simon Bligh is one of the many Store comics who admires Izzard for never compromising his creativity. 'Eddie always had his own agenda, so he'd go on and he'd do what he wanted to do,' says Bligh. 'He was the first career person, it seemed to me. Eddie seemed to be the first person who actually took control of it all.'

Izzard first played The Store in the mid-Eighties, as one half of a double act. Back then, he was still a street performer, working mainly down the road in Covent Garden, and the routine they brought indoors consisted mainly of stuff that didn't work so well on the Covent Garden piazza. A disappearing bowl of cornflakes, a fake knife-throwing routine, and a toy beaver who leaped through a hoop on a piece of elastic. These tricks were supposed to be insanely crap, but sometimes, if they didn't pitch it properly, they didn't seem insane, just crap. They also did a sword-fighting routine on the piazza which they took to Jongleurs, but they never did it at The Store. There wasn't enough room.

In 1987, Izzard went solo on the street, in 1988, he started doing stand-up, and within a few months he was trying out at The Store. He played several open spots, but that was when wannabes didn't go on until the end of the show, often straight after barnstorming headliners like Jerry Sadowitz had bled all the laughter out of the room. 'I was dying,' he says. 'It was a miserable way of starting, and I couldn't quite work out why they did it.' Just like Jack Dee, Izzard decided to leave The Store alone, and only come back when he was ready. He returned a year or so later, in a stand-up contest. Nobody wanted to go on first, but Izzard wasn't bothered. Not only did he go on first, he also ad-libbed his entire set. Jeff Green won and Izzard only finished about halfway down the field, but he knew he'd done pretty well in the circumstances. Not long after, he went back and did an open spot on a normal night, and after that, he was in. 'I think I'm cooking now,' he told Bob Mills, after he'd nailed it one night. 'Well, I suppose I can talk to you now,' joked Mills, but like all the best jokes, this quip concealed an underlying truth. One night, Izzard turned up at The Store with a double act called The Nice People. The bouncers let in The Nice People and shut the door in Izzard's face.

Even onstage, it was never easy, especially after midnight on a Friday night. His solution was a lot like Ben Elton's, at the old Soho Store a few years before. 'Do it really fast, and never take a breath, because in that breath, if I went "er" they'd go "fuck off, you cunt." They weren't going to do anything except stop the gig.' And once he'd won the audience around, the hecklers were much easier to pacify. 'If someone heckles, they want you to grab him and destroy him,' he says. 'They actually want you to kill him, as long as you're doing well. If you're going down the toilet, it's a different thing.' But that was increasingly rare, and one night, when the mikes went dead, Izzard stayed onstage and finished off his set unplugged.

'Being white, male and middle class is useless if you're a comedian,' ran one of his one-liners, 'so thank god I'm a transvestite.' Yet it was still a while before Izzard wore a skirt onstage, at the Meccano Club in Islington, and until he did, I'm sure I wasn't the only one who thought this was probably just a joke. And it was even longer before he wore a skirt at The Store. The West End punters who use The Store have never been as alternative as audiences at local gigs. 'I thought they'd kill me,' he says. Eventually, Izzard played The Store in a dress and lived to tell the tale, but it was the other comics who took the piss. 'Everybody's going, "Oh, hello, Eddie," as if nothing's happened,' says Newcastle comic Dave Johns. 'We're all thinking, "We're talking to a bloke in a dress," but everybody was trying to be dead cool and be liberal about it.' It was Mickey Hutton who broke the ice. 'Eddie, you've got a dress on, You look awful in it. Even I wouldn't wear that, and I've got the figure for it.'

'I remember the first time he showed up at the back bar in his skirt and his nail polish,' says Bob Mills, who was backstage with Johns and Hutton. 'You know, don't you, that you're wearing a dress?' they asked him. 'Yes,' replied the future superstar. 'You know you look like a twat, don't you?' they asked. 'No,' he replied. 'Come on, we love you, it don't matter,' they told him. 'Just in case you put it on by mistake and hadn't noticed.'

Comediennes

When the Store celebrated its tenth birthday in 1989, the highlights of this gala week were two all-female bills. 'A quip and a quim we called it,' says Jenny Eclair, who was on the bill. 'Cunts in comedy.'

'For once, the dressing room smelled of perfume and hairspray instead of chips and beer,' recalls stage manager Ali Day. 'I could walk in knowing I wasn't going to see somebody's genitals.' It was a step up from performing in a strip club, but it was still scarcely a level playing field. All-male bills are the norm – it's rare to find more than one woman on a bill of four or five – and women-only bills usually attract women-only crowds. What made this show so special was that it wasn't advertised as an all-female line-up, so the audience was the usual cross-section, not a self-selecting clique. Yet staff still felt they had to warn waiting punters that this wasn't a normal night, and so did some of the comediennes.

'The women were really worried that the audience would feel disappointed,' says Ali Day. 'You shouldn't have to say to the audience, "It's all women on the bill,"' she told them. 'If it was all men on the bill, there's no way you'd walk up the queue and say, "It's only men on the bill tonight."' In the end, only two punters walked away, and both of them were women. 'Everyone wanted to be the most filthy, foul-mouthed repulsive person onstage,' says Jenny Lecoat. 'The men not being there had left a gap which we felt we had to fill with our own testosterone.'

Both shows went down well, and the crowd was bolstered by a cluster of male comics, curious to see how their female colleagues would fare. 'I certainly didn't want to fail in front of that mob,' says Eclair. 'All the male comics were incredibly sceptical about it, and pooh poohed it, and said, "It's never going to work, you're all going to die,"' says Jo Brand. 'They all came out and watched pretty much the whole show, but in the sense of being vultures waiting for it to go wrong, rather than wanting to enjoy it.' And despite their best efforts, with gutsy comediennes like Donna McPhail on the bill, enjoy it they did. 'The boys just couldn't keep up with her,' says Eddie Izzard. 'The lads in there thought, "She's more of a lad than we are."' 'Sandi Toksvig compered brilliantly, despite the fact that some appalling City type had lobbed out his lobber for her viewing pleasure in Leicester Square,' recalled Jo Brand. 'It certainly did destroy the myth that The Store is too blokey blokey for the lady performers.'[1]

Mandy Knight

'Have we got a shepherd in?' asks Mandy Knight, as wolf whistles greet her entrance. 'Was that my coil? Is that what's setting it off?' She's far too smart to admit any offence, even if she feels it. She knows the softly softly approach is far more effective. 'Who is that whistling? Let's have a look. You're very sweet but I do draw the line at charity work.' Unlike a lot of comediennes, she doesn't build barriers between genders, and that's her greatest strength. 'Am I going too quickly?' she asks a blond woman in the front row. 'I'll keep moving,' she tells us. 'They like the colours.' There's a refreshing lack of sisterly solidarity in her act. 'I'm getting a disapproving look down here from the lady with the white wine.' But her best gags target men and women simultaneously. 'Please patronise me because as a woman I see that as affection,' she says. 'I'm too bright. No wonder I can't get a fuck.' And the same goes for class. 'Nothing against the working classes,' she says, 'as long as they stay in documentaries.' No wonder she's been compared with Dorothy Parker. The audience all adore her, and her departure after her allotted twenty minutes feels like twenty minutes too soon. Only the frog in her throat gives any hint of how unwell she really feels.

'You pray the adrenalin keeps kicking in until you finish,' says Knight. 'As soon as you come off, you're ill again. It's really odd.' She was coughing her guts up into the toilet before she went on, and again after she came off, but onstage she felt fine. The show must go on is a showbiz cliché, but like most clichés, it's largely true. 'When I was filming the Jo Brand series, I found out my father was dead two hours before we filmed the first one. I couldn't tell anybody. You just have to do the job.' The same goes for The Store. 'Everybody just shits themselves the first time,' she says. 'Until you can actually get that out of your head and think of it as just another gig, you'll never do that well there.' Yet after getting spat at by drunken kids at college gigs, and entertaining a few thousand spaced-out muddy punters in a tent at Glastonbury, The Store doesn't seem so tough after all.

John Moloney gave her two useful tips. First, if you're on here the audience assumes you are the best, and all you have to do is not prove them wrong. And second, the main thing on their minds isn't the show, but whether they've got time for a Chinese before they pay the babysitter.

Her Store debut was at the Leicester Square venue. 'I'd never actually performed to that many people in one room at any one time,' she says. 'Performing to thirty people is a lot harder because they can see the whites of your eyes. They see every flaw and every nuance and every twitch and every insecurity.' Like Phill Jupitus, the comedian formerly known as Porky The Poet, Knight was a performance poet before she became a stand-up. For years, she watched comedians and thought, 'I'd love to be able to do that.' Jo Brand told her she ought to do stand-up. 'I can't,' she told Brand, 'I don't know how to do it.' She could only write jokes that rhymed. Yet that night, she discovered she *could* do stand-up. 'I'm actually here at The Store,' she thought, midway through her debut, 'and there's people laughing!'

'You'll be all right tonight,' male comics often tell her, 'because there are lots of women in.' But Knight finds female punters far harder to win round, and she's not the only comedienne who thinks so. 'Hen nights are worse than stag nights,' says Donna McPhail. 'When a woman gets drunk she's much more dangerous than a man because she won't shut up.' Women don't heckle as much as men, but when they do, they can be much more cruel. 'You're sad,' a woman once shouted at a male comic. 'You could virtually feel the air being vacuumed out of the room,' recalls McPhail. 'What she was saying is exactly what happens when you're dying. You've got no friends and you're humiliating yourself, but at least the boys just say, "Fuck off" or "Tell us a joke." A man wouldn't dream of being that cruel and that starkly accurate.' Even when they keep quiet, Knight worries they sit there thinking, 'Is she thinner than me? Is she fatter than me?' She even fears if she makes their boyfriends laugh, they might hate her for it. Men are much more pliable. She learned the art of seduction doing stand-up in front of blokes. If you tickle them, they roll over. 'The room is dominated by men because their laughter's louder, and often the women take the lead from their boyfriend,' she says.

Yet women, unlike men, value wit over looks. 'Women first and foremost like a bloke with a sense of humour,' she says. 'That's why so many ugly blokes on the circuit can get a shag.' 'Freud says men go onstage for the love of a beautiful woman,' says Arthur Smith. 'A lot of stand-ups want to show off and cop off, so that's actually not so good for the girls. Women don't get shags after gigs. Men do.' Although it was the first Alternative Comedy club, The Store is one of the most macho venues on this circuit. 'Sadly, the comedy business is a male-dominated affair,' claimed Jo Brand, 'especially at The Store, where many female comics simply cannot be arsed to stand up in front of a group of alcohol-sodden misfits and be abused.'[2]

Lately, Knight has cut back on her gigs. 'When you're working seven nights a week you just don't know what you're doing anymore,' she says. 'You don't actually improve.' At first, she was too scared to show any sort of frailty. 'I was like a little armadillo,' she says. 'I had such little self-confidence when I started that the jokes were everything.' Now she knows one-liners are only part of the package, and that her hard-headed, hard-hearted humour actually allows her to show the audience a softer, more human side.

She's never had to walk off, but like all comediennes, she's had to weather far nastier heckling than most men. 'Don't wink at me, you filthy whore,' a heckler told her. Incensed, she laid into him, but most punters hadn't heard him and didn't understand why she'd suddenly become so cross. If she'd only repeated what he'd said, they would have been on her side. She came off feeling awful, knowing one punter had turned the whole room against her. No wonder such hatred sometimes reduces her to tears as soon as she reaches the sanctuary of the dressing room. Yet although she's guaranteed a certain degree of respect backstage, even the dressing room is a relatively male environment. 'Resistance comes much more from your peers than the audience.'

Even though the audience is half and half, most hecklers are men, and even when there are women on the bill, the compere is also almost always male. 'I'm happy to be on an all-female bill because that can actually illuminate how different women are, and stops perpetrating the myth that we all only do the same thing,' says Knight.

But it hardly ever happens. 'You have to be one of the boys,' says Brooklyn comedienne Emmy Gay. 'It's a boys' club. They give the information to each other, what booker to call.' Men don't show the same solidarity towards women. 'There's usually something you've got to do in return, or they're helping you out because they think you're cute,' says Gay. Gay's post-feminist perspective is reflected in her act. 'I want to make as much money as my boyfriend,' she says. 'It's just when we go out, I'm not spending it.' She's gigged as far afield as the United Nations Women's Conference in China, attended by over 30,000 women from more than 170 countries. 'They actually called me one of America's leading feminist comediennes,' she quips. 'But the Chinese don't have a word for feminist, so they just wrote China Welcomes Funny Bitch.'

'Cowardly men attack women first, before they attack men,' says Eddie Izzard. 'That's the injustice of it. Women will get more gigs because there are fewer women, but they have to deal with more shit.' Men don't have to try so hard. As Helen Lederer says, 'They don't even have to have clean clothes.' 'I don't like female comedians, but you were brilliant,' an English punter told New Yorker Maria Falzone. 'What is it about female comedians that you usually don't like?' she replied. 'They're vulgar,' said her new English fan. 'Did you fucking hear what I said up there?' asked Falzone. 'I have a clitoris that comes down to here. I'm fucking filthy.' 'No, no, you were brilliant,' he said. 'Funny yet feminine?' says Falzone. 'It sounds like a new douche.'

Quick laughs aren't always the way comediennes like to work. 'In the late show you have to establish yourself onstage very quickly,' explains Simon Bligh. 'That's harder for a woman to do because it comes across as aggressive, and maybe the people who come to the late show don't expect a female comedian and possibly don't want one.' Knight can cut it, at a price, and so can Rhona Cameron and Donna McPhail, but even Jo Brand had to revert to basic gags about her figure to control the room. 'It's a waste of time for her,' says Bligh. 'She's reached the stage where she doesn't have to do it any-more.' 'Women who played The Store had to become honorary blokes,' says Bob Mills. 'Otherwise there wasn't a place for them. There was nowhere for them to go.'

'A male comic gets much longer before anyone will start on him,' says Hattie Hayridge. 'As soon as a female name is mentioned, people think they're going to be crap.' Yet despite this testosterone-ridden atmosphere, Knight knows that down here, less is often much more. 'Sometimes you can actually whisper and the whole room is totally mesmerised,' she says. 'You can win by pulling them in, rather than banging it out.' But sometimes she's stormed it only to be told by male comics that the reason she went down so well was because there were so many women in the audience. What can you do? As she says, you can sit and cry and say it's not fair because they're all sexist bastards, or you can find a way of dealing with it. And she has. Even if she's furious, she's learned never to show it. 'You can't fight them,' she says. 'The second you lose your charm, you're on a losing battle. The minute they don't like you, you know you're going to lose.'

Jo Brand never went to the Soho Store. 'I kept meaning to,' she says, 'but because I was a student at the time, I was always too busy getting drunk.' By the time she started doing stand-up herself, The Store had moved to Leicester Square, and she still hadn't been. 'I preferred to paddle around in the shallows of the liberal, non-racist, non-sexist little North London clubs rather than the shark-infested waters of the West End. Friendly, discerning polytechnic lecturers were more my cup of tea than homicidally tanked-up lads on stag nights.'[3] When she finally went along to see what all the fuss was about, she'd played virtually every other club on the circuit, but she still thought the atmosphere was amazing. It was after midnight, the late show had already started, the room was full of smoke and people, and Mark Thomas was onstage, ranting at a drunken crowd. 'If Mark Thomas can do it,' she thought, 'I'll have to be able to do it as well.' So when Kim Kinnie asked her to do an open spot, rather than the other way around, she said yes.

'The Store was never really part of the Alternative Circuit,' she says. 'It was always slightly American and slightly glitzy.' Most Alternative clubs catered for local middle-class audiences. The Store was a much wider mix. 'Arseholes from the City,' she says, 'plus a few girls from Essex, one of whom was getting married the next day.' At other clubs Brand would be told to 'Fuck off, you fat cow.' Here, they just called her a cunt. 'It used to pain me to know that there were friends of mine in the audience,' she says, 'having to listen to me being called these various sorts of awful names.' So she soon learned not to invite them. 'An audience could smell your fear better there than they could anywhere else.'

After midnight, drink sent one half of the crowd to sleep, and drove the other half into a frenzy. 'It's a hideous combination. Half the audience aren't aware you're actually up there and the other half want to kill you.' At these late shows, the testosterone level soars. 'Because it's all blokes together, it tends to be far more vicious. By the time the late show's on, they're so drunk they really couldn't care what they're saying or what they're doing.' Sometimes, they were so horrid that she did gags she regretted, simply to survive. 'I ended up being pushed into a corner and making remarks to hecklers that I was a bit ashamed of after-wards,' she admits. 'To lose your temper with an audience is the worst thing you can do, but I've done it, and just launched into a stream of abuse, which isn't very funny, but it makes me feel better.'

Jo Brand

But it was compering that set her on the path to becoming Britain's best live stand-up comedienne. 'She had this problem with her delivery, which was quite monotone,' says Eddie Izzard, who found his own feet compering Screaming Blue Murder, a sub-urban comedy club chain in South London. 'Then she started compering. She started talking to people and she broke that and became herself onstage.' And so Jo Brand became the first domestic comedienne to compere The Store (the first comedienne was Australian Wendy Harmer). It had taken her a while to crack it, but with the best comics there's always something special there, right from the beginning, and Brand was no different. 'Look at that fat ugly cow,' Donna McPhail recalls some bloke saying, as Brand walked up to the mike for her very first Store gig. 'I was in the Nativity play at school,' said Brand, by way of an introduction. 'I played Bethlehem.' She'd done a big woman gag before any bloke could, and her hecklers were struck dumb. From then on, they were docile. 'She dismissed them with one line,' says McPhail. 'They loved her from that moment on.' 'She didn't make it on being pretty pretty,' says comedienne Jo Jo Smith. 'She made it on being bloody funny and being able to hold her own against four other men on the bill. She could top that bill. She could MC that show. She could do whatever the men could.'

Brand achieved the success she deserved, but she also took the flak that went with it, and in doing so, she opened doors for several fine feminist comediennes who, thanks to Brand, went about their funny business with a bit less hassle than before. Comediennes like Jenny Eclair, Hattie Hayridge, Jenny Lecoat, Helen Lederer and Donna McPhail. 'I don't know how she took the pressure,' says McPhail. But no heck-ler could ever be as abusive as the patients she had to put up with as a psychiatric nurse – at the Maudsley Hospital, where Paul Merton was once a patient – and at least now she was allowed to answer back. As a student nurse, she was sent to the canteen to pacify a hyperactive female patient. Brand ended up with a plate of roast pork, peas and potatoes sliding down her face. 'What's for pudding?' she asked.

'Kim always said, "Men have to be one hundred per cent here and women have to be one hundred and fifty per cent,"' says Donna McPhail, a striking thirtysomething woman with the androgynous good looks of a professional athlete.

McPhail was already a regular in the back bar before she played The Store. 'When are you going to do it?' Kim kept asking her. So she did it. She'd already been gigging for a few years, but it still felt like way too soon. This wasn't like any of the other clubs she'd played. 'Everyone was packed in really tight, so they were all really aggressive and hot and waiting hours for the toilet, so when you came on they wanted their money's worth within two minutes,' she says. The compere was Arthur Smith, who'd compered her first ever gig. 'I saw this woman when she first started,' Smith told the audience. 'She is fantastic. You are going to love her.' But Smith's gushing introduction only made matters worse. 'I managed seventeen minutes and got off with my dignity,' she says. 'My mistake,' Smith told the audience. 'She was shit.' Afterwards, Smith apologised but McPhail wouldn't hear of it. 'You shouldn't have set me up like that in the first place but you're absolutely right,' she told him. 'I was shit.' She can't have been too bad to last seventeen minutes, but all the best comics are their own toughest critics, and McPhail started out the way she meant to carry on. 'You must state your authority onstage,' Kinnie told her. She didn't know what he was on about. It was two years before she went back again. 'It did my ego in big time,' says McPhail. 'It really shook me.' But by the time she went back, she'd sussed out what Kim meant.

Even closing her first late show went fine, since the punters who'd heckled in the first half were asleep under their chairs by the second. And from then on she was flying. 'Are you a lesbian?' blokes shouted at her. 'Are you the alternative?' she replied. 'I've got a better dick than you. In fact, I've got three of them. They're all in a drawer at home.'

When a gig goes really badly, she virtually invites hecklers. 'If I'm not doing well I'm desperate for a heckle,' she says. 'I've got no chance unless they heckle me.' 'Get your cunt out,' shouted one particularly unenlightened punter. 'I don't bring my cunt to work,' she said. 'I usually find there's at least one cunt in the audience already.' And that turned the gig around. 'He saved my bacon. Stupid man. What an idiot. What a foul idiot.'

It's over six hours from the start of the early show to the end of the late show, but unlike a lot of other comics, she doesn't like to do another gig inbetween, in case she ends up repeating herself onstage. 'If you show them the mechanism then you're fucked. Fair enough. If somebody tells the same joke twice they deserve to die, especially when they don't get a laugh and they haven't even noticed. Another reason I don't like to treble up is you don't know what the other acts have done.'

She still gets nervous backstage, even after all these years, and she's not the only one. 'Someone is going to get it on the late show, and we're all good enough, but we know it could be any of us,' she says. 'One little slip up and it could be you.' And the odds are only one in four. 'It's twelve o'clock. They've been queuing since eleven. On a Friday they've been drinking since half past five. The Saturday late is all right because they've had a kip and they haven't been drinking, but the Friday late is nasty. It can get very unpleasant.' You're onstage for only twenty minutes, but from the early morning until the small hours, the travelling and the waiting add up to an entire day. 'It's a marathon,' she says.

Donna McPhail

'I was probably drinking quite a lot then, so I don't remember an awful lot about the first few years,' says Rhona Cameron. 'When I started out I was amazingly confident onstage. My material was really quite crap, but I probably had much larger performing skills.' Now her writing has caught up. We're talking at the BBC Club at Television Centre, across the corridor from the office where she's writing her first sitcom, *Rhona*. With her dark cropped hair and darker brow, she looks more Italian American than Scots, but her clipped accent is Heart of Midlothian. 'A lot of the gigs I did, I felt quite tough, but I used to drink before them, and I obviously spent a lot of time covering insecurities up with that kind of bravado.' She was amazed to see Jeff Green reading a book backstage between gigs, like it was just another job.

In 1992, Cameron won Channel 4's *So You Think You're Funny?* She's since won the Paper Boat Award for Best Stand-Up at Glasgow's Mayfest in 1995, but she actually won her first award way back in 1969, when she was crowned Rosebud Princess at the tender age of four.

She'll never forget the first night of this new Piccadilly Circus Store. 'At the opening night party I burst my vocal chords and I had to have an operation,' she says. 'The first few years of my career, I had a very husky voice. I suppose because I'd been drinking for quite a long time and had quite a rough time living in Scotland.' When she started to do stand-up too, all that shouting made her increasingly hoarse. She'd been in a band as well, and when she started singing at that first-night party, it finally gave way. 'I had to get an operation and I couldn't speak for two weeks,' she recalls. 'It was a thousand pounds – I remember that,' she adds. 'I had to completely retrain my voice.'

She likes to arrive early, to sniff the atmosphere around the room. On her way in, she asks the bouncers how the audience has been, and once she's inside she also asks Stan Nelson, but he usually just makes a joke about how nervous she always is. 'If the room is rowdy I will change the order of my jokes about, and I will do an automatically guaranteed opening line, and I will not fuck about when I go onstage.' However many times they've stormed The Store, even the best comics never take this crowd for granted. 'I have to sharpen up all my tools for The Store,' she says. 'It's not a trendy, middle-class, try-out-new-material kind of gig. It's not the intelligentsia of the Banana Cabaret in Balham or the King's Head.' Both those clubs are suburban, and attract a regular, local crowd. The Store is a big night out Up West.

Cameron is one of relatively few female comics who've really cracked The Store, but it's tougher for any woman to break into this male clique. She used to dread hecklers shouting out 'Get off, slag,' or 'Show us your tits.' And it wasn't only new comediennes who suffered. Even seasoned comics like Donna McPhail were often apprehensive, and rightly so. 'She got very nervous,' says Cameron. 'That was interesting for me because I was having a relationship with Donna, who was further on in her career.' Watching McPhail gave Cameron a sneak preview of the sort of abuse that was to come. 'I always get a heckler. I just think they like to test women.' And like a lot of ordeals, the secret is to look like you're enjoying it, even if you're not. 'If I stop smiling, I notice my gigs really fall apart.'

'The prospect of The Store spoiled my whole weekend,' says Jenny Eclair, in a baritone voice that belies her petite frame and impish face. 'Despite the reputation I have as a female hard nut of comedy, I'm actually a complete coward.' Indeed, if it wasn't for her friend Julie Balloo, she might never have played there in the first place. Balloo was going out with Paul Merton, so after her gigs in pub function rooms, Eclair would join Balloo backstage to eat and chat and show off and act daft. She didn't have to do an open spot, because back then there were so few female comics. She was never booed off, but disinterest was even worse, that sickening dread that turns to hopeless despair when punters start talking amongst themselves. 'I'd refuse to leave the stage even though it was quite obvious they weren't interested, but a sort of petulance takes over.' What's more, she was strong enough not to take it personally. 'You have to be able to fail at The Store and walk away with your dignity intact, because at the end of the day, who's shouting at you? Just a load of people with very red faces that probably wouldn't even remember what you'd been talking about in the morning anyway.'

She started out as a performance poet, 'I was so frightened of being myself. It took me years to develop the in-between poem patter.' It was The Store that made her shift to stand-up. 'It suddenly became a bit namby pamby in that environment, and I realised I had to toughen up.' Store comics were less arty farty. 'Tim Clark and Mickey Hutton, people that didn't actually need to do their act, probably survived best,' she says. 'It bred people that actually didn't write material.' And people who were pissed off, with anything, everything. 'It bred angry comedy because you had to shout to be listened to,' she says. 'It's a survival mechanism.'

She's phlegmatic about her Store success, and that of her female peers. 'I don't think me, Jenny Lecoat or Helen Lederer were that strong as stand-up comics at all. I got better, Helen was a character actress and Jenny ended up hating performing.' The odd

Jenny Eclair, the first, and so far the only, female comic to have won the Perrier Award

woman out was Jo Brand. 'I always got too frantic. I was inches away from losing control of my bowels. Jo always looked like her bowels were firmly under control, so for me it was a real kick up the arse. I've always been very jealous and very competitive and I realised very quickly that she was stealing my thunder.'

More theatrical than Clark or Hutton, less political than Brand, Eclair's post-feminist persona, unrepentantly posh yet gynaecologically graphic, rubbed a fair few female punters up the wrong way. 'Often the women would be the most vicious. Women have turned on me at The Store and that's really hurtful. It's a betrayal. You think, "I'm only having a go," but it's not about having a go. It's about being good enough to hack it. To go down well at The Store doesn't necessarily mean you're a fantastic stand-up comic. It means you're very good at dealing with people whose concentration is quite limited, and if you've got any survival instincts, you tailor your act to suit that.'

In 1989, she had a baby, Phoebe, but carried on gigging throughout the pregnancy. 'It's very cruel to heckle a pregnant woman, so those were probably some of my easiest gigs. In fact, I should have just put a cushion up there and pretended I was still pregnant for a couple more years. That was when my stand-up came into its own. It wouldn't have happened ten years on because it's commonplace now, but at that time it was quite a new thing to work through pregnancy and childbirth.' After gigs she'd go home and breastfeed Phoebe. After she became the first woman to win the Perrier Awar in 1995, she got a bigger welcome at other clubs, but here at The Store she was just a name on a bill. 'They haven't come to see me at all,' she realised. 'They couldn't actually give a shit.' This club doesn't respect reputations, just results.

Bill Bailey

At The Store, the closing comic isn't the headline turn, but tonight you could be forgiven for thinking so. Bill Bailey is a pretty self-deprecating fellow; when you're this funny, and this talented, you can afford to be. Bailey could comfortably cut it as a straight stand-up comic, but he's also an immaculate musician, who can morph effortlessly from one musical style to another, on keyboard or guitar. With his long, lank receding hair, goatee beard and Catweazel eyes, he looks more like a roadie than a comic. As he says himself, he could pass as the secret fifth member of ABBA, or an Eighties Meatloaf off of *Stars In Their Eyes*. And tonight, Matthew, his incongruous hits include a Satanic Heavy Metal lullaby and a cockney knees-up cover version of Lou Reed's 'Perfect Day'. It's after two in the morning, but the crowd demand an encore. At the very end of their evening out, the entire room has woken up.

When Bill Bailey first went to The Store, it still doubled as a funk nightclub called The Cat In The Hat, and Bailey was still in a manic musical double act called The Rubber Bishops. Ali Day saw them do a gig at The Canal Café pub theatre and recommended them to The Store. Invited down to do an open spot, they went the week before to see what they were letting themselves in for. They found anarchic clown Chris Lynam on a tiny stage throwing ice cubes at a cellar full of shouting drunks. Bailey felt as if he'd stumbled across something wonderful.

'I'd been on tour with a theatre company in Japan and I had this date in my diary – Comedy Store, big bold letters, must get back, can't be in Asia for this gig,' says Bailey. 'Now I think it's mad to come back for an open spot but I suppose then it meant a lot.'

But if it hadn't been for the inadvertent intervention of the People's Republic of China, Bailey might never have made it to that first Store open spot. 'We'd got tickets to go to Beijing and then it all kicked off in Tiananmen Square, so all the visas were cancelled and we couldn't go,' he says. 'It worked out very well for me. Obviously not so well for the Chinese dissidents.'

Bill Bailey

Bailey got back in time for his open spot. And far from being too late, he was far too early. 'We got there right at the beginning of the show and just sat there and got more and more nervous.' When their turn came, it was two in the morning. 'It's so late now, they're so drunk, they won't even notice, we might just get away with it,' thought Bailey, but the crowd was still up for it, and they went down really well. 'Very good,' said Kim Kinnie, afterwards. 'One of the best new acts I've seen in a while.'

Even after all these years, those first few gigs still feel magical to recall. 'I can't believe it,' thought Bailey. 'We're actually here.' He'd imagined they might get a booking, but to close the show and be brought back on for an encore – that was beyond belief. After gigs, Bailey would sit in that little dressing room, sweating, still wired with all the elation. After late shows he wouldn't get home until three or four in the morning, but still he couldn't sleep, so he'd sit up and play cards until seven. It was even worth the struggle of lugging his guitar around on the tube.

One night, a bloke a few rows back stood up right in the middle of Bailey's set. Straight away Bailey thought, 'This is going to be trouble.' He took something out of his pocket and walked towards the stage. 'At the side of the stage, people were going, "Oh my god,"' recalls Bailey. 'We just stood there and for one moment I thought, "That's it. He's going to lunge at us."' The stage lights were shining in Bailey's eyes, making this bloke seem even more menacing. 'When the light is behind someone, you can't see,' says Bailey. 'I couldn't see his other hand. He had something behind his back.' While everyone else sat and watched, this bloke stepped onto the stage and thrust out his hidden arm. It was in a cast. 'Can you sign that, mate?' he asked, handing Bailey a pen.

Another evening Bailey spotted a sleeping punter and persuaded the entire audience to keep absolutely quiet before he woke him from his very public slumber. 'You've got to go home, mate,' said Bailey. 'The club's finished.' 'All right,' mumbled the drunk, still half asleep, thinking he was the last person left inside, before turning round to be awoken by a deafening cheer from the entire audience.

When Bailey did The Cutting Edge in the early Nineties he realised he had a future as a solo act. He'd been at Glastonbury Festival all weekend and didn't get back until Tuesday. He couldn't have been more badly prepared. He didn't have a clue what had been going on. He'd not read a newspaper for a week. Quite a handicap in a supposedly topical show. 'I just had to go on and busk and make stuff up.' Somehow, in his mud-encrusted clothes, he got away with it.

During the Gulf War, The Cutting Edge had a whole section of the show which was devoted to the conflict. 'There was a real atmosphere in the place when you did material about it.' After one such show, Bailey was on his way upstairs when a man from the audience grabbed him. He was emotional, fluctuating between tears and laughter. 'I'd just like to thank you for doing that,' the bloke told Bailey. 'You've really cheered me up. I'm a Harrier pilot. I've got to go out to the Gulf next week.' It was a cathartic reaction. His wife, friends and family had all avoided any mention of the war, and he was so relieved to hear the subject discussed irreverently that he'd been laughing fit to burst.

Patrick Marber

A good comedy club helps to produce first-class stand-up comics. What makes The Store a great comedy club is that the comedians who've played here have moved into so many different spheres. From newspapers to novels, from television to theatre, there's scarcely a form of writing or performance that hasn't been invaded by Store veterans, and one of the most prolific invaders is Patrick Marber. Like a lot of fine character actors, Marber has a curiously anonymous face and a classless manner. You feel he could comfortably slot into any supporting part, in any play, in any period. But although he's done some acting, it's as a writer and director that he's made his name.

Still only in his mid-thirties, Patrick Marber isn't merely promising. He's already an accomplished playwright and theatre director, with two huge stage hits behind him: *Dealer's Choice* and *Closer* have played the National Theatre, the West End, Broadway, even the Atlanta Olympics. Today's comics tend to be bombarded with writing deals, but Marber's plays are a completely separate case, on two counts. First, although he was a competent and comparatively successful club comic, Marber was never famous enough for his stand-up reputation to open doors for him in different fields. And second, there's the sheer quality of Marber's work. But I'm not here to talk to him about his first play, a profound and funny piece about poker, or his second, a haunting drama of erotic dislocation, or even his work with Steve Coogan on Alan Partridge, the most potent English archetype since Basil Fawlty. I'm here to talk about The Store. Because Marber didn't serve his stage apprenticeship at Stratford, the Barbican, or even BBC TV Centre, but in front of a bunch of drunks in a claustrophobic cellar beneath Leicester Square.

'It was quite unlike any other experience I'd ever had,' explains Marber, recalling his first trip to The Store, when he was still a student at Oxford University. 'It was unique.' He'd seen Ben Elton and Rik Mayall, Mel Smith and Griff Rhys Jones before, but that was in big, anonymous theatres. 'There was a blister of excitement to be a member of the audience,' he says. But he felt scared too, because almost as soon as the show started, he realised that being a member of the audience wasn't enough. 'There's no way I'd be able to do this,' he thought, 'but I want to be doing this.' And six months later, he did. 'The Store is a place of pilgrimage,' he says. 'It's what got me started.'

Barely twenty-one, and still at college, he wrote five minutes of comedy, went back to The Store, watched the show, and in the interval he asked if he could do an open spot. It was a Friday night, but by the time he finally got to go on it was three o'clock on Saturday morning. It was the death spot, but he got two laughs early on. 'Oh my god,' he thought. 'It's going to work.' But after a few minutes, the heckles started, and he was utterly incapable of dealing with them. He got heckled off, but those laughs made it all worthwhile. 'I'd gone onstage at The Comedy Store and got a laugh,' he says. 'A genuine laugh, rather than a piteous, sarcastic cackle.' That night, Marber couldn't sleep. He was still buzzing. 'Something had happened to me.'

For the next five years, The Store was under his skin. And the oxygen of that laughter made him determined to return. 'One day, I will come back,' he thought. 'And win.' He did another open spot, in a double act with a friend from Oxford, on the same bill as Jack Dee, who was doing his first ever open spot at The Store. He went to the comedy workshops at Jackson's Lane community centre in Highgate, North London, in the same class as a street performer called Eddie Izzard. 'Eddie was the no-hoper of the class,' says Marber. 'He had something. He had sparkle. He was rubbish for two or three years, but over a period of years, he just got good, and he was doing exactly the same kind of stuff as he was when he was bad, but he was funny now. It's really weird.'

At the 1992 Edinburgh Festival, Marber directed Steve Coogan and John Thomson's Perrier-winning show. TV work with Coogan followed, on *The Day Today* and *Knowing Me Knowing You*, and he stopped playing the circuit. 'I didn't need to earn my living performing stand-up comedy anymore,' he says. 'A good comedian needs to be a comedian, and I didn't.' Marber was a good comedian, but stand-up wasn't in his bones. All the greatest comics are driven by that compulsion, and some of the worst ones, too. Good or bad, they all know this is what they do best, better than anything else they know. That's why Robin Williams still performed for free at The Store after he became a movie star, and why comics you've never heard of still can't quit the circuit after twenty years, although they'll never get any better, and may even be getting worse. Marber was better than some of them, but he found something else that he did best of all. And although writing plays may seem like a million miles away, his Store apprenticeship wasn't wasted.

'I learned more about myself,' he says. 'I learned about the discipline of language. I learned about instinct. I learned how to hear an audience, which has stood me in good stead as a playwright. I learned not to be afraid of changing my material. I work on a play like I used to work on a set, so there isn't a word that doesn't need to be said in it. I learned that from stand-up. Less said the better. Get to the point quickly. Don't flannel about. And how a laugh is entirely dependent on inflection and circumstance.' His circumstances have changed too much for him to return. 'There's no way I could go on at The Store now and do my old act and survive,' he says. 'It would be terrifying.'

Comperes

'First show in the New Year,' announces Tim Clark, strolling out into the spotlight with the casual confidence of someone who's as comfortable up on that small stage as he is in his own home. And so he should be, for, by common backstage consent, Clark is the best compere on the circuit, a host who makes his audience and his fellow comics feel utterly at ease. From the twilit shelter of the balcony, you can only sit back and marvel at the immaculate, audacious artifice of it all. When you see a top compere, it looks so simple that you wonder what all the fuss is about. It's only when you watch a bad one that you realise what a subtle, thankless trick it is to build a bridge between stage and stalls, to control a baying crowd and still come across as two parts comic and one part punter. And the mark of doing it really well is when spectators scarcely know you're there. Forget soap opera. Compering is the acme of naturalistic acting, The Store is the ultimate arbiter of this unsung yet essential craft, and Clark is about as good as it gets. 'Tim Clark is the master compere,' says Alan Davies. 'He can operate at a really slow pace in what appears to be a very hostile environment.'

'A lovely welcome,' says Clark, soaking up the ripple of spontaneous applause that greets his self-assured entrance. 'Apart from this bloke,' he adds, selecting a sap from the front row, without so much as missing a beat. 'You just put your coat down and looked at me as much as to say, "Make me laugh, you bald bastard."' Dressed all in black, with his trim build and bare pate, Clark looks a lot like Yul Brynner's gunslinging android in Westworld. 'So what's your name, sir, seeing as I'm going to be taking the piss out of you the entire night?' Yet just as the rest of the front row shares a selfish sigh of relief, Clark switches his assault to a different scapegoat. 'I was going to be taking the piss out of you the entire night. Then I spotted you, who's come in dressed like one of the Dukes of Hazzard.' However, at the very moment that his first victim is settling back into his seat, thankful for his surprise reprieve, Clark returns to his former prey. 'I could go back to you for the cheap ones,' he warns, before turning again to the Duke Boys lookalike. 'So what's your name?' asks Clark. 'Darren?' Clark raises his eyes to the heavens in reverential gratitude. 'Thank you, comedy god. Darren, where have you parked the Capri?' And just as Darren's pals start to enjoy his acute discomfort, Clark turns to the woman beside him. 'Madam, you look mortified. Are you Darren's good lady? You're not?' Clark apes mock surprise. 'Because you're between Darren and what's your name? Darren and Ben? I think I'll call you Bo and Luke. So, Daisy.' A belly laugh of recognition floods through the room, as 400 beery babyboomers clock the Seventies TV reference. Punters admire a comic who thinks on his feet, but not half as much as they relish the *schadenfreude* of seeing a stranger suffer.

Compere Tim Clark

'What is your name, madam?' continues Clark, pressing home his advantage. 'Jemma? You're posh, aren't you, Jemma. You've never been in a Capri in your life. Unlike you, madam,' he adds, turning his attention to another woman in a different party. 'The one on the end is only fifteen,' he adds. 'What are you doing in here? You should be outside with some pop and crisps. How old are you? What year were you born?' Pause. 'He had to think about that, didn't he?' Clark tells his audience. 'I don't want your ID. Are you from America? Darren, you're off the hook.' Clark works the Yank for a while, and then rips the piss out of a South African. He also does some established material, but he doesn't really need to. The crowd is on his side now, and unless something goes badly wrong, his authority is assured for the rest of the night. He knows they'll laugh at anything now, or nothing at all, and Clark is even bold enough to tell them so, and tear apart the illusion he's so meticulously created.

'See what happened then?' he challenges us, daring us to rip into him, as well we all might, because there's nothing quite so precarious for a comic as deconstructing their own set onstage. But nobody comes back at him. We're beaten before we've even begun. 'I was getting no laughs and I just said something stupid. Got a laugh. That's technique.' And so it is. Everyone laughs again, without really knowing why; by now it's become a habit. We're ready for the first act. His task completed, for the next twenty minutes, at least, Clark retreats to the temporary sanctuary of the dressing room. 'The compere needs to be the strongest on the bill and orchestrate the night,'

Compere Tim Clark (centre) backstage at The Comedy Store with: (left to right) Dominic Holland (seated), Eddie Izzard, Owen O'Neill, Rhona Cameron, Gina Yashere, Felix Dexter, Jim Tavare

says Ali Day, and tonight, Clark's comic conducting has turned this restless crowd into an attentive audience.

'It's the most glorious gig in the world compering here,' says Clark, backstage, at the start of yet another long working weekend. 'I learned everything I know about working a room standing up in The Store. I learned everything about dealing with hecklers from being heckled here.' A compere must create a link between the audience and the acts. If an act dies, he has to bring the mood back up before he brings on the next. If an act storms it, he has to bring the audience back down to earth. But if the show is steaming along, he's quite happy to do one gag and get the next act on straight away. 'It is always a compliment as a compere when people say to you, "You were really good, you should try and get yourself a spot,"' says Mark Lamarr, one of The Store's most audacious MCs. 'And you say, "Well, I've actually been on for forty-five minutes tonight. I've been on a lot longer than anyone else." People do assume that you happen to work there. You're the janitor.'

'An act is in charge of himself,' says veteran Store compere Lee Cornes. 'You're in charge of the evening.' Compering isn't just about making the punters laugh. It's about showing them who's boss. 'If anybody's celebrating anything tonight, like they've got a birthday, or they're getting married, write that down on a piece of card or paper in the interval, and post it to Radio One,' Boothby Graffoe tells Store punters. 'This is a comedy club. If you want that sort of shit, fuck off to Jongleurs.'

'Tim Clark is the compere's compere,' says Hattie Hayridge. 'You've got to be very unselfish as a compere. You're not there as the star of the show. You're the Polyfilla. You're not the Victorian antique tiles.' The best comperes are always very good comics, but they're rarely comedic greats. Maybe compering prevents a good comedian from becoming great – in a sense, you're sacrificing your own act. Backstage, most stand-ups are much the same, but onstage, a star turn must act unique while a compere has to play the everyman. It's the difference between being a first-class centre forward and a first-class centre half.

Mandy Knight, the first comedienne to compere Jongleurs, reckons the main reason good comperes are so rare is down to ego. 'It's an entirely different skill to stand-up.' John Mann is a good example. He's hardly the most mesmeric comic on the circuit, but star quality can be more of a hindrance for a club compere. Far better, Mann has that blokey bonhomie, calm under fire, which all the best comperes share. 'The first thing you do as a compere, you throw your ego away,' says Mann. Stand-up is a solitary, selfish trade, and making other comics shine brighter than you often goes against the grain. Acts on a bill aren't in direct competition, but there are far too many good wags for every turn who deserves it to graduate from club circuit to TV and national tours. Some make it. Most don't. The best ones will and the worst ones won't, but for the competent majority, it's a lot more hit and miss. It's no coincidence that Clark is in his forties, with a different career behind him, and the less self-absorbed perspective a longer life's lessons bring. 'His strength is really working the room,' says Knight, 'but he always makes sure everybody's absolutely focused.' Bad comperes milk tamer crowds, but bail out if it's rowdy, chucking on an act to sink or swim without establishing control. Not Clark.

'Oh, baldy's on, we'll piss off,' says Clark, as his return onstage prompts a rush to the toilets, but the audience can tell it's only mock indignation. At plenty of other clubs, the compere is a commercial break, but here, it's his show. Clark's comic links are so smooth, from Bill Clinton to Chelsea Clinton to Chelsea Football Club, that he achieves stand-up's ultimate illusion: it really does feel as if he's making it up as he goes along. Clark uses his pet American punter as a sounding board for a few gags about Stateside sport. American football is rugby league in fancy dress and baseball is really rounders. We're away.

'You need to be able to talk to the audience,' says Simon Bligh, another regular Store compere. 'If you do too much material, you've failed.' The first time Bligh hosted here was as a sudden substitute for another comic. 'They did the first show and they were so crap that Don told them to do a set on the second show and asked me to do the compering.' For the last few years, he's compered here once a month.

Bligh's animated stand-up style is a welcome antidote to most British comics, who only perform from the neck up. He doesn't hide behind the mike stand, or even a hand-held microphone. Instead he wears a personal radio mike, like The Comedy Store Players. And like The Players, this device gives him the freedom to roam around the stage, and even into the audience. If anyone heckles, Bligh can step offstage and hunt them down. 'For a while, he had to work off the stand and he didn't look comfortable, but now he's got a personal mike and he's like a man who's been liberated,' says Lee Hurst. 'It's fantastic to see.'

Bligh's first experience of Alternative Comedy was hearing Alexei Sayle on a Comic Strip LP in the early Eighties. That record inspired him to do an open spot at the Soho Store. On a Friday night, he squeezed into the tiny lift and took his turn among ten open spots. By the time the compere, Jim Barclay, brought him on, it was already Saturday morning. 'I never went there again.' And so despite his relatively successful Store debut, it wasn't until the late Eighties that he began to play London's booming comedy club circuit.

He never needed to try out at the Leicester Square Store because *Time Out* comedy editor Malcolm Hay recommended him to Don Ward, and Ward actually phoned Bligh and offered him a gig. This was lucky for Bligh, who never mastered one of the most crucial parts of a rookie comic's craft: cold calling. 'I always find it harder to ring up for a gig than anything else,' he says. 'I'd rather do the gig.' Yet even this short cut didn't guarantee instant success. 'I was always the worst on,' says Bligh. 'If anyone was going to die, it would be me.' From the moment he woke up in the morning, he was terrified. 'Comedy Store tonight, Comedy Store tonight,' he'd think all day at work. He was right to worry. Come show time, he had no armoury. 'I didn't have any stage skills then. I used to just do my set. I'd stand onstage and do my set word for word, no matter what happened.'

Bligh's turning point came on a night when Phill Jupitus was compering. His act was hijacked by four big black American marines who'd been drinking wine all evening. 'Stop serving them wine,' Don Ward told the bouncers. 'You stop serving them wine,' they told him. 'Chuck them out,' Ward told them. 'You chuck them out,' they told him. Bligh was on last, and was actually doing pretty well, until one of the marines got up onstage and grabbed him. Bligh is over six foot, but this marine was at least six inches taller. 'You're a funny guy, sir,' said the marine. 'Thank you very much,' replied Bligh, politely. 'Now can you leave the stage?' But the marine wouldn't budge. Then the sergeant got up. 'I'm telling you to leave the stage,' said the sergeant. 'With respect, sir,' replied the marine, 'fuck you.' The two marines stood eyeball to eyeball. 'The show's over,' said Jupitus, demonstrating another important compering skill – knowing when to cut your losses. Bligh left the marines to sort it out among themselves, but after that, nothing scared him. 'I've pushed people offstage,' he says. 'I never let people on. Since the American marines incident I'll never let anyone get onstage.' Now Bligh fills that space like he owns it, and even an American marine wouldn't try to take it away.

Back out front, Tim Clark gets the second half underway. 'What's your name, sir? Dylan? Named after the great man Bob? Or the other great man Thomas? Or the one from The Magic Roundabout?' 'Do some jokes, for god's sake,' shouts a heckler, slouched against a pillar. The crowd whoops in mock shock horror. He's challenged Clark's authority, and Clark must put him in his place before he can carry on. 'I'm the compere,' says Clark, with the patient air of a professor patronising a half-wit. 'We call this working the room.' Clark isn't remotely flustered, but he knows he has to show the heckler, and the audience, that he's the boss. And soon. 'OK, I'm going to have to take the piss out of you now, sir. Go on. What d'you want to talk about? And I'll see if I've got anything. You're leaning there in a very aggressive fashion, as well, sir. Aren't you? It's a sort of "I'll take you out, skinhead." To dinner, maybe.' The house howls. Clark is back on track, and he barely missed a beat. But not all hecklers need crushing. 'Do either of these beautiful ladies have a relationship with you?' he asks a man in the front row. 'Both of them? And then he wakes up? I rather like that, madam. That's called doing my job for me.'

'The compere is a sort of conduit,' says Mark Lamarr. 'Sometimes you have to be on the audience's side. You have to say, "Yes, they were shit, sorry about that."'

Yet one night the audience was so abusive, Lamarr had no option but to berate them. 'What's the fucking matter with you?' he asked them. 'You're just being a bunch of cunts.' At last the show ended. 'The whole evening had just been a disaster,' recalls Lamarr. 'Ben Elton was in watching.' And Elton was full of praise. 'He's such a lovely fella,' says Lamarr. 'He came up and he went, "That was the best piece of compering I have ever seen."' Quite a compliment from a comic who'd compered The Store himself with such distinction. 'It was really lovely of him,' says Lamarr. 'As he was doing this, this couple come up with a pen and paper, and he just turned to them and he went, "You don't want my autograph. You want this man's." And they went, "Yeah, we've come for his." But they hadn't. That was what I thought was amazing. They fucking hadn't, and they just like rubbed his nose in it.' 'Only joking,' they told Elton. 'Can we have your autograph?'

'Is she your girlfriend? No? She's not going to be either, is she, sir?' Tim Clark is baiting yet another luckless front-row punter. 'How old are you? Nineteen next month? You're twelve. Don't stay out too late. You've got that paper round in the morning. If it gets a bit rude later, put your satchel over your knee. No one will ever know.' Clark turns his attention to a gaggle of girls from Bath. 'You're a bit posh, aren't you?' he asks them. 'You're more used to Chardonnay and vol au vents, aren't you? I'll just explain to the lads. Vol au vents. It's this kind of pastry type thing. You've all obviously been in work today because if you've gone home and got changed it's a bit tragic. You work for BT?' The audience boos. 'I heard all that hissing and I thought he was letting his girlfriend down for a second. Do your mum and dad let you use the phone? Sometimes? He's playing along with it. I like it.' And so do we.

Although it doesn't always look that way, the compere wants the other acts to do well. 'If an act dies, you've got to go on and get it back,' says compere Mickey Hutton, in the dressing room. 'This woman went on and she said, "Men are from Mars, women are from Venus," and this guy shouted out, "If you weren't so fat, I'd let you suck my penis."' This open spot left the stage in tears. 'Birds,' said Hutton, when he went back on. 'No sense of humour.' A compere is nothing without the confidence of the crowd. 'I'll always say, "This act's going to be great. Give them some support."' But that support breaks both ways. 'If they die, you've got to go out and say, "They were shit, weren't they?" Otherwise they won't trust you.'

Compering an early show, from eight until ten, can be tricky, but a compere hasn't really won his wings until he's compered a late show, after midnight. 'Any questions?' Mickey Hutton asks the late-show crowd. 'Why don't you give up stand-up comedy?' asks a punter, invisible in this translucent tobacco haze. Not quite the sort of question Hutton had in mind. 'You can't scare me,' says Hutton. 'But you can bore us,' says another punter. There are several boos and whistles, and even a few sporadic chants of 'Off, off, off,' but although it looks like he might be about to lose it, Hutton doesn't panic. Unlike acts, comperes have to keep coming back for more. Hutton knows that if he leaves now, with the room against him, there's no way he'll be able to return in twenty minutes and keep his authority intact. So he sticks around, even though it must be the last thing he feels like doing, does a bit of pre-prepared material, and against all odds, he gets them back. 'I've still got it,' he says. 'You love us now, don't you?'

Mark Lamarr and
Sean Lock

In a smart yet anonymous office block on Wardour Street, the tin pan alley of Britain's movie industry, Mark Lamarr and Sean Lock are busy writing a television series. In this room, at this table, they act like equal partners. But although Lock's name will be on the final credits, only his friends and family and a few media insiders will notice it. Because even though Lamarr and Lock are writing this show together, Lamarr alone is fronting it, and so for the millions of viewers, every single gag in *Leaving The Twentieth Century* will seem like Lamarr's alone.

Lamarr and Lock are both top stand-ups, but in a way, they're at opposite ends of the comedy spectrum. Lamarr's prolific appearances on a fleet of flagship shows, from *The Word* and *The Big Breakfast* to *Shooting Stars* and *Never Mind The Buzzcocks*, have made him a familiar face for the best part of a decade. First and foremost, he's one of Britain's best stand-ups, but millions more have seen him on TV than have ever seen him live. Conversely, Lock has contributed to TV shows for Bill Bailey, Lee Evans and Newman & Baddiel, with whom he appeared in the first ever comedy show at Wembley Arena, but without a TV series of his own, he's still not a household name. Yet he's acknowledged as one of the top stand-ups at The Store, and maybe, in the long run, this kudos is worth just as much, if not more. Lamarr is one of a small number of comics who've broken into television on their own terms, but many lesser wags would be wise to trade their few fleeting minutes of small screen fame for the more lasting rewards of Lock's solid reputation.

'I couldn't even believe I was allowed in, never mind on the stage,' says Lamarr, recalling his teenage Store debut. 'The Comedy Store for me was for people on telly.' Now he's one of those people, but it wasn't always that way. 'I did an open spot, when the open spots were at the end of the show,' he says. 'That cruel fucking system where you had to go on at half two.' Against all odds, he had a good gig, although he often suffered thereafter. That was in Leicester Square. 'The atmosphere was much more intense because they were right on top of you,' says Lock, recalling that claustrophobic collision of stage and stalls. 'There was a much clearer point of contact between the comedians and the punters.'

Lamarr went down there every weekend, whether he was on the bill or not, but today's Store isn't quite the same. Resting comics must squat in the dressing room or watch the show out front, with the paying punters. 'If you're randy young comics and you want to pull birds after a gig, this new Store must be rubbish because you have to come offstage

Mark Lamarr in the back bar at the Leicester Square Store

and run out round the back,' says Lock. 'In the old days you just had to sit in the club.' It's not the only thing that's changed. 'Comperes now come offstage at The Store and say, "Right, there's a bloke on the left, it's his birthday. There's a fella up the back there, he's just got a new job. Steve here works for BT, and there's a hen party over there." I say, "Why are you telling me this? How many years have I been doing it? Have you seen my act? I'm never going to make any use of that. Why tell me?"' Because the circuit, and The Store, has changed. 'Nobody would ever have said that to you,' says Lock, of the way things used to be. 'Nobody would have found out those banal details.' So what's changed? 'The sense of fun, excitement and experimentation, and the fact that you could fail, do what you wanted and just go off and talk bollocks in a new way, or just make stuff up,' says Lock. 'You don't have that freedom now. When you do it, it's usually when it doesn't really matter. Like the late show, Don's gone home and half the audience are asleep.'

Comics used to muck about more because there was a lot less to lose. 'All the people you thought were really good were the ones who just had a bit of fun,' says Lock. 'They were obviously never going to become huge stars because they didn't really take it that seriously. It was almost like ambition was something you'd be embarrassed about. You'd never talk about what you wanted to be, or where you wanted to get to.' Until one night, Lee Evans arrived, 'really late and in a real hurry as usual', and when they got talking, Lock realised times had changed. 'He said, "I'm fed up with this, I want to move on. This isn't enough for me. I want more."' 'What are you talking about?' marvelled Lock. 'Where do you want to go? We're playing in the heart of London's West End.' Evans ended up in Hollywood. 'You can't even think beyond that bubble,' agrees Lamarr. 'I always used to think there isn't anywhere bigger than The Store.' But in the end, all bubbles burst.

Sean Lock

'Comedians have become so safe, reliable and cautious that audiences expect something which is easily digestible,' says Lock. 'It does make it more difficult for new acts to experiment.'

But more experienced acts like Lock still find plenty of opportunities to muck about. Lock turned up one night and started heckling Bill Bailey and Mickey Hutton, in mid-musical duet. He ended up onstage, singing 'Satisfaction' as Donald Duck. Once he even heckled an Australian stand-up from the dressing room. 'He was going, "England's shit, England's crap," but he didn't actually have any kind of angle to it,' says Lock. 'The audience were turning into a mob and he wouldn't get off.' Lock opened the dressing-room door and poked his head out. 'Get off,' he said. 'You're shit.'

Since Lamarr started out, comedy has expanded beyond his wildest expectations. 'I couldn't even fucking comprehend making a living at comedy,' he says. 'There weren't that many clubs.' Sean Hughes gave him some good advice. 'He said, "All you need to do on the comedy circuit is to have a tight twenty minutes,"' says Lamarr. 'I didn't even realise. I used to just go on and fuck around and see what would happen and try different material every night.' But even after he realised, he didn't stop fucking around. He once spent an entire twenty-minute set ad-libbing with a couple in the stalls. 'You'd just be so bored of sitting in that dressing room, you'd go, "Right, let's go and fuck this up for a while and see what happens," and I've always liked doing that,' he says. 'It's the easiest job in the world to charm some strangers for twenty minutes and them to leave liking you. It's really simple. So I used to try and go on and wind them up and then make them laugh, and I used to think that's a little bit more of a challenge at least, because making a load of drunk people in a room laugh for twenty minutes isn't that hard.' It's certainly far too easy for Lamarr. 'Loads of shitty acts every night of the week do it. It's not that big a trick really, so sometimes I'd go on and try and make them hate me as much as I could just to see where that would go.'

'We've had your money, you've had your show,' he'd tell the audience at the end of the night, staying onstage and daring them to leave before he did. 'It's finished now. Go on. Fuck off.'

Open Spots

'At the beginning of the night I lied,' says Tim Clark. 'I said there were two acts in this first half. Ladies and gentlemen, there are in fact three.' The audience cheers on cue. 'Someone's going to come up and do five minutes for you.' Regulars will know from his clue that this turn will be a beginner, but while Clark is careful to drop a subtle hint to more seasoned and sympathetic spectators to go easy on this rookie, he doesn't give the game away to tipsy first-time punters, who often labour under the old delusion that heckling actually helps an act along. Top comics can indeed turn a heckle to their advantage, but for an apprentice stand-up, with only a short time in which to shine, hecklers are nothing but a hindrance. Old hands like Clark can weave together impromptu put-downs and proper material into one flawless whole, but this open spot will have to stray off his rehearsed set and shed some of his best gags to deal with any unprompted interruptions. He'll be hoping, praying, that we all shut up and listen. 'Look the punters full in the eyes,' Don Ward tells open spots. 'Don't show them you're nervous, because they'll smell it, and be on to you.' But will he heed Ward's advice?

Jay Sodagar is Anglo-Asian, and although The Store's core philosophy may be anti-racist, he's still shrewd to begin by pre-empting and debunking a prevalent old Asian stereotype, asking if anyone needs a minicab, before moving on to the more sophisticated routines that make up the substantial part of his set. Arranged marriages are the Indian equivalent of *Blind Date*. Students who go to India in their gap year to find themselves are really going to find out what life would be like if their parents cut off their allowance. But not all his material is about his ethnic roots. 'I went into university an A-level boffin and came out a stand-up comedian,' he says, building a bridge between the stage and every graduate in the room. 'I'll keep it to a tight five,' he says, quitting while he's still ahead.

'Ladies and gentlemen, what I didn't say about Jay before he came on was Jay was what we call the open spot, which means he's just started out in the business and came here to do five minutes as a try out to see how he did,' says Clark, returning to the mike. 'And I thought he did all right.' The audience claps, on cue. It's not the loudest or longest round of applause I've ever heard, but it's far warmer and more heartfelt than the tepid sound of polite sympathy. Sodagar's delivery was a bit hesitant, and none of his gags brought the house down. Yet the laughter, though quiet, was consistent, and nobody in the audience took him on. He needs nursing along, but he already has the makings of a good comic.

'I was crapping myself,' admits Sodagar, at the bar during the interval, still breathless from his first five minutes on The Store stage. He played a pub gig last night, but even then, The Store was on his mind. 'I died on my arse because I was so nervous about tonight.' But you're only as bad as your last gig, and he didn't die tonight, so yesterday's defeat is already irrelevant. He also performs on the fledgling Asian comedy circuit, where he can use references that audiences in other clubs won't understand. Yet these shows make up only a minority of his work. Ironically, like black comedians, he refers to non-ethnic gigs as 'mainstream', a term once used by Alternative acts to denote trad comedy.

To a casual punter, a Store open spot may look like the bottom rung on the stand-up ladder, but although any untried wannabe can turn up and take their chances, almost every try out who hits a home run here is already an established act elsewhere. In the past two years, Sodagar has done 200 gigs and has even been running and compering his own comedy club, in nearby Covent Garden, before tonight's unpaid debut at the club where he first saw stand-up live.

Later in the evening, Sodagar is buzzing. Ward has offered him ten minutes on a Friday in March. From five minutes to ten is a step up, and so is Thursday to Friday. It's still unpaid, but he doesn't mind. 'I'm just glad to be working.' He still works afternoons, but mornings are free for writing new material. He'll probably ditch about 90 per cent of this fresh stuff straight away, but 10 per cent might end up in his regular twenty minutes, and a bit may even make his half-spot at The Store in two months' time. Meantime, he's off home to Upton Park in London's East End, and a fridge containing five cans of lager. 'I'm just going to down them all in one go,' he says. 'Get completely pissed.'

'A lot of people who were doing open spots, it was the first place they'd ever played,' marvels Mark Lamarr. 'Their first ever gig would be at half two on a Friday night in front of people who didn't want to watch acts who'd been doing it for years.' On nights like these, nobody could compete with the crowd, and American comic magician John Lenahan would tell the open spots waiting backstage to go home. 'You're going to die,' he'd say. 'Kim and Don will respect you more for leaving.' But none of them ever left. 'They would always go up and die.'

Smarter rookies cut their teeth in smaller clubs, but the greenest beginners head straight for The Store, simply because it's the only comedy club they've ever heard of. 'I don't know whether it was the height of arrogance or the height of ignorance, but the fact that they would try there first was really fucking stupid,' says Lamarr. 'You get people who turn up and they've really got some kind of genuine psychological problem,' says Sean Lock, recalling one woman's first, and final, open spot. 'She started getting angry, which was obviously very funny at the start, but she just carried on getting angrier. She ended up on her knees, slumped on the stage, weeping, saying, "It's all fucking shit." Her whole life collapsed onstage.'

'She had a bag of vegetables,' says Bob Mills, recalling one American who came sensationally unstuck in the open spot. 'She went onstage and she took out a vegetable and said, "Hi, my name's Tommy Turnip. Who's in my bag? Hey, it's my old friend Ronnie Radish."' The audience simply sat and stared, while Tommy and Ronnie talked among themselves. As Mills says, you always give an open spot a few minutes, just in case they're a genius. 'If you only watched a minute of Eddie Izzard or Harry Hill, you'd probably boo them off.' But after four minutes, Cindy Celery started singing, and these punters finally lost their patience. 'She came in the dressing room and she put the bag of vegetables down, and she said, "I guess you people have different vegetables."'

But another American comedienne won a place in Mills' heart, by dying a truly heroic death. 'The five minutes she did seemed to be some kind of rambling introduction to her philosophy on life and comedy, so it was rather churlish to pull her off then because she hadn't actually started, so she did another five, and then she did another five, and then another five, and then she played a tune and it was going absolutely nowhere and not getting any laughs at all.' The red light went on, but she didn't budge, so Kim Kinnie came backstage and told Mills to go on and get her off. Mills hated doing that, especially when punters started laughing, simply to prolong the agony, but she was dying on her arse and he knew he had no choice. Yet before he could haul her off, she suddenly stopped her set and spoke directly to the audience. 'Can I just tell you something about me?' she said. 'I was brought up in the Sixties, in California, and when I left college, I went to work as an environmental crusader. I wanted to become part of that movement. Not an important part. Just a small cog in a movement that somehow made the world a slightly better place to live in. And now I'm forty-nine years old, and all I want to do is get off this stage with a shred of my dignity intact.' And she did. 'The audience threw ash trays,' says Mills, 'but she did.'

'All those people have got a very special place in my heart,' says Mills. 'The people who thought, "I'd like to have a go at that," and had a go. I don't like the ones that hung around too long. Sometimes, you'd see a bad open spot five or six times, and then they became a bore, but the ones who just did one and died gloriously, and then went out the door and never came back, they're special people, because, wherever they are, when you're talking about the history of Alternative Comedy, they can say, "Yes, Alexei Sayle, Ben Elton, Ade and Rik, Paul Merton, Eddie Izzard, Harry Hill, me, we all played there." They're part of it. Of course they are. They've got just as much right as anyone else. Their pictures aren't on the wall but they were there. They had a little go at it and they were shit and god bless them.'

Open spots who admit defeat are readmitted to the fold with a gentle, 'Don't worry about it, mate, everyone does it, it doesn't matter, keep going round the pubs, don't let it get to you.' But some try outs who stiffed still thought they should be getting proper paid gigs. 'How can you tell within five minutes?' they'd ask Kim Kinnie. 'You can within thirty seconds,' says Alan Davies. 'Just the way they go up to the mike, and start moving. How they say hello.'

'I've seen open spots die terribly, and you know they're going to be good,' says Store compere John Mann. 'Material's secondary to presence and persona. If you look comfy onstage and you can carry it off then material will come. Not the other way around.' 'Calm down,' he tells open spots. 'There really is no need to be stressed out here. It's the nicest room in the world.'

Mann's point was proved a few years ago, when he introduced an open spot who froze as soon as he reached the mike. 'Sorry,' said the open spot. 'It's gone. I can't remember any of it.' 'Well, what do you normally do?' asked a punter. 'I don't know,' replied the open spot. 'I just can't remember.' 'Have you got any notes?' asked another helpful punter. 'Yes,' replied the open spot, rummaging through his pockets. 'They're in my jacket.' His jacket was backstage. 'Ask the compere to come back on again,' suggested the first punter. Mann came back on again while the open spot went backstage to check his notes. 'I reintroduced him and he got the most enormous applause when he walked back on,' says Mann. 'And he was dreadful. But nonetheless, it does restore your faith in audiences. Audiences aren't as nasty as you think they are.'

'I couldn't talk to anyone for about a week,' says award-winning stand-up Dominic Holland, recalling his first open spot here. 'When I actually got to The Store, I couldn't even look at anyone. I was bouncing off the walls.' Backstage, he paced up and down, ploughing a lone furrow in the linoleum. When people spoke to him, he couldn't even hear them. But once the compere called his name, his head cleared. He'd been playing the circuit for a couple of years, and had fifteen minutes to choose from, so his best five went down a storm. 'I came off and I went into the dressing room and I was the only person there. I don't think I've ever been as excited in my life, because I'd done The Store, and even if I never got a gig there, I would always say I'd done The Store. It was only five minutes and I didn't get paid, but I did it.' And he still does it, even though a corporate gig pays ten times as much.

Once in a while, along comes an open spot who needs no help from anyone. 'I need you to fill in for eight minutes while I set up,' one newcomer told John Lenahan. Eight minutes stage time is an eternity, but Lenahan obliged, while this try out sawed and hammered away onstage behind him. 'I turn around and he's built this wooden New York skyline,' recalls Lenahan. '"New York, New York" started playing and he walked on wearing these huge wooden Cadillacs on his feet, and he climbed onstage and did this dance to "New York, New York" and then all the lights went out and the New York skyline lit up and the headlights of the cars lit up.' The crowd went wild. 'That was amazing,' Kim Kinnie told him afterwards. 'Do you want a booking?' 'No,' said the open spot. 'I just wanted to see if I could do it.'

Yet Store crowds can kill an open spot with fake kindness. Lenahan brought on one act who got a sarcastic standing ovation for some bog standard impressions of James Cagney and Tommy Cooper. 'You should be ashamed of yourselves,' Lenahan told the crowd, after bringing him back on for several encores. 'I'm not doing it anymore.' 'I have no idea what just happened, but I just have to book you,' Kim Kinnie told the open spot afterwards. 'I don't know when I'm free,' he said. 'Call me,' said Kinnie, but he never did. 'We never heard from him again,' says Lenahan. 'He disappeared into the night.'

'Up your bum, I've had your mum, who hasn't, mate?' Daniel Kitson tells an impertinent punter who strolls along the front row, and across his line of vision. 'Even you?' he asks another punter. 'Has she got no taste?' Kitson is actually an open spot, but you'd never guess it from the casual way he parries this unwanted interruption. 'I've been fucking storming, mate,' he tells another latecomer. 'You've missed a treat.' Kitson's right. He has. But not many open spots would have the balls to say so.

'You've got a very stern face, haven't you, mate?' Kitson asks a morose spectator. 'I'm going to have you tittering before I leave this stage. I might have to tickle you but I don't care.' Open spots often have to fend off hecklers, but they usually leave unresponsive punters well alone. Not Kitson. 'Unfold your arms and let your tits hang free,' he tells a fat bloke in the front row. He even seeks out unheard heckles and makes them public property. 'Don't try protecting him now, madam,' he tells the heckler's girlfriend. 'You said, "You've got a crap jumper," didn't you? Well, I think you'll find it's a tank top. No, I didn't get it off my nan, but I did get it off my grandma. What a funeral that was.'

He's silenced this particular heckler, but his put downs have established a precedent, and now his sleeveless pullover is attracting even more abuse. 'Off, off, off,' chants the crowd, reviving the lynch mob politics of the playground. 'Do you want me to take my tank top off?' he asks. 'We live in a democratic society. We'll put it to the vote. Who wants me to keep the tank top on?' Cheers. 'Who wants me to take the tank top off?' Louder cheers. 'Who wants me to take all my clothes off?' Even louder cheers. 'No, I'm not going to take it off,' he tells us. 'Up your bum.'

Kitson is still ahead on points, but his actual material has become a distant memory. 'Take your glasses off,' shouts another heckler. 'No,' retorts Kitson. 'I've got a mind like a fucking blow torch, haven't I?' he adds, even heckling his own lame attempt at a put down. 'Oh god, it's all gone a bit pear shaped, hasn't it?' And until he returns to his set,

Rising star Daniel Kitson

the best he can do is parry the punches, rather than take control and land some clean blows of his own. 'Have you noticed how it was all going quite well until you opened your mouth, mate?' he tells his initial heckler, in a belated admission that he's bitten off a fair bit more than he can comfortably chew. Yet his brief set has been hilarious, and he departs to a ferocious cheer.

'What a lovely welcome back to the stage,' quips Tim Clark, a tacit admission that despite leaving his pre-prepared set behind, this open spot has very nearly stormed it. Clark is clearly impressed. And so are we. Don Ward sees only a few storming open spots every year. Despite his baptism of fire, or maybe even because of it, Kitson will be back.

A week after Kitson's explosive Store debut, we're in the pub next door to Malcolm Hardee's cosy yet raucous comedy club Up The Creek. Kitson isn't on tonight's bill, although he's played this sometime snooker hall and seaman's mission before, but he lives around the corner. Kitson is one of The Store's newest faces, and, funnily enough, one of its oldest recruits, Malcolm Hardee, is playing pool only a few feet away. Kitson and Hardee are a generation apart, but they look uncommonly alike, and as Hardee finishes his frame of pool and ambles across to meet us, the resemblance becomes uncanny. They could be father and son. Is Daniel Kitson Malcolm Hardee's secret love child? Of course not. But if this book was a novel or a fairy tale, he would be.

Kitson first visited The Store in 1995. He was so transfixed by all the old photos in the stairwell that the door staff had to move him on so other punters could make their way inside. The first show he saw was The Comedy Store Players. 'I couldn't take my eyes off Paul Merton, even when he was offstage,' says Kitson. 'He was the person who got me into stand-up in the first place. I watched him on *Have I Got News For You?* and *Whose Line Is It Anyway?* He was completely debunking the whole thing.' Suitably inspired, he phoned The Store, but they told him they were all booked up, so he decided to leave it for a few years. He was still only in his teens, so time was on his side. He did a drama degree, graduated in the summer of 1998, and tried out for the first time in the autumn. Only a few months later, he was compering London's Comedy Café, doing twenty-minute sets around town, and now his first Store try-out has landed him a half-spot. There's still an awful lot of open road ahead of him, but he's well on his way. By 2001 his act was stong enough to be shortlisted for the Perrier Award.

Nevertheless, it was still nervewracking turning up for his Store debut. 'Hello, I'm Daniel Kitson, I'm the open spot,' Kitson meant to say when he arrived at The Store, but he has an acute stammer from which the stage is his only refuge, and he could barely force the words out. Luckily, he'd often chatted to the bouncers on the door as a punter in the past, and this huge doorman soon put him at his ease. 'Hello, mate, you're a bit of a regular,' said the bouncer, recognising Kitson in his jam jar specs. 'In you go.' Stan Nelson, the stage manager, took him backstage, into the dressing room, where the working comics made him feel at home. 'I'm not sure what it would have been like if I'd died on my arse,' he says. 'I don't know if they'd have been quite as friendly.'

Yet as his time drew near, stagefright overwhelmed him. 'I just started going really shaky,' he recalls. 'I must have been hyperventilating.' 'I'm going to faint,' said Kitson. 'No, you're not,' Paul Zenon reassured him. And as soon as he walked through the door, onto the stage and into the spotlight, all of a sudden he felt fine, and he knew it was going to be all right. 'As soon as I went on and that bloke walked across the front and I went, "I've had your mum," and that got a big laugh, I thought, "Gosh, going to be a piece of piss, this." You know if that gets a big laugh, it's going to be lovely. So from then on I felt completely at home.' Kitson's girlfriend doesn't usually go to his gigs. 'She gets incredibly nervous, far more nervous than me,' he reveals. 'Like she can't stand up. That sort of nervous.' But she was there that night, and she was made up, especially when a punter congratulated him on their way out. Kitson should have many more congratulations to look forward to in future, but whatever else he achieves, it might never feel quite so sweet again.

Lee Hurst

Lee Hurst first phoned The Store for an open spot in February 1991, and was booked in for the following August. 'You mustn't be longer than five minutes,' he was told. 'That's an instruction,' thought Hurst. 'I have to stick to that.' Six months later, he still remembered the five-minute rule. 'I got heckled by a guy, and I nailed him straight away, and it was meat and drink to me – it still is,' he says, of his first try-out, on a Thursday night at the Leicester Square Store. 'I was half ready to tear him apart, lay the law down. And all I could hear in the back of my mind was tick, tick, tick, and I thought, "I haven't got time."'

Don Ward watched his five minutes. 'I'm not going to give you a booking after that,' he told Hurst afterwards. 'I wasn't going to ask for one,' replied Hurst. Hurst never asked for a booking unless he'd ripped the place apart. 'Come down Friday week and do another five minutes,' said Ward.

That Friday, Hurst met Ward back at The Store. 'Listen, Don,' said Hurst. 'I find it very difficult to do five. It takes me that long to say hello some nights.' 'Don't worry about that,' said Ward. Hurst laid the law down that night, and Ward gave him a full booking. Hurst stormed that gig, but neither Don Ward nor Kim Kinnie was there to watch, so Kinnie agreed to see him at The Red Rose, a comedy club in North London. Unluckily, the gig sucked. Luckily, Kinnie never made it. Even luckier, he felt so bad that he hadn't been there, he gave Hurst a gig. The front row was full of policemen, and Hurst did nearly twenty minutes about them off the top of his head. Kinnie was stunned. Only the most seasoned comics stray off their tightest twenty at The Store. Hurst was still trying out, yet he'd had the cheek to busk all but a few minutes. He didn't need to call Kinnie. Kinnie called him. 'What are you doing Friday, Saturday?' asked Kinnie. 'Nothing much,' said Hurst. 'Come and compere The Store,' said Kinnie. Hurst had never even been in the audience on a Friday or a Saturday before, let alone onstage. 'Sure,' he said.

Hurst was confident, but he would have been a fool not to feel nervous. 'I'd just started dating this girl who'd come up for the weekend,' he recalls. 'I had to dump her on my friend because I didn't want her there while I did my first gig.' Nick Revell was on the bill that weekend, and during the break between the early and late shows, he gave Hurst some welcome tips. Kinnie came backstage and overheard their conversation. 'Have you not done a Friday or a Saturday here?' asked Kinnie. 'No,' replied Hurst. 'So you've never done a late show?' said Kinnie. 'Boy, have I been a cunt to you.' Yet neither of them need have worried. Hurst was pumped up, the late show went even better than the early one, and after that he compered a weekend every month. 'Even though it was a smaller room, there was still that big snap of a laugh because it was packed.' And that big snap has never left him.

I went to visit Hurst at his own Backyard Comedy Club in Bethnal Green. It's a converted warehouse, behind a brewery, opposite the old site of an asylum now commonly known as Nutter's Park. It's called The Backyard because it's around the corner from his lifelong East End home. Hurst was born in Tower Hamlets, and he's lived in this London borough ever since. Back in the late Eighties, he ran a local comedy club, The Friday Approach, then Backyard Cabaret, and only packed it in to build a big enough reputation to open his own permanent local venue. A decade later, he's finally come home. When he hosts a show here, his passion for the place shows in the warmth he generates around the room, but his labour of love isn't confined to show times. Hurst has been here all morning, mucking in with the painting and decorating. This should be his lunch break, but he merely stops to talk, not eat. 'No matter how good I make this club, it will never be The Store,' he says. 'I've had nights here that have been superb, and I've had nights at The Store that have been superb, but it's that difference between a team that can win a league and a team that can win a cup. The Store will always be at the top of the league.'

Hurst reckons the toughest Store show is late-night Friday. The crowd is pumped up in the first half, and so for the first few acts, this boozy atmosphere is a bonus. But acts further down the bill pick up the tab. 'The energy has just been sapped out of them by the interval,' he says. 'It's like the air rushing out of a balloon.' Not many comics can whip up a drunken audience in the small hours. 'I don't think I've ever seen more than half a dozen comics who can regularly close the late show and blow it away.' Many more are defeated by the weight of The Store's reputation. 'They shit themselves,' says Hurst. 'They're trying too hard.' And so, sadly, lots of fine comics never crack it. For them, that clock is still ticking. 'Not playing The Store doesn't mean you're a bad comic,' he says. 'But playing The Store means you're a good one.'

Backstage

Keep Out, scolds a sign on the dressing room door, but nobody takes a lot of notice, at least not after hours. People stroll in and out without knocking. Lots of Store acts tend to double up, especially at weekends, rushing across town to play another club, and dashing back, like stand-up Cinderellas, just in time for their midnight turn. Close up, outside the spotlight, these comics look older than they did onstage, and their smart stage clothes seem incongruous in this scruffy back room, like dinner dress by daylight. This discrepancy isn't unusual. It's a good sign. Natural-born comics tend to look most at home onstage, and a bit out of place off it.

The cramped dressing room is pretty rudimentary, but it's a palace compared to what the same comics had to put up with only a few years before. Now there's even a shower. Mr Tim Clark, Suite 23, reads a requisitioned sign stuck on the bathroom door. Not many comics use the shower, although the toilet comes in handy. There's a mirror, framed within a vaudeville necklace of light bulbs, but nobody ever pays it much attention, at least not while anyone else is looking. Character acts have never really clicked here, and comediennes tend to be treated like honorary lads, backstage as well as onstage. Hence there's not much call for make-up. The noticeboard is festooned with tabloid press cuttings: Bob Mills in his birthday suit, and a boyhood Lee Hurst, sporting a full head of hair. 'Clive Borr is Nick Wilty,' reads Wilty's surreal, self-deprecating small ad, from the lookalikes corner of *The Stage*. Even curiouser, Geordie comic Dave Johns has placed a similar advert, offering his services as a Michael Jackson impersonator. Despite looking nothing like the prince of pop, apparently he actually had a few replies.

There's a blackboard with tonight's turns chalked upon it, and a monitor mounted on the wall above, so waiting comics can watch what's happening onstage. The small screen growls and flickers as Stan replays the video of tonight's show. More than any other art form, stand-up is all about being there, in one particular place at one un-repeatable moment. An instant later, it's gone for good, like it never even happened. And so seeing an act that you saw in the flesh less than an hour before repeated on tape feels irreverent, even strangely ghoulish, like a home movie of an old friend or a dead relative. Spontaneity, feigned and practised, is stand-up's fundamental illusion. Seen for a second time, so soon after, carefully rehearsed gags that felt like sudden flashes of inspiration first time around now sound tired and mechanical, trapped in suspended animation. Nick Wilty reaches up and turns the telly off.

'The Store is like a family,' says American comic Dave Fulton, backstage, straight after a show, amid the gaggle of working and resting comics who gather in this dressing room after virtually every gig. 'You know it's a good club when comics come here just to hang out. There's a lot of comedy clubs in England right now but there's very few that comics would come to after they've done their shows.' 'In the dressing room, the banter's brilliant,' said Harry Hill, 'everyone trying to outdo everyone else.' 'They should film the dressing room,' agrees Phil Davey. 'Sometimes, it's a disappointment to go out onstage and do a gig because you're having such a good time, and by the time you get back you know you've missed twenty minutes of top gags.'

However that doesn't make it the best place to prepare for a pressure gig. 'You really have to make the grade, or else people don't even talk to you,' claims Davey. 'If they do, they talk to you until someone important walks in and then they immediately talk to them. They all talk about their latest TV show and their latest offer from Channel 4.' 'It's always very precious,' concurs the up-and-coming comedienne Gina Yashere. 'You've got a whole load of egos, a whole bundle of nerves in there. Everybody's nervous. You can't concentrate.' Gina prefers to sit and watch the show on the monitor, or out front with Stan Nelson in the sound booth. 'I like to get a feel of the audience, and see what they're laughing at,' she explains. 'Some audiences like it a bit more rude. Some audiences like a little bit of surrealism. Some audiences may be a little bit rowdy, or a bit subdued. You have to try and read the audience and see what they want, see what they like and don't like. You get that by watching the other comedians, and seeing what gets the biggest laughs.' Laughter is the final arbiter. Unlike applause, you can't fake it, and its absence is deafening.

For open spots, going backstage can be even more intimidating than doing the actual gig. 'I can remember all the comics being really silent with me, and I felt it was a really horrible atmosphere, and they spoke a different language to me, because they was quite educated and they were speaking on a different level to what I know,' says ex-boxer and -hairdresser Ricky Grover, recalling the long wait backstage before his Store debut. 'You cunts,' he thought. 'You could have made me feel all right.' 'Now, I always make a point, when there's a new open spot, to try and make them feel comfortable.' He felt comfortable with Don Ward. 'Don spoke my language,' he says. He felt far more at home with the bouncers than he did backstage. 'When I went in that dressing room, I thought "All these comics, they know something I don't,"' he says. 'I couldn't sort of read and write until a few years before I started comedy. I weren't into all that, so I felt like we was just worlds apart. I thought these people were better than me.'

'It's very easy for a young comic to screw up his chances by being a cunt in the dressing room,' says Jenny Eclair. 'There's got to be a little bit of deferential treatment to the right people.' 'If they were a bit quiet and a bit nervous and they were asking for advice, that was fine,' says Jo Brand, remembering the open spots who shared her dressing room under Leicester Square. 'People were fairly kind to them.' But if they sprawled all over the furniture and announced, 'I'm going to blow this fucking place apart,' that encouragement quickly curdled. 'In which case people were pleased that they died on their arse.' 'People would cut you down if you were cocky,' agrees Sean Lock. 'When you were an open spot it was a terrifying place.' Phil Davey believes the dressing room is the worst place to be for open spots, and that it's far better to wait your turn in the back stalls. 'Don't go into this bloody madhouse, where you'll just feel like a complete wanker.'

'You're on next,' Geordie comic Mickey Hutton would tell open spots. 'By the way, you're shit and you're going to die.' 'I used to hate it backstage here,' says comedian Mike Gunn, recalling his open spot apprenticeship. 'Everyone was really relaxed and Mickey Hutton was strolling about going, "You're going to die."' Hutton said that to every open spot, but back then Gunn didn't realise that this was simply a rougher, tougher way of saying break a leg. 'I didn't realise he did it to everybody. I just thought he hated me. And I wasn't able to take that as a joke at the time.' 'Mickey wouldn't give you an inch,' agrees Jeff Green. 'He was always saying, "You're going to die tonight."' But eventually, Green got his sweet revenge. 'I took the mike from the sound desk and every time Mickey went to do a routine I'd finish his punchline for him, offstage, and so he'd try something else, and I'd do it again.'

'Harry Hill tells a story about when he did his open spot here,' says Mickey Hutton. 'I was compering. As he walks in, I was going, "Dead man walking, dead man walking," and he always mentions that every time I see him. I'd seen Harry before and I knew he was going to be brilliant. I wouldn't do that to somebody who I knew couldn't hack it.'

At least Hutton doesn't ignore open spots. If anything, that feels even worse. But established turns are wary of being too welcoming to try outs backstage. 'Chances are, you could be nice to someone and they'll get up and tell the most hideous racist fucking bollocks,' says Hutton's fellow Geordie comic John Fothergill. 'No one knows until the first gag.' Several open spots told me how comic magician Paul Zenon wished them luck while other acts ignored them. 'Don't worry about it,' he tells them. 'It's not the end of the world if you have a bad one. It's only fucking comedy.' Zenon's trad roots may be one reason why he looks out for other acts. 'Something I did notice about doing the old mainstream stuff years ago, there was more camaraderie at that time.' Zenon had to wait only five weeks for his open spot. Now it's more like five months. He needed no recommendation. Then as now, The Store accepts all comers, no questions asked. 'That was very healthy, from their point of view as well, because it meant that some acts, although they were dreadful, were very funny because they were so bad, whereas nowadays even the open spots tend to be quite good.'

Today's backstage buzz isn't so much sex and drugs and rock and roll as parenthood, mineral water and mortgages. 'A few years ago everyone would be talking about the party they'd been to and the drug they were experimenting with,' says John Mann. 'Now people are saying, "I've been up all night because the baby's not well."' Football is a perennial source of dressing-room debate, and like soccer itself, the comedy circuit has been transformed by telly, from a world where everyone earned similarly paltry sums into a two-tier league. Relatively impoverished losers in the Nationwide, big money winners in the Premier League. 'Some people, particularly the ones that have done quite ordinary mundane jobs before comedy, it's just a great way of earning a living compared to getting up at six in the morning and going to a factory,' says Zenon.

'So there are some jobbing comics, there are some career comics, and the good thing is that anybody who is very obviously a career comic gets taken down a peg or two.'

The dressing room is a waiting room, where workers dawdle between shifts. 'Frank Skinner is my favourite act of all time because he makes me laugh in the dressing room,' says Mickey Hutton. 'There's lots of people who you'd never want to get stuck in the dressing room with.' Some of the funniest stand-ups have the least to say back-stage, and when they insist on trying out material in the dressing room, Mandy Knight feels like killing them. 'Can't you talk like a normal person?' she thinks. And then she remembers normal people don't do this job. No wonder she sometimes tells them, 'I think I'll watch it from the front today.'

Sean Meo

The first time Sean Meo went to The Store, Julian Clary was on the bill. Afterwards, he peeped into the dressing room, told Clary, 'That was really good,' and felt like a complete arse. In the late Eighties, he was a full-time snooker player, reaching the last eight of the English Amateur Championships. Now he'd stopped playing snooker, he was looking for something else, and he finally found it at The Store. But when Meo first tried out there, he had to follow Jerry Sadowitz. 'He was going off the boil, and ranting at everyone and he just wound the whole audience up and then left before they had a chance to turn around. I went straight into the cauldron of hate.' 'I can't believe that people can get through this,' thought Meo. 'You're just popping your head up above the trenches in no man's land and waiting for them to kill you.'

Ten years later, he's one of the top stand-ups on the circuit, but it wasn't an easy ride. 'I've talked to a lot of comedians about how long it takes them to get to the point where they have a bookable twenty minutes, and it took me a lot longer than most. It took me a good two or three years of really slogging away and thinking about giving up quite a lot, although I always think every year I'm going to.'

We're sat upstairs at Up The Creek. On the wall above us is a painting of the Last Supper, with Store veterans like Julian Clary, Harry Enfield, Jerry Sadowitz and French and Saunders gathered around the Christlike central figure of Malcolm Hardee. Coincidentally, Hardee tells me, Ben Elton occupies the position of Judas Iscariot in this fresco. Downstairs, Hardee is hosting his traditional Sunday night show, a haphazard, jovial mish mash of old pros, young rookies and hopeless amateurs. Meo is closing. Last year he did over 200 gigs. 'The only places people really die, probably, are

The Store and Up The Creek,' says Mark Lamarr. And they're probably the only places where people really raise the roof.

'It's no good to be adequate,' says Meo, a dapper, balding man, with the quiet self-assurance of a professional sportsman, in a snatched half-hour before his finale. 'You've got to rip the roof off the place, because Don Ward does not need you. He's fielding two or three hundred calls a day from wannabes. So I took it upon myself to get that good.' And in the end, he did. 'I wanted a half-spot and he gave me twenty, and then I was in big trouble.' Once you graduate to a full twenty-minute spot, the goodwill that greets beginners is gone for good. Suddenly, he was on a bill alongside rising stars like Bob Mills, Bill Bailey and Steve Coogan, in front of punters who assumed he'd be just as good. 'When you're quite raw, you don't know where all the breaks are,' says Meo, as distant laughter rumbles down below. 'You don't know how to sit on the laughs and let it go quiet. You're scared of all that. You're scared that someone will snipe you before you get going, and you rely very heavily on your opening gag, and if that doesn't bite, if someone walks past with a tray of drinks, and they don't listen to the set-up, you can be sunk.'

At first, Meo found fighting his way into The Store almost as scary as performing. 'I was so scared to actually go to the front of the queue and say, "I'm performing," that I queued up,' he says. These close encounters with prospective punters were scarcely risk free. One night, Meo found himself queuing behind a bloke who was so drunk that he'd become handcuffed to his briefcase. 'Oh Christ,' thought Meo, mindful of the chaos this pissed-up wage mule could cause inside. 'We're going to The Store, we're going to The Store, we're going to The Store,' chanted the drunk, utterly indifferent to the stares of spectators all around him. 'We're going in, we're going in, we're going in,' he chanted, as the queue started to shuffle forward. 'We're nearly there, we're nearly there, we're nearly there,' he chanted, as the queue snaked around the corner. 'They're chucking me out, they're chucking me out, they're chucking me out,' he chanted, as the bouncers dispatched him from whence he came. 'Thank God for that,' thought Meo, but his relief lasted only until he stepped onstage. 'As I walked on, just as I was about to say, "Good evening," this voice bellowed out from the audience, "I've sneaked back in, I've sneaked back in, I've sneaked back in."'

Since then, he's followed Lee Evans and Eddie Izzard. 'They might be famous, but it doesn't bother me.' In fact it's often the biggest names who feel bothered. Last time Jack Dee played The Store, he told Meo he felt a bit nervous to be back in a smaller room. 'I've done gigs in theatres,' says Meo. 'You can still get the banter but it's not so immediate.' Which is why the big stars keep coming back, to test drive new material, or just to take a look. 'You get a lot of people dropping in,' says Meo. 'People who don't play anymore, people who play it rarely, people who've just been touring pop in. You see them at the back.'

Doing a weekend at The Store is a sign that a comedian has arrived. 'There are some people who lie about it on their CV,' says Meo. '"Regular at The Comedy Store", and you know that they regularly buy a ticket to get in and that's about it.' Yet once you've fought to get into The Store, you're fighting to get out of it. 'You don't get anywhere unless you really push it. Adam Bloom's testament to that. I remember him doing his first gig down there, and he said, "You'd better be really nice to me, or I won't put you on my TV show."' It was bloody presumptuous, but Bloom is now beginning to bridge that big gap between the club circuit and national theatre tours. 'At least he believes in himself,' thought Meo. 'He's got a lot more confidence than I had at his stage.'

For rookies, getting those early gigs can be nearly as nervewracking as doing them. 'They'll be hunting down the owners of The Store, and frequently getting someone at the office door saying, "He's not in today," and you're sure he is.' Meo knew he'd cracked it when they told him to bring his diary. 'Before that it was always me going up with a diary and going, "Is the owner around?" And knowing he was in the office, hiding. And I don't blame him either, because he doesn't have to book you.' But when he became a real insider, and ate his first half-price club sandwich in the inner sanctum of the Leicester Square Store back bar, he felt like the youngest member of The Magnificent Seven.

Yet in that spartan dressing room, not every comic was magnificently kind. 'I'll never forget how they ignored you,' he says. 'One of them came up and said, "Are you on tonight?" And I said, "Yeah." And he said, "You're going to die." And I thought, "That really isn't what I want to hear. That's not helping at all." I thought, "If I ever get to your stage, I'm never going to fucking say that," and I don't. I try not to. It's very easy to go on after someone's died and belittle them onstage and ignore them off, and I try not to do that.' Some acts were supportive, some didn't care either way, and others made him think, 'I hope they're not in the dressing room, and if they are I'll have to leave.' But this was easier said than done. 'There's nowhere to hide.' And for all the atmosphere of the Leicester Square Store, the Piccadilly Circus Store plays far better. 'It's not a pretty room to look at,' he says, 'but when it's full, it's the best gig in England.'

Peter Kay

Peter Kay is still only in his mid-twenties, with only a few years' stage time behind him, but this portly, babyfaced comic is the closest thing I've seen to a stand-up prodigy. Like all prodigies, his talent is elusive. The actual material is nothing to write home about: a rag bag of everyday observation and shameless groaners, but the delivery is a dream. I've never seen a comic so young and relatively raw who looks so utterly at home onstage. 'What's up with them?' he asks, as a commotion at the bar disrupts his set. 'Someone got a car boot sale on or something?' He's equally unphased when enthusiastic punters try to join in. 'Shut up!' he protests. 'I've only just got on! I've only got eight minutes!' Even when an invitation to clap along with his musical finale elicits a minimal response, he takes this potential humiliation in his stride. 'What the fuck d'you need?' he asks, unabashed. 'A metronome?' And when a Carry On cackle punctuates one of his punchlines, he quips, 'I thought Sid James were dead.' More like reincarnated.

Peter Kay's first taste of comedy was a best man's speech at his mate's wedding, which turned into a twenty-minute routine. Encouraged, he entered the 1996 North-west Comedian Of The Year, first won in 1992 by Caroline Aherne. In his first formal gig, he won his heat. In his second, he won the final. 'He came on last at the end of a very long night,' says Dave Spikey, the compere that night, who now writes and performs with Kay in Channel 4's *Phoenix Nights*. 'He came on and just blew them away.' As Spikey told his wife when he got home that night, 'He's only done four gigs and he's funnier than I am.'

Less than a year later, Kay went to the Edinburgh Festival for the first time, where he won So You Think You're Funny? The following year, back in Edinburgh, he was shortlisted for the Perrier Award. He's presented *The Big Breakfast*, played a carpenter in *Coronation Street*, and even appeared at the Royal Variety Performance. He's also been nominated for Top Stand Up and Top TV Comedy Newcomer at the British Comedy Awards, and racked up two Channel 4 series all of his own. Not bad for a cinema usher from Bolton who claimed, with his usual flair for comedic licence, to have been sacked from his job as head of fruit and veg at a cash and carry for pricing an iceberg lettuce as a cabbage; from behind the bar at Yates's Wine Lodge for trying to get a head on a pint of lager; from a bingo hall for putting the wrong fluid in the dishwasher and almost poisoning 300 pensioners; and from a front of house job at Bolton's Octagon Theatre for telling Des Barnes out of *Coronation Street* he couldn't come in wearing white jeans. 'I didn't do anything bad,' he says, in The Store's crowded dressing room straight after tonight's show. 'I weren't pushing people off ladders. I just kept messing about.'

Kay first played The Store when he came down to London to warm up for *Parkinson*. His dad came too, to celebrate his fiftieth birthday, and took a photo of his son outside The Store, in front of his billing on the noticeboard. 'Don't think about who's played here,' he told himself. 'It's just like any other club anywhere.' But it wasn't. Kay went down well, yet uniquely, he opted to quit while he was ahead. 'I've done that now,' he decided. 'I don't want to go back.' And he never did. Until tonight. 'If I keep doing it all the time it just becomes like another club.' He still lives with his mum. 'When I'm at home, I feel safe,' he says. 'There's something about London that frightens me.'

He finds The Store's tight twenty-minute sets constricting. 'I've got a bit of a reputation for going on and on and on,' he says. 'As long as they're having a good time I'm not bothered. If they weren't, then I would go off. I'm not that much of an egomaniac to keep going until they're all bloody asleep.' But he does like to do more than merely rattle out one-liners. 'I always try and go full circle on a story,' he adds. 'It becomes more like a piece of theatre then to me.' Since there still aren't nearly so many clubs up North as there are down South, northern comics can't imitate their southern counterparts and keep on polishing the same old twenty-minute set. 'People tell you if you've done stuff before. They'll say, "I've heard it," so you're always pushing yourself to do more material. Down here, you can go round and round and round.

'Comedians are miserable,' he says. 'They'll come off and say, "The lighting weren't right, that microphone's fucked, they're a bit dead tonight, what's the matter with them lot?" And then I'll go on and do it and I come off and it's fine.' Audiences sense his confidence from the moment he steps onto that stage, and almost always respond in kind. Kay seems fearless behind the mike, but he wasn't always quite so confident. 'I had fears when I first started that I wouldn't translate outside the North-west.' He had no need to be afraid. 'It's the rhythm, isn't it? Sometimes you can tell a joke and if it's said a certain way, they'll laugh even though they don't even know what they're bloody laughing at.' Unlike a lot of other acts, he doesn't want to trek around the country, which is one reason he's done only a couple of gigs at The Store. 'A lot of comedians sleep on people's floors,' he says. 'I don't like doing that. If I wanted a life like that I'd go and work in a bloody all-night garage like I used to.'

'The last time I were here, I threw a pint of beer over someone's head. I came on and some lad had been really noisy out front and I picked a pint up and there were only a bit left and I threw it over his head.' Kay also picked up a fork from the floor. 'I were gonna throw it at him.' Luckily, he decided not to. 'Don were laughing about it, but I heard that later he were a bit pissed off.' It only goes to show that all good comics suffer from first-night nerves. 'I were that scared,' he says. 'I weren't doing it for attention. I think I just did it because I were angry, and I wanted it to go so well.' But like all the best comics, he's learned to hide his stagefright, and channel his adrenalin. 'I'm not as scared as I used to be.' Sounds like punters' pints are a bit safer from now on.

Punters

There are really only three rules for watching comedy: don't arrive late, don't sit at the front and don't answer back. And if you must break any of these rules, whatever you do, never break more than one of them at once. 'Where are you from?' compere John Mann asks two punters who are breaking rules one and two simultaneously. 'There's a guy here from Halifax. He got here on time.' But at least they're wise enough to leave rule number three unbroken. So long as you smile and nod and admit defeat, the compere will soon move on in search of the next gag.

A weekend at The Store has a rhythm that's all its own, and comics ignore these collective mood swings at their peril. 'Thursday's a nice crowd,' says observational stand-up Mark Maier. 'Friday, they can be a little bit pissed up, a bit lethargic.' Midnight shows can go either way, but Saturday's early show is acknowledged as the best club gig in the land. And since London is currently recognised as the world's stand-up capital, it may even be the best one on the planet. At eight o'clock, The Store's 400 punters can feel like 4,000.

Mandy Knight isn't the only comic who sometimes tires of midnight shows. So many times, she's stood up there and thought, 'You're pissed. I don't want to be here. It's really late. What are you doing here, you fools? Why are you asleep at a comedy club that you've paid twelve quid to get into? Why don't you just go home?' In time, high hopes make way for weary pragmatism. 'I know I'm good,' she thinks. 'I'm not going to try and prove it to you just because you're pissed.'

The proximity of the audience also takes some getting used to. 'They're right in your

face, eating chips and burgers and swigging beer, and you can see every expression on all the faces in the front six or seven rows,' says Cutting Edge regular Paul Thorne. 'The ones that aren't laughing, the ones that don't get it because they're Swedish, the ones that you know don't get it because they don't like you or they want to do the talking.' And some punters present problems even when they're having fun. One night, Thorne was constantly interrupted by a man who kept snorting like a pig. Thorne went off on a long flight of fancy about him sniffing for truffles. After several minutes of this tirade, this snorter and his girlfriend got up and walked out. He'd driven away the punter who'd been laughing loudest at his gags.

'There was a woman in the audience who had this astonishing laugh,' recalls Lee Hurst. 'It just continued through the whole set, and I had to keep referring to it. You ask any comic, somebody with an obscure laugh is actually a potential nightmare, but I managed to keep it evenly paced all the way through, and then I finally met her about three years later. It was Yvette Fielding off of *Blue Peter*. And it was just so bizarre, and the funny thing was, it was a very dirty joke as well, so it was quite ironic. Here's one I prepared earlier.'

'What a show we've got for you tonight,' says Mickey Hutton. 'It's shite. Lock the doors. I'm the best on.' A woman shouts something nonsensical, but Hutton is hard to rattle. One late show, he went on in a power cut without sound or lights, and did his set with a hand-held torch. 'I don't speak slapper,' he tells her. But she isn't the only lippy punter in tonight, and soon Hutton barely has time to pause between put downs. 'Save your breath. You've got girlfriends to blow up when you get home.' It's all basic stuff, but how sophisticated do you feel after a hard day's toil, followed by a hard night's drinking in a West End bar? 'I'm a professional,' Hutton reassures the rest of us. 'Like their mums.' His female heckler isn't finished yet, so Hutton resorts to a more drastic remedy. 'Put the lights up, sound man,' says Hutton, but the stage manager has gone AWOL, so Hutton has to dash offstage into the sound booth, bring up the house lights himself, and then sprint back onstage. 'She's not much of a looker, is she?' he asks us, surveying his female foe. 'Have I seen you and your mate in *Viz*?' His stand-up radar is remarkably acute. Like The Fat Slags, and Hutton, she's from Newcastle. She's also a physics student. 'I don't believe it,' says Hutton, suitably impressed. 'I've met a brainy Geordie. I bet you wear knickers and everything. One pair of knickers in the whole of Newcastle and she's wearing them.'

A late-night audience at The Store is like a heckling hydra. You chop off one talking head, and two sprout up in its place. Sure enough, no sooner has Hutton subdued his female heckler than a male troublemaker takes over where she left off. 'Does the building site know you've left yet?' Hutton asks him, but it turns out he's a student, too. This show is starting to feel like an episode of *University Challenge*. Does anyone in this audience actually work for a living, or are undergraduates the only punters stupid enough to join in? This student is reading biochemistry. 'You couldn't knock me up a woman?' asks Hutton.

Hutton can tame the rowdiest audience, but the heckles still hurt. 'One night, I went on and the whole audience was shouting, "Fuck off,"' he recalls. 'In the end, they realised there was nothing they could say to us, and they realised that I had complete disdain for them.' 'You really hate them, don't you?' said Lee Hurst, backstage. 'Yes I really hate them,' replied Hutton. 'They weren't fun. They've got to be fun. Just to shout "Fuck off" isn't funny. It's vicious and it's nasty. Other times, people heckle under their breath, and you can't say anything to them because if you do, people at the back don't realise what you're talking about.'

The best heckles of all are the ones that take the evening onto another level. 'A good heckle is great,' says Hutton. 'I love a good heckle.' One night, he was doing everything right, but the audience remained unresponsive. 'What's wrong with you?' asked Hutton. 'You're using the wrong mike,' replied a punter. 'What do you mean?' asked Hutton, confused. 'That mike over there's funnier,' said the heckler, pointing to another mike stand upstage, so Hutton divided the rest of his set between two different microphones. The audience groaned at the gags he did on one of them, and laughed at the gags he did on the other.

And when there's a celebrity in the audience, Hutton turns the tables. 'Do you remember Chesney Hawkes?' he asks me. 'He was in the audience one night.' So

Hutton and Bill Bailey sang 'I Am The One And Only – This Is My One And Only Hit'. 'Chesney Hawkes to his credit came backstage with a couple of beers and said, "You wankers," and laughed about it.'

The Store audience isn't static. It's changing all the time. 'The audience and the performer had much more of a relationship,' says performer and punter Vivienne Soan, of the atmosphere at the Soho Store. 'The actual success of the show depended on give and take between the two, whereas now, either the performer is in control or the audience is. If the audience is in control then the performer doesn't get to do his act, and if the performer's in control then the audience laugh.' Her fellow Soho Store veteran Tom Tickell believes that to succeed, The Store had to conform. 'The number of people who found radical comedy funny was pretty small. This is not surprising because I don't think it is funny. If it was going to be a success, it had to become mainstream, and I'm all in favour of that.' And today's audience feels much the same. 'They're not into alternatives and looking for radical solutions. They're looking for something funny.' Tickell feels far more comfortable in today's mainstream crowd than in the more radical audience of 1979. 'It's much warmer. It's much less self-conscious. It goes to be entertained. It doesn't want to change the world.'

Paul Zenon reckons today's late-show crowd is 'composed partly of kind of *Guardian*-reading right-on liberal-educated middle classes, and partly of drunken rugby players who want to hear up-the-bum jokes.' Leicester Square spectators were a lot less diverse. 'They were a hell of a lot more PC than now. Now, The Store is so well established, I go and do shows abroad where they've heard of The Store, and this is middle-aged businessmen in Italy. At that time it was very much a young, middle-class liberal kind of community that went to live comedy.' Once, he cracked a joke about men and added, 'Isn't that right, girls?' A female punter stood up and said, 'We're not girls – we're women.' He hadn't meant any harm, but he learned his lesson soon enough. 'You had to tread carefully, particularly being a Northern end of the pier oik.'

Nevertheless, Zenon still found Alternative audiences more receptive than the trad punters he'd left behind. 'You could actually do something that was a bit more tangential, esoteric and experimental and people would go with it and understand what you were trying to do.' Not like working men's clubs, then or now. 'They still have to have a punchline that rhymes with the word tits,' he says. 'It might sound a bit superior, but I can say that, being northern and working class.'

Sometimes the house can turn in the few hours between an early show and a late show. Two of Paul Zenon's best and worst Store gigs were on the same night. The early show was a breeze. 'Probably one of the best shows I've ever had,' he says. 'There are just some gigs where you go on and you come off and you know you can't do anything wrong. You're tempted to piss off at that point because it ain't gonna get any better.' And then in the late show, only a few hours later, punters were booing. 'I did the same venue with the same number of people and the same type of people and I'm doing the same set virtually word for word, and I've had the best and worst gig I've ever had the same night, so what's changed?' he wondered. 'Alcohol is the answer. For me or them, I'm not sure.' Other crowds are too quiet. 'Sometimes you get a very polite audience which you appreciate but they're just not going for it. Other times you get that little bit of heckling that helps and you can feed off it.' And the dynamics of The Store tend to push an audience one way or the other. 'It's the best gig on the circuit and the best room to work, but if it goes badly it can make it one of the worst rooms because everybody is so tight,' he says. 'There's no escape. There's people on all three sides of you and they're very close because of the seating, so if you are having a hard time you really feel like you're in the middle of a load of people that hate you.'

Late shows are always a lottery, however good you are. Before his first late show, comedian Mike Gunn was so worried that he'd get heckled that he drove his workmates mad by telling them to heckle him throughout the day. It was useless preparation. The only way you can practise heckle put-downs is by doing them for real. 'You and me could have been a double act,' he tells hecklers now, 'but I've already got one arsehole.' And if things get really tough, he can always fall back on his impressions. 'I can do one of your girlfriend having an orgasm,' he tells unruly punters. 'I doubt you'd recognise it. Some of the bouncers will.' And now he quite likes a bit of heckling, even though when he came to watch he never would have dreamt of joining in. 'I certainly never sat in the front row as a punter. I always wanted to be out of sight, out of mind. I would hate to have been picked on by a comic.'

'Friday late show at The Store is as near as you'll get to a fight,' says Ricky Grover. 'You've got to really be able to hit them. If you give them a minute, you're going to get KO'd.' So he never gave them a second. 'It's the nearest thing you can get to boxing,' explains Grover an ex-boxer himself. 'Dying is like getting knocked out. You're on your own. There's no one there to help you. The build-up is exactly the same. "What am I doing here? What am I standing here for?" Then all of a sudden, you're out there, the light's in your face, you're away, and as soon as you get that first laugh, it's like throwing your first good punch.' Unlike some other comics, he's never been physically attacked on stage. 'I had a tangerine thrown at my head once,' he says. 'That's the nearest I've got.'

'I'm scared,' lorry driver turned stand-up Kevin McCarthy told Jack Dee in the dressing room before his Store debut. 'We all are,' said Dee. Dee gave him some tips and told him to have a good time, but McCarthy, a bearded barrel of a bloke, walked onstage to a barrage of abuse. 'You fat bastard!' yelled the whole room. 'For fuck's sake, somebody say something nice,' pleaded McCarthy. A punter stood up. 'He was enormous. I didn't know whether to hit him or climb him.' 'I think you're fucking lovely,' said the punter. 'The whole place went up, and I was off.'

'Are you heckling?' Simon Bligh asks a loud-mouthed punter, compering a Friday night show. 'Or are you shouting out all the words you know?' On comes Paul Tonkinson. Tonkinson won the 1992 *Time Out* comedy award, but what the press giveth, the press soon taketh away. He's since been called the most annoying stand-up in the world by London's *Evening Standard*. Actually, that's one of those critical quotes that's so bad it's rather good, and he was sufficiently shrewd and sporting to reproduce it in the programme for his solo show at the subsequent Edinburgh Festival. But tonight, bad reviews are the least of his worries, because he's just met the most annoying heckler in the world.

'You've got a nice jumper,' shouts his heckler. Tonkinson is wearing the sort of patterned pullover that grandmas knit for their grandsons. In any other art form, this wouldn't matter. 'This is not a catwalk,' counters Tonkinson. 'This is a comedy club.' But comedy clubs obey the politics of the playground, and his heckler won't let it lie. 'Light up,' Tonkinson tells the sound booth. 'I want to see this cunt. What are you wearing?' The house lights go up, but this heckler is too drunk or daft to be embarrassed. When Orwell wrote that ignorance is strength, this probably wasn't what he had in mind, but it's a pretty good illustration of invincible stupidity. Tonkinson tries to laugh it off. 'I'm paranoid now. People in the front row are slagging off my trainers.'

He's doing everything right, but tonight it's to no avail. 'I'm Paul and I've got a shit jumper and a shit haircut, but I'm a funny cunt so give me a fucking chance.' Yet his heckler has found allies around the room. 'Off, off, off,' chants this growing throng. 'I'm not taking my jumper off because you'll hate my T-shirt,' says Tonkinson, but this only fans the flames. Eventually, he gives in and peels off the offending pullover, to reveal a Manchester United top. Tonkinson was right. The barrage of abuse is now overwhelming. 'Doesn't football bring people together in a wonderful way?' says Tonkinson. 'Put your jumper on,' says his heckler. 'What sort of gig is this?' asks Tonkinson, but he already knows the answer. It's just another Friday night at The Store.

It may look like Tonkinson is dying, but the fact that everyone is having so much fun shows he's still in control, if not in charge. Watching comics die can be compulsive viewing, but it's never half this funny. 'I'm going to put my jumper back on,' says Tonkinson. 'Burn it,' shouts his heckler. 'Get over it,' snaps Tonkinson, losing his cool for an instant. 'Get your hair cut,' replies his heckler. Sometimes it's best to simply roll with the punches, rather than try to impose your authority upon a rowdy room, and this is one of those unruly nights where the best form of defence is to simply keep smiling through. Tonkinson has done his job. He's made us laugh for twenty minutes. And does it really matter if during these twenty minutes we laughed at him rather than with him? Of course his actual material is far funnier, so in a way we've wasted our own time tonight, as our teachers always told us. But a comedy club is one of the few places where adults can muck about like kids in a classroom. And without this ability to shape events, punters might as well sit in silence in the cinema, or stay home and watch TV. Tonkinson will have another opportunity to do his proper set, back here at midnight tonight.

'That was Paul Tonkinson and his car boot sale jumper,' declares Simon Bligh. Next on is Boothby Graffoe. He enters wearing a coat, as if he's only just arrived, straight from another gig. He takes off his coat to reveal Tonkinson's jumper. The audience shriek with hysterical delight. 'Burn it,' shouts that heckler. Graffoe removes the pullover and gives it to Tonkinson, already en route to his next gig. He wades through the crowd, holding it aloft, like a severed head or a sporting trophy. It's a glorious mock heroic end to a set that could quite easily have finished in failure, but was rescued by his refusal to take himself too seriously.

'Where's your jumper?' the heckler asks Graffoe, but Graffoe is a tougher type of stand-up than Tonkinson. 'My punchline was so much better than yours, and now we'll never know,' says Graffoe. 'Have you ever considered that the reason your father spent so much time with his cock in your mouth was to keep you fucking quiet?'

'It's always better to be heckled by someone at the back, because if you put them down, you have to shout at them and everyone hears it,' says Phill Jupitus. It's the quiet hecklers at the front whom comics really fear. Yet unlike some comedians, he doesn't begrudge hecklers, good or bad. 'At The Store, you've paid not only to sit and watch a good show, but, if you wish, to participate,' he says. 'The audience feel the evening is theirs as much as yours.' And there's no accounting for an audience's taste. He's seen Harry Hill and Eddie Izzard die down here.

Tim Clark heckles his hecklers before they can heckle him. 'It's getting your retaliation in first, as Don Revie used to say.' But there's a fine line between controlling a crowd and assaulting them, and the comic who taught Clark where that line lies is Bruce Forsyth. 'I used to watch him on *The Generation Game*, and he had a wonderful way of taking the piss out of people but at the same time saying, "Look, it's all right, you're not going to be hurt."' If a punter doesn't want to play along, Clark can see it in their eyes. If they don't, he leaves them alone. 'If people start having a go at the acts or having a go at me, I'm quite happy to bury them, but I wouldn't do it gratuitously because then there's no enjoyment for me and there's no enjoyment for them and audiences can see it. They can see nastiness and they don't like it. I get it wrong sometimes, I know I do, but generally that's the rule I try to stick by.'

Rhona Cameron adopts a more conciliatory tone. 'You've got a happy nice life, haven't you?' she tells her hecklers. 'You're all right. It's fine, isn't it? I'm jealous. I need you. I need your love. It's not nice to have a room full of people against you every day.' As she quells a female revolt stage left, a male rebellion breaks out stage right. 'No. Be louder please. It's only me. There's nothing more interesting until another man comes on. I'm just a girl. You wouldn't want to know. I'm talking about vaginas for ten minutes.' But the bloke keeps talking to his mate. 'Hello? Me. My life, written down in pain, turned into humour, for you. Thank you. I need the attention. That's not funny. That's sad. You laughed at my tragedy.' But Cameron is playing up these minor insurrections for comic effect. Despite her self-deprecation, she's totally in charge. 'It's nice to have a profound heckler,' she tells a punter. 'It's usually just bollocks. Get off. Shit.

Lesbian. But that was really nice. It was beautiful. Are you in therapy or something? That was really moving.'

One of stand-up's persistent mysteries is hecklers who think comics will welcome their endless interruptions. 'Nice one, mate, really enjoyed that – you didn't mind me joining in because it helps, doesn't it?' hecklers tell Mark Maier after a gig. 'You need a bit of that – everyone else was a bit quiet, but it helps you along, doesn't it?' Maier always tells them it doesn't, and yet these helpful pests persevere. 'People genuinely believe that shouting out inane drivel at you for half an hour is really what you want.' Maier wants to do stand-up, not crowd control, but such altruistic tormenters are insatiable.

But for some comics heckling at The Store can be an invaluable survival course for the harsher glare of TV's intrusive yet autistic stare. 'Hecklers in here will give you a hard time, especially after they've had a pint or two, but that's a good training ground for any comedian,' says Richard Blackwood, who's graduated from The Store to MTV and Channel 4. 'You have to be that strong, you have to be that tough, because once you come from the comedy circuit into TV, anything can go wrong, the cameras are on you, and the people behind the scenes, they're not the ones that are gonna take the rap. It's you.'

Sean Lock once left the stage to deal with a persistent heckler. 'I put him down loads and loads of times. There was nothing which was going to shut this guy up, and then I just lost it.' Luckily the bouncers beat him to it. 'Never leave the stage in my club,' Kim Kinnie told Lock afterwards, but sometimes a comic has little choice. 'This guy was charging towards the stage,' says Lock, recalling the only other time he lost it. 'He's coming for me,' thought Lock. 'What am I going to do? Well, the best thing to do is to just grab him before he gets here.' Lock grabbed him and threw him into the audience, but the audience threw him back. 'Just before I was about to intervene again, the bouncers lifted him up by his elbows and I just saw him disappearing out of the room.' 'I just had a joke for him,' protested the punter, as the bouncers hauled him out. 'We had to throw out eighteen people after you were on,' they told Lock. 'And they was just the ringleaders.' Yet the bouncers haven't always been quite so quick to help. 'Can the bouncers come over here and remove these people?' asked Mark Lamarr one night. Nothing happened. 'They thought I was joking.'

Hattie Hayridge's first trip to The Store, around midnight, one Friday night in 1985, could scarcely have been more dramatic. She thought it was strange that the only empty seats were in the front row, but she and her friend sat there all the same. They soon wished they hadn't. To their left was a young couple. 'They had that uneasy air of being on a first date, and the young man looked as though he was out to make an impression,' recalled Hayridge. 'By the time the second comic came onstage he had plucked up a bit of courage.' 'Shut up!' yelled the young man. 'You shut up,' laughed the comic, unflustered by such a lame heckle, but a few minutes later, he came back for more. 'Go on, shut up!' yelled the heckler. By now, the comic was not amused. 'Piss off, you sad wanker,' he replied. 'Angrily, the young man hurled his beer up into the comic's face,' recounts Hayridge. 'The comic picked up his own drink and emptied the glass of beer over the punter.' The heckler grabbed the foot of the mike stand and started pulling. The comic grabbed the top.

'Everybody's laughing, and the microphone is going backwards and forwards and backwards and forwards,' recalls Don Ward. 'Let go, you wanker!' shouted the comic, but the heckler wouldn't. 'Well, if you want it so bad, you can have it,' said the comic, and he let go. 'The microphone flies off the top of the stand and hits the girl above her eye,' remembers Ward. From her ringside seat, Hayridge saw it all. 'The girl screamed and blood spattered along the row towards us. The young man was on his feet, jumping this way and that, torn between protecting his girlfriend and thumping the comic. The girl was sobbing and angrily pushed him away.' So the heckler got up onstage.

'The comic was distraught. Still fending off the boyfriend, he was trying to see if the girl was all right, and now he had the manager's anger to contend with too.'[1] Hayridge grabbed the manager's arm. 'It wasn't the comic's fault!' she told him. It was her first meeting with Don Ward. 'Clive!' Ward told Clive Anderson. 'You're on!' 'What, now?' asked Anderson. 'Especially now,' said Ward. 'Just get on and calm it all down.' Anderson could be forgiven for not feeling overly keen. 'There was blood all over the place and a fight was about to break out,' he says, but he went on and did his duty. 'What's this audience going to be like when they've seen one of their number taken away bleeding?' wondered Anderson, as he stepped up to the bloody microphone. But although punters hunt in packs, they rarely feel much loyalty to one another.

'It had no effect on them at all,' remembers Anderson. '"Never mind, don't apologise, don't even refer to it, just get on with it. We're here for a good time." Presumably, they just thought this is what always happened at The Comedy Store. This is what you come for. A bit of audience interaction. They always said don't sit at the front. Now I know why.' 'Quite reluctantly, Clive went on and did his piece,' says Ward. 'That's the last time he ever appeared at The Store.'

Meanwhile, Ward called an ambulance and got the injured girl a brandy. 'Big deal,' said her boyfriend. 'Multi-millionaire Don Ward, owner of The Comedy Store, or should I say Casualty Store, giving her a brandy. I bet it'll be three star.' 'Actually, it is,' replied Ward. 'It's all we have for now.'

'I thought we were in for a huge law suit,' says Kim Kinnie. For a while, it looked as if they were. 'The litigation went on for five years,' says Ward. Eventually, they settled for a few hundred pounds.

One night, John Lenahan was onstage when he saw a punter marching straight at him. 'He had psycho killer written all over him and I knew he was coming onstage. The secret when somebody comes onstage is to make sure you have the microphone, because the guy with the microphone wins. If the guy grabs the microphone, you just stand there going "Come on, give me the microphone back," and you look like an idiot.' Yet unfortunately for Lenahan, this punter had something else in mind. "He took out a can of silly string and he sprayed it right in my face. Silly string is like a pie. The rule in comedy is if somebody comes at you with a pie, you don't duck. You have to stand there. When you duck, you look like an asshole. So I just stood there, and it kept coming at me, until I couldn't see anymore, and it had completely covered my face.' Lenahan couldn't even see the punter throw the empty can at him. Luckily, it missed. When he heard the clatter, he took off his glasses, and his silly string mask came off with them. 'I have a rule onstage, which is "you can tell me to fuck off, You can do anything, but as soon as you start throwing stuff, I'm done,"' he says. 'I'm not working here unless you have bouncers,' he told Don Ward, as soon as he got offstage. Next week, the bouncers arrived.

Head bouncer Julian Moses

The Management

'You say to yourself, "We'll give this guy about five minutes, see if he's just going to take the put-down, or if he's going to keep on trying to surpass the comic,"' says doorman Mark Skeete, standing guard outside The Store. 'If they continue, then you step in and you have a quick word with them. If you can see that this person's really trying to enjoy theirselves, just give them a little warning. Say, "Hey, we don't mind you heckling, but you've got to calm down. You can't be on them every minute because we have a time schedule to go by." Most people understand that, keep their mouth shut. Some people do still heckle afterwards, but it's just a game. You're onstage and you're an open target for anyone.'

You can't imagine anyone in their right mind heckling Mark Skeete. As this huge bear of a man stands in the doorway of The Store, surveying the swelling queue that snakes up the road and around the corner into Coventry Street, he towers over the waiting punters, a foot taller than most of them, and almost twice as wide. And yet he has that special softness that only goes with great strength, that quiet civility which almost borders on diffidence. 'If someone's pissing me off,' he's tough enough to tell me, 'I just walk away.' Skeete's kindness and his courtesy shouldn't come as any surprise. Bouncers and comedians have a lot in common. They're both in the crowd control business, and the best of them have long since learned that less is a whole lot more. 'People get offended by the littlest thing,' he says. 'People get offended by you telling them to keep quiet, because as far as they're concerned, they've paid for the evening. You can't treat people like shit when they're paying for their evening. They're not paying to watch me.'

Mark Skeete, Carl Frith and Julian Moses at the entrance to The Store

But they're not paying to watch hecklers either. They're paying to see comics. His biggest headache isn't lone hecklers, but large gangs of lads. 'You get big groups come in. Some of the groups are maybe even having fights before they even get to The Store.' But trouble can come from the most unexpected quarters. 'A group of police lads came down and started insulting all the staff,' he says. 'That was kind of strange. Out of everybody you expect to keep theirselves in a certain manner, they become the biggest thugs when they're out among their friends.' Drink is the biggest factor, the final arbiter between good behaviour and bad. 'The first show starts at eight. Pubs are open but they haven't had enough time to get totally legless, so they're just in a nice, happy-go-lucky sort of mood when they get here. The first show they usually thoroughly enjoy theirselves. They don't want to leave at the end of it. They want to sit down and hear a little bit more.' The midnight show is a different story. 'You see someone staggering all over the place, can barely stand up, you have to turn them away,' he says. 'You tell their friends to put them in a cab and send them home.' And the main thing for Skeete is never to lose his remarkable sang froid. 'It's not easy. It's nowhere near easy because you get some strange people out there. But you have to get on with it. Even though they're making you scream inside, you have to make it look like everything's cool.'

'They're the best in the whole country,' says Australian comic Phil Davey of Skeete and his colleagues. 'At other clubs, when someone has been thrown out while I'm onstage, kids have kicked up a fuss, tables and chairs have gone flying. I've seen a bouncer put a bloke in a headlock and knock him unconscious.' Skeete adopts a more softly softly approach.

Sometimes, his services even go beyond the club door. When a local minicab firm took Davey's kid brother home the long way round, Davey asked Skeete to go with him to get his money back. 'I'll never forget it. He goes, "This is Phil, right? Phil's my people, right?" I couldn't believe it. I'm this weasly little Australian guy. He's this massive bloke. To think we could be related.' But Skeete got Davey's money. 'He knows exactly how to control somebody. That's why he's so good at his job. Very quiet. Very assertive. Very persistent. He just kept repeating the same thing over and over again.'

'They're really subtle and gentle about the way they deal with people,' agrees Martin Coyote, who once even conquered a stag night of Millwall fans, confident in the knowledge that the bouncers were there to back him up. 'There's never any scuffles. It makes you feel very secure, and then, of course, because you feel secure, you get more swagger.' Coyote once watched Skeete silence a persistent heckler merely by putting a paternal hand on his shoulder and whispering in his ear. 'It was great the way you handled that,' Coyote told Skeete afterwards. 'What people can't see is when I'm bending down like that, I'm breaking his shoulder,' said Skeete.

'Because they've been at The Store themselves for years, they know the rhythm of an audience just as well as the comedians,' says stand-up John Moloney, whose old day job as a teacher taught him all about crowd control. 'What are they like?' Moloney will ask Mark Skeete, on his way in. 'They're all right, bit feisty,' Skeete will reply. 'Stage left there's a couple of fucking idiots.' But Skeete won't wade straight in. His understated skill is a blend of authority and good grace. Moloney has seen him talk punters down for fifteen minutes until the interval and then tell them, 'If you behave, you can stay.'

'There have been a couple of occasions when I wish security had waded in, but afterwards they've said, "That's a compliment – we left it to the end of your act because we know you can handle it,"' says Paul Zenon. 'Half of you is thinking, "Well, that's nice," and the other half is thinking, "I wish you had got them outside and given them a good punch for me."'

But it isn't only bouncers, or even comics, who keep this house in order. One night, two hecklers were giving Julian Clary such a hard time that the chef came out of the kitchen and stood between them clutching a meat cleaver. The chef didn't say a word, and everyone else saw him standing there long before either of the hecklers. Eventually one of the hecklers turned round, saw what the chef was holding, nudged his mate, and they both became as quiet as pussycats.

'Get back in your box, you big monster,' compere Mickey Hutton tells Stan Nelson, who's deserted his post in the sound booth. 'Go on, you big stupid bald git.' Obediently

Stan returns to his box, and Hutton returns his attention to his midnight audience, but when he speaks, the rest is silence. Stan has killed the sound, and Hutton has to stand and shuffle for a few foolish moments, stranded in suspended stand-up animation, as these pissed-up punters stop laughing with him, and start laughing at him instead. Eventually, Stan relents and the sound resumes. 'Thank god he can't do anything else,' says Hutton, whereupon the entire room is plunged into darkness. Stan has killed the lights. The whole house howls with mock horror, like hysterical kids on a fairground ride. 'I shagged his girlfriend, ladies and gentlemen,' says Hutton. 'And she said you were shit,' booms Nelson's disembodied baritone. 'I hate it when the stage manager's funnier than you,' says Hutton. 'Every fucking night down here,' says Stan.

'You're actually paying less for each comic than you are for a pint of beer behind the bar,' says Stan Nelson, in that last orders limbo between shows. For thirteen quid you get five acts, including the compere, plus open spots. A Store pint costs three quid. 'Why not stick five pints of beer onstage?' says Stan. 'You can watch them for two and a half hours.'

Nelson loves comedy, and the comics love him. 'He's a diamond,' says Terry Alderton, speaking for virtually every comic who's played here in the last decade. 'He's as artistic as all of us.' It's this artistry that makes the shows run so smoothly. 'It runs through Stan and it runs better than any other place,' says Alderton. 'You walk out on that stage and your arse is being wiped for you. You know there is nothing that won't be right, and if it's not right, he's up there at a hundred miles an hour, and it's fixed before you know it.'

From his twilit cockpit in the sound booth, Stan's heard more heckles than most comics. 'You get bad heckles. You get drunk mad heckles.' You even get heckles from other comics. 'I remember somebody at the old Store getting heckled from offstage by Arthur Smith and Paul Merton and Owen O'Neill, who'd all been out on the piss.' Smith, Merton and O'Neill ended up onstage, singing. No wonder the biggest stars remain wary of this small stage. 'Jackie Mason standing in the box with me, two nights running, didn't want to go on. He still knows there's an element of danger here.' But Mason is happy to play the Palladium. 'I remember Ben Elton coming down the old Store, and Ben wouldn't go onstage for love nor money.' Jo Brand asked him, but Elton wasn't tempted. 'He said, "You're mad. I'm not going up there. No. Why should I?" You can understand that because anything can happen.'

The job description can be pretty broad. 'There's been times when I've had to steam into the audience.' And once, when the sprinklers went off, he even rescued a damsel in distress. 'I had to carry Jo Brand across the room, which she was actually pissed off about, because the fire brigade turned up and she'd rather have had one of them carry her out.'

'Stan the man is a fucking genius,' declared John Moloney, onstage at The Store's twentieth birthday party. 'He's watched my act for the last ten years.' To prove it, Stan provided the punchlines to some of Moloney's most familiar feeds. 'Went to a

dyslexic rave,' said Moloney. 'Loads of people taking F,' said Stan. 'What was the bloke in the corner trying to inject?' asked Moloney. 'A heron,' replied Stan. 'I went bob sleighing,' said Moloney. 'Killed twenty bobs,' said Stan. 'I got stung by a bee yesterday,' said Moloney. 'Twenty quid for a jar of honey,' said Stan, to groans around the room. 'Fuck off,' said Moloney. 'Like you could do better.' We couldn't. The groans subside.

Nelson counts many of the comics as his friends, and the feeling is mutual. 'Stan's been more like a fucking therapist to me than anything else over the last ten years,' says Phill Jupitus. 'Why do you never compliment me?' Terry Alderton once asked him. 'Keep your fucking feet on the ground,' said Stan. Nelson saves his compliments for when comics really need them. 'Don't worry, babe, it'll be all right,' he tells good comedians who've had bad gigs. 'You'll have a great one later on.'

Just as many open spots scarcely know of the existence of Don Ward, most would be surprised to discover that this testosterone-heavy club is in fact run by women. In 1985 Ward's wife suggested that a young friend of hers would make an ideal manager. Barbara Herbin had been a teacher and had worked as head cashier in a casino. In the early days at Leicester Square, she and Kinnie took the helm and while Kinnie dealt with the performers, Herbin set in place the administration that makes the Store one of the best-run businesses in the West End. Along with Ward they worked the box office, cashed up and were very much hands-on bosses. In 1990, as another bar manager bit the dust, Wendy Frediani joined the company. From a show business background and having run her own small business prior to a divorce, Frediani set about turning round the deficit on the bar. This led to a confrontation with Kinnie who was outraged to discover she had put an embargo on staff acquiring drinks from the notorious back bar. The girls stuck to their guns and Kinnie graciously accepted defeat.

The move to Piccadilly taxed Frediani and Herbin's resources to the limit. 'The show came down at ten o'clock on Sunday 12 December and the gala opening in Piccadilly was set for seven o'clock the next evening,' recalls Frediani. 'Barbara and I had to organise the move overnight.' It was a nightmare. 'Not only did Stan and Jon have to strike the lighting and sound, but we also had to clear the bars and transport things like the ice machines. All in one small vehicle that Stan had hired, as Don couldn't see the necessity of a removal company! The staff were wonderful and trailed across Leicester Square with trolleys.'

Arriving at the new venue, they were dismayed to find that it wasn't really finished. There was still a pile of rubble in front of the bar, which was covered with a thick film of dust. The office had no desks and even worse, there was nowhere to lock-up the takings. The auditorium looked splendid with its rows of shining red seats, but the bar had no shelves on which to store the glasses. They laboured through the night. 'Don wandered in with his wife at around two o'clock to see how it was going. I asked if he'd instructed the cleaners to clean the bar and he said, "Don't worry, it's all taken care of."' Famous last words.

On the afternoon of the opening night they arrived to find builders and electricians still scurrying about. Of Ward there was no sign: he was with his lawyers ensuring all the licences were in order. Herbin concentrated on the office and the box office. She sent the Store's building maintenance man, Roy Saunders, to buy a lockable cabinet for the takings. Meanwhile Wendy was horrified to discover that the cleaners hadn't touched the bar. She had no alternative but to clean it herself. The staff arrived at four p.m., and began stocking the bar. 'I had been swearing and cursing in frustration all afternoon,' she remembers. 'At about five o'clock, an Irish electrician broke the tension. 'Sure and now you'll know how Anneka Rice feels.'

At six o'clock it was clear that the new till system was not going to work. Roy Saunders was once more dispatched to the old venue in Leicester Square to disconnect the tills and bring them into service in Piccadilly. 'It was a race against time that had us all wrung out with nervous exhaustion,' says Herbin. 'But we opened the doors on time, everyone had a great evening, and no one could have guessed the obstacles we overcame that day.'

Today Herbin and Frediani, joint general managers, administer the rapidly expanded business from the comfort of their bright new offices at the Prince of Wales theatre. 'After years of working in a basement, it's a joy to see daylight,' remarks Herbin. It is in these offices that she has catalogued and stored the archives and history from day one of The Comedy Store. Every diary, newspaper cutting and photograph has been conscientiously filed or framed and displayed in the venue.

Meanwhile Ward, as a natural progression from discovering raw talent, has started a management agency. He found a perfect person to build the agency in Charlotte Foley, a young graduate who was already working for The Store. She now works alongside Herbin and Frediani at the Prince of Wales office, and the comics, at first wary, then intrigued, began to make enquiries. She now handles Store regulars such as Simon Bligh, Ian Stone, Boothy Graffoe, Mike Gunn, the American Tom Rhodes and a new young comic discovered in Manchester, Justin Moorhouse.

The success of the Store as a venue is not only due to the perspicacity and business acumen of Don Ward but also the dedication of these hardworking women. Together they have assembled a team of employees of remarkable longevity. The bouncers, led by Julian Moses, have been with the company for twelve years. Stan Nelson and Jono McGrath, stage managers for ten years. Bill Green worked as barman, head barman and finally night manager for ten years. When he eventually moved on a young Australian, Loki Mackay, took over. 'I have no doubt that he will be with us for some years as well,' says Frediani. 'The comics love the fact that when they come to work they will be greeted by familiar faces, that we know their ways and the door staff will keep an eye out for their cars. They feel at home and that is why so many say that this is the best gig in the country. No only is the room built for them to display their gifts to the best advantage, but the staff are like family to them.'

But the man behind all these comics, bouncers, bar and backstage staff remains a surprisingly anonymous figure. Don Ward is so low key that some open spots scarcely realise he even works here, let alone that he owns and runs one of the world's top comedy clubs. When Ward came backstage after Bennett Arron's first open spot and shook his hand and said how much he'd enjoyed it, Arron had no idea who he was, since he'd only spoken to him on the phone. 'I said, "Who are you?", which I think threw him a bit, because I think he expected me to know who he was and I didn't, so he introduced himself. Up until then we'd been having a very relaxed conversation and I was just thinking to myself, "This is just an audience member who's allowed in to have a chat."' But Ward's softly spoken approach pays bigger dividends than self-important bluster. 'Don is a businessman,' says Sean Meo. 'He's very loyal to people who've made the effort. He's always been very loyal to me, because I've never committed the cardinal sin of not showing up, or showing up late, or letting him down, and he knows.'

And despite his club's success, Ward still isn't too grand to stick around and watch an open spot, and come backstage afterwards and give try outs a few tips. 'The feedback was just amazing, the way he takes time to explain where he thinks you could do better,' says open spot Nik Coppin. 'Don actually sits down and asks you how you think you did.' Coppin never got this feedback in any of the smaller clubs he played. But Ward knows it's worth keeping a careful eye on the open spots. A few try outs are future stars, and a few more make far more trouble than any heckler, like the tattooed

Geordie nudist who turned up in Leicester Square. 'He went onstage naked, covered in tattoos, shouting and screaming in a high-pitched Northumberland accent, and then simulated masturbation and left,' recalls Phill Jupitus. Don Ward and Kim Kinnie's contrasting reactions to such strange try outs were almost as amusing. 'Didn't go too well, did it?' Ward would say, laconically, afterwards. 'We don't really do that here.' Kinnie, on the other hand, was rather more direct. 'Get out and never come back,' he'd say. And who's to say which one was kinder? 'Don would always be like the friendly headmaster,' says Jupitus. 'Kim was much more the psycho deputy head, and Stan was the PE teacher who was quite genial, but could kick your head in if he really wanted.'

Jeff Green

Jeff Green first went to The Store in 1987. 'There was all the photos of all these people who, if you're my age, you were brought up on in your most formative years,' says this handsome, boyish stand-up. 'Rik Mayall and Ade Edmondson and Alexei Sayle.' He didn't see a brilliant bill, but maybe that was for the best. 'If they'd been any good, I probably would never have done it.' 'I want to be a part of this,' he thought. 'How can I be a part of this?' He decided to become a barman, and work his way up from there, so he took a day off from his job as an engineer in Newport, travelled all the way from South Wales to Leicester Square, and rang the bell. Barbara, who still works here, answered the door and gave him a number to call. Nothing came of it, but a friend spotted an ad for comedy workshops at Jacksons Lane, the community arts centre in Highgate, North London. Green got a transfer to Guildford, and every Tuesday night he'd change out of his suit and into his jeans and trek across town to Highgate. 'I hadn't even set foot onstage until I became a comedian, so it was all absolutely brand new to me.' There were fifteen hopefuls in his class. Several stuck at it. One was Eddie Izzard.

Green kept going back to The Store, but only to watch. 'I used to get butterflies,' he says, recalling the thrill of queuing outside. 'By the time you get down there, you're at fever pitch.' Green even brought his mum along. 'Come down,' he said. 'I'll show you. I've found what I want to do.' 'Oh god,' he thought, as they sat and watched Paul Merton. 'Everyone's swearing and people are heckling.' But she loved it. 'She loved the show and she loved the fact that I wanted to do it.' When he did his solo show in a West End theatre, his mum was in the audience.

His first Store gig was in 1988. 'Your material's shit,' Kim Kinnie told him. 'Get rid of that, but you're quite good. You've got something about you which I really like. Go away, don't come back for six months, and then come back and see me again.' Kinnie gave Green a crucial incentive. 'That's what kept me going for the first six months,' he says. 'That's what drove me on. Otherwise, maybe I'd have given up.'

Jeff Green

Green got his first paid booking later that year. 'I'd no interest in what the audience thought. I wanted to know what Kim thought.' He had work the next day, but afterwards he lay in bed, wide awake, still too excited to sleep. 'I miss all that now,' he says. 'I don't know what could possibly give me that sense of achievement now.' His hands would sweat. 'I never used to take the mike out. I used to hold onto it and just scream into the mike, as much as I could, with this incredible nervous energy, which some people might call charisma, but I would actually call fear. I remember the first time I ever took the mike out. It's like getting your dick out.' Suddenly, he was no longer rooted to one spot. 'I always wonder how the fuck I managed to get away with some of the crappy jokes I used to do, but I think it was nervous energy that got me through it.' One night, in 1989, the crowd started shouting for an encore, and finally he felt part of something he'd always wanted to be a part of. 'Do you want to do some more?' the compere asked him, but he didn't have any more to do. 'You used to have to do twenty minutes, but I'd only have eleven minutes and hope laughs would bring me to seventeen.'

'I've been booed off,' he says. 'We've all been booed off.' But he finds no fun in seeing other acts go down the toilet. 'I've never been a one for watching people die onstage, I hate it,' he says. 'I always go, "There but for the grace of god go I." Some people love it. "Look! There's somebody dying onstage!" I just think that's cruel, so I never watched too many deaths.' At Leicester Square, there were fewer tourists, and the regulars all knew the score. 'If there was a chink in your armour, they were allowed to attack you, and there were plenty of chinks in my armour.' Yet they could also be utterly indifferent. 'There'd be people asleep in the front row.' Those punters were even closer than today. 'That also contributed to your sense of fear,' he says. 'They were all around you, on all three sides. You were actually hemmed in.'

In 1989, to celebrate its tenth birthday, The Store held a talent contest, and Kim Kinnie asked Green to enter. There were over twenty up and coming comics on the bill, including Eddie Izzard, but Green won. He was awarded £500, an ornamental gong, and a weekend at The Store. 'What am I going to do now?' he wondered, on the tube home. 'Have I got enough material? Do I give up the day job?' Five years later, he was nominated for the Perrier Award, and even got a backstage visit from Billy Connolly. He's since played festivals as far afield as Australia, and his solo West End shows have been broadcast on ITV.

'I've got to get out of here,' he thought, a few years ago. 'Otherwise I'll just be a very one-dimensional Store act, with lots of knob gags, lots of heckle put-downs, lots of attitude.' And now he's older, he's not really interested in going down that route. 'I had to leave The Store. In a way, The Store was bad for me. Being accepted so early on down The Store, I became a Store act, and I stopped growing. I couldn't develop my softer side, a more gentle side.' And so he never found out where that would take him. 'When I stopped playing The Store and started playing other places where I didn't need to be so nasty and so gag orientated, I actually started to develop.'

But The Store is still the ultimate test for new material. 'It's a benchmark. Will it work in a late show at The Store? It still has to stand up down here.' There are some routines he won't do here. 'In the late show, the last thing they want is, "Let's talk about my mother and father's divorce." If it's a laid-back night, you can give yourself room, but if it's a Friday late show and you're fifth on and it's two o'clock in the morning, the last thing you're going to do is start messing around.' And yet in longer gigs he loses something else instead. 'You miss the immediate reaction once you get a Comedy Store audience on a roll,' he says. 'In terms of adrenalin and buzz there's nowhere like doing twenty strong minutes at The Store.'

Vaudeville

Martin Soan strides onstage carrying the biggest book you've ever seen. Entitled *101 Ways To Stop Feeling Small*, it's about the same size as a suitcase, and that's precisely what it is. This book is his bag of tricks, and prop-based stunts pour unabated from within its outsized covers. His other visual gags include a portable window frame complete with net curtains, a squirrel on the end of an electric drill, and a self-soiling nappy. He even cracks jokes in semaphore, with a pair of hand-held flags. 'Never take drugs at a maypole dance,' he warns, producing a tangled web of multi-coloured ribbons. The only device that refuses to function properly is his *Ancient Book Of Comedy*. 'Come back and see me another time and it'll work,' he says, after several abortive attempts. 'Owing to a lack of material, there will now be an Elizabethan interlude,' he announces, putting on a huge white ruff and rolling up his trousers to reveal a pair of Dayglo stockings, before winding up with some elastic band gurning, transforming his face into a grotesque caricature of Michael Jackson, and leaping into the audience to snog an unsuspecting punter.

'One of his influences is drugs,' reveals the compere, Stephen Frost, telling the audience a strange but true story about the time he drove Soan from London down to a gig in Penzance, via Stonehenge and Bodmin Moor. As Alan Davies says, you have to tune into Martin Soan, but if you let him fly the rewards are huge.

Martin Soan's performances have always been unusual, especially in the troupe he formed with Malcolm Hardee, The Greatest Show On Legs. They played snooker with punters dressed in different coloured crash helmets. Malcolm even did a ventriloquist's act with Martin sat on his lap. One night, during the interval, Martin got inside a big

metal box and Malcolm dragged it out onstage. 'The interval ran over and I was in this box for about half an hour. When Malcolm got me out I was half dead and no one took a blind bit of notice anyway.'

After all, they weren't the only ones using The Store to test drive their weird and wonderful routines. Soan remembers a street performer who trawled Soho for discarded junk and incorporated it into his act. And then there were the meat jugglers, 'these three pristine laundered butchers that came on and juggled with meat,' recalls Martin. 'Kidneys and liver,' adds Martin's wife Vivienne. 'At the end the whole backdrop was just splattered with blood,' says Martin.

'I've only just learned how to do that,' says the next act up, Boothby Graffoe, as he taps the strings on his amplified acoustic guitar to make a percussive yet melodic noise that sounds a lot like wind chimes. 'I got it off a bloke who sits outside Kentucky Fried Chicken, outside Leicester Square. Paul his name is. Very good. Just plays harmonics. He's much better at it than I am, but it's warmer in here.' Boothby Graffoe isn't just the only comic in the world named after a market town in Lincolnshire. He's also one of the most unusual and accomplished acts to play The Store in recent years. He's toured Europe, America and Australia, and entertained the Edinburgh Festival in his own fitted kitchen. TV Variety may be dead, but on this midsummer Monday night at The Store, the old Vaudeville tradition is alive and kicking.

Nowadays, The Store is mainly a stand-up club, but it wasn't always that way. Back in the early Eighties, the sort of shows you saw at The Store were still called cabaret, not comedy. 'There was a lot more variety involved,' says comedian Mark Billingham. 'All sorts of strange people.' The atmosphere was much more gladiatorial. 'If you saw four straight stand-ups do OK and then a try out do OK, you'd leave feeling a little bit disappointed because that wasn't quite what it was about. You wanted something live and interesting to happen that wasn't like watching TV.' But although the circuit, and The Store, have since been swamped by straight, white twentysomething blokes doing observational stand-up, a few of those variety artistes have, thankfully, survived.

'Fantastic to be at The Comedy Store on a Monday night, and that's the end of the topical material,' announces Paul Zenon. 'I do comedy and magic. So if something's not

funny, it's a fucking trick.' But this comic magician can do both, at the same time. 'Some of the people sat down at the sides might actually spot how I do a couple of these tricks. And the same goes for the people in front.' Self-mockery is a mainstay of his act, but only top-class entertainers can risk such self-deprecation. 'Good job the floor was there,' he says as he drops a prop. 'That could have gone for fucking miles.'

He soon has this audience eating out of his hand. 'You're not entirely indispensable,' he warns us, playing pre-recorded applause on a portable tape recorder, but there's no need for warnings. We're all on our best behaviour. Like all the best stand-up conjurers, he could crack jokes or do tricks and keep us entertained, so both together is twice the fun. 'You know when comedians come onstage they always go, "A funny thing happened to me on the way here?" To be honest, in years of this, nothing the slightest bit fucking funny has ever happened to me on the way anywhere ever. Until tonight.' Gags and stunts flow thick and fast. 'Most magicians come on and pull bunnies out of hats,' he says, producing a toy rabbit from his trousers. 'I pull hares out of my arse.' But he can get away with the corniest gag because the actual illusions are the business. 'That last bit never gets a laugh, but I keep it in because I like it,' he says. You have to be very good to get away with sending up your own tricks and jokes, and Paul Zenon is very good indeed.

Zenon hauls a volunteer up onstage. He's called Tim. 'Not so lippy now, are we, Tim?' says Zenon, producing a flick knife. Zenon relieves Tim of his leather jacket. 'Razor sharp,' says Zenon, brandishing his blade. 'Unlike the jacket.' Tim tries to escape, but remembers his jacket and thinks better of it. 'I know it might sound like bollocks, but it got me out of the army,' says Zenon, describing how he plans to transport a knife through leather. 'Shit,' he says, as he impales Tim's jacket. 'It's fucking happened again.' But all is not lost. 'I think we could be worrying about nothing,' adds Zenon, with heartfelt relief. 'I think the knife might be all right.' The audience howls with heartless laughter as Zenon rips the lining out of Tim's jacket. 'Seeing as it's fucked, we might as well have a bit of a laugh with it,' says Zenon, lighting up a cigarette and plunging it into the ugly gash his knife has left behind. 'Smoking jacket,' says Zenon. 'Leave it a minute. It might be a blazer.' Yet miraculously, Tim's jacket is completely unharmed. 'No damage, no applause either,' says Zenon, prompting a rigorous round of clapping.

'You know some tricks look quite dangerous but when you know the secret, they're actually fairly safe?' he asks, as he sets up his finale, a precarious party piece involving a dog lead, a snooker triangle and a pint of Newcastle Brown Ale. 'This one doesn't look much but it's bloody dangerous.' A clumsy punter kicks over their drink. 'I'm going to spin a pint of beer round my head,' says Zenon. 'You can't even leave a glass stood on the floor.' As Zenon explains, this stunt works on the same principle as the old trick of spinning a bucketful of water above your head. 'Because of the weight of the water and centrifugal force, the bucket would snap off the handle, fly off, make a right mess everywhere, and you'd get a smack round the head from your dad,' says Zenon. 'Well, this is going to be similar, but don't worry if it goes wrong. My dad's not here.' He pours the Newcastle Brown into a pint glass, balances the glass on the snooker triangle, and clips the triangle to the dog lead. 'If anybody wants to check this after the show, try to get out more. Meet people. It's only a trick.' And with that, he swings the entire contraption in a wide arc above his head. Incredibly, the full pint pot stays put, but a trail of froth confirms the liquidity of Zenon's assets. 'Seriously, if it does fly off and injure someone it's just a bit of fun, all right?' A punter in the front row gets up to go. 'Three years to learn this, and you're going for a piss?' The punter sits down again. 'If I were you, I'd start clapping at some point,' says Zenon, but his audience is too transfixed to provide more than a polite ripple.

'As you've probably gathered, the hard part is stopping it, so I won't. Just ignore me for the rest of the night. Work round me. We've got some short comics in the second half.' But he does stop, and a front-row punter verifies that his pint isn't stuck down with anything stronger than centrifugal force. This innocuous piece of audience participation is the only bit of this curtain call that's ever come unstuck. Once, after Zenon had spun the pint around his head without spilling a single drop, a cack-handed volunteer dropped it as they lifted it off the triangle. Thankfully this punter picks up the pint without dropping it, and hands it back to Zenon, who downs it in one, to tumultuous cheers. 'Interesting to note that the biggest round of applause in the act was for drinking a fucking pint of beer,' he says, belching into the mike.

Paul Zenon first went to The Store in the mid-Eighties. Still only in his early twenties, he was already working as a comic magician, but that was on the trad circuit, and back then, those two worlds could hardly have been less alike. 'It was like one extreme to another,' he says, in the bar at Jongleurs Battersea before a gig. 'It was very experimental.' Jeremy Hardy, Jerry Sadowitz and Ruby Wax were all on the bill. It was certainly a dramatic contrast to appearing in end-of-the-pier shows alongside comics doing routines about going home drunk to the wife, or summer season in Jersey. 'We used to call it Club Eighty To Dead because it was all Saga Holidays.' Nevertheless, he went backstage afterwards and asked for an open spot. 'Living up North at the time, the only way I could perform was in very traditional surroundings – working men's clubs, summer camps,' he explains, 'but I was always interested in people who were doing different stuff.'

Straight stand-ups have it tough enough, but magic can be even harder. 'People need to concentrate on the plot,' he says. 'You can't bail out like you can with a joke. If you're doing a routine verbally, and it's going down and it's not getting a laugh, you can change direction. If I brought out two props and joined them together, there's a logical plot to what I'm doing. I have to carry it out to its conclusion, otherwise you're admitting it's going wrong.' Stage magic still suffers from the same naff reputation that stand-up endured before The Store. There's also a more practical problem. 'You have to carry a load of shit about.' Stand-ups only have to show up on time. Magicians must make time to check they haven't forgotten any props. 'There's nothing worse than arriving slightly late at a gig, rushing to go on, and not being quite sure whether you've got the right shit in your pockets.' It's an uphill struggle in the early show, but the late show is even harder. 'Late night, people are generally more interested in people talking about anal sex, problems with condoms,' says Zenon. 'They don't want to watch a fucking card trick and I don't want to watch a card trick and I don't want to do one.'

Lately he's seen Alternative comics adopt trad techniques and values, professionalism and showmanship that were always the norm among Variety acts in the mainstream clubs. 'There's not a lot of room to be bad anymore,' he says. 'The performers and the venues are adapting more to the audience that pays the wages, so they have to deliver all the time.' And so those speciality acts, the Variety turns, and Vaudeville eccentrics wither away. 'There ain't no room for manoeuvre anymore,' he concludes. 'Years ago, when you used to go in, you'd go, "Well, two of the acts were brilliant, one was shit and that other one was just weird," and you still felt as though you had a good night. Nowadays, they come out and they go, "Well, four acts were very good but that one was shit," and they feel as though they've had a bad night.'

John Lenahan is a magician from Philadelphia. He first came to London for a short break. Sixteen years later, he has a wife and son and a house in Cricklewood. He started busking magic on the streets of London. Within a year, he won an award from *Time Out*, and took his act indoors, mainly to stay out of the rain. 'This would be a great country,' he quips, 'if only it had a roof.' He toured with Ronnie Corbett, and even did summer season with Little & Large (he's an American – what did he know?), but his transatlantic blend of mesmeric tricks and smart stand-up patter also made him one of the best turns on the club circuit, and one of the top comperes at the Leicester Square Store. He became the first magician ever to be thrown out of the Magic Circle after revealing the mechanics of the three card trick, Find The Lady, on TV's *How Do They Do That?*

However he's also pulled off a few successful scams at the Piccadilly Circus Store. When Paul Daniels played The Prince Of Wales over the road, Lenahan sent out invitations to the press, saying 'Come and see Paul Daniels' show, and if you want to leave halfway through, come and see me at The Comedy Store.' The only problem was, Lenahan wasn't booked at The Store that week, so he had to bribe Sean Lock into giving him his spot on the bill. It was a brilliant publicity stunt but a pretty poor business proposition. Lenahan did Lock's spot, but Lock still got paid.

But he owes his most magical Store moment to a mystery punter. One night, he picked a punter at random and asked him to name a card. 'King of Diamonds,' said the punter. 'Wouldn't it be amazing if I reached in my pocket and took out your card?' asked Lenahan. 'Yes,' said the punter. Lenahan reached in his pocket and pulled out a huge card with all fifty-two playing cards printed on it. 'That's not amazing,' said the punter. 'This is amazing.' The punter reached in his mouth and pulled out a folded playing card. He unfolded it. It was the King. Of Clubs.

'Where's the lasagne?' shouts a heckler, as Otiz Canneloni arrives. 'If only life could be as simple as you,' replies Otiz. Canneloni is a comic conjurer, but unlike fellow Store illusionists John Lenahan or Paul Zenon, his tricks are a foil for his humour rather than the other way around, and so his style feels far closer to Tommy Cooper than David Copperfield. He describes his act as mystery, madness and magic. The mystery is 'who the fuck is this guy?' The madness is 'who the fuck booked him?' And the magic is 'how the hell will he get out of here?'

When Otiz started out, at the Soho Store, there was more variety, in both senses of the word. 'Lots of double acts, lots of musical acts, you usually finished off the bill with a band,' he recalls. 'That doesn't seem to be the case anymore. It's just straight stand-up, and people aren't interested in listening to many long stories, either. They want it kept pretty short so they can laugh a lot. I don't know whether it's a sign of the times that we need more laughter, or we're just getting more specific in what we want.' His own attitude is closer to classic Variety. 'I've never really thought about it as a career, which is why I'm where I am today,' he says. 'I've always thought of it as just something I enjoy doing. I'm a natural performer. I like being onstage and I'm quite happy to be up there. I'm not up there to make a point. I'm just up there to make people laugh.' Yet The Store provided a forum for a different sort of laughter. 'People could get up and say what they liked, and I suppose that's the job of the artist, isn't it? To live on the edge and to be able to say things that normal people wouldn't say. Hopefully we're all artists in one way or another, and I've always thought of my act as alternative in as much as it's non-sexist and non-racist. I've always thought of myself as a political act, even though I don't do political material.'

The Leicester Square Store hosted several fine comic magicians, but the most incredible Variety act to grace that tiny cellar stage was Phil Herbert, aka Hugh Jelly, aka Hubert Haddock, aka Randolph The Remarkable, whose act involved fire eating, fish juggling and lifting a tub of water with the suction from his massive stomach. 'Balancing flat out upon it in an impressive display of agility for one so big, he forces the folds of his enormous belly inside the bowl,' reported the *Independent* in 1990. 'At the climax of his performance, he leaps to his feet and raises his arms above his head to allow the audience to marvel at the sight of a twenty-stone man standing on a stage with a washing-up bowl stuck limpet like to his body.' 'It was a subversion of all that bland, end-of-the-pier stuff,' says Jim Barclay. But at a club increasingly dominated by stand-up, it was a celebration, too.

'I was an actor,' explains an older, slimmer Herbert. 'I'd learned how to fire eat in a show.' When he was resting, he'd busk in Covent Garden or Camden Lock, until a punter who saw his street show said he should do a turn at a new club in Soho called The Comedy Store. 'They won't want a fire act,' thought Herbert, but he went along anyway to take a look, watched a naked poet who hid his manhood behind a briefcase, and got roped into the open spot. He hadn't brought any of his props, and ended up doing his pyrotechnic act with a cigarette lighter. It was risky, but it went down well. If I can do the act with a borrowed lighter, he thought, I might as well come back and do it properly. And so Herbert, aka Randolph The Remarkable, became a regular at The Store.

'You got three drinks tokens for the night,' he says. 'Quite a few of the comics wouldn't drink, so I used to get their drinks cards. It'd be a sort of solo drinking adventure for me.' The women talked about periods, the men talked about ejaculation, subjects he'd never heard discussed onstage. 'You could see people sinking into their seats, not quite sure whether to laugh or not.' His fire eating was a welcome antidote, but there were a few practical problems. 'I used to smoke the place out,' he says. 'They used to have to turn the alarms off.'

Fire wasn't the only problem. There was also the water. When he lifted a bucket of water with his belly, the suction from his ample girth kept most of the water in the pail, but the floor would inevitably be a bit wet by the time he'd finished his act. 'Tony Allen used to complain about following me because I used to leave a wet puddle on the stage,' he says, 'so I took to the habit of going back on and mopping it up.' At least it was only water. A comedian called Mac MacDonald used to eat yoghurt sandwiches onstage.

Herbert's fire eating and bucket lifting usually went down well. 'I've never actually walked off,' he says. 'I've always finished the act. I've always left the stage with grace to applause. I've never left it to a sick silence.' However the highlight of his Store career was the double act he formed with Jane Janovic, his friend and flatmate from drama school. When she did her belly dancing, fire eating and bed of nails act in Covent Garden, she was Fatima The Fantastic, but at The Store, they became The Haddocks, or Hubert & Hilary Haddock With A Fish And Fire Fantasy, for short.

'It was a cod act,' explains Janovic. 'It was based on magic acts you'd see at Butlins and on cruise ships, except there was no magic involved. It was just dancing with fish.' They did a mackerel dance, a fish finger dance, a gold fish a gogo, and a finale called What The World Needs Now Is Sprats, Fresh Sprats, during which they threw white-bait at the audience. 'Whitebait are the best,' says Janovic. 'You can throw out a lot of whitebait.' However, despite this provocation, punters were usually stunned into silence rather than incited to riot. 'If anyone got out of hand, they used to get a slap round the face with a wet fish,' says Janovic. 'Give us more variety,' yelled a heckler, one evening, at every stand-up on the bill. 'How's this for variety?' asked Herbert, and smacked him across the cheeks with a mackerel.

At the Leicester Square Store, even the open spots shunned straight stand-up. 'The act before me was this bloke who went on, dressed in a black dinner suit and a bow tie,' says Hattie Hayridge, recalling her Store debut. 'He got this bottle of tomato sauce out of his pocket and tipped it into his mouth really slowly and filled his mouth up with tomato sauce and got this plastic gun out of his pocket and put it to his head and splattered tomato sauce all over the audience.' This stunt got laughs from punters safely out of range, but the punters who got splattered were furious. 'They were standing up, wiping it off their clothes and shouting at him.' But the Sauce Man played dead, and the other punters got up to leave. 'Get up now,' Kinnie ordered Hayridge, nudging her in the back. The compere dashed on and called her name, so Hayridge went on and spoke into a microphone for the first time. She didn't take her coat off because she doubted she'd be stopping long. 'I wasn't heckled,' she recalls. 'It was mostly people leaving and wiping tomato sauce off themselves.' The Sauce Man was still lying beneath her. 'I was standing over him,' she says. 'Luckily, I had a long coat on.' Half way through her set, he crawled out from between her legs, got up and walked off-stage, so she said goodnight and followed him.

However, the variety act that every Soho Store veteran raves about is Andrew Bailey. He's become a sort of symbol of what Alternative Comedy used to be. The Store never persevered with his oddball, other worldly humour, but Bailey's rarity is part of his appeal. Countless comedians talk about his strange act, his uncompromising attitude, how he performed his bizarre routines with total commitment, and a heroic indifference to the reaction of his audience. 'He made no distinction between success and failure,' explains Nick Hancock. 'His only distinction was his own, and he would perform at exactly the same pitch and same level, no matter whether there were two people that loved him or four hundred people that hated him.' For anyone who did get it, it was unique. 'He was my favourite Variety act,' says Nick Revell. 'He'd do a striptease. He'd take off his red nose and there'd be a white one underneath.'

The Store is a lot saner and safer nowadays, and even the few novelty acts that still play here have had to tone down their routines to survive. Pierre Hollins used to ride a unicycle, in tights and goggles, juggling five eggs and a rubber chicken. Now he just plays an electric squash racquet. However, Hollins still has a special sympathy with those eccentric turns who once entertained The Store, like that charming old man who could repeat any sentence backwards, or the Ice Man, whose entire act consisted of trying to melt a big block of ice in a wide variety of ways. 'That's all he did. He didn't have any lines. There was nothing funny. It was just an event. He had a blow torch, and he'd lick it, and he'd blow hot breath on it.' He also died the fastest death Hollins has ever seen. The Ice Man wore a huge fur coat, and one night, as he came on, someone shouted, 'Give it a saucer of milk.' He never even reached the microphone.

One of Pierre's favourite eccentrics was anarchic clown Chris Lynam. 'He was the master,' says Hollins. 'I don't think anybody could touch him for the energy and madness he brought to what he did.' Lynam's party piece was clutching a lit firework between his clenched buttocks, but he'd also set off fire extinguishers, hurl ice cubes at the audience, do swan dives into the front few rows, and then raise the roof with a heart-rending banjo rendition of Louis Armstrong's 'Wonderful World'. 'You weren't ever sure if Chris was an entertainer or an actual mad bloke,' says Hollins. And this fine line was what made his act so special.

Kevin McCarthy saw Lynam perform his combustible curtain call at Malcolm Hardee's notorious Tunnel Club. Even at Hardee's riotous dive, Lynam wasn't allowed to perform this stunt inside, so the audience followed him outside. 'He went out into the car park, stood on top of his own car, stuck the Roman candle up his arse, they played the music, and it wasn't until about ten seconds before the first flash went up that we realised his arse was facing the gasworks, which was literally just behind the place, and everybody ran away thinking they were all going to die.'

Anarchic turns like Lynam are almost all long gone, but a few speciality acts endure, and one subgenre that's proved more durable than most is impressionists. Chris Barrie and Steve Coogan both cut their teeth at The Store, and the latest mimic to break into peaktime terrestrial telly is also a graduate of this influential stand-up cellar. Alistair McGowan first went to The Store in the late Eighties, with a friend from drama school. He loved the show but he wasn't sure if he fitted in. 'It was quite intimidating,' he says. 'I felt a bit uncool, but then I saw Mark Thomas at the bar after he'd been on, wearing this blue mohair v-necked jumper, and I thought, "Oh well, even the comics don't look that cool."' He started doing impressions in the spring of 1989, and that summer, he did his first open spot at The Store.

McGowan had a flair for mimicry that most stand-ups could only dream of, and he also had a useful tip about playing this lopsided room. 'Bit of advice, mate, if it's your first time,' Jeff Green told him, beforehand. 'Do all your set-ups at the front, and do all your punchlines down the side.' 'I always did it, every time I played there, and I never asked anybody else if that's what they did, and I never mentioned it to Jeff,' he says, 'but it was the best advice anyone ever gave me.'

However, Kim Kinnie was looking for something more. 'Very good voices, but I wanted to see a bit more of you in there, and when I can see you and your attitude, not just showing off, then we'll have to think about you doing it again,' Kinnie told him afterwards. 'Come back in maybe a couple of years.' McGowan was devastated. 'A couple of years?' he thought. 'Forget it. What's the point?' But the next day, McGowan thought, 'He's probably right.' And now McGowan knows he was. 'What he said was absolutely true, and I started to work differently and have a different attitude about what I was doing,' he says. 'That was invaluable advice.' A couple of years later Kinnie saw his show at the Edinburgh Festival, and phoned him up and asked him to play The Store. McGowan was ready.

Whenever his mother was in London, she'd walk past The Store and check the board to see if her son was on that night's bill. 'I saw your name outside,' she'd tell him. He was thrilled that she was so excited, so the next time he was on, he took her along. They got past the bouncers, but at the bottom of the stairs his mother grabbed his arm. 'I can't go in there,' she said. 'Why not?' he asked her. 'It's all dark and it's full,' she replied. 'I really don't think I can go in there.' McGowan took her in and found her a seat at the back and she was fine. But it reminded him that for an outsider, The Store hadn't lost its capacity to intimidate, even if the star turn wears a blue mohair v-necked jumper.

Luck of the Irish

'Luck of the Irish? Hold on. Invasion, conquest, colonisation, famine, mass emigration, sectarian strife. How jammy can one small nation be? That's why we don't do the Lottery. We're afraid we'd get lucky and end up owing Camelot twenty-five million quid.'

Kevin Hayes[1]

The Thick Paddy joke was one of traditional stand-up's most persistent jibes, so it's apt that Alternative Comedy has always had a subtle yet distinctly Irish flavour. Estuary English comics subscribe to the notion that the shortest distance between two points of view is a straight one liner. Ireland's comedians take the scenic route. 'The Irish have elevated the art of beating around the bush to a level where the bush no longer exists,' observed Irish comic Kevin Gildea. 'Their language is rich because it is the language of avoiding the subject.'[2]

Early Irish emigres like Ian MacPherson and Michael Redmond introduced a more literate comic style to British comedy clubs in the Eighties, and in the Nineties, three Irish acts, Sean Hughes, Dylan Moran and Tommy Tiernan, all won the Perrier Award. 'The only thing you can do as a comic is create your own world and hope people will find it funny,' MacPherson once told me, and now a new generation of Irish comics are teaching the English how that's done. 'There's a bit more of a surreal element in Irish comedy which I suppose comes from Flann O'Brien or Joyce,' says Kevin Hayes, one of the new breed of Irish acts who've become established on the

British circuit. TV has been less pervasive in Ireland, while literature has kept its cultural kudos.

The discursive and tangential wit that Southern Irish comics brought to Britain works less well here in Piccadilly Circus than it did in Soho or even Leicester Square. Irish comics like Dylan Moran, Graham Norton, Ardal O'Hanlon and Tommy Tiernan all became TV stars without much help from The Store, and it was playing The Store that persuaded MacPherson to leave a circuit he felt had already left him. 'There was one gig I did which convinced me that I had to get out of the stand-up circuit, in which every single person onstage, including the compere and two open spots, made a joke about Linford Christie's penis, and the thing that frightened me about it was that the audience laughed every single time.'[3] A stag night party with a blow-up sheep watched with bemusement as this brilliant but uncompromising comic discussed Samuel Beckett and Seamus Heaney.

Yet Sean Hughes and Owen O'Neill have both been Store regulars, and Ed Byrne, one of Ireland's brightest rising stand-up stars, is a current Store favourite. Byrne's stand-up persona is less eccentric, and his material is more direct, but Kevin Gildea's quirky wit is also popular down here. Despite the casual bigotry of traditional English acts and the reluctance of modern comedy clubs to embrace Ireland's less commercial comics, humour has always travelled remarkably well across the Irish Sea, in both directions. One comic who epitomises this special relationship is Anglo-Irish stand-up John Moloney, and tonight he's hosting The Store's Saint Patrick's Day show. Actually, it's the day before the day before St Patrick's Day, but Wednesday is a Players night, and after several pints of stout, who's counting?

'Did you say Norway or Galway?' Moloney asks a Scandinavian visitor. 'It's the same thing really, isn't it? Can't understand either of them.' It's still early but Moloney looks at home up there and so he should be. He's already been onstage for three-quarters of an hour, playing sublime accordion music with his three-piece Irish band. Well, he is a former All-England & Ireland accordion champion. This St Patrick's show was his idea, and on its third year running, it's an annual Store event, drawing an eclectic crowd of Irish emigres and wannabes. As Kevin Gildea puts it, on Paddy's Day, even Oliver Cromwell's Irish.

'Hello, I'm Irish,' says Kevin Gildea as he reaches the mike. 'You're not serious,' shouts an Irish punter. 'Great talking to you,' retorts Gildea. 'Now shut up.' 'And you,' answers his heckler. 'They say you are what you eat,' says Gildea. 'You must have eaten a stupid cunt this morning.' Gildea's put-downs are effective, but his rehearsed material is far funnier. 'Irish pubs are so popular, they're building them in Ireland now,' he reveals. 'We're always the last to catch on.'

I first saw Gildea in the 1994 Hackney Empire New Act Of The Year. He finished runner-up behind future *Father Ted* star Ardal O'Hanlon. But although *Gildea* and O'Hanlon were new acts on the London comedy circuit, back in Ireland, they were already old hands. Five years before, with Dermot Carmody and Barry Murphy, they'd formed a sketch troupe, Mr Trellis, and set up a club called The Comedy Cellar, in a narrow attic above Dublin's International Bar. Like The Store, this club became the focal point for a national comedy renaissance, but unlike The Store, it was never a business. They simply handed it down to a new generation of local comics. And over a decade later, it's still going strong. 'We knew about The Store,' says Gildea, the morning after the night before, in a café around the corner from The Store. 'We knew about Alternative Comedy.' They performed once a fortnight for the first few months, in front of friends. There was no gong and hardly any heckling, but there was the same sense of turns and punters both making it up as they go along, both learning from one another.

Five years ago, Gildea started doing stand-up, a process that inevitably lured him towards London. 'It's like playing soccer. If you want to play soccer you want to play in one of the best leagues, and in terms of comedy, London's probably got the best league in the world.' After the informal ambience of Dublin's Comedy Cellar, phoning round for gigs in London was a culture shock. Despite living in Dublin for ten years he still felt sheltered, fearful of London audiences, whom he thought might be more misanthropic than the cheerful crowds at The Cellar. On the whole, he thought right, but it wasn't as bad as he first feared. Once, at The Store, someone shouted, 'Go home, Paddy,' but he's only heard that a few times. He thought it would happen a lot more. As he says, 'There's a lilt and a softness of delivery, a gentleness,' about many Southern Irish comics that's bound up with accent as much as anything. Northern Ireland has a more direct dialect and the humour follows suit. 'It is a very harsh, in your face sort of comedy,' says Gildea. 'They're more up front.' Pioneering Irish comics like Michael Redmond and Ian MacPherson had a more oblique relationship with an audience. 'It was almost as if they were delivering their material sideways.' It's a world away from the humour that succeeds on today's circuit. 'The material's not that great. It's more about noise and colour.'

'Yes, I am from Northern Ireland,' growls shaven-headed, ear-ringed Michael Smiley, taking Gildea's place at the mike. 'It's about fucking time there was a couple of us on this stage.' Some of Smiley's humour is specific to The Troubles. 'I love spotlights,' he quips. 'They make me feel at home.' But the poignant childhood memories that make up the vast bulk of his bittersweet set play equally well on either side of the border, or either side of the water. 'Are you my sister?' he asks a woman shrieking with laughter at an evocative routine about his father. 'Because I think we're talking about the same man.'

Yet there's a rough edge to his insistent wit that's uniquely Northern Irish. 'It's great to be here amongst all yous treaty-signing bastards,' he tells these Southern Irish punters. 'I'll stand over here and you do your best to ignore me for eighty years.'

'I don't really have much time for St Patrick's Day,' says Michael Smiley. 'It's just an excuse for you to get drunk and maybe get your leg over if you're lucky.' He's refreshingly disparaging about Ireland. 'There seems to be a global love affair with the Irish,' he says. 'I can't see it myself.' He's also amiably irreverent about surreal Southern Irish comics. 'I love them all, they're all my mates, but I had to be the opposite,' he says, in a clipped nasal accent. It's a dialect suited to fast, in your face one-liners, unlike the South, where delivery and material are summed up by his quip, 'Why say a word when a monologue will do?' His hard, dark humour is its antidote. 'You need that light and shade.'

Growing up in Northern Ireland was a good training ground for stand-up. 'Belfast has a tradition of slagging,' he says. 'You stand around with your mates and take the piss out of each other from the moment you walk in the door. If you're meeting your mates on a Friday night for a drink you'd better be on your best form.' It sounds a lot like performing at The Store. Before he became a comic, he was a cycle courier and Acid House DJ. He'd only been doing comedy for a few months when Kim Kinnie gave him twenty minutes, straight off, at The Store, without an open spot. Smiley went once as a punter before he played it, to see Lee Evans. The room was far smaller than he'd imagined, and Evans made it seem even smaller. 'Because of its reputation I expected it to be massive.' He'd been to a comedy club only once before, and got thrown out for shouting, 'Show us your gusset.'

Yet on the day of his Store debut, he was still pacing around his house, sweating, going through his notes, trying on different outfits, like some adolescent girl going out on her first date. One of his best friends gave birth at four o'clock that afternoon, and four hours later he was onstage. Smiley had supported Phill Jupitus on tour in Ireland, and Jupitus just happened to be compering that night. Jupitus gave Smiley a generous introduction, and despite his first-night nerves – 'I must have been going at about four hundred mile an hour' – the gig went like a dream. Afterwards Kim Kinnie bought him a bottle of champagne. 'Where did you come from?' Kim asked him. 'Nobody's talked about you. How come I haven't heard about you before?'

Within a few weeks the Leicester Square Store had closed, and so he did his second Store gig at the current premises in Piccadilly Circus, after midnight on a Friday. 'I was closing which I thought was fantastic because as far as I was concerned, I was headlining, but the reality is you're not really headlining because everybody's headliners down here anyway,' he says. 'If you're on late on a Friday night it means you're the sacrificial lamb.' Punters were dropping drinks and shouting abuse and trying to cop off with one another. 'Half the front row was asleep, the other half was throwing up, people at the back were shouting, "Fuck off, you Paddy cunt,"' he says. 'It felt like you were a rabbit in the headlights.' 'Do a tight sixteen, I'll light you at fourteen,' said Stan Nelson. 'They're a bunch of cunts. Let's get this over with.' It was sound advice. This was the sort of evening when the funniest guy in the photocopying room decides it's going to be his night, but Celtic aggression carried him through. 'All right then, bring it on, come on, do your worst,' he thought. 'I'm the one with the microphone and I've got a big pair of boots on, so as long as nobody makes their way towards the stage and I don't need to kick anybody in the head we should get through this OK.' He still felt panic stricken but he got away

with it and had another good gig. He got paid and went straight out clubbing, to dance away the energy.

'I just got back from Northern Ireland,' announces Owen O'Neill, a wiry Northern Irishman whose gaunt face is half hidden beneath a thick mop of rich red hair. 'I was there three weeks. I think I've got the accent off to a tee.' O'Neill left his home and eleven siblings in Cookstown, County Tyrone, when he was seventeen, to work and drink his way through a string of Big Smoke building sites. 'He finally escaped to London in 1980, boarded an underground train at Hounslow West and wasn't seen for two years,' reads O'Neill's biog. 'In 1982 he arrived at Holborn tube station with twenty poems and read them to passers-by. In 1983 he performed some comic poetry with Roger McGough and Brian Patten. He went to the 1984 Glastonbury Festival, did a stand-up comedy routine in the peace tent, was carried off after two minutes and has never looked back.'

Plenty of modern comics do a range of showbiz jobs, but O'Neill is that rare thing, a proper creative polymath. Stand-up, actor, poet, playwright and screenwriter, he's done solo shows about being a labourer, an alcoholic, even a comedian. 'There's a ceasefire in Northern Ireland which is brilliant because I live in London,' he says. 'This is where all the fucking bombs are going off.' A joke is a problem shared and the audience responds with a gutsy laugh and a communal sigh of relief. 'Ten years ago, I probably wouldn't have had anything to do with it,' he says, later. 'Maybe because I'm getting older I think, well, why not?' And there are upsides to any theme night. 'It was a bit like doing a gig in Ireland because they did get things that English audiences wouldn't get.' And he relished the opportunity to do stuff about the IRA for Irish punters, not because they give him an easier ride but for quite the opposite reason. 'Sometimes it's more edgy, actually, to do that sort of material with an Irish audience than it is with an English audience.'

Owen O'Neill first played The Store in the early Eighties. It was the first time he'd ever even been inside. 'I was really disappointed,' he says. 'It was like an underground car park.' The normal thing to do was phone up and pester Kim Kinnie for an open spot, but O'Neill simply turned up and blagged his way in, and on. 'Tony Allen was in the doorway and he was having an argument with Kim,' recalls O'Neill. He could scarcely have bumped into two more seminal antagonists. 'I don't think Don had really that much to do with it during those years,' says O'Neill. 'If you wanted to go on, you went to see Kim Kinnie. You didn't go and see Don Ward.' However O'Neill didn't have a clue who any of them were, and they didn't know him either.

'Who are you?' Kim asked him. 'I'm the open spot,' lied O'Neill. 'Go in and see the compere,' said Kinnie, his hands already full with Allen. 'Your name should be in the book.' Of course it wasn't, but O'Neill went in anyway, and found the compere, Tony Morewood, a Mancunian who's actually better known in America, having toured over half the United States. 'I'm just doing five minutes,' O'Neill told him. Morewood checked the running order. Naturally, O'Neill's name wasn't on it. 'I rang up,' lied O'Neill. 'I don't remember you ringing me up,' said Kinnie, finally free from his altercation with Allen. 'I did,' persisted O'Neill. 'I rang you up twice.' 'Who did you speak to?' asked Kinnie. 'I spoke to you,' insisted O'Neill. 'Well you're not down here,' said Kinnie. Kinnie told him to come back next week. 'I can't, I'm going back to Ireland,' lied O'Neill. 'I've come all the way from Ireland.' 'Can you squeeze him in somewhere?' Kinnie asked Morewood. 'It's up to you,' said Morewood. 'OK,' relented Kinnie. 'You can go on after the interval.' O'Neill opened with a poem, to total silence. 'It wasn't a dying silence,' recalls O'Neill. 'It was a bemused kind of silence.' He did another poem, a comic poem, got a laugh, and followed up with a routine about how he came to write it.

'That was different,' Kinnie told him afterwards, still unaware he'd been hustled. 'You don't have any jokes but it was very interesting. You didn't die.' It wasn't a rave, but O'Neill got what he was after. 'Come back next week,' Kinnie told him, 'but come back with some jokes.' The Leicester Square Store was stand-up, not cabaret or variety. 'It had to have a political edge,' says O'Neill. 'No fucking jugglers. No stupid double acts with hats. The Store set that standard and Kim was the man there.' There weren't many other comics who could pull the wool over his eyes.

Although O'Neill had no jokes, Kinnie had seen something he liked, and when he went back, he didn't have to hoodwink his way in. He spent the whole week writing, and then an IRA bomb went off in London. One of his newly written gags had suddenly acquired a potent topicality. 'There's this sign on the tube that says if you see an unattended package, please go and tell someone,' said O'Neill, 'but not if you've got a Northern Irish accent.' That gag got the biggest laugh he'd ever had. 'To my horror, I'm still doing it,' he says, fifteen years later.

Yet not all O'Neill's Northern Irish material went down so well at The Store. Once, he did a routine about tabloid coverage of The Troubles, and enraged some squaddies who'd recently returned from Northern Ireland. 'These soldiers got up, they're going, "You're fucking dead, you bastard, you fucking IRA sympathiser,"' he recalls. 'It all went off. It was really ugly, and the whole audience just went against me.' One punter stood up and said, 'You can't do jokes like that.' 'I can fucking do jokes like that if I want,' retorted O'Neill. Not now he couldn't. 'It was impossible for me to do any jokes. They just weren't going to listen.' Yet he refused to leave the stage. 'I stayed up there and I tried to explain what it was I was doing and how I came from there.' His routine was about the red top papers, rather than the army, but these troops were still angry. 'I've just been to Belfast,' said one soldier. 'As far as I'm concerned, you're a gunman,' said O'Neill. 'I'm protecting the Catholic community from Protestants,' said the soldier. 'If that's what you're doing, fantastic, but you're not all doing that,' replied O'Neill. 'We had this big argument,' recalls O'Neill. 'It became more than comedy.' O'Neill felt there was something very vital going on, but he also sensed a degree of danger. 'They'd just come off a tour of Northern Ireland and they'd had their mates shot so it was quite a volatile situation,' says O'Neill. 'They were soldiers who'd been in the Falls Road so they weren't going to give a fuck about one bouncer in The Store, so it could have been pretty nasty.'

Finally, O'Neill left the stage. 'Bunch of fuckers,' said his fellow comics, who'd left the dressing room to watch this rumpus unfold from the wings. 'People were saying, "Throw them out," and Kim was saying, "No, I'm not throwing them out, because they were heckling, and they've got their say, and they were upset, and let them stay."' They stayed. 'I can't just go out there and do material willy nilly,' realised O'Neill. 'If you're doing stuff about Northern Ireland then you have to at least feel that you know what you're talking about and if anybody does challenge you then you've got an answer for them.' From where I'm sitting, casual racism seems far more insidious than genuine outrage. Another night at The Store, a heckler taunted O'Neill throughout his set with the slight: 'Paddy, where's your shovel?'

Yet even unruly hecklers are a picnic compared to some quieter punters back home. 'I don't want to censor you,' a guy who ran a gig in Northern Ireland told O'Neill before the show, 'but you know that material you do about the IRA?' 'Yes?' said O'Neill. 'Well, you see that table over there?' 'Those four lads?' asked O'Neill. 'You're fucking winding me up.' 'I'm not winding you up,' said the guy who ran the gig. 'Take it from me. I'm not saying don't do it. But.' 'For fuck's sake,' thought O'Neill.

But once any comic steps up onto that stage, it's a different story. A stand-up set is an isolated moment, where even the shadow of a gunman seems less tangible than a far more urgent task, to make an audience laugh, and keep them laughing. Once a comic is in the spotlight, every other imperative is lost in another distant elsewhere. Real life must wait. 'You just feel impervious to everything,' says O'Neill. 'I thought, "If I don't

Ed Byrne

do this now, I'm the biggest fucking hypocrite that ever walked."' And so he did it. The light was in his eyes and the audience was cloaked in darkness, so he couldn't see if those four lads were laughing or not. The gig went well, but the instant he stopped, the spell was broken. 'As soon as I put the microphone back in the stand and I came offstage, I thought, "Oh fuck, I shouldn't have done that."' But by now it was too late. O'Neill was at the bar when one of the four lads walked up to him. 'Excuse me,' he said. O'Neill turned around. 'Yes?' asked O'Neill. 'You did one thing right tonight, son,' he said. 'What was that?' asked O'Neill. 'You didn't take the piss out of my jumper,' he said. And he turned and walked away.

'It's nice to be back here again because I haven't played here since the last Saint Patrick's Day,' says Ed Byrne. 'I've been touring the world apologising for *Riverdance*.' Actor, playwright and broadcaster, this scrawny long-haired Dubliner is still in his twenties. It's only five years since his first open spot at The Store. 'Say something funny,' shouts a heckler, as Byrne returns for an encore after a seamless stand-up set. 'What?' asks Byrne, with simple surprise. 'Say something funny,' repeats the heckler, but he's on his own and Byrne doesn't even need to put him down. His dissent simply dies away.

'It was the one gig where you're sure no one's going to heckle you and make a derogatory comment about your nationality,' says Byrne, in the dressing room. In a few days' time, he'll be down here again for another five gigs, crammed into three nights. He even dropped in last weekend, even though he wasn't on, and saw Kevin Hayes bear the brunt of some anti-Irish abuse. 'He was asking if someone was Irish and somebody else says, "No, they don't sound stupid," and the rest of the audience didn't boo,' he marvels. 'The audience didn't seem to see anything particularly harmful about that remark and that's a bit of a worry.' Hayes told me he thought British punters were becoming more broadminded about Ireland, but as Byrne says, this incident, and the audience's indifferent reaction, suggests things may be getting worse. 'Ten years ago that kind of remark wouldn't have been welcome at all.' Actually, they're probably both right, in different ways. England as a whole has become less bigoted towards the Irish, but The Store now attracts an increasingly broad cross-section of punters, liberal enough to want to go and watch right-on modern comics instead of old trad stand-ups, but insufficiently militant to shout down the bigots in their midst. 'I remember doing the Comedy Café and going on after an Irish comic who'd died on their arse,' says

Byrne. 'As soon as I opened me mouth, some guy shouted out, "Oh no, not another fucking paddy."'

The Store's first Saint Patrick's night show two years ago was especially memorable for Byrne. 'I'd met this girl a few days beforehand,' he says. 'I was too shy to ask for her phone number. Canadian comic Simon B. Cotter, who's married and therefore lives vicariously through young folk got her phone number for me.' Byrne called her up, but even then he didn't want to ask her out on a date. 'I'm doing a gig on Monday night,' he told her. 'Do you want to come to watch? I'll put you on the list. You can bring some people with you.' And she came along. 'I had a routine all about Freudian psychology and then when I got off I was talking to her and it turned out she was a student of psychology. She had a degree in psychology and drama, and she was very impressed with my psychological comedy. I remember thinking, "I'm in here!" And then when her friends all said, "Right, that's it, we're heading home now," she stayed. 'We live together now. A year later we went to see *Cosi Fan Tuti* for our anniversary and I wrote a show about it and took it to Edinburgh last year and got nominated for the Perrier, so that night was a very important turning point in my love life and my comedy career.' But there's a down side to beginning a beautiful relationship on Saint Patrick's Day. 'Now our anniversary is Saint Patrick's Night and that's just fucked things up for me.'

'You'll play the fucking anthem, won't you?' a punter at last year's show asked John Moloney. So Moloney played the Irish national anthem, and he'll play it again tonight. 'You may react to this in any way that you feel fit, but I was told to play it by someone very tall with a very scary accent,' he says, strapping on his accordion, before playing the first few bars of 'God Save The Queen'. It's just a joke, and he soon reverts to the proper tune. Some punters stand, some sing along, and British punters get a fleeting glimpse of how it feels to be a member of a cultural if not an ethnic minority, for whom joining in and opting out both feel uncomfortable, if not plain foolish.

'It was quite strong stuff about Republicanism or Loyalism but within an Irish context,' explains Moloney, later. 'Irish people understand. People weren't leaving going, "Hoorah! Fuck the Royal Family!" It wasn't like that. It wasn't revolutionary talk but it was just honest talk about how the Irish ethnic community itself abuses Republicanism, abuses Loyalism, abuses Catholicism.' These shows tend to attract a slightly older crowd. Over half are ethnic Irish, rather than one in ten on a normal night. There's a common bond between these acts and their audience, so the atmosphere is less confrontational, more convivial. 'Irish people have a respect for other people's entertainment ability. English people can be a bit more cynical about it.' It's not just a celebration of Irish comedy, but Irish culture, too. 'Everybody has to be able to do something, whether it's sing a song or dance or play an instrument or recite a bit of poetry,' he says, confirming the half-truth in the stereotype of singing, dancing Irish family life. 'Irish people celebrate that ability.'

Phill Jupitus

'If you have a good one at The Store, it's a reminder of why you did this in the first place,' says Phill Jupitus, above the early evening racket of gossiping media hacks in the Groucho Club. 'If I ever got jaded and was thinking about chucking it in, I'd risk a weekend at The Store. I'd probably have four shit ones.' But the one good one would remind him why he stopped doing poetry and started doing stand-up instead. 'I'm feeling the tug again now,' he says. 'The Store's the place that's got the strongest pull.' And in half an hour, he's heading straight back there to do his first Store show this year.

Nowadays, his stand-up shows fill theatres throughout the land, but Jupitus started out as a performance poet. And even though he was well received at other venues around the club circuit, for years he reckoned his live verse wouldn't be welcome at The Store, where straight stand-up reigned supreme. Eventually, Mark Thomas persuaded him to give it a go. 'You're funny enough to do The Store,' said Thomas, so Jupitus rang Kim Kinnie. 'I was wondering if it would be possible to come and do a gig?' asked Jupitus. 'What's your name?' asked Kinnie. 'Porky The Poet,' said Jupitus. 'We don't book poets,' said Kinnie. Jupitus packed in the poetry and went into the music business. He worked as a press officer for The Housemartins, then illustrated record sleeves and directed videos for Billy Bragg and Kirsty MacColl, all good training for his future starring role in TV's *Never Mind The Buzzcocks.*

After a few years, Jupitus gave up his day job to try comedy full-time. He got an open spot from Store stage manager Kevin Luton, and by the time Kim Kinnie saw him, he'd already done several try outs. This time, Kinnie booked him for a weekend.

His first paid gig was following Denis Leary. 'Friday late show was supposed to be the nightmare one, but those were my favourite memories.' One Friday, just after an IRA bomb, there were barely forty punters in the building. 'It was always terrorism that tended to keep the crowds away. Never the turns.' Jupitus built his entire set around trying to remember all their names.

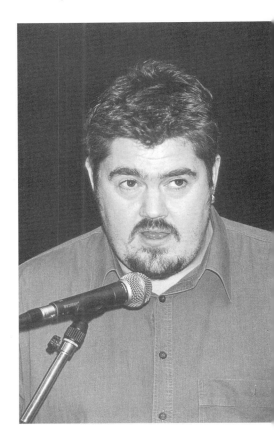

Soon, he was doing five gigs a night at weekends: early and late shows at The Store and Jongleurs, plus another club inbetween. 'An awful lot of money for one night's work,' says Jupitus, who'd worked in a Job Centre for five years. 'That's more money than I made in a month when I was a civil servant.' But doubling up brought occupational hazards. 'You've already done this,' said a heckler, so quietly that nobody else could hear, as he was closing the late show. Repeating a gag is every comic's worst nightmare, and after five gigs in one night, Jupitus wasn't too sure himself. 'Have I done this yet?' he asked Stan Nelson, in the sound booth. 'No,' said Stan. His heckler was bluffing, but he'd found his Achilles' heel. Jupitus stopped doubling up soon after.

Now he's become a TV star, he no longer has the luxury of anonymity. 'They know who I am,' he explains. 'I've not got the advantage of surprise anymore. They know you too well and that takes a little bit of the magic away, but I've always upped my game in the past. I don't know if I'll up my game now. You just have to learn to be a bigger man. I'll be back.'

Americans

You drive out of Santa Monica, away from the ocean, with the setting sun behind you, through Beverly Hills, along Sunset Boulevard and into Hollywood, until the driver stops and drops you outside a smart roadside club called The Comedy Store. Today there are two Comedy Stores in England, and two more long since come and gone, but there are four Stores up and running in America. There's The Comedy Store Playhouse here in Hollywood, a Comedy Store at The Dunes Hotel in Las Vegas, one in LaJolla, just outside San Diego, and this, the original all-comedy workshop nightclub. Stood here, with that warm Pacific breeze blowing through your hair, watching the sleek convertibles sailing down Sunset Strip, you can see why Peter Rosengard and Don Ward both felt so inspired.

Absolutely No Fire Arms, reads a notice outside the nightclub along the street, and the bouncer shines a torch into your handbag on the way in, just in case nobody saw the sign, but there's nothing like that out here. It all feels perfectly safe and fairly friendly. I step inside. There are three stages: the Main Room, the Belly Room and the Original Room, where Richard Pryor made his comeback in 1972, creating three groundbreaking stand-up albums that inspired a million aspiring stand-ups, including a teenage impressionist from Dudley called Lenny Henry. Roseanne Barr, David Letterman and Garry Shandling all played here too. Today, the big names play the Main Room, but the Original Room is where the ghosts will be, and so I buy a ticket for the arena where it all began. In this dark, slick studio, tonight's show has already started, and the waitresses have to stoop down over the tables to stay out of the spotlight. The compere is already up onstage. And he's English.

His name is Adrian Neil and I've never heard of him, but he's been in *Frasier* and *Sabrina The Teenage Witch* in the States, and even *The Bill*, back in Britain. He's played Chaucer and Shakespeare in London, but seeing him onstage, he seems so, well, American. He's a lot better than a lot of Brits I've seen back home, but tonight his accent is the only remotely British thing about him. He introduces half a dozen acts, including a comedienne called Harriet Rose, who's been on *Saturday Night Live*, and another called Elizabeth Kuyper, who's done stand-up in pubs and clubs in London. The closing head-liner, Carlos Alazraqui, is a class act, and the rest of them aren't too far off. The material is intelligent and inoffensive, the delivery polished and accomplished, and even though I stick to the two drink minimum, the only time I'm not smiling is when I laugh out loud. It's as much fun as you can have for ten bucks, alone and sober, without doing anything you'd wake up feeling miserable about. Yet as soon as I step back into the cool Californian dusk outside, apart from Carlos, I can barely remember a word they've said.

Mitzi Shore started her Comedy Store in 1972. She sold tickets, handed out free gum and cigarettes, and poured drinks for stand-ups like Kelly Monteith. The Westwood Store opened in 1975, showcasing future movie stars like Jim Carrey, Michael Keaton and Robin Williams. In 1984, The Dunes Hotel pioneered modern stand-up on the Las Vegas strip, and now The Comedy Store Playhouse nearby provides a unique platform for solo shows and comic plays.

This is what Peter Rosengard wanted to emulate. Instead he ended up in a Soho strip club with Keith Allen and Alexei Sayle. Was he lucky or unlucky? I can't decide. But either way, the Soho Store was nothing like tonight. And nor was Don Ward's Leicester Square Store. His Piccadilly Circus and Manchester Stores do bear some passing resemblance to New York clubs like Caroline's On Broadway, but out here, on the other side of America, the other side of the world, Manhattan is 3,000 miles away, and London feels more like a million.

'Good evening, and in case you're wondering, twenty stone,' says Phill Jupitus, kicking off Independence, The Day After. As the title implies, despite the brace of star-spangled banners hung behind him, it's a somewhat belated celebration. This year, Independence Day was on Sunday, and Sunday is a Players Night. What's more, Jupitus isn't American. But he is a lifelong fan of the land of the free and easy. As he says himself, he may not be American, but he does look like he comes from Arkansas. 'I'm here because I fucking love America,' he declares.

'Get your wig off!' shouts a heckler, at Arj Barker. Barker can't comply. He doesn't wear a wig. His hair is all his own, although he does crack a gag that attests to its unusual shape and style. 'Never get your hair cut at a Star Trek convention,' he drawls. He's still only in his twenties, but this laid back San Franciscan slacker has already come a long way. He's even done David Letterman's flagship show back in the USA. It's a lively audience, but they appreciate transatlantic class, and by the end of his set, this rising star has them eating out of his hand.

Nowadays, he makes it look so easy, but it took Barker a while to work out how British punters tick. 'When I first came over here, I felt like I had to really win over an audience or they'd all turn on me,' he says. 'I didn't know anything. I'd never been here.' His second gig reduced him to tears. 'There was dead silence and I really thought I'd failed.' 'Have a tissue,' said one of the other comics. 'You should take the piss out of being American.' Barker dried his eyes and took the tip. It worked. His third British gig was better. The fourth was better still. He'd imagined Englishmen wearing monocles, but he soon learned not everyone here wears a bowler hat and takes afternoon tea. He also learned to send up his own All-American assumptions. British punters loved it.

'About fifty-five years ago, my nan would drop her knickers for this stuff,' says Jupitus, tucking into a Hershey Bar. 'This is probably the reason I'm here tonight. And a pair of nylons.' He chews thoughtfully, then delivers his considered gourmet verdict. 'It's fucking horrible, but I'm going to carry on fucking eating it,' he says. 'This stuff is vile,' he adds, as he finishes off the entire bar. And despite the distractions of transatlantic confectionery, he's still fighting fit. 'Not unlike World War Two, you came in halfway though and spoiled everything,' he tells an American heckler, as he brings on another US comic.

'I know it sucks when you come out for a chat,' Eddie Brill tells two talkative punters, 'and they build a comedy club around you. It fucks up your whole night.'

'I've always loved British comedy,' says Brill, sat in The Store's cramped windowless office, still sweating slightly from his set, as the show carries on outside. 'I feel like I belong here.' British punters are allowed to answer back, unlike punters back in the States, but this cuddly comic relishes the challenge. And although he's already a seasoned stand-up, you can still sense his boyish enthusiasm as he talks about the craft he so clearly adores. 'It's rewarding to go to another culture and make people laugh,' he says. 'It really makes me work hard.' Especially when hecklers force you off your set. 'I hadn't done three-quarters of the session I did last night, because I was dealing with hecklers tonight,' he explains. 'I don't mind that. If you're so rote that you're doing the exact same thing every single night, you're never going to grow.' And he only notices how much his act has grown when he gets home. 'In England, you can do so many more things with comedy, because you have to deal with the crowd. You have to deal with being in another culture.' He's even worked a few British put-downs into his act. If a punter drops a beer bottle in the middle of his punchline, he's learned to say, 'Sack the juggler,' and if a heckler calls him fat, he's learned to say, 'That's because every time I fuck your mother, she makes me sandwiches.' And though he's played other British comedy clubs, The Store is something special. 'It's my home,' he says. 'People here treat me like family.'

Not every Stateside act is so popular. 'I'm going to tear the roof off,' boasted one visiting American comic, backstage before the show. He lasted less than ten minutes before he was booed offstage. Afterwards, he was sat in the dressing room, totally dejected, when Don Ward came in. Ward chatted to the other comics for a while, then looked up at the ceiling. 'Roof still here then?' asked Ward.

Brill has Denis Leary's son to thank for introducing him to The Store, even though Jack Leary was only a few weeks old at the time. In 1990, before he became a Hollywood film actor, Leary flew from his New York home to London for a long weekend to do a set on the BBC stand-up show *Paramount City*, hosted by Arthur Smith. His wife came with him. She was six months pregnant. They planned to stay three nights. On the morning of the show, her waters broke. They took a cab to the hospital, where they were told she'd have to stay until her child was born, which could be three months away.

That night, Leary played *Paramount City*, around the corner from The Store. He assumed the backstage chat about a riot was a reference to the success of his short set. In fact it was a reference to Britain's biggest poll tax riot since the Peasant's Revolt. Policemen blocked his exit. Rioters burned cars in the streets outside. It was three hours before he could leave the theatre. It took another three to walk to the hospital. Leary played *Paramount City* again the next weekend. Two days later, his son Jack was born, twelve weeks premature. The family was advised not to leave the country for another five months, and Leary spent much of this impromptu sabbatical at The Store.

'Please come and visit me,' Leary told Brill. When Brill arrived, Leary was playing The Store. Brill was amazed at the transformation Leary's act had undergone. 'It was the best thing that ever happened to him,' says Brill. 'He really grew over here. He had a confidence that I'd never seen before.'

Brill didn't want to drop Leary's name, so he just asked Kim Kinnie for an open spot, incognito. Contacts can help open doors, but in the end, it isn't about who or even what you know, it's about whether you know how to make an audience laugh. Kinnie gave Brill ten minutes, but as soon as he'd seen him work, he booked him for a whole weekend. Since then he's been back here several times a year. He'd play here even more if it wasn't for his regular gig back home in New York, warming up studio audiences for David Letterman.

Transatlantic travel has broadened Brill's Stateside perspective. 'Now, when I write, I write for every audience,' he says. 'I don't write for just New York audiences, or for an American audience. I write gags that human beings will laugh at.' But there are gags he can crack here that he could never crack back in the States. 'America is so uptight about religion, you really can't joke about it,' he says. 'My favourite comedy show is *Father Ted*. You can never have that in the States, because America's too uptight. They'll boycott the show before they even know what it's about.' He wasn't entirely surprised by our British latitude. 'I always thought British audiences would be smarter than American audiences,' he adds. 'British comedy to me was always much funnier.'

And several of his fellow Americans have also found fresh audiences over here, such as Greg Proops. 'I met him in Los Angeles and he couldn't get onstage,' says Brill. 'He came to England and then you found out he's a smart guy, a funny guy, and he did very well here. Denis Leary was a decent comic, but he came here and it was fantastic. That's what I loved about this culture. They will embrace you if you're smart, if you take the time to understand them and if you talk about human nature.'

'Of course the Kennedys were from Boston,' Jupitus tells the Bostonian in the front row, kicking off the second half. 'Did your mum fuck any of them?' The Americans boo, but Jupitus isn't bothered. 'What?' he asks. 'The fucking Kennedys were at it like knives, twenty-four hours a day. When they weren't being shot.' More boos, but Jupitus doesn't care. 'The clue is in the name, sweetheart,' he says, pointing to the grinning logo behind him. Jupitus asks American punters to shout out what state they come from. 'Manchester,' bellows an English heckler. 'That is a fucking state,' concurs Jupitus, 'but not the sort I mean.'

Maria Falzone has been a visiting Store act for several years, but it took her a while to find the wavelength. 'I thought people were going to be really polite,' says this dark, Rubensesque New Yorker, backstage, between shows. 'I was waiting for people to serve me tea.' Falzone's England was Merchant Ivory movies and *Upstairs Downstairs* on TV, not a late show at The Store. 'You could tell just coming in that they were rowdy,' she says, remembering her first midnight show, compered by Phill Jupitus. 'You don't have to do your full twenty,' Stan Nelson told her. 'No, I've got to do my twenty,' she replied. 'If I need back up, I'm just going to call,' she told the bouncers, 'because I'm going to kick the shit out of somebody.' She'd already done an early show that night, but she still felt overwhelmed. 'It was like I was being assaulted.'

'Show us your piss flaps,' a heckler shouted at her. 'What are piss flaps?' asked Falzone. So the heckler got up onstage and showed her. 'No one was offering me tea,' she says. 'Security had to calm down this woman in the front row who was going to help me kick the shit out of the people that were heckling. It was close to a riot.' The bouncers threw out the bloke who'd got up onstage and pointed at Falzone's 'piss flaps', but while they were about it, they had to remove most of the front row. 'I'd rather lick a bloody gash than talk to you fucking people,' she said, and returned to the dressing room. She couldn't talk to anyone. 'I was in complete shock. When I started comedy, I never planned to say, "I'd rather lick a bloody gash". That was never part of the game plan.' And the next night she had to go back and do it all over again.

She walked onstage to a barrage of boos, but this time she was ready for them. 'Boo?' she said. 'Boo? I'm from New York. Fucking boo? You've hurt my feelings. Boo? You don't impress me, you people. Maybe if you have a knife you'll impress me.' This shut them up, but by the end of her set, they were yelling for an encore. 'Excuse me, but who was fucking booing me twenty minutes ago?' asked Falzone. 'I'm not going to stay up here any longer. Fuck you.' She exited to applause, but she's still a bit wary of this room. 'I'm always a little nervous before I get up here, because I don't know what's going to happen,' she says. 'In a minute, they can turn.' But now she turns on them. 'When I first came here I had this idea that I had to be gentle and I had to be nice.' But that all changed the night she doubled up, and took a cab between The Red Rose and The King's Head, two North London comedy clubs. It wasn't a black cab, the car was a wreck, and the driver couldn't find the club and yelled at her when they got lost. By the time she got onstage, she was livid, and the crowd loved it.

'The comedy scene here is incredible, and I hope they don't do what we did in America, because we bled it dry,' she says. 'So many clubs opened up and there weren't enough comedians.' Open mikers were hosting. Also-rans were headlining. 'It got to the point where you'd say, "Can the guy stay onstage for ten minutes without shitting himself? All right, he's the opening act."' After fifteen years doing stand-up Stateside, she was bored. She isn't bored here. 'When I come out of the tube in Leicester Square, people are coming out of there in throngs,' she says. 'People say New York is overwhelming. No, this is overwhelming. I've never walked out of a subway station with that many people just pouring out.' Know-alls say humour doesn't travel, so when yours does, you know you're good. 'If you can come to another culture and make people laugh, then you're funny.'

'God bless the eighty-three people who showed up tonight,' says Rich Hall. 'Look at the big sea of red industrial leather furniture to my left, ladies and gentlemen. The old "you're not sold out again" reminder.' You have to be a pretty good comic to draw attention to a sparse turn out and get away with it, but Hall can take risks that lesser comics wouldn't dare to contemplate, and still look like he's treading water. 'If there's someone that looks as though they don't give a shit onstage, chances are it's because they've spent a long time learning that, because no one in their right mind actually goes onstage not giving a shit,' says Paul Zenon, of Hall's immaculately indifferent style. He's even good enough to send up his own act. 'If I can make even one person laugh? What a shitty percentage that is, ladies and gentlemen.' And when a heckler pokes fun at his camp cowboy shirt, Hall joins in. 'That's right, sir, it's called a Kansas City faggot shirt,' he agrees. 'You never know when a gun fight could break out in Old Compton Street.'

But although his off-the-cuff repartee is better than many other people's pre-prepared stuff, his proper material is better still. 'Stop fucking trying to be like America,' he pleads. 'We make the best snacks anywhere on the goddamn planet and also the most exercise equipment. We're just getting the world fat and helping them to lose weight again.' But his finale is interrupted by another heckle about that shirt. 'I'll never wear this shirt again,' he promises. 'I'll take it home and burn it. Does that make you happy? And the American flag. No, you can't do that. It's actually against the law to burn an American flag in the United States. How fucked up is that? And yet I guess in a way I agree with it because those people in Malaysia work really hard to make

Greg Proops in front of The Comedy Store's dressing-room mirror

you don't get your show then you're a writer on a show and if you're not a writer on a show, what are you? That comedian hasn't made it as far as America is concerned.' Stateside comics usually have only one objective – 'to get into Hollywood and make as much money as you can.' These British comics were less interested in plugging their latest project than ripping the piss out of each other. 'Here, they come down to have a pint and a laugh and watch their mates make people laugh.' Like the time Tony Slattery stripped off and confronted Sandi Toksvig in mid-sketch, completely naked. Toksvig went so red, she looked like a ham wearing a blond wig.

Mike McShane was the American impro king, and Rich Hall is the stand-up champ, but one American comic shone in both genres. 'The Americans brought a crispness that a lot of reserved British comics didn't have,' says Philip Herbert, and no American comedian is crisper than Greg Proops. Proops first came to London to do *Whose Line Is It Anyway?*, and his fellow San Franciscan Will Durst recommended him to Kim Kinnie. Durst had done a lot of stand-up here, and his say-so was worth a dozen open spots. Kinnie booked Proops blind. He didn't regret it, but for the first few minutes, it looked as if he might.

Before the gig, Proops had dinner with Paul Merton. 'I never really travelled to any other foreign countries before I came to England,' says Proops, backstage, before a Players show. 'I went over my whole routine, boring Paul to tears.' But it didn't do much good. 'I walked on, told the first joke backwards, told the punchline first and thought of a hilarious joke that I just completely fucked up.' And then someone heckled. When a bad comic begins badly, one heckle can push them under, but when a good comic begins badly, that same heckle can save him from himself. 'What do you do?' he asked, grateful to grab a lifeline. 'I'm a male prostitute,' said the heckler. 'Well,' said Proops, 'you must be the butt ugliest one in Leicester Square.' After that it went OK. His second gig went even better. 'Things that were erudite and troublesome in the States got big laughs here,' he says. 'I used to do a bit about being lost in my freezer and finding the diary of an Arctic explorer, which always got OK laughs in the States. But when you come to the home of dying Arctic explorers, that joke is very funny.' By the time he met his first hen night, he was ready for almost anything. 'Listen, sister,' he told a woman who took the piss out of his suit. 'This suit is worth more than your whole shitty wedding tomorrow.'

Richard Vranch was playing piano on *Whose Line*, and asked Proops along to a Players show. 'This is Greg,' Richard Vranch told the team, bringing Proops backstage. Proops sensed a huge wall of resentment. 'I'm going to go out and get a beer,' he said, and walked straight out again. 'Shit,' he thought. 'They hate me. I'm over here doing *Whose Line* and it's their bowl of rice.' But onstage, this Arctic freeze soon thawed. The joke that really broke the ice was his crucifixion gag. 'I can see your house from here,' he said, suspended on an imaginary cross.

Proops discovered British impro audiences have longer attention spans. 'People listen here and people want it to work and they are very harsh when it doesn't work, but you do have the first three or four minutes,' he says. 'The audience is more relaxed about letting people take their time.' Literary references are easier too. 'You ask for authors and playwrights in the States. You often get Stephen King as a movie director and John Steinbeck as a playwright. People are a little confused sometimes over literature. Here, people are more involved in reading.'

Even our hecklers are smarter, yet the atmosphere is more laid back. 'In LA it's really a showcase,' he says. 'People are trying to get seen.' Here, it's so informal that Americans can trip each other up. 'You told me a very interesting poem and every line rhymed and it was very funny,' Proops told Mike McShane, onstage. 'Would you do it for us now?' It seemed Proops was putting McShane on the spot, but he was really helping him. 'Failing is just as funny as succeeding, if you do it right,' he says. And if McShane played it right, as he would, he'd win both ways.

'I've absorbed a great deal of English culture simply by being in this room,' says Proops. 'I know who *The Clangers* are and what *Blue Peter* is.' He even learned how to parody pantomime and Carry On, but he's never pandered to English tastes. 'They don't want you to be watered down,' warned his wife. 'They want you to be yourself.' And he's passed her advice on to other American comics who've followed him across the pond. 'It's not a matter of translating the jokes,' he tells them. 'They'll get your jokes and the few references they don't get really don't matter. Just tell the jokes and be yourself.' He's found us happy to hear all about his frustrated loathing of the States, but also willing to mop up just as many jokes at our own expense. 'Americans don't want to be told they're wrong,' he says. 'Although we have a sense of humour about ourselves, it's not as highly developed as the English one.'

It was great to get away from the laughs per minute mentality of Stateside club comedy, but there are some things American comics do better. 'Americans tend to be a little more uninhibited,' he says. 'Our sense of embarrassment is not as keenly developed. We're not quite as apologetic. We're definitely pushier and on *Whose Line* it really pushed the show into a different area.' And so he was surprised to hear Brits call American comics slick, and mean it as an insult. 'In America, you strive to be slick,' he says. 'I never think of it as slick. I just think of it as professional.' Proops soon discovered that even looking professional isn't essential at The Store. 'They shamble on, they look a mess, their hair's fucked up, they look like they slept in their clothes, and it still works.' But he's not one to moan about how much better comics are treated in the States. 'Corporate places with rugs on the floor and nice lighting and seating are comfortable for the punters, but to me, comedy is telling jokes to drunks in bars.'

In The House

'Burt Laurent and Marcus Simmons for In The House Productions in association with The Comedy Store present In The House at The Comedy Store,' reads the poster on a pillar at the back of The Store stalls. 'The first Monday in each month.' That was how it all started. 'A first at the home of comedy,' declared black newspaper *The Voice*. 'History in the making.' And about time too, on a circuit where, for all its politically correct pretensions, equal opportunities for black acts, and consequently equal representation among black audiences, can be summed up in four short words: too little, too late. Until now.

Anti-racism was the first commandment of Alternative Comedy's unwritten manifesto. And initially, this ideological amendment seemed successful. Alternative Comics resolved not to crack those crude, demeaning jokes that caricatured black people as stupid, workshy and libidinous. This fresh philosophy even made some small impact on the mainstream, making trad acts temper their xenophobic attitudes, if only on TV, but the influx of black comics and black punters never really happened. Felix Dexter did an open spot, but although he eventually became a regular at The Store, even ten years later he was still a rarity. And despite his prolific talent, Dexter is hardly a household name.

'The audiences are not very well integrated,' says Reginald D. Hunter, a Black American comic who's built a stand-up career in Britain. 'Very often in the clubs that I play in, there may be two black people in the audience, or two people of colour in the building. Oftentimes, they're the bar staff.' But audiences will only follow where entertainers lead, and historically the number of black turns who've been accepted onto the club circuit has been pitiful. Black comedy's response has been to take the mountain to Mohammed, by mounting its own gigs for a predominantly black public. And nowhere has this been more significant than at The Store. With In The House, Laurent and Simmons have put black stand-up at the centre of the comedy club circuit.

'Black people make some noise!' yells tonight's host, Marcus Simmons. A fat cheer rings around the room. 'White people make some noise!' he yells. This chorus is far thinner, yet there are still a fair few white folk inside. 'Did you know it was a black night?' Simmons asks one of them. 'No? Well, you do now!' It's a Monday night, and unless someone hires it out for a special function, The Store usually closes to recover from the weekend. Yet tonight, the place is packed, and the atmosphere is like a week-end party. This audience is loud, like a late-show crowd, but they're in much better spirits. 'Hold onto your handbags,' Simmons tells his Caucasian guests, and the laugh-ter that ripples through the stalls pays testament to a stereotype revealed and vanquished. 'Do you know Bernie Grant and Diane Abbott are the same person?' says Simmons, of the two black MPs. 'Only black people can tell that.'

Simmons scores PC points by stating that not all black men are well hung, but blots his right-on copybook by claiming that those that aren't date white women. This is ethnic humour with its gloves off. 'I got educated in London and when I used to go to school the white boys used to say to me, "Why don't you go back home to the jungle and swing from the trees?"' he says. 'I never knew any black man who swing from trees. I knew one man who swing from trees and he's white. And his name is Tarzan.'

Such is the racial bias in Alternative Comedy that largely unknown black comics on the white stand-up circuit have become so big in the black underground that, like pop stars, Simmons can bill them by their Christian names alone. 'We've got Curtis, we've got Gina, we've got Richard,' he boasts, reeling off the names on tonight's bill. That's Curtis Walker, Gina Yashere and Richard Blackwood. Walker has been a vital corner-stone of the black circuit for the best part of a decade, Yashere is among its best and brightest rising stars, and Blackwood's name draws whoops from his female fans in the audience. 'He's already spoken for, ladies,' says Simmons. But these women won't be told. Like rap, rock and roll or civil rights, the white establishment usually catches up eventually. By the autumn, Blackwood was presenting his own Channel 4 show, but these black punters knew about him ages ago. 'You guys were very late,' Blackwood told the *Evening Standard*. 'Very, very late. All it boils down to is you are very scared.'

'I'd done all the clubs on the white circuit,' says Simmons, at a table by the bar, in that edgy hour before showtime. There are white gigs all over London, but black gigs are usually confined to venues like South London's Lewisham Theatre and the East End's Hackney Empire, islands of enlightened programming in centres of black population. Both these venues are crucial bastions of black comedy, but Simmons was well aware that too few white punters, press and producers were watching. 'You're on the white circuit and you get recognised,' he says. 'If you're on the black circuit, no one knows the shit what's going on.'

So Simmons and promoter Burt Laurent asked Don Ward if they could do their own gig at The Store. 'Down the West End is more prestige,' says Simmons. 'The white people come down and see you. We didn't want to be just underground.'

Simmons made his Store debut in Leicester Square. 'I was crap,' he says. 'I didn't know anything about structuring material.' Yet it hardly helped that he was sent on at the end of a late show. 'They were all drunk and they weren't really listening.' Simmons died, but decided he'd be back. He went to the Jackson's Lane comedy workshop in Highgate with future stars like Jack Dee, Eddie Izzard, Jeff Green and Patrick Marber. 'They couldn't teach you how to be funny, but they taught you how to go about getting gigs.'

For five years, he juggled a day job as store manager for Moss Bros, with shows in pub function rooms. These gigs were mainly white, simply because they weren't the sort of places where black punters tended to drink. 'Most of the clubs and pubs where the shows are, black people don't come out.' Not that he minded. 'I don't have a problem with performing in front of predominantly white audiences. My comedy was basically trying to break down barriers.' Yet playing to black punters brings its own rewards. 'We're very vocal in a positive way.' And a negative way, too. 'A white audience would let you go through your set, even if you're dying on your arse.' Black audiences aren't so indulgent. 'They'd say, "Get off! I've heard it!"'

Some bookers, like Kim Kinnie and Don Ward at The Store, and Malcolm Hardee at Up The Creek, helped him get started. Others weren't quite so helpful. 'No one would talk to you. They think like you're from another planet.' When he phoned up for open spots, bookers didn't know he was black, but when he got to the gig, he could feel their attitude alter. 'I've got to go up there and change the world. When you're a black comic, being average isn't enough. You've got to go up there and really kick it.' White comics say similar stuff, but they don't know the half of it.

In The House shows that it's not just black punters who want to watch black comedy. Sometimes, half this audience is white. 'Ideally, we're putting the show out for a black audience, but bums on seats, I don't give a damn. I don't care what fucking colour you are.' The biggest divide isn't between black and white, but rich and poor. In The House books white comics, like Ricky Grover, who understand the street. White punters are also becoming more familiar with black culture. 'You can go up there and talk dialect or patois and they'll know what you're saying.'

Once the number of black stand-ups and spectators on a normal Store night finally reflects London's black population, Simmons sees no further need for In The House shows. 'They will disappear because that will be a day I dream of.' And why not? After all, he's been on an entirely black bill on a normal night elsewhere, Downstairs At The King's Head, in Crouch End, one of Alternative Comedy's oldest venues. 'All-white audience, all-black comics, and it worked.' Simmons dreams of seeing an all-black bill play a weekend at The Store. 'I don't know when, but it will happen,' he says. 'I've been here when there are two black comics on the same night and to me that's a start, and it will get better and better.' But until that day, In The House is here to stay.

In some ways, the black circuit is still more conservative, especially about that stubborn black taboo, homosexuality. Burt Laurent, the main man behind In The House, had to ask one comedian not to do some homophobic material at The Store. He did it regardless, and went down a storm. Laurent reckons In The House will be the first black show to bill a white homosexual act on a black night, but right now he thinks it's still too soon to do it. But among straight black acts and audiences, at least, there's solidarity. 'Comedy's about trust,' says Laurent. 'The circuit is so small and they're all stars so they trust you straight away.' And although, out in the wider world, not all black folk act like brothers, down here that solidarity still counts for something.

Laurent doesn't like black acts baiting white punters. 'I can remember going to see Jim Davidson at the Circus Tavern, and it was me and one other black person and we were the only black people in the audience. We were the butt of his jokes virtually all night. Every time there was a little lull in his stuff, he'd pick on us two and I just feel that too many black comics these days do that.' Of course it's not the same. One white punter in an all-black crowd is only a minority in one room for a few hours, but even a multitude of wrongs don't make a single right. Conversely, one black punter in an all-white crowd has become a sort of politically correct barometer. 'White comics can say a joke which is taking the piss out of the black race to some degree and the white audiences will look to see whether or not you as a black person find it funny, and if you find it funny it's now acceptable for them to find it funny and they laugh.'

'A black man can never be a punk rocker,' says the next act, Jocelyn Jee. 'What? Mash up his system?' She's of Nigerian origin, but her reference points, from The Spice Girls to *Stars In Their Eyes*, are resolutely Middle England, and her impressions, Whitney Houston milking slow ballads, Kate Moss hamming up TV commercials, or Michael Jackson strutting his androgynous stuff onstage, are all similarly mainstream. Routines about her dad fielding calls from boyfriends or her mum embarrassing her on shopping trips both show just how much common ground we all share, wherever our families are from.

'It doesn't really come from being a woman and it doesn't really come from having Nigerian parents,' says Jee, of a routine that Nigerian, West Indian and white punters can all relate to. It's more to do with the way we all live today. 'What we see on TV, and the music we listen to, and the adverts.' These are the influences that can unify an audience. If anything sets her apart from some punters, it isn't being Nigerian but being a Londoner. 'When I do gigs out of London, there's certain jokes I can't do because it's so London based.

'I never really wanted to set out as a black female comedian,' she says. 'I never really wanted to do black jokes and female jokes. I just want to be funny, and stick to universal things. Lots of black comedians have to change their set when they go to a mainstream audience, but I'm doing practically the same set on both circuits.'

'Who thinks Paul Condon should be sacked?' asks Marcus Simmons, as Jocelyn Jee returns to the dressing room. A loud cheer roars around the room. 'White people?' No cheers now, merely a few muffled murmurs of consent. 'You whites elected the Prime Minister and you can get that done because they're not listening to us. Black people been telling them that since Windrush, since we came over here, that the police are racist. They ain't listening to shit. So you write a letter tomorrow to Prime Minister Blair and get that done.'

The Stephen Lawrence Report is fresh off the press, and the room feels raw with indignant grief. 'You can kill a black man and nothing happens and that's an injustice,' Simmons told me, later. 'Had it been the other way round, black guys are locked up, keys thrown away, no one has heard about them, and that's happened every day in our community.' In times of communal crisis, strangers need to gather together, to drink and dance and talk, and especially to laugh.

Simmons is articulating the suppressed pain and fury around the room, giving a voice to the silent, the dispossessed. Tonight, for once, black comics can talk freely about injustice, without jeopardising future bookings. 'They're all dummies. They've got to be fucking dummies. Check it. They put a camera up with no film in it. What the fuck is that about?' But there is film in The Store's video camera, to record his impassioned plea. And with the economy of anger, he brings on Curtis Walker.

'Institutionalised racism, it's a new word, let's all learn it,' says Walker. 'It's been re-invented for us. We're constantly told about chips on our shoulders. "Relax, it's only a joke, innit? Only a joke, you black cunt. Go on, laugh at it, it's a fucking joke, innit?"

'I was born in England, lived in England, but certain English things I can't get with. So what you going to do? Beat me up at a bus stop?' He follows this requiem with a poignant tale about buying his niece a Barbie doll. She didn't want the black one he bought for her. Walker alleviates his polemic with lighter humour. 'Go to any of our countries of origin. They don't queue. They fight but they don't queue. Whoever shouts the loudest gets served first.' In an another instant, he switches to a sterner note. 'Jamaican people talk with their hands,' he says. 'That's what gets misconstrued as aggression.' A hum of confirmation runs through the room. Yet as soon as that shot hits home, he leavens his heavy rhetoric with another dose of wry wit. 'There's so much of our culture that is beautiful for England,' says Walker. 'If black people never came here in numbers you'd all still think George Formby was the don, leaning on a fucking lamp post.'

And then once more, he leaves comedy behind, in a stunning soliloquy on the evolution of racism. 'We want to assimilate, we want to be a part of England. We do, but at what price? Do we throw away everything our fathers fought for?' He concludes by enacting a black woman, 'desperate to get along', suppressing her culture to fit in with her white employers, in a routine that's both funny and profound. 'I'm preaching but fuck it, man, it pisses me off,' he says, but tonight his audience is pissed off too, and his preaching lifts them up to a special place no joke can ever take them. 'Give it up for Curtis Walker,' shouts Simmons, 'the king of black comedy.'

'I like to challenge the status quo,' says Walker, at a table by The Store bar. 'In The House gigs allow me to do that.' Walker can be more honest when he's performing for a black audience. 'It's louder,' he says. 'There's a lot more emotion in the room.' This show is a case in point. 'It was a very good evening,' he says. 'The audience was fantastic. A lot of electricity.' Yet this isn't a typical Store crowd. 'A black audience wouldn't really come here on the whole. You'd get one or two black people coming, but they wouldn't really come here regularly.' It was ever thus. 'You didn't see black teenagers at The Comedy Store,' said Charlie Hanson, producer of the black sitcom *Desmond's*, in 1990. 'They were all down at Soul II Soul gigs at The Fridge. Comedy was just not a black thing to do.'[1] A decade later, things are gradually beginning to change.

Walker doesn't do different material for white crowds, but he does alter his delivery, speaking more slowly and articulately, with less patois. 'I'll try and make it intelligible for the audience,' he says, 'but that's the only concession I'll make.' However it's hard when white crowds even recoil from the word 'white'. 'I find that really ironic because as a black person growing up in England, black is an everyday word.'

As society changes, his white audience changes, but the white media still lags far behind. 'When you turn on the TV, I don't really exist,' claims Walker. 'What is that saying to a nation of people who, when they leave their house, are going to meet a non-white person?' And so he shuns such shows. 'I switch them off. I don't let my children watch them because I don't think it's representative.'

In The House is a pragmatic response to unrepresentative TV. 'You can be out in the cold for years, working hard, and nobody really sees it or appreciates it or interviews people about it until it's performed at The Store because that's a stamp of approval.' Apart from In The House, he's only ever played a few shows here. Not for him the workaday grind of five shows every weekend. 'Comedy for me is something to do out of inspiration, not out of necessity,' he says. 'I've always admired and respected what goes on down here, but I don't know if I could get on that treadmill.' For him, reacting to real events is far more important than repeating the same set ad infinitum. 'I can't afford a psychiatrist, so I take it out onstage,' he says. 'I had to remind myself that I was there to entertain and not to educate.' I reckon he did both, but scant TV exposure creates a glass ceiling above this circuit within a circuit that prevents Walker and his colleagues from rising up to fulfil their true potential. 'We've got a lot of talent, writing and performing, but no avenue to express it,' he says. 'There's no through line.'

Walker has had some small-screen credits, including *The Lenny Henry Show*, and he's written for Richard Blackwood. With his former double act partner, Ishmael, he appeared in the landmark black sketch show *The Real McCoy*, and presented *Paramount City*, both for the BBC. But doing TV on someone else's terms can be a very mixed blessing. 'When me and Ishmael started as a double act in the late Eighties we had social content, we really did, we talked about issues, and then during the TV period of the Nineties, we lost that.'

And so Walker went back to basics. 'I made a conscious effort, once me and Ishmael split up, to really go back to what I enjoyed about my comedy,' he says, 'which was actually commenting on things.' His rewards are less tangible than mainstream wealth and fame, but they're less transient, too. 'I love the work too much to disrespect it,' he says. 'I've realised how important social comment is.' And comedy can seduce bigots like straight polemic never can. 'We have to talk to them gently and comedy is the easiest way to do it because if you fill their heads with factual information they wouldn't be able to absorb it,' he says. 'That's what comedy is all about. Stimulating people's emotions, stimulating their thoughts.'

'They blame the recession on America, they blame the unemployment on the blacks and Asians,' says Simmons, kicking off the second half. '"Coming over here, taking our fucking jobs. Why don't you fuck off back home?" So I did. To Leyton.' Yet before he brings on Gina Yashere, there are more mundane matters to attend to. 'Are you an actress?' he asks a female punter. 'Well get your fucking foot off the stage.'

'Don't try and hide,' Gina Yashere tells her white spectators. 'You glow in the dark.' Yet her black fans bear the brunt of her amiable abuse. A Nigerian Londoner, like Jocelyn Jee, she contrasts the formal chat-up lines she gets from Africans with the more upfront approach of the men she met on holiday in Jamaica. 'Everything's so laid back in the West Indies,' she says. 'Even the serial killers.' But her funniest, most heartfelt stuff focuses on those relationships that bridge the racial divide. 'I remember when white guys were scared to chat to black women,' she says. '"Fucking hell, Terry, leave it. Fucking hell, I don't want a fucking machete in my head."' Yet like all the most sensitive and subversive comics, she's the ultimate target of her own invective. 'You can probably tell after my rantings and ravings, I am single,' she admits. 'White people, I'm going to do one more joke about you and then I swear I won't bother you again,' she concludes, introducing a courageous routine about mixed-race adoption. Most comics would shy away from such risqué material, but that's where the big laughs are, and she exits amid a barrage of generous yet justified applause.

When Yashere started out, in the mid-Nineties, there were very few Anglo-African performers around. 'It was mostly West Indian comics, and a lot of their stuff was based on taking the mick out of African minicab drivers, or African students,' she says. 'The only one who did it quite well was Felix Dexter.' The others did caricatures, not characters, and Yashere didn't find them funny. 'They used to do a lot of stuff denigrating Africans,' she says. 'There's a big divide between West Indians and Africans. The West Indians used to take the piss out of Africans a lot.'

Yashere felt this was derogatory, so she resolved to present an African perspective

Gina Yashere

instead. 'I used to do a lot of stuff about being African, the difference between Africans and West Indians, why West Indians used to take the piss out of me at school,' she says. 'It's a lot more blurred now because there's more second generation blacks being born here. You can't tell the difference between a London-born Nigerian and a London-born Jamaican, because we're all brought up here.'

She took voluntary redundancy from her job as an engineer in 1994, and spent a year 'spending the money and lazing about', before starting doing comedy, signing on the dole and living off the Giro. 'I was more hungry because I was skint, so it made me work a lot harder towards getting to my goals a lot quicker, because I didn't have a job to fall back on, so I had to make a go of it.'

By the time she did her Store debut, she'd already done over fifty gigs. She'd always thought, 'You're not a comedian, until you've played The Store.' She knew not to come here until she was ready to handle a rowdy room. She had trouble tracking down Don Ward, but she wouldn't be deterred. 'I had no problem ringing around for gigs. I was actually pestering people. If they said ring me back in six weeks' time, I'd put in my diary six weeks to the day.' But the dressing room was more intimidating. 'There was lots of established acts sitting there, talking amongst themselves about gigs they'd done for telly.' It must have felt like her first day at a new school. 'I don't know any of them and I don't feel like I've reached that level where I can actually make conversation with them, because they're so much further ahead than me, so I sat there like a little mouse.' But before nerves could overwhelm her, she was on. 'It was terrifying when I walked out on the stage, but once I picked up the mike and got my first laugh, it was pretty much plain sailing.'

Yashere believes that the white middle-class perspective still dominates down here. 'The only time I ever see black people in The Store really is people who are on a work do, or they have a white partner, or if they know a particular black comic that they want to see is on the bill.' Getting pissed, that staple topic of all bog-standard stand-ups, is also far less fascinating for black punters. 'Black people don't drink as much as white people,' she says. 'We used to run a little comedy club for a while, and we used to get in trouble with the patrons of the building because our audiences were mostly black and they didn't drink enough. They used to get pissed off because they weren't earning money at the bar.' Jokes about booze and kebabs almost seemed compulsory, but she didn't want to write for a white audience. 'I'll just write about myself,' she thought. 'If it's funny, it should work.' And although her humour plays well with white punters, black audiences tend to be more responsive. 'If you say something that really touches them, they will make a lot more noise. They all shout, they'll scream, they'll cheer.'

Yashere is in a minority thrice over, not just because she's black and Nigerian, but because she's a woman, too. 'I'm still quite quiet in the dressing room,' she says. 'All these white guys around me, talking about when they went out and when they shagged.' Alternative Comedy may be anti-racist and anti-sexist, but it's still a white boys' club. 'Audiences are more likely to listen to a man,' she says. 'It's very hard for a woman to come out and hold a room.' Her dynamic delivery is a conscious response to this imbalance. 'My comedy has been described as laddish because I do run about a bit,' she says. 'I tend to be a lot more energetic.' And for as long as audiences stack the deck against female comics, Yashere will have to meet them halfway. 'They almost want you to fail, and if you are going to fail, they're going to eat you alive.'

It's time for tonight's star turn. 'He's the only black comic who never had to do the white circuit to get where he's going,' says Simmons. 'Respect to that.' Enter Richard Blackwood.

'White people, I'm sorry,' says Blackwood, in a Caucasian cockney accent. 'I've been round the fucking back, listening to these fucking black cunts talking about ya.' Black and white punters both laugh, but with that element of unease that attends all the best humour. 'I love white people,' he adds, 'because white people don't take no shit. White people will stand up for themselves.' However, the caricature that follows pokes amiable fun at such macho posturing. And before the black punters can relax, Blackwood turns the tables. 'We got shit in our race that we need to deal with, too.' Like when treading on someone's shoe can be a capital offence. 'We don't stick behind each other man,' he says. 'We always want to put each other down.' And yet he's too incisive a comic to pretend that black and white are all alike. 'We are different in a lot of respects,' he says, tackling those two particularly black taboos – homosexuality and the oral sex double standard of cunnilingus. 'Just try me,' he says. A woman in the audience stands up, ready to take him at his word. 'You can't say that, man,' says a black punter, crying with laughter. But Blackwood can.

Black comedians such as Lenny Henry and Richard Pryor were among Blackwood's early inspirations. 'We saw somebody that came from the same nest as us get on TV, so we thought OK, well maybe we can do it.' It's less than a decade since his first gig, yet he's already had several hit series on Channel 4, a couple of singles and an album, and he's still in his mid-twenties. No wonder he's been called the British Will Smith. Fame runs in the family. His uncle, Junior Giscombe, had a number one in the early Eighties with 'Mama Used To Say', and his step-sister is the supermodel Naomi Campbell.

'There were white people in the audience, not as much as maybe there would be on

Richard Blackwood

a normal night, but they laughed just as much as the black people,' says Blackwood, recalling his In The House debut. 'If it's funny, it doesn't matter who says it.' He's one of a new generation of black comics, entertaining black and white crowds united by a common popular culture in a way their respective parents never were. 'We're watching all the same programmes,' he says. 'There's not a channel specifically for black people or a channel specifically for whites.' This reflects an even broader ethnic fusion. 'Races are actually getting together, there are interracial relationships,' he says, 'so therefore there's no need for any comedians, or anybody in any form of entertainment, to segregate themselves, because we're in a melting pot.' Blackwood is maybe the only black comic who's broken through without playing the mainstream circuit, but being billed outside The Store still felt wicked. 'They probably don't even know who you are, but the fact remains your name's there, so you must be good.'

He still felt apprehensive before his first regular Store gig, in front of a predominantly white crowd. In the early show, he did the sort of stuff he thought white punters would want to hear. 'It went OK,' he recalls, 'but it wasn't the huge roaring laughter I'm used to.' In the break between shows, he went to get some food with a friend. 'Fuck it,' his friend told him. 'Go out there and do what you do.' Blackwood took his advice. In the late show, he did his proper set, and tore the place down. Afterwards a white couple approached him. 'You was fucking brilliant, you were the best man on the show,' said the bloke. 'You must have been intimidated when you came out there and you saw nothing but white people looking at you, but your attitude was just, like, fuck it.' 'I told you,' said Blackwood's friend. 'You were brilliant,' said the bloke's girlfriend, giving Blackwood a hug. 'You're gonna be a star.' Blackwood was called into the office and was handed a thick brown envelope. He can still remember sitting in the car, counting the money.

'Some black comedians, when they come on the mainstream circuit, they kind of forget where their heart is, and they end up doing what they feel the audience want to see,' he says. 'The mainstream circuit for me was wonderful because no one judged you on your colour, race, creed, nothing. It was just what do you have to offer us? And that's what it's supposed to be about.' And so white comics at The Store have always been supportive, united by the knowledge that laughter is one of life's great levellers. 'They don't see you for a colour, they see you as a comedian,' he says. 'You're just like everybody else in here, and that's exactly how you're gonna be judged when you go out there, on your skill, nothing to do with your colour.'

It was a gig at The Store that secured his MTV slot. 'If you come in here, and you're recognised in here, the sky's the limit.' And The Store is a fine preparation for the unpredictable rigours of live TV. 'When you go on that stage, even though your material might be slamming, somebody could throw you off and you've got to be ready to come away from your material.' Like all top comics, he can now slip between pre-prepared and spontaneous humour so smoothly, you can barely see the join.

But after Stephen Lawrence, even comedy cannot conceal the reservoir of sadness at the centre of the Black British story. 'Comedy is therapy, it's a way of venting anger,' he says. 'It's like talking to a counsellor. It's like you're lying on the couch, people are there listening to you and saying, "Well, tell me what happened?" But instead of being silent, they're giving you a response, and that's the response that you need in order to clear your head.' Humour, it seems, can sweeten the bitterest pill. 'You want to listen because you want to laugh,' he concludes. 'If a comedian can get across a point in a way that makes you laugh, trust me, you will walk away repeating that joke, not realising that there was a message in that, and you probably will end up picking it up, and saying, "God, I understand what he's saying."' Loud and clear.

'Forty-five per cent of the audience were white and they went home happy – they weren't patronised,' says black promoter and stand-up John Simmit, afterwards. 'It was literally half and half,' agrees young black stand-up Toju. 'It was like apartheid. White people on one side, black people on the other side. But in a sense, there wasn't no real separation apart from how they were sitting. So it's gonna get to a point soon where it's gonna be like a regular night down here.' But Simmit doesn't believe In The House should primarily be about educating or even pleasing white punters. 'The black audience at the same time went home happy,' he says. 'They're having their lives actually put up into the spotlight and they're accurately reflected because we all know comedy's true. If they ain't gonna laugh, it's bullshit.'

The comedian who paved the way for all these comics was Felix Dexter, the first, and for a long time the only, black comic at The Store. He wasn't afraid to tackle racism head on, but unlike some Caucasian stand-ups, there was nothing remotely po-faced, tokenistic or politically correct about his polemical wit. 'The golliwog is not offending us. No one is going to mistake me for a jar of jam. What is offending me is bricks through the window while I am watching television.'

Dexter was born in St Kitts, in the Leeward Islands. Like a lot of comics, black and white, he was inspired by Richard Pryor's seminal live movie, which he watched in a downtown cinema in Watts, Los Angeles. Dexter went to The Store a few times with friends, while he was still a student. He'd actually been to the same building before, to a reggae club in the basement, but this was much more fun than clubbing. Dexter was amazed to hear comics crack jokes about events he'd just read about in the evening paper, and eventually, he decided to have a go himself. 'I was in a state of total terror,' he recalls. 'It went awfully.' His mouth went dry, he could barely speak, and everything seemed to happen in slow motion. Dexter was shocked and upset. 'They were like heroes, and I was envious of this special place they held,' he says. 'I fancied the glory that I felt they were getting, and I thought, "I can do that," but I couldn't.' Afterwards, one of the regulars, Ronnie Golden, told him to try The Earth Exchange, a gentler comedy club in a vegetarian restaurant in Archway, North London, but Dexter felt too humiliated to try again. He never went back to the Soho Store, not even to watch.

Dexter left it alone for over five years, until he went to Jongleurs in Battersea, just to watch, and the compere, Arthur Smith, asked if anyone in the audience wanted to do an open spot. Dexter got up and had another go, went down well, and never looked back. He started playing the circuit, and eventually wound up at the Leicester Square Store. He was only there as a punter, but on the spur of the moment, he asked if he could do a try-out. In those days, there was no waiting list, and this time he had a joyous stormer and got a booking straight away. He was delighted. 'Oh my god,' he thought. 'This is unbelievable.'

Starting out in stand-up is never easy, but Dexter had an extra couple of crosses to bear. 'There were two big reactions I had to overcome. The look of amazement on the faces of those who had never seen a black person up there attempting to be funny. And those trying so hard to be right-on and generous that they would laugh even when I wasn't any good.'[2] Yet despite these two opposing handicaps, Dexter quickly became one of the most prolific stand-ups on the circuit, sometimes playing as many as six gigs in one night. It still scared him, but even that became a bonus. 'I was really attracted by that,' he says. 'Every time I did it, I felt such a sense of conquest over my fear.'

However many gigs he did elsewhere, Store crowds were special. 'They were there to see a big event, like a gladiatorial combat,' he says. 'There was always a sense of tension in the air which you never found anywhere else.' And although he became a firm fixture here, he still got some racist heckles. 'You black cunt,' shouted a heckler. 'I'm a black cunt?' repeated Dexter. 'You must have a really hard time going around trying to have sexual intercourse with people that look like me because a vagina doesn't actually look like me. You must spend your time getting beaten up by black guys because if you think I look like a cunt you must be trying to fuck black guys the whole time.' The punters loved his put-down, but they didn't seem particularly shocked by the actual heckle.

'It was never my experience that the audience in The Store were racist,' he says, 'but also, I don't think they were politically correct, or would've been outraged if somebody said anything racist. They were politically apathetic, because many times people would go on and do really sexist, homophobic or even arguably racist material, and do OK. I remember a couple of mainstream comics on occasions coming down there and doing stuff to that effect and storming it.' He remembers one act in particular. 'He did a whole stream of racist, sexist, homophobic jokes,' says Dexter, 'and he did very well.' 'That's comedy,' he told the other comics, when he came off.

'Yes,' thought Dexter, 'but not one of the things you said is an original thought of your own.'

But what about Asian comics? That's another story, and one that is even more under-represented than Black British stand-up. But again, The Store is making small but significant inroads, even if the best Asian comic down here is actually Canadian. Russell Peters' Asian heritage allows him to rip the piss out of other Asians. 'How old are you?' he asks an Asian punter. 'Thirty-one? Are you married? Not yet? Talk to your parents. They'll hook something up for you.' And his Canuk upbringing enables him to tackle Anglo-Indian relations. 'Wait, we're coming with you,' he tells his Caucasian spectators. 'You can't just come here and leave. What the hell are you going to eat when you get drunk?'

Since 1995 Peters has played here dozens of times, gigging alongside stars like Harry Hill and even Lee Evans. Last month alone, he played Barbados, Trinidad and Hong Kong. But The Store is still his favourite club.

He's been called a racist by a drunken heckler, simply because he's happy to play around with racial identity in a way that's still rare in Britain. 'People think it's politically incorrect to talk about that stuff, and that's what makes it fun for me.' With our history of racist comedy, so many British comics say nothing, for fear of saying the wrong thing. Peters has no such qualms. 'That's wicked,' he adlibbed during one show down here, while talking to an Italian man and a Jamaican woman in the audience. 'They're going to go home and make little pastafarians.'

'There's certain things that white people don't say to black people,' says Marcus Simmons, kicking off another In The House show a few months later. 'Like, "Can you hold my purse for me?"' Never a truer word, as the nervous laughter all around attests. And with that he brings on an angry young black comic called Toju.

'When I say, "Make some," you say, "Noise,"' yells Toju, above the fierce, ferocious bellow of the rap track that heralds his indignant entrance. 'Make some,' he shouts. 'Noise,' shouts his audience. 'Make some.' 'Noise.' 'Make some.' 'Noise.' 'When I say, "Make some," you say, "Noise." Make some.' 'Noise.' 'Make some.' 'Noise.' As ice-breakers go, it certainly beats 'Good evening, ladies and gentlemen'. After less than a minute, the entire room feels fired up, and so does he. He doesn't ask if we're sitting comfortably. Without a pause to catch his breath, he launches into an indignant high-speed rant about the banal commercialism of modern pop. But it isn't all doom and gloom – he also bats about a few familiar film and telly references: *Goodfellas*, *The Six Million Dollar Man*, Kung Fu movies, complete with badly dubbed Bruce Lee impressions, and that grumpy green giant, The Incredible Hulk. 'If The Hulk was black he'd be changing every five minutes because brothers get frustrated quick.' His finale, about an all-black *Blind Date*, is rewarded with whoops, roars and a stampede of pounding feet. 'Well, Tasha, will your blind date be number one, from Lagos, who's just got out of jail for giro fraud, or will it be number two, from Peckham, who's got a mobile phone but can't pay the fucking bills, or how about number three? He says he doesn't eat pussy, but he has chunks of pubic hair between his teeth. The decision, Tasha, is yours.'

'You can talk to me,' Junior Simpson reassures the white punters in the front row. 'I am a comedian. I'm not security.' Simpson is the closing act on tonight's In The House bill, and right from the very start of his set it's clear he's every inch a headliner. Yet it's barely five years since I first saw him, in the final of the annual Hackney Empire New Act Of The Year Award. He cracked the most trenchant one liner of the night: 'I can't call myself Jamaican, because I wasn't born there,' he said, 'and I can't call myself British, because I'm not an athlete.' Simpson didn't even make the final frame of four, but it didn't matter. With his all-round flair for stand-up, music and mimicry, this lapsed Pentecostal choirboy was bound to make it in the end. Three years later, he was hosting Channel 4's *Nights Out At The Empire*.

'I don't gig that much in London anymore since I found out from the Macpherson report into the Stephen Lawrence inquiry that the Metropolitan Police in London are in fact institutionally racist,' he says. 'Who knew? I've been in London for seven years. I just thought they had a problem with only me.' But he can switch effortlessly from such incisive invective to the lighter side of life. 'It's about time that we as people transcended things like colour, race, religion, class, all the things which keeps us apart. All of us get together, lobby parliament to ensure that one day, finally, Sean Connery gets to play a Scotsman.'

Simpson first went to The Store with a few colleagues one night after work. 'Though I was joking round the office with clients, I never ever thought I'd be able to translate that to this,' he says, in the dressing room. 'It was the furthest thing from my mind.' The show he saw that night was The Cutting Edge, with Mark Thomas. 'It was stuff I'd read in the news that morning, and they were making gags about it that night, and I thought that was fantastic. As a punter I never imagined that I'd actually one day be up there, or anywhere.'

By the early Nineties, he'd become friends with Felix Dexter. One night, Simpson returned to The Store to see Dexter do a set. Dexter had a word with Stan Nelson, and the next thing Simpson knew, he was doing an open spot. 'I must have spent about half an hour in the toilet,' he says. 'I was very, very nervous and I must have gone through about fifteen minutes of material in about six and a half minutes.' But despite his first-night nerves, or maybe even because of them, his open spot went so well that he was booked to do a Saturday night half-spot. 'Lee Hurst was hosting,' he recalls. 'I said to myself, "That's about as close as I'm gonna get to working with someone like Lee Hurst."' But on the strength of this half-spot, he was invited back for an anti-racism benefit, alongside Hurst, plus Steve Coogan, Harry Hill and Eddie Izzard. 'I've just shared the bill with these guys,' he thought, as he drove home, 'and when I was onstage the audience were laughing just as much.' He did his first full weekend last year. 'It was almost like an out-of-body experience,' he says, of this seal of approval. 'I was standing in the same place where Robin Williams had played, and Lee Evans, and Jack Dee.'

Since then, Simpson has followed in Dexter's footsteps, to become one of the most successful black crossover comics in the country. No wonder *The Times* called him the new Lenny Henry. 'Doing a show in front of a black audience seemed a lot easier,' he explains. 'These people are the same colour as me so therefore their experiences have been the same as mine.' But playing predominantly white clubs forced him to find a far broader base, and eventually, he even became a regular guest with The Cutting Edge. 'I didn't want it to be that the reason why I was in the show was because I was a black guy.' And so beforehand he read the newspapers as if he was revising for an exam. 'It was important for me to make sure that I was being judged by the team, by the promoter, and also by the audience on my merit as a comedian and nothing else.' His preparation paid off. 'I don't feel like the poor relative that's turned up for Christmas Dinner anymore.' He knows it's vital to keep on writing new material for Cutting Edge shows, and not just to please the other acts. He wants the audience to feel the same frisson of excitement that he felt on his first visit to The Store, when he saw The Cutting Edge crew crack jokes fresh from the day's breaking news.

Most In The House punters aren't Store regulars, but fans of black acts from TV shows like *The A Force* or *The Real McCoy*. 'They're more expressive and enthusiastic than the regular audience.' And there are still some nuances he can do here that a regular audience won't get. 'I can't talk about a friend of mine from Barbados, because the audience will not be able to make the distinction between someone from St Lucia or Barbados or St Kitts or Trinidad. As far as they're concerned it's still all West Indians, all black, so therefore there's no difference.'

And on those rare occasions when most of the comics on a bill are black, then so are most of the punters. 'White people feel that if it's a total, or near total black audience, black bill, then it's not gonna relate to them, which is ridiculous,' says Simpson. 'Black comics who are performing on the circuit were born and grew up in this country, so therefore the stuff that we talk about will be things that you experience.'

'White people, did you enjoy that?' asks Marcus Simmons, prompting a big, boozy cheer. 'Did you love what we were saying?' A much smaller cheer this time, but a big laugh from the black folks in this crowd. 'Now you can go home and tell your friends about this shit, and bring your black friends with you as well,' he says. 'I know some of you haven't got none,' he adds, 'but you must have some in the work place.' And the laughter that follows this backhanded quip is even bigger still.

John Hegley

John Hegley fell in love with poetry on the night bus on his way back from The Store. He'd get the bus at about four in the morning, home was over an hour away, so by the time he finally got back to Forest Gate, it was already five o'clock, sometimes even later, and in summertime it was often already light. 'That's where I used to read my poetry,' says Hegley, above the falsetto shriek of an espresso machine, in a crowded coffee bar around the corner from The Store's first Soho hideaway. 'I used to feel I could understand it.' At first, he used to sing songs at The Store, but these late-night, early-morning poetry bus-bound readings persuaded him to recite one of his songs without music, to see if it worked as a poem. And it did. Twenty years later, he's probably Britain's best performance poet.

After fulfilling his childhood ambition, by working for a year as a bus conductor, John Hegley read European Literature, The History of Ideas and Sociology at Bradford University, a degree which left him eminently qualified for a career in children's theatre. He also worked as a clerk in a social security office and a nurse in a mental hospital. He was doing street shows and playing in a band called The Popticians, when a few misguided pals persuaded him to try out at The Store. 'Some friends advised me that my sense of the whimsical might be appreciated at a late-night comedy venue,' he writes in *Beyond Our Kennel*, one of his fine books of funny yet surprisingly profound comic verse. 'They were wrong.' He went down well the first time, but got gonged off the second time, and the third time, and the fourth time, and the fifth. Yet Hegley had something far more useful than instant talent. Staying power. And so, pretty soon, he turned this audience around.

'He would look like he'd cut his own hair with a pair of blunt scissors,' says musical comic Pierre Hollins, 'but he always used to storm. I never ever saw him go badly.' Hegley's concentration and confidence would silence most rooms, and if it didn't, he'd work hecklers into the show. 'He came on as a rather naff teacher that couldn't control the class,' recalls Jenny Lecoat. So even when he failed, he was still funny. 'It's like good acting,' says Jack Dee. 'He's completely absorbed in his character.' And like all good actors, Hegley is always completely in the moment. 'He's got such a strong hold on being funny without overplaying it in the least, without ever being facetious or self-conscious,' says Dee. But who knows what Hegley might have been without that night bus home from The Store?

Nick Hancock

'The first time I ever set foot in The Comedy Store was to perform,' says Nick Hancock, one sunny summer afternoon on the balcony of the BBC club bar at Television Centre. 'I'd never worked anywhere else. I'd never done any stand-up or any live paid performing.' However, he had performed, unpaid, with Neil Mullarkey, who went on to create a double act with Mike Myers. When Myers returned to Canada and ultimate stardom, Mullarkey asked Hancock to take his place.

In an outdoor market in Bury St Edmunds, Hancock found an old LP record of TV theme tunes: *Colditz*, *Ironside*, *Dad's Army*, *Hawaii Five O* and *Alias Smith & Jones*, and the two of them created a series of cod re-enactments to match the music. 'It only lasted twelve minutes,' says Hugh Dennis 'It was so stupid. It was fantastic.'

Under the pseudonym Bleep & Booster, Mullarkey and Hancock launched their own Go With Noakes campaign, whose demands included bringing back The Osmonds, The Banana Splits and John Pertwee's *Doctor Who*. Bleep & Booster's Seventies revival was a decade ahead of its time.

Their Store debut was on a Tuesday night in the early Eighties, still a quiet night in those days. Hancock and Mullarkey did the first half. Harry Enfield did the second. 'It was very nerve-wracking for me, but it was also a bit of an adventure because it wasn't my job,' says Hancock, during a brief break from filming *They Think It's All Over*, which he chairs in the studio downstairs. At the Leicester Square Store he could stand at the bar for a few minutes before he went on, and nobody would know who he was, but those days are long gone.

They did four Tuesdays that month, alongside unknown open spots like Jim Tavare,

Jack Dee and Eddie Izzard. 'They weren't fantastically good when they started and they really worked at it, and that was something I never understood, because to me it would just be too toe-curlingly upsetting to live through that, but they obviously really wanted to do it. When I first started I didn't believe people could get better if they hadn't cracked it immediately. Now all three of them are much better exponents of stand-up than I am.'

But although he's too modest to say so, in that time and place, Hancock was among the best, something that Kim Kinnie spotted from the start. After a few weeks watching him perform alongside Mullarkey, Kinnie suggested he try a solo stand-up act, and offered him an open spot the following Saturday. So that weekend, after watching his beloved Stoke City, he travelled down to London on the train from his native Potteries. 'I wrote my set on the train on the way down. In an hour and forty minutes, I wrote about twelve minutes and I think I used that twelve minutes for the rest of my stand-up career.' 'He never added any new material,' confirms Steve Punt. Yet that hour and forty minutes on the train, and those twelve stage minutes, were enough. His one liners were user friendly, middle of the road and inoffensive (unless you happened to be bald) but they were delivered with boundless charm and aplomb.

Nick Hancock and Neil Mullarkey, aka Bleep & Booster

'Stand-up is a much easier discipline to carry off in front of a baying audience, whereas if you ever try and do character comedy, or any sort of sketch-based stuff, it's quite difficult,' says Hancock, of his effortless transition from double act to solo spot, but the mark of true talent is making something most folk find hard look so easy.

'I've said this to my wife, who's never seen me do stand-up. When I look back, I don't recognise that person. I can't think how I had the balls to do it, because now I don't think I would. I'm quite glad I've done it but it feels like my cycling proficiency test. I know I've got the certificate, but I don't remember anything about it, or believe I ever had the discipline to go through with it.'

Thankfully, his colleagues have better memories. And no other comic attracts such unconditional praise.

'People would always come out and watch Nick Hancock,' says Mark Lamarr, recalling how all the comics vacated the back bar as soon as Hancock arrived onstage. 'He did exactly the same act, word for word, every single fucking show, yet everyone would flock out and watch.' Jo Brand agrees. 'He never changed his act, ever, and a lot of the time about five of us would go and stand out the back and just repeat his act over with him as he did it onstage. But that wasn't because people wanted to put him down. It was because they were so fond of him, and he was so funny that he didn't need to write a new act. It was just brilliant every time he did it.'

'I used to love it,' says impressionist Alistair McGowan, who saw Hancock on his first trip to The Store. 'He did the same thing again and again, but I was thrilled.' McGowan was delighted Hancock didn't change his set, because he told a friend all about it, and brought him along to watch the next time.

Although Hancock's set remained the same, his responses to hecklers were always completely off the cuff. 'Nick Hancock did one of the best put-downs I ever saw,' recalls Sean Lock. 'He used to do a joke about how shit Dudley was. This woman got really upset. She was going, "We're from Dudley," and started giving him a hard time. This woman threw her drink at him and it splashed on his face. He tasted it and said, "Champagne! So pleased to be out of Dudley!"' 'There was some cockneys in,' recalls Lamarr. 'They just wouldn't fucking shut up and you could see him boil up, and he went, "Oh, go and sell some fruit!"'

'The comedian I used to love the most of all was Nick Hancock,' says Jeff Green. 'I loved his confidence, and I used to get a pain in the back of my head from laughing at him.' And he made it seem so simple, even backstage. 'I saw him eating a cheeseburger before going on to compere the late show, and I couldn't believe it,' says Green. 'I hadn't eaten for days.' But when Hancock went on, it became clear why he was so laid back. 'He wasn't political,' says Green. 'He was just funny and cheeky and rude.'

And like all great comedians, hilarious things seemed to happen all around him. 'I can do better,' one heckler boasted, one night, so Hancock invited him up onstage to have a go himself. The heckler took the mike and started to talk, and his false teeth flew out. 'He was only about thirty,' remembers David Baddiel. 'It was complete fucking mayhem.'

Punt & Dennis

'I started performing because I wanted to write and the easiest way to get your material performed is to perform it yourself,' says Steve Punt, over an afternoon drink in a pub on Wimbledon Common. Ben Elton's motivation for performing at The Store was much the same, and like Elton, Punt has done pretty well as a performer, starring in two series of *The Imaginatively Titled Punt & Dennis Show*, with his double act partner Hugh Dennis, and in one of the most talked about comedy series of the Nineties, *The Mary Whitehouse Experience*, alongside Dennis, again, plus Rob Newman and David Baddiel.

Punt first heard about The Store from Nick Hancock, when they were both students at Cambridge University. Hancock had a Comic Strip LP, and Punt listened to it in Hancock's room in halls. Punt was a Monty Python fan, but this was something completely different. 'It was weird to know this album had only been recorded a couple of years earlier,' he says, some twenty years later. The stars of this LP, such as Alexei Sayle, Rik Mayall and French & Saunders, had already headed off into the comedy stratosphere (or onto telly at any rate) and there was a tangible prospect of playing the actual place where they'd started out. Punt's Python records suddenly felt old and distant.

As a sixth former, Punt had lapped up *Not The Nine O'Clock News*, but despite its contemporary flavour, it was a pretty traditional sketch show. At the end of his first year, he went to see some live comedy at the Edinburgh Festival. One of the shows he saw was a revue called 'A Sense Of Nonsense', starring Stephen Fry, Hugh Laurie, Emma Thompson, and most of the Footlights team who'd won the first ever Perrier Award in Edinburgh the summer before.

'The Mary Whitehouse Experience' in 1992: Rob Newman, David Baddiel, Hugh Dennis and Steve Punt

Yet it was another show in the same venue that made Punt realise how much comedy had changed. Ben Elton and Rik Mayall were both performing on the same bill, alongside Andy de la Tour, and after the languid monologues in 'A Sense Of Nonsense', what amazed him most was Elton and Mayall's breakneck pace. 'The audience didn't know Ben Elton at all, but he had a gallon of material squeezed into a pint-sized set, at a million miles an hour, obviously an incredibly gifted writer,' he recalls. 'Rik Mayall, completely the opposite. He had no material at all, and the audience were helpless with laughter.' The reason for this disparity of speeds was simple. Fry and Laurie's sketches had evolved in front of polite and sympathetic theatre audiences. Elton and Mayall's stand-up had evolved in front of a drunken rabble after midnight in a Soho strip club.

Back at Cambridge, Punt watched Elton and Mayall's *Young Ones* sitcom religiously, and started doing his own Footlights stuff with Hancock and Hugh Dennis. After they'd all graduated, Hancock stayed on to do teacher training, while Punt and Dennis came to London. They did an open spot at Malcolm Hardee's Tunnel Club and got a booking, and by the time they played The Store, they were already an established circuit act. They made their Store debut in *Cabaret Upstairs*, a radio show hosted by Clive Anderson. Kim Kinnie was there, and afterwards he invited them to play the club. Punt and Dennis had cannily avoided the dreaded open spot.

The Store's central location made it a convenient showcase, but inviting showbiz contacts was tempting fate. 'You'd get heckled,' says Punt. 'That's when you could guarantee something would go wrong.' Nevertheless, Jasper Carrott saw them at The Store, and asked them to appear on his TV show, and subsequently on national tour. It was their big break, but at The Store, things were never quite the same again. 'Where's Jasper?' yelled the hecklers. 'Excuse me,' Punt felt like telling them. 'We've done this venue many times before we were on telly and we're not here because of that.' But he never did, because in a way, they were right. His relationship with The Store had changed. 'It's not a place where you go to see people who you can see on the telly,' he says. 'It's a place where you go to see working comics on the way up.'

Now he's doing what he does best of all, but he still misses the special togetherness of those late nights in Leicester Square. 'You feel terribly magnanimous towards the world if your act goes well, so it's great to be on first and then relax and watch the other acts,' he explains. 'You could hear laughter from every corner of the building. It was all around you, wherever you went, even in the dressing room.'

'It was certainly less scary,' says Hugh Dennis, in a Soho café a few weeks later, describing the companionship that came from starting out with Steve Punt. 'I would never have done it on my own.' However, after the relatively cut-throat world of Footlights, where everyone tried to outdo everyone else, Dennis actually found The Store far more generous, and a lot less competitive. 'You might get some very vain people who demanded they headlined at eight o'clock, but because the midnight show started so bloody late, it was the worst job in the world to headline, so everybody vied to go on as early as they could.'

There was another reason why Dennis was relatively relaxed about his prospects. For the first six years of his comic career, he was also working as a brand manager for Unilever. 'I didn't have much angst about [comedy],' he explains. 'I was just doing it for fun.' And even when Punt & Dennis went on peaktime TV with Jasper Carrott, he was back in the office on Monday morning. 'The night that Jasper Carrott came to see us, Steve didn't tell me he was in the audience. And even when we were asked to go on *Carrott Confidential* – twelve million viewers on a Saturday night – I didn't take it that seriously, because I was still thinking, "I am a marketing man." I was in charge of a shampoo.'[1] It was a sign of changing times at The Store. After all, it was scarcely the sort of job that Soho Store veterans like Keith or Tony Allen would have done. It was only when *The Mary Whitehouse Experience* transferred from radio to TV that Dennis gave up his day job, and even then it wasn't easy. 'Sad to say, I actually quite liked it,' he says. 'I liked the power.' But now Dennis has no regrets. 'I'm glad I did it,' he says, of his decision to swap shampoo for comedy. 'There's no better way to earn a living.'

Television

Today, thanks to The Store and all the other comedy clubs that copied it, a comedian can make a very comfortable, comparatively easy living without ever becoming a star. The national circuit is so large, and its audiences so far flung, that less ambitious comics can tour more or less the same set ad infinitum, like old Music Hall turns. And who's to say that touring pubs and clubs for an admiring if modest clique isn't more fun in the long run than the indiscriminate curiosity and tabloid intrusion that accompanies nationwide notoriety? Well, maybe, but for every journeyman who's perfectly happy with his lot, there are several undiscovered stars who closed the shows in which today's champions did their first free try-outs. That memory must weigh mighty heavy as they fend off yet another stag night, rowdy rugby club or office party at one more weekend midnight show. 'Some people go off into hyperspace,' says Alan Davies, who's done exactly that. 'There's only a fraction of a difference between them and the next guy. He just hasn't got factor X.' 'This is a nasty business sometimes,' says John Moloney, a big success by most people's terms, but hardly an inhabitant of Davies' hyperspace. 'It can be very hurtful.'

Playing The Store offers a ringside view of Britain's top stand-ups at that special moment when they break through from solid club act to star turn. Store comic Milton Jones was backstage with Lee Hurst before Hurst compered here for the first time. Hurst had a few first-night nerves in the early show, but he stormed the late show so well, The Store booked him up for loads more thereafter. Another time, Jones was backstage, chatting with Eddie Izzard. Then Izzard went on and transformed their conversation into a storming ten-minute set. 'It's not fair,' says Jones. 'I have to sit at a computer.' Not for Izzard, it seems, the tedium of honing the intonation of every word. As Arthur Conan Doyle observed, 'mediocrity knows nothing higher than itself, but talent instantly recognises genius.' You've got something I haven't got, thought Jones, and good luck to you. Sportsmen talk about being in the zone, and it's similar for comics. When a comic finds this sort of form, it's almost as if they could walk across a motorway blindfold and escape unscathed.

Being a newcomer is tough, but stardom also has its pitfalls. Once people start paying to see a particular comic in the flesh, because they've seen them on the telly, they stop behaving like proper punters, and start coming on like cheerleaders instead. Sometimes, this gives comics the confidence to be daring and creative. Often, it makes them flabby and self-indulgent. Either way, it's a far tamer evening when the fans of the famous leave their critical faculties at the door. They've made a specific investment in a single share rather than buying a lottery ticket for a lucky dip. At first these devotees are a welcome break after all those drunken batterings at The Store. 'The great thing about people coming to pay to see you specifically is they'll give you incredible slack,' says David Baddiel. 'People who pay to see you trust that you're funny already, and people who come to The Store don't really trust that about any of the comics.' But eventually, a devoted crowd can blunt a comic's cutting edge. Comedy cannot bear too much adulation.

Stardom builds a fourth wall between stage and stalls, and the adulation that comes with it can corrupt the necessarily suspicious relationship between act and audience, the shared illusion that the heckler and the comic could swap places. 'Without us here,' a heckler once told comedian Simon Bligh, 'you're just rehearsing.' Sceptical fans want to be won over, giving comics something to wrestle with along the way. Starstruck fans surrender before the battle has even begun, leaving comics with nothing to push against, no friction to overcome. 'Fame and comedy don't go together,' says Donna McPhail. 'I've seen Victoria Wood and people like that in big theatres and they stop talking and audiences piss themselves laughing, and you think, "How difficult must it be to know whether you're actually funny, or whether they're going to laugh at anything you say because you're so famous."'

But The Store is still a great leveller, and greatness is no guarantee of a good gig. 'There's nowhere to hide,' says Simon Bligh, who's outplayed many stars at The Store without ever landing the TV vehicle that would make him a household name. 'You get two minutes of clapping, but then you've got to be funny.' The stars who still return have got little to gain and a lot to lose. 'Lee Evans had a hard time here relatively recently, and it was brave of Lee because he was trying stuff out for the tour,' says Bligh. 'He came on and they went mad and then he said, "I'm just going to try this stuff out," and it wasn't finished off. He had it very difficult and he ended up doing some old stuff.' Izzard, one of very few comics who've reached the top without much help from TV, returned to The Store straight after he played Wembley Arena, but while his fellow performers mingled with the punters at the bar, he had to shelter in the dressing room and leave by the back door. 'If you can play The Store, you can play anywhere,' says Izzard, who advanced from here to Hollywood, without passing Go.

Most Store comics needn't worry about Hollywood, but they do worry, and rightly so, about fame's more familiar motor, TV. Before TV fame, a twenty-minute Store set is an imperial standard against which every comic can be measured. 'If you didn't play The Store, you weren't a real comedian,' says Jenny Lecoat. 'It's a tough audience,' says Steve Punt. 'You can't get away with flab.' Beginners blame tough audiences, but deep down, they know Izzard wouldn't have died on his arse out there.

Fame disrupts the delicate balance between the comic and the crowd. 'It makes it impossible for you to just do stand up,' says Jo Brand. 'People are so desperate to get it, but when you do get it, and I'm not being ungrateful, it's a fucking nightmare. I hate it, and I know a lot of people like it, and I'm very pleased for them that they do, and I wish I did but I don't. I just find it embarrassing and humiliating.' Playing The Store before you become a star can feel like the best sort of fame. Inside, you're a local hero, but outside, nobody knows your name. 'It's like being in a really famous rock band and being the one at the back that no one recognises,' says Brand. 'That's what I'd like to be, because you get all the perks of the money and the touring and the fame, but you don't get recognised all the time and abused.' 'It destroyed my confidence,' says Donna McPhail, of her return to the circuit after a spell on telly. 'All of a sudden it's just "that bird off the telly."' Punters didn't seem to care that, like virtually every other comic on telly, she'd been doing live stand up for far longer. 'I don't know one stand up who hasn't had problems getting back to live work after doing telly,' she says. 'I found it very insulting and very upsetting that they didn't want to know my stand up. They didn't want to hear my jokes.'

'Notice to all artists,' reads the sign, scrawled in fat black felt tip, stuck up on the back of the dressing-room door. 'Tonight we have a very tight schedule to stick to and nine acts. The red light will be in operation. You have twelve minutes stage time. The red light comes on at ten. If you are selfish and over-run the acts after you suffer and we suffer. Red lights equals two minutes. Then off. Keep it tight you cunts and enjoy.' The author of this informal yet emphatic memo is Stan Nelson, and the tight schedule is for tonight's filming of a new series of Channel 5's stand-up show, *The Comedy Store*.

The room is already full and the air is alive with restless expectation. Most of tonight's turns have done this show, or others a lot like it, many times before, but there are quite a few first timers on both sides of the black curtain, and their adrenalin is infectious. Even tonight's compere, Richard Morton, an old hand who's seen it all before, is pacing up and down in the galley between the bar and the back stalls, like a prize fighter warming up before a title fight.

It's no coincidence that you rarely have to pay for the dubious privilege of sitting through a televised comedy show. Free tickets are a lot like free lunches, and television never distributes comps out of the kindness of its cheating heart. 'Red Indians believe the camera steals your soul,' says Michael Smiley, who's done this show before. 'TV comedy cuts the balls off it. When you see it live, you know the performer can step away from their material.' Unusually, performers on this show do stray from their rehearsed sets, and short of screening it as it happens, tonight's show is about as live as televised stand-up is ever going to get. But there's still that scary sense you never get on a normal club night, that these gags are forever. The feeling that every wisecrack will vanish in an instant gives comics their bravado, but tonight, no comic can quite forget that their every fleeting utterance will be recorded for posterity. 'You've handed over material,' explains Smiley. 'If it's been done on TV, it's in the public forum, so now you're less willing to do that stuff again.'

'People say, "Treat it like a gig," but it's not a gig because there's cameras everywhere and it's a special audience who haven't paid,' agrees Gina Yashere, who's doing this show for the first time tonight. 'My experience of audiences that haven't paid is, they don't care.' She isn't the only one who thinks so. The worst audience, said the late great Eric Morecambe, is the one who hasn't paid. And the worst comedian is the one who'd really much rather be doing something else. 'There's lots of stand-ups who are using the circuit and who don't really envisage staying on it or working and becoming a great stand-up,' says Steve Punt. 'The first presenting job they get offered, they'll take it.'

'You don't get the atmosphere on TV,' says Jim Tavare. 'You can't heckle your TV set.' But the production company, Open Mike, make a point of filming the interviews for the show here, in The Store's usual spartan setting, in front of the dressing room mirror framed within the ubiquitous garland of bare light bulbs, or out front, amid the empty rows of crimson seats. And although for the show itself, lights and drapes transform the spare black stage and backdrop into a lurid sea of pastel, Open Mike have managed to create a TV studio inside a comedy club, rather than the other way around, and the reward for their restraint is a show that actually looks and feels a lot like a night out at a proper comedy club. Apart from the cameras, which steal some standing room in the aisles, the mood around the room is almost like any other night. Punters park their coats, fetch drinks from the bar and fast food from the diner. They talk to the acts. They even talk to one another.

'This is watched by about a million people,' announces Open Mike's floor manager. 'So, a little tip. Anyone that's come down here with anyone they shouldn't be with tonight, just move, now.' This floor manager is fine, but he's not a natural comic, and watching him makes you realise how hard a compere's task really is. Only comics who do it well make it look so easy, and as Richard Morton takes the mike, you can see the difference between amateur and professional. 'Is this a staring match?' he asks, as the audience greets his entrance with less than rapturous applause. 'I feel like Glenn Hoddle at a Mencap benefit.'

Ed Byrne breezes through a honed-down version of his normal twenty-minute club set, his standard routines stripped down to the bare one-liners. It's a perfect televisual twelve minutes, it'll cut down dead easy in the edit, and he leaves to a wave of applause without breaking sweat. But the second act, Ben Norris, has a much harder time of it, although his hecklers aren't around the room. Far worse: they're in his head. 'I'm going to have to stop now, because I've lost the plot here completely,' says Norris, bailing out in mid-routine. 'Can we edit this?' he asks the producer, half hidden in the sound booth, as another floor manager dashes onstage. 'Where shall I pick it up from?' asks Norris. 'Wherever you feel comfortable,' says the floor manager. After a brief consultation, Norris decides to go off and come back on again.

'You'll never guess who's coming on now,' says Morton, as Norris makes his second entrance of the evening. 'Will you laugh again?' asks Norris, pensively, but his reappearance is greeted by the biggest cheer so far, and the gags that follow all get larger laughs than they deserve. Norris leaves to an even bigger cheer than the one that greeted his second entrance, but it still feels as if something has been lost along the way. Now we all know there's an emergency exit that doesn't exist on a normal club night. Half the thrill of stand-up is the cold, cruel certainty that these entertainers will sink or swim for your amusement. But now that spell has been broken. It's like a conjurer showing you how a trick is done, or a trapeze artiste falling off the high wire into a safety net you didn't know was there. Would Norris have even dried at all without this second chance to fall back on? It doesn't make it any less skilful, but it does make it less dangerous, less real.

'How many people recognise me off the telly?' asks Gina Yashere. 'In the black community, I'm a celebrity. I can say that because there's no black people here.' She's almost right, on both counts. Even though this is her debut on this show, she's done stacks of other late-night telly, and for the handful of black punters here, she's already a star. But melanin isn't her main gripe. 'Male comics get all the groupies. They get women queuing up outside the dressing rooms. I don't get shit.' By now she's going great, and the only false note is her unexpectedly rapid exit.

'I felt a little bit out of my depth and I was very nervous,' she says at the bar, a few weeks later. 'I came back and did it again last Monday, and I was a lot calmer.' The producers said it was good enough first time around, so what went wrong? 'I knew the audience appreciated it, but deep down I knew I could do much better. I knew I'd done well, but it wasn't well enough for me. I'm quite a perfectionist and I came off early because I'd been put off by a cameraman who walked up in front of the stage. Somebody was obviously saying something in his ear piece and he was waving his arms about. Beforehand, they beat it into us, "When the red light comes on, get off, don't go over," so when I saw this cameraman waving his arms about I thought, "My god, I've gone over, I've done something wrong," and the rest of my set went completely out of my head. Then I forgot the rest of my material, and that's why I came off early.' Yet she'd still far rather do televised stand-up in a club than a studio. 'You don't get the buzz you get with a normal comedy club,' she says. 'All the comedians know The Store. They know the room. It's much easier to play it than going into a studio.'

'My name is Scott Capurro and I really want a clitoris,' explains the next act. 'I want it so bad, I can taste it. I'm gay and I was born a Caesarean, so I've never been near one, but I know how to spell it and I know it's not the capital of Cyprus.' And he'd love to have one in his ear. 'Those family functions would just fly by.' Capurro is from San Francisco, and his catty yet sensitive set is a wonderful contrast to the comedy by numbers of so many identikit Britpop comics. 'Don't point at her like this is your girl-friend, like I didn't know about her already,' he scolds a man in the front row. 'They've all got a girlfriend. Two girlfriends? D'you want to pee around them so we know that's your area?' But compared to his family, his audience gets off lightly. 'When she's dead I get four thousand dollars a month for the rest of my life,' he says, talking about his grandmother, a recurrent theme in his sharp, camp act. 'With that kind of cash, I won't be telling dick jokes at The Comedy Store to make a living anymore.' And more's the pity. 'Scott Capurro, ladies and gentlemen,' announces Morton, putting his fist in his mouth. 'Available for children's parties.'

'Don won't book me,' says Capurro, in the dressing room during the interval. But later that night, Ward walked up to him and offered him a gig the following autumn, his first here in over four years.

'I was very nervous because I didn't think Don Ward liked me,' says Capurro. 'I knew he hadn't returned my management's calls, and didn't want to book me, so I felt odd doing a TV show when I knew he was sitting there.' Ward was eating dinner by the bar when Capurro walked by. 'I didn't know how to respond,' he says. 'The whole time I was onstage, I had in the back of my mind that he was back there, watching.' Yet watching Capurro go to work, you never would have guessed he had other things on his mind. 'It felt like a club gig,' he says. 'It didn't feel like a TV gig. It wasn't lit like a TV gig. I didn't feel like I was burning under the lights.' The cameras were so far back, he could barely see them. In the end, he forgot all about them, and did a great gig, but he also forgot to mind his language. 'They said you get one cunt in your set,' he says. 'I just used mine inappropriately, apparently.'

Comedy has always endured an uneasy marriage of convenience with TV. Both parties often feel let down and badly served by one another, yet neither partner is sufficiently bold or foolhardy to go it alone. It wasn't always that way. 'A lot of comics in the early days didn't want to do television,' says Phil Herbert, who appeared on Julian Clary's Alternative TV game show, *Sticky Moments*. But now those idealistic days are long gone, and most times, TV fails to trap the frisson of live club comedy, and transfer that 'you had to be there' excitement onto the idiot box. 'How can I make a joke about a person's world when they're sitting there on the sofa and I don't even know what their lounge looks like?' asks Phil Davey. 'We're only funny if there's atmosphere. Smoke, drink, lots of people packed in that are already up for a night out.' And it's not just comics who feel exposed. Even the studio audience feels more nervous and self-conscious. 'You're trying to relax them and let them laugh,' says Davey. 'They're trying to look their best, just in case the camera finds them.' 'The most exciting thing about seeing live comedy is that it's live, and so therefore to put it on television immediately puts up a barrier,' explains Nick Hancock. 'You think, "Those people are having a good time and I'm not there."'

Occasionally, against all odds, TV captures some of The Store's strange moondust. Lee Hurst's invective, cultivated with The Cutting Edge, eventually surfaced in *They Think It's All Over*, and Paul Merton's surreal flights of fancy, honed in The Comedy Store Players, bore fruit on *Have I Got News For You?* Jack Dee's Channel 4 series, which cast Dee as the host of his own mythic club, Bohemia, felt like a real-life stand-up show. It wasn't shot in an antiseptic studio, but amid the faded chic of London's Embassy Rooms, which once hosted Miss World. Yet although stand-up still hasn't really found its *Old Grey Whistle Test*, let alone its *Later With Jools Holland*, both sides keep coming back for more. Like a vampire with a drink problem, television must feed its insatiable thirst for fresh blood, while otherwise streetwise comics are happy to be sucked dry, for the vague promise of a bigger stage and a smarter dressing room. And nowhere are the hard-nosed terms of this arranged marriage more apparent or pertinent than here at The Store.

'If you want to be seen on telly, you have to be seen down The Store,' says Bob Boyton. 'If a TV researcher wants to go and see comedy, nine times out of ten they'll go to The Store.' The Store is the top rung of the club ladder, but promotion from this first division to the premier league is far from automatic. After they've stormed The Store, the problem for lots of comics is there's nowhere else to go. And in the end, it all comes down to TV.

'In the Eighties, the circuit led to nowhere,' explains Eddie Izzard. 'Television was very sceptical about taking anybody on.' Izzard shunned television's witless stare until he'd built a word-of-mouth reputation that gave him secret insider status, but only the best and worst comics can afford to ignore the one-eyed god. Most aren't as brave or talented enough to gamble everything on such high stakes. After The Store, the next step up is regional theatres, and it's a very big jump indeed from topping bills at a club where punters pile in whoever's playing to persuading a provincial audience to fork out for a special trip to see you, and you alone. And unless you're Eddie Izzard, the only way to bridge that gap is via the mass exposure of TV.

Live or televised, Alternative Comedy fed off an immaculate double standard. Thatcherism gave comics something to moan about, and the means to do so. 'The huge explosion in radical anti-government comedy on television was made possible only by Thatcher's insistence that the BBC take twenty-five per cent of programming from independent television companies,' observed *They Think It's All Over* producer Harry Thompson. 'Many of the comics became very rich by attacking the principles which led to their creation.'[1]

When the previous generation of comedians played The Store, television was still

The Comic Strip Presents . . . the cast of the 1993 programme, 'Queen of the Wild Frontier'. Left to right: Peter Richardson, Dawn French, Nigel Planer, Miranda Richardson, Julie T. Wallace, Jennifer Saunders and Keith Allen

learning what it could and couldn't do with stand-up comedy, and inevitably, it made many mistakes along the way. Soho Store stars like Rik Mayall, Adrian Edmondson, Dawn French and Jennifer Saunders all adapted very well to telly, and this brand recognition helped them fill big halls on national tours. But the best TV comics aren't always the best live comics. Stand-up, the most prolific format in club comedy, is especially hard to transfer. Plenty of fine comics are scuppered by lousy small screen concepts, and on telly, second chances are rare.

Deregulation played an essential part in giving good comedians the sort of TV they deserve. The most resourceful and successful comics now make programmes on their own terms, through their own independent production companies, and both the BBC and Channel 4 have responded by becoming far more inventive, devising tailor-made formats to fit the talents of individual comics like Graham Norton and Frank Skinner. On ITV, comics like Lily Savage have colonised mainstream strands once reserved for seaside special turns, and Channel 5 has provided user-friendly slots for comedians who haven't quite acquired the clout to command a network vehicle of their own. For today's rising stars, the relationship with telly need no longer be all or nothing, but in a world where yoof and novelty are treasured far more than talent or integrity, for a generation of older acts, it's often too late.

The Comic Strip found mass success after the foundation of Channel 4. Their daft yet artful Enid Blyton skit, *Five Go Mad In Dorset*, was screened on Channel 4's opening night in November 1982, and it infuriated critics in all the right places. 'A send up of Enid Blyton with *Crossroads* star Ronald Allen playing a homosexual,' fumed a leader in the *Sun*. 'Is that supposed to be funny?' At its inception, at least, this new channel felt like a televisual third way, a world away from the BBC's civil service imperialism or the coarser but equally conservative supermarket commercialism of ITV. And if Channel 4 no longer seems quite so radical today, that's partly because its revolutionary style and content has since been flattered by the imitation of its terrestrial rivals.

The BBC caught up pretty quick (ITV never quite cracked the code) and eventually brought The Comic Strip back to the corporation in 1990 for the last fifteen of its thirty-five televisual outings. Yet although The Comic Strip actors came from The Store, it was only when they moved to The Boulevard Theatre that they attracted the attention of TV producers, who saw far more potential in character comedy than in the straight stand-up favoured by The Store's conveyer-belt format. It wasn't until the Nineties that Store regulars like Jo Brand and Jack Dee made pure and simple stand-up truly attractive to television, and it took young pretender Channel 5 to build a successful series around The Store itself.

Meanwhile, meat and potatoes stand-up at The Store was more or less left alone, and away from the camera's intrusive stare, Store comedians were able to develop their own identities, instead of pandering to the conventional tastes of Light Ent producers. Media anonymity let new acts test drive their material, without worrying too much whether it hit or missed. TV may have introduced a huge new audience to modern stand-up in the Nineties, but it standardised and simplified the product in the process.

'Nobody was interested,' says Don Ward, of his early attempts to attract broadcasters to The Store. 'The attitude was "this is too hot to handle".' Twenty years ago, attitudes to swearing and profanity were far more conservative. 'You'll never get anywhere with this stuff as far as television and radio are concerned,' a man from London Management, a top mainstream agency, told him. 'The language. It's impossible. Can't be used.' Peter Rosengard received the same feedback, or lack of it. 'I had hoped that agents, TV producers and journalists would regularly come to discover new people. This didn't happen. The showbiz establishment regarded us as a threat. They didn't see any wider audience for a bunch of foul-mouthed amateurs. TV was out of the question. So they didn't come down. One exception was a young BBC TV producer called Paul Jackson.'[2]

Jackson was wise to this new wave, and it's a measure of Alternative Comedy's invasion and conquest of the Light Ent mainstream that this pioneering Store punter subsequently became Controller of BBC Entertainment, a £120 million business employing over 400 people. Jackson's fruitful involvement resulted from the right blend of good luck and good judgement. He was in the right place at the right time, but so were a lot of people. Jackson was the only one with both the desire and the know-how to make it happen. 'He was the first guy to spot the television potential and sell it to the powers that be,' says Rosengard. 'Everybody else was saying, "These guys will never work on TV because of the swearing."'

Paul Jackson first went to The Store a few weeks after it opened. He'd seen the adverts and heard about the bizarre blend of radical acts and traditional frilly-shirted, bow-tied comics that collided on the first night, but even so, he still didn't anticipate anything all that different from the trad showcases he attended to spot new talent. 'Getting in and out was a bloody nightmare,' he recalls. But he was glad he persevered. Over the first few nights, he saw Alexei Sayle, Keith Allen, Tony Allen, Rik Mayall, Adrian Edmondson, Nigel Planer and Peter Richardson.

Jackson worked for the BBC, but he was there as an ordinary punter. 'I had no real access to making anything happen,' he says. 'I didn't have the clout.' Nonetheless, although he didn't know it yet, this would be his big break, as well as theirs. 'Ultimately, it became the most important thing I ever got involved in.' And maybe the reason he saw and seized an opportunity that other producers spurned was because he went along as a regular, rather than a VIP. 'I'd gone because I wanted to be entertained on a Saturday night.' And he was. 'I just loved it.'

It was Jackson who took Alternative Comedy where its musical equivalent, punk rock, had never ventured – onto peaktime TV. 'It was a punk statement that transferred into comedy,' he says. 'That generation who emerged now were a generation who'd listened to punk music in their youth and as students.' They applied this punk ethos, of 'fuck concept albums and stadium rock' to humour. 'They were an alternative to the very strong and very successful tradition of heavily produced, carefully written, carefully crafted, by and large big, expensive, long-laboured-over shows,' he explains. 'You don't need to have a BBC budget and six weeks filming and eight weeks prep time. You can just stand up and be funny in the union bar.' Or as one punk fanzine put it, 'This Is A Chord, This Is Another, This Is A Third, Now Form A Band'.

Jackson soon realised that not every alternative comic was anti-trad comedy. 'There's no greater respecter of the traditions of show business than people like Rik and Ade. One thing they did have an issue with was all the racism and the sexism. They didn't find that funny. They found it insidious and dangerous and they wanted to stop that.' But the most important and immediate element was punk's can-do attitude, or, to use a more trad term, 'let's do the show right here'. 'We've got to get some of this on telly,' thought Jackson, on his way home after that first night. 'I've seen the future of comedy and it's The Comedy Store.'

He went back to the BBC and submitted a completely impractical proposal for an entire series. Luckily, he was still relatively naïve about TV. 'Otherwise I'd never have done it.' Even luckier, his boss was Robin Nash, who's worked with comedians from Les Dawson to Harry Hill. 'He always wanted to look at new stuff,' says Jackson. Nash had just seen a musical entertainment called *George*, performed in a little café theatre in the back room of a pizza restaurant, by several of the cast of *Angels*, a BBC soap about student nurses. 'I've noticed this new kind of club cabaret theatre thing's going on,' agreed Nash. 'Have you seen this thing called *George*?' 'No,' said Jackson. 'Well, go and see that,' said Nash. Jackson enjoyed *George*, but this medley of Cole Porterish songs, strung into a sweet twentysomething storyline, was totally different from the comedy he'd seen at The Store. 'I'll do you a deal,' said Nash. 'I'll give you two days studio if you'll do *George*, which I like, on the first day and you can do whatever you like on the second day.' The man who commissioned TV's first Alternative Comedy show had never even seen any Alternative Comedy, and the man who produced and directed it had never produced or directed anything in his life.

It was just as well Nash didn't say yes to Jackson's plan for an entire series. Jackson had told Nash there was a whole circuit out there, but when he visited other venues, he saw the same acts he'd already seen at The Store. 'There's only us,' they told him. 'We're doing three or four nights a week.' So Jackson recruited an American actress from the RSC who was performing in a two-woman comic act called The Johnson Wax Floor Show and writing for a new BBC show called *Not The Nine O'Clock News*. Her name was Ruby Wax. She already knew Rik Mayall. 'She's always been a spotter for talent,' says Jackson. But her set didn't even make the final cut. 'We over-recorded by miles.'

Jackson recorded *George* on the first studio day, and *Boom Boom – Out Go The Lights* on the second. His meagre budget didn't even stretch to commissioning a signature tune, so he made do with an existing song by guest musicians Paul Jones and the Blues Band. Jackson's choice of band betrayed the age gap between him and his comics. Already nudging thirty, his teenage years ran in rough parallel to The Beatles. But he was a fast learner, and for the follow-up show, less than a year later, he enlisted Dexy's Midnight Runners, whose general dogsbody, Jo Jo Smith, later became a comedienne at The Store.

'I remember sitting in the gallery while Alexei said, "Fuck – I just said fuck – they'll fucking kill me,"' recalls Jackson. 'There were all these faces in the gallery turning around to look at me.' His apprenticeship on *The Two Ronnies* had given him a grounding in most TV comedy genres, but Ronnie Barker's spoonerisms hadn't prepared him for this sort of problem. 'Shall I stop the tape?' asked the technical manager. 'There's no point in recording this because it's completely unusable.' 'No,' replied Jackson. 'Keep it going.' By the end, he was pretty pleased. He cut the two shows together and reported back to Nash. 'You've screwed it up,' said Nash. 'It doesn't work.' *Boom Boom – Out Go The Lights* went out in October 1980. *George* still hasn't seen the light of day.

The first show begins with Keith Allen, his face hidden beneath a back to front balaclava, falling offstage. 'What a flop,' he says, as he clambers back onstage. 'It's a bit like being a geology student,' he quips, with a disparaging nod at The Blues Band. 'Looking at old rock formations.' Mainstream comics only ever slagged off the house band as a form of friendly leg pulling, and there was nothing overtly affectionate about Allen's withering aside.

Tony Allen took Keith Allen's musical criticism several stages further, even deconstructing the misogynistic lyrics of the show's signature tune. '"If I get her in my sights, boom, boom, out go the lights"?' he asks. 'He's going to smack her one. What is this? Open door for wife beaters?' Uneasy laughter erupts into a ripple of applause, from a studio audience who'd been obediently chanting the chorus a few minutes before. Allen even criticised TV itself, calling it the 'greatest breakthrough in anaesthetic since chloroform', and describing how a BBC producer saw him play The Store. '"Even if you go down badly and it's a bit wishy washy and you don't say what you're going to say, you can veto it,"' he mimics, in a passable imitation of Jackson. '"But on the other hand, you may come across with a lot of pungent political satire." And I said, "And then you'll veto it."' This wasn't normal Light Ent etiquette. Aspiring comics on *Opportunity Knocks* or *New Faces* didn't dare slag off the one-eyed god, let alone spill the beans about backstage squabbles with producers.

Allen seemed torn between an instinctive mistrust of the mass media and its attraction as a means of speaking to more people in a single session than he could ever hope to persuade from the far smaller platform of the Soho Store. Could he hope to use the tube, or would it end up using him? He soon found out. One of his typically uncompromising routines ended with a woman telling a man to 'get your ego out of my cunt'. Allen knew the line would never be broadcast, but he told Jackson he wanted to do the whole routine in the studio, so as not to break his flow. However, the BBC cut his amplification so even the studio audience couldn't hear. 'This is not for me,' thought Allen. 'I've got to steer clear of this one.' So Allen stopped doing TV, and TV stopped doing Allen.

Unlike Tony Allen, the next act in the show was clearly already en route to stardom. Rik Mayall's earnest poet persona, which eventually evolved into his *Young Ones* namesake, is crisp, accessible and utterly unencumbered by any problematic content. The poems themselves are pretty standard skits. Mayall's mock fury as he flicks two fingers at laughing punters is the only really radical detail. 'Don't clap,' Mayall admonishes his delighted audience. 'You're so hypocritical.' It's the actual performance that really sets him apart. Despite his youth and relative inexperience, Mayall is remarkably focused and at ease in front of the cameras.

Nigel Planer appears as depressive hippy Neil, later immortalised in *The Young Ones*, playing two downbeat numbers from an album called *Despair*. 'They're both pretty bad,' he says. 'I'm going to do the worst one first so the second one won't sound quite so bad.' Alexei Sayle, eyes obscured under pork pie hat, introduces himself as 'Britain's first mod two-tone poet'. One such poem is 'Hello John Got A New Motor', which subsequently became a souped-up hit single.

'They showed *Boom Boom* to the worst audience response in the history of the department,' revealed Jackson. 'It went out to a very small audience.'[3] The Appreciation Index was 46/100. Apparently, anything under sixty is pretty bad news. Yet the *Financial Times*, of all places, quite liked it, and the BBC commissioned a second show.

Broadcast fewer than eighteen months after The Store opened, and a few weeks after The Comic Strip left The Store, the first show was very raw. The second, transmitted in May 1981, still only two years after The Store opened, was far slicker. These comics had already learned how to play to the camera, without forsaking their radical edge. 'You're going to really love these next two guys,' says Alexei Sayle, introducing the opening act, 'because they really love themselves.'

Nigel Planer revives his *Young Ones* hippy prototype, Peter Richardson plays a traffic cop who books him for speeding, and Rik Mayall gets an unlikely laugh from some earlobe origami, but Tony Allen puts them in the shade, saying this was the studio where *Dixon Of Dock Green* was made, contrasting that benign bobby on the beat with a routine about policy brutality. The most topical material comes from Pauline Melville, like Jim Barclay a veteran of radical theatre troupe 7-84. Now a novelist, she did stand-up disguised as a wide-eyed, well-intentioned housewife called Edie. 'Lady Diana Spencer, Prince Charles's girlfriend, she's getting ever so thin,' says Edie. 'She was always slender but now she's getting really thin. I do hope she hasn't got worms.'

Andy de la Tour argues that the British media play down the Northern Irish conflict, likening coverage of The Troubles with World War II-style reports that 'in the disturbances in Western Europe today, there was a short delay in the cross Channel ferry service from Dunkirk.' And although not every viewer would have agreed with his claim that 'TV companies have a policy of telling us that what's going on in Northern Ireland is a minor civil disorder, whereas in truth there's been a war going on,' it's impressive to hear him say so, especially on the national network that bears the brunt of his attack.

Sayle, conversely, was already honing a pragmatic relationship with the medium Alternative Comedy tried so hard to despise. 'Because this is BBC2,' he says, a philosophising yob in a pork pie hat, like one of Steven Berkoff's Shakespearean bovver boys, 'I've gotta do a couple of poems for ya.'

Rik Mayall and Adrian Edmondson finish off with a classic squabbling double act. The actual material, an old-fashioned groaner spun out and torn apart, would scarcely have looked out of place in old time Music Hall, but the dynamic, manic delivery is very new wave. 'I hope you've enjoyed it,' concludes Sayle. 'We certainly haven't.' But despite his protestations, it certainly looked as if they had. 'If you'd like to see us again, please write to your MPs because we'd like to come back here. I'd like to come back here because I'm getting a lift home and I've got a return ticket on the tube.'

By the time the second *Boom Boom* was broadcast, Jackson's best show was already waiting in the wings. *The Young Ones* made stars of Rik Mayall, Adrian Edmondson and Nigel Planer, and established Ben Elton as a new sitcom writer par excellence. Rik Mayall's

ranting poet and Neil, Nigel Planer's gloomy hippy, had both surfaced in the first *Boom Boom*. However Mayall normally worked with Adrian Edmondson, while Planer usually appeared alongside Peter Richardson; already, TV was disrupting live partnerships that had flourished at The Store. And although Jackson reunited Edmondson and Richardson with their respective partners in the second *Boom Boom* the damage was done. Edmondson became a *Young Ones* star but Richardson didn't. 'Paul had meddled a bit in that he'd split up the double acts,' says Sayle. 'He'd taken the two funny ones out of Pete & Nigel and Rik & Ade.' This was only possible with Mayall and Planer's co-operation. 'Comedians being the way they are, they immediately betrayed their partners,' says Sayle. 'He put Rik with Nigel, not understanding the kind of chemistry that exists between a double act.' But Jackson understood that a different chemistry exists on TV.

'There is something very TV unfriendly about stand-up,' says Jackson. 'The act gives you their best five minutes, which they've probably spent three years writing.' And TV needs another five minutes every week. Modern TV sidesteps this problem by trawling today's vast stand-up reservoir, but back in the early Eighties, there simply weren't enough comics to go round. *Boom Boom* was a pale imitation of the real thing partly because it wasn't filmed from The Store. Hence, Jackson was delighted when these comics adapted their work to suit TV, rather than the other way around. The result was a sitcom which, more than any televised stand-up, put Alternative Comedy on the map.

'It was a brilliant TV encapsulation of that mood of the moment that was driving that comedy,' says Jackson, of *The Young Ones.* 'Almost all the rhythms and streams and jokes and personalities and ideas that were being done on The Comic Strip and Comedy Store stages were represented in a very television friendly way.' 'They found a kind of metaphor for The Comedy Store,' agrees Alexei Sayle, who wrote and played a supporting role, slum landlord Jerzy Balowski. 'The Comedy Store disrupted the conventional atmosphere of cabaret. *The Young Ones* disrupted the conventional atmosphere of sitcom.'

The supporting cast list doubles as a Comedy Store who's who: Mark Arden, Keith Allen, Jim Barclay, Chris Barrie, Arnold Brown, Lee Cornes, Ben Elton, Dawn French, Steve Frost, Ronnie Golden, Helen Lederer, Norman Lovett, Paul Merton, Jennifer Saunders and Andy de la Tour. Most of the main characters and even many cameos were derived from routines these comics had performed at The Store. Adrian Dangerous, Edmondson's manic punk rocker, was already a familiar feature of Rik & Ade's live show, alongside Mayall's Richard Dangerous in The Dangerous Brothers. But *The Young Ones* reached a far wider audience than a Soho strip club ever could.

It was *Saturday Live*, broadcast between 1985 and 1987 on Channel 4, which finally made the wider world aware of the new stand-up circuit The Store had spawned, providing a TV platform for countless other Store regulars. Edmondson and Mayall's Dangerous Brothers, plus Mark Arden and Stephen Frost's The Oblivion Boys, were among the most regular acts. Chris Barrie, Nick Hancock, Neil Mullarkey, Jeremy Hardy, Helen Lederer, Andy de la Tour and French & Saunders all made more than one appearance. Julian Clary, Josie Lawrence, Jenny Lecoat, Norman Lovett, Paul Merton, Nigel Planer and Punt & Dennis appeared once apiece. Even visiting Americans such as Will Durst, Charles Fleischer and Emo Philips played The Store and its closest small-screen equivalent, broadcast live from London Weekend's South Bank studios. Once more, the brains behind this innovation was Jackson.

But not every Store comic fared so well, or was half as happy. 'I hated *Saturday Live,*' says Owen O'Neill. 'I'd no idea what television was like. They told me to get there at half eleven in the morning, and I went on at ten to eleven at night. They cut my act to bits,' he says. 'It was just dreadful.'

Even today, many Alternative veterans feel very uneasy about TV. 'I remember Rik Mayall and all of them always used to say, "We're going to use television, it's not going to use us," which is a load of fucking crap,' says Oscar McLennan, an innovative performance artist ignored by TV. 'Television's too big. It ends up swallowing you up and eating you alive and spitting you out again.' Despite Jackson's talent for transforming Store stars into popular TV personalities, for most comics, most times, there's still no substitute for doing, and seeing, comedy live.

Alan Davies

'I kind of avoided The Store because it had a bit of a fearsome reputation,' reveals Alan Davies. In the end, in a reversal of conventional fortunes most comics could only envy, Kim Kinnie invited him in. 'Have you phoned up for an open spot?' asked Kinnie. Davies admitted he hadn't, and told him why. 'Don't be daft, it's just a comedy club,' said Kinnie. 'Why don't you come down?' So Davies went down to the Leicester Square Store and tried out. 'I remember his first gig down there,' says Ainsley Harriott. 'There are certain people that walk onstage and you just know. I always knew he was something special.'

Davies attributes The Store's reputation to its drunken late shows, but his one chronic Store death owed nothing to drink, and everything to backstage banter. 'That day the IRA had put a bomb in a sandwich box,' he says. 'We were in the dressing room, making jokes about sandwiches.' Often, private fun behind the scenes feels even funnier than the public events out front, but humour is always the first casualty of translation, and Davies discovered to his cost that green room gags don't travel. 'I went on and thought I'd open up this IRA sandwich box bomb gag that had just been knocking around in the dressing room. The audience stared at me, bewildered,' recalls Davies. 'And then it all went quiet.' That loud silence is a sound no comic ever wants to hear. 'In the front row there were two women and one said to her mate, "He's lost it," just quietly to herself, but I could hear it because it was so silent in the room.' Then, in that dark, distant corner by the bar, the heckling began. 'Get off. Get on with it. It's not funny. You're shit.' Nothing out of the ordinary, but even back then, it wasn't what Davies was used to. Nevertheless, he admitted defeat with dignity. 'I don't think this is working out,' he said. That was the end of his gig, but it wasn't the end of his evening. It was only the early show, and he had to go back on a few hours later. Luckily, he was fired up and so he did the business. Unluckily, Kim saw the early show and not the late one. Davies didn't get another Store gig for the next six months. Everyone dies at The Store sometime, yet every time it's a serious set back that costs comics time and money.

But nothing good in life ever came easy, and Davies was determined to bounce back. He can still recall the date of his first paid spot: January 20, 1990. 'I remember it because Arsenal played Tottenham at home and they'd won and I'd been to the game.' He was already in a good mood. 'Then the phone rang. "We're stuck. Someone's dropped out. Help."' His fee was £70. Arsenal won that afternoon and Davies won that evening, but for stand-up football fans, both results can just as easily break the other way. His fellow Arsenal fan Keith Dover died at The Store straight after seeing The Gunners snatch defeat from the gaping jaws of victory, losing three–two to outsiders Luton Town in the 1988 League Cup final at Wembley. 'That Luton defeat really did for Keith, he took that really hard,' says Davies. 'Much harder than the gig. There's always another gig. There aren't many cup finals.'

But Davies had plenty more stand-up cup finals to come. He played the opening night at the Piccadilly Circus Store, and even encored a couple of times, always a rarity at The Store. The second time, he wasn't even on the bill. He'd only dropped in for drink, but there'd been a balls up with the booking. A comic hadn't turned up and the bill was an act short so he went on and did the best Store gig he'd ever done.

'The new Store's a great club but the old Store has special memories for people because a lot of the people who are now very famous started there. I can remember when I was doing an open spot, Jack Dee turning up on his motorbike.' And ripping the place apart. 'He was untouchable,' says Davies. 'He was devastating.' Nevertheless, for a while no one knew who he was, and that was the magic of The Store. 'That was where we all started,' says Davies, of the basement club where he first met Arthur Smith and Paul Merton. 'I felt like a first year, sitting in there with the sixth formers.' But Davies soon graduated to the senior common room, and despite this backstage hierarchy, there were no stars at that Store. 'One of the great joys of the club at that time, there weren't any famous people,' he says. 'You were just working in total anonymity.' Nowadays, he fills big theatres on solo tours, but the adrenalin of that midnight audience remains hard to beat. 'They'd queued up to get in, been out in Leicester Square, which was a hellish place, especially that time of night.'

At its best, that hellish place was also a great leveller. 'There's someone in the dressing room,' Kevin Day once warned him, on his way in. 'You'll probably recognise him.' That someone was Lenny Henry. 'Are you doing a spot here tonight?' asked Henry. 'Yeah,' replied Davies. 'I'm just a comic.' Henry corrected him. Nobody who played The Store was just a comic. 'Can I borrow your watch?' asked Henry. Davies was happy to oblige. Henry went on and did ten minutes of new material. 'He came off and he got his stuff ready to go and I went after him. I tapped him on the shoulder. I said, "Lenny," and he said, "Oh yeah, nice to meet you. Have a good gig." I said, "No, Lenny, you've got my watch."'

His strangest Store gig was on the night of the Poll Tax riots in the spring of 1990. Davies went on the march with a couple of other comics, but he had a more pressing prior engagement. 'Arsenal were playing at home, so I left for the match about two.' The Gunners beat Everton one–nil, and afterwards he headed back into town to play The Store. But that was a lot easier said than done. All the local tubes were shut. He had to get out at Goodge Street and walk. 'Tottenham Court Road, Charing Cross Road, debris everywhere, broken glass, all the musical instrument shops looted, which became my joke when I went onstage. "If anyone's interested, I've got two trombones out the back."' At Centrepoint, he had to cross a police riot shield barricade, but eventually he made it to The Store, where, despite all the chaos and the carnage, a few hundred people were waiting to see some comedy. 'Nothing would deter someone who wanted a good night out down The Store.'

Davies' most bizarre backstage moment involved an open spot. 'The majority are young men who want to be comics. Some can do it and some can't.' However, some try-outs are rather more eccentric, as Davies discovered to his cost. He was in the dressing room before a gig when an American woman came in, dressed in a short skirt. 'She wasn't a young woman but she was sort of slim and she wasn't unattractive,' recalls Davies. 'Can you help me with my make-up?' she asked him, as she changed into an even shorter skirt, indifferent to the sniggers of the other male comics in the dressing room. 'She lifts her skirt up and she's got a map – as far as I remember it was the Polynesian Islands.' Davies was entrusted to paint these islands onto her bum. By now the other comics couldn't contain themselves, so they all left the dressing room, but every now and then the door would open wide, as the compere, Bob Mills, brought another few people in to witness a blushing Davies with a paintbrush in his hand and a woman's posterior in his face.

By the time she went on, the word had gone round, and the auditorium was full of comics. Bob Mills can still recall every detail of her turn. 'She did about five minutes of material and then she said, "Have I shown you my tattoos? I have a map of the world." And she flipped around and she said, "This is the United States of America." And then she showed them the other cheek and said, "This is Mexico," and then bent over, pointed to her arsehole and said, "And this is Guam."' The crowd just sat and stared. They'd never even heard of Guam. 'It's the only time I've ever seen a comedy audience ever so slightly embarrassed.'

Only Mills could have followed that. 'He went on and he said, "I need ten strong men and a chamois leather," and no one really knew what it meant,' remembers Davies. 'Did he mean to clean her bum? To clean the stage? To clean himself? What does it mean?' It didn't matter. Mills' daft turn of phrase released all the bewildered tension around the room. 'And this woman went in and cleaned her bum without any assistance from me and was never seen again.'

You Lend Some People a Fiver (And You Never See Them Again)

It's eleven o'clock, pub closing time, but here at The Store it's only half time, that strange, listless limbo between early and late shows. I hadn't planned to stay for the midnight show, but Stan Nelson has had a tip that Glaswegian Jewish iconoclast Jerry Sadowitz might be dropping in to do an impromptu ten minutes, and there's that potent tang of expectation in the air, the sense that something exciting is about to happen. Sadowitz is one of the most extraordinary acts to ever appear at The Store, and no one can quite remember the last time he played here, so I decide to stick around.

Samuel Beckett said nothing is as funny as unhappiness, and no comic was so hilariously unhappy as Jerry Sadowitz. With nihilistic equality, this indignant, aggressive, politically incorrect rebel raged against the creative poverty of mainstream entertainers and Alternative Comedy's right-on piety. Within a few years, what had started as an anarchic free-for-all had acquired its own manifesto of received values. Unlike most trad comics, Alternative Comedy attacked the strong and not the weak, but many new performers soon became complacent and self-satisfied. This wasn't what The Store was for. 'It's not for people to try out their act that with a bit of tweaking and editing could turn up on the *Des O'Connor Show*,' says Clive Anderson. 'It should be an act that almost couldn't get on to late-night telly.' Such an act was Jerry Sadowitz. 'He was like a man on the verge of murder, bursting with hate and ideas,' recalls Arthur Smith. 'There were things you wouldn't say onstage which Jerry would. People were genuinely excited to see him exploding myths.' As Owen O'Neill says, 'Everything else just paled into insignificance.'

Yet if you'd seen him backstage, you never would have guessed. 'There was this funny little bloke just sitting hunched at a table with a peaked cap and a Dennis The Menace jumper,' says Jack Dee. 'I didn't know who he was and I had no idea he wasn't a punter,' And then he went on and tore his spectators to pieces. 'It just blew everyone away,' says Mark Lamarr. 'And he went on at the half-two slot as well.' 'That was a defining moment,' remembers Dave Cohen. 'Everyone was knackered and he went on and did ten minutes of absolutely phenomenal comedy. It was the first time he'd ever done a gig in London and he was already as good as he ever got.' Cohen had never seen anything like it before, and nor had anyone else. 'There was so much anger and aggression in there,' he says. 'It all came spewing out.' Yet the moment he finished, Sadowitz reverted to his shy offstage persona. 'You were fantastic,' the other comics all told him. 'No, don't say that,' he replied. 'But it's brilliant,' they all told him. Usually, the more unusual the comic, the longer it takes them to find their own true voice – Jack Dee took a year; Eddie Izzard took even longer. But Sadowitz was instantly unique. That raw reality was there right from the start. 'You've got to come back,' said Kim Kinnie, and gave him a paid booking for the following week.

'The great thing about Sadowitz was that he didn't give a fuck about the audience,' says Pierre Hollins. 'That's what made it work, the fact that he wasn't pandering to an audience at all. Most people wanted it to work, but he could snatch defeat from victory just out of pure belligerence.' 'He didn't give a flying fuck whether they liked him or not, and they couldn't work out whether they liked him or not, but they had to watch him,' agrees Nick Hancock. 'Everybody watched Sadowitz because you wouldn't know what way it would go.' 'Comics would put down their drinks and start peering round and watching what was happening,' says Mark Billingham. 'There was always something electric about Sadowitz coming on and just not knowing what was going to happen.' 'He was relentless,' says Martin Soan, of a set that reduced act and audience alike to a state of near nervous exhaustion. 'You'd sit there wondering when it was going to be your turn.'

Sadowitz seemed to set out to alienate everyone, striving to locate the particular topic that would offend every individual in the room. This fearless attitude made him equally detested and adored. 'I found it hilarious that people actually took it seriously, even if Jerry in his mixed-up madness meant it,' says Soan. 'Old people, social workers, teachers, anything, everything, and that's the real attraction of Jerry Sadowitz for me. He would not stop. He was like a dog.' And like a dog, once he'd sunk his teeth into the ankle of your liberal sensibility, he would not let go.

Jerry Sadowitz

'What the fuck can I say that's going to really fucking piss them off?' Owen O'Neill recalls Sadowitz asking backstage before a show. 'Why don't you say, "Nelson Mandela, what a cunt?"' suggested Nick Revell. They all fell about at the thought of uniting the world's most revered personality with the most reviled word in the language, but they never thought Sadowitz would actually say it. 'It was a Friday night, the place was packed and across the road at South Africa House there was a big demonstration,' recalls O'Neill. 'His opening line was, "Ladies and gentlemen, Nelson Mandela, what a cunt," but he didn't have any punchline.' The rest was classic Sadowitz. 'He fought them and got them back and lost them again.' 'You've got to have a punchline,' the other comics told him, afterwards. 'What do I need a punchline for?' he asked, but in the end he relented. 'OK,' he said. 'I'll have a punchline tomorrow night.' And he did. 'Nelson Mandela, what a cunt, you lend some people a fiver, you never fucking see them again.' The room erupted, but O'Neill reckons he actually liked it better before.

This quip was a cheeky poke at the liberal left's pious preoccupation with Mandela, so often demonstrated in token gestures like renaming student union bars in his honour. However, more reactionary punters were immune to the gag's inherent irony. 'He'd get a reaction from racists in the audience,' says Pierre Hollins. 'The whole audience would laugh together but for entirely different reasons.' Gay comics face a comparable dilemma, as liberals laugh at the searing insights of their gay material, alongside homophobes who howl at the hilarious spectacle of someone actually admitting they're gay. 'Because Ben Elton became so popular on telly, that started a backlash of people who saw somebody being left wing and not terribly funny,' says Cohen. 'Mark Thomas was always going on about what you can say and what you can't say and it was really tiresome,' says Jim Tavare. 'They were right in one sense because they made the world a better place.' But they didn't always make it funnier. 'It was a pain in the arse and Jerry just put that to rights.'

Yet like all the best abstract artists, this anarchic act was underpinned by a sound understanding of the traditions of the form. 'He had a genuine interest in comedy,' adds Tavare. 'He wasn't just saying it all for effect. He had a real understanding of what being a comedian was all about.' 'He was the real thing and you knew he was,' says Patrick Marber. 'There were people who didn't like it, who were offended and upset, but he really worked. He always had craft. He was always a comedian's comedian. Even if people didn't like what he was saying, he had such skill, and enormous charm. He was tougher on himself than he was on anyone else. He was the business.'

Offstage, Sadowitz was quiet, reasonable and intelligent, yet his stage persona left a residue that was difficult to dispel. 'He scared me,' says Pierre Hollins. 'He was quite a scary bloke, not easy to make friends with him, although I did get on with him fine on a one to one.' 'He was an uncomfortable person so it was a relief when he was onstage rather than backstage,' confirms Jenny Eclair. 'There were some nights when you'd really rather sit on the toilet than be in the dressing room, because there were some people who'd unnerve you. Sadowitz could be unnerving, but when he was onstage, he was more comfortable in his skin, however vile that skin was.' Sadowitz opened a lot of doors for a lot of people, but he was always a hard act to follow. 'People didn't really want to go out and be angry or really on the edge and mad because that's what Jerry was doing,' says Owen O'Neill. 'We all had an act. Jerry didn't. He was the real thing.' 'He's either absolutely brilliant or he's shit because his anger is just rampant,' confirms Ronnie Golden. 'It's just an inferno. It's his driving force.'

'There was nobody else who could say such offensive things but at the same time have the audience killing themselves laughing,' says Simon Clayton. 'He created the opportunity for people to laugh at their own prejudices. For a comedian to do that is special. It's not something you can do permanently. It never lasts very long.' 'He had such an intensity of vision that he was bound to burn himself out,' concurs Arthur Smith. 'In the end, I fell foul of him,' he adds, 'because he started doing Pakistani jokes.' Sadowitz could bend the old orthodoxy, but he couldn't break it, and his explosive delivery gave him less leeway than other more softly spoken comics. 'I'd been talking about abortion, I'd been talking about religion, I'd been talking about all sorts of issues, and he said he couldn't understand why I was allowed time and space to talk about those things, but if he'd even mentioned some of them, people would be up in arms,' says Kevin Day. 'It was a difference in styles. Even if he'd been talking about kittens, there was the assumption that everything he said was full of anger and bitterness, so people never gave him any time and space.'

A decade after his Store heyday, Sadowitz finally found a telly forum that reflected at least a smidgen of his huge, strange talent, in *The People Versus Jerry Sadowitz*, an anarchic anti-chat show in which random all-comers did verbal battle with Sadowitz, and, on one occasion, physical battle with his celebrity bouncer. His subsequent TV vehicle, *The Jerry Atric Show*, which combined mesmeric stage magic, pre-prepared stand-up and off-the-cuff banter, was even better. Because above all, Sadowitz is a great close-up magician. John Lenahan calls him one of the best card men in the country. And coming from the best magician to cross the pond, that's high praise indeed.

Store punter turned stand-up Ian Stone is one of many who call Sadowitz the best comic they've ever seen. 'I never heckled again after seeing him because I thought, "There's no way I'm going to take you on – no way," because he just looked like he'd eat me. I was really scared of him, actually. I was scared of him when I met him and I'm still scared of him.' True talent of any sort is scary. There's something alien, amoral and unfathomable about it. 'I went to see him with my girlfriend,' says Stone. 'She thought the men liked him more than the women.' But like all the greatest comics, his biggest target was himself. 'I never saw him do bad shows. I always saw him just blow it away.'

And despite the accusations of sexism in his act, there's no shortage of comediennes who attest to his comic genius. 'Even though people think he's the most appalling misogynist, I actually don't think he's a bad bloke underneath,' says Jo Brand, who still has a soft spot for him. 'He's actually a really brilliant stand-up.' It's difficult to call him sexist when his abuse is so universal. 'He had a whack at everybody,' says Vivienne Soan. 'Nobody was safe.' 'I still don't think there's anyone better than Sadowitz,' says Mandy Knight. 'I still think he's the king.'

'I've played some fucking toilets in my time but never have I seen so many pieces of shit in the one fucking sewer, and you're fucking ugly cunts as well,' drawls Sadowitz, his eyes hidden behind dark shades. 'If I had my way, I'd have you all ethnically cleansed, you bastards. I can fucking smell you from fucking here.' Sadowitz, safe to say, isn't trying to ingratiate himself with this audience. 'Is that your face or is it an advert for Pizza Hut?' he asks one punter. 'Is that your hair or is your face unravelling?' he asks another. 'How you doing, Miss? Oh, it's a fucking guy. Fuck you.' This undiluted onslaught does get a few laughs, but Sadowitz is actually playing an unfamiliar comic character, a tough-talking American, and this added baggage tips the balance from acceptance into confusion. 'I just flew in from the fucking Bronx,' snorts Sadowitz, in a thick Noo Yawk accent. 'You know the fucking Bronx. The kind of fucking place you put all the Kosovan Albanians there it would improve the fucking stink. No offence, ladies and gentlemen, but fucking Albanians, fucking gypsy thieving fucking bastards. If you're not paying any attention they'll steal the fucking protein from your fucking shit stools.' At the Leicester Square Store, in the politically correct Eighties, this racial rant would have incited outrage all around the room, but this crowd have no right-on sensitivities to scandalise. Their only reaction is irritation.

'I'm actually a bisexual necrophiliac,' explains Sadowitz, retreating to an older banker. 'I'll fuck anything that doesn't move.' But it's twice as hard for a character comic to quell an unruly room, which is why they're increasingly uncommon here. 'You'll need to get that guy's cock out of your fucking mouth before I can hear what you're fucking saying,' he tells a heckler. 'Don't heckle me in Esperanto, you fucking dickhead.' But by now, this crowd is booing, not with outrage, merely boredom and bemusement. 'Where I come from that means you fucking like me, you fucking fucks,' he says, but he's pushing against an open door. This house is giving him nothing to fight against, only the passive resistance of mild disdain. 'I can see I'm not going to follow the last act so I'm going to fuck off,' he says, with admirable dignity, nothing becoming his act like the leaving of it. 'I find it very difficult to say goodnight to an audience so I'll phone you. Wednesday, about three o'clock. Fuck you.' And he walks off to the sound of his own footsteps. 'We want Jerry,' chant the crowd, perversely, as soon as he's safely gone. Sadowitz has left the building. Will he ever be back here again?

Stand-up metaphors are always vivid, and often violent. It's not a matter of life and death, but it often feels that way. Tonight we saw someone stiff who's ripped this place apart more times than anyone. And if there's any justice in stand-up comedy, which there isn't, he'll be back sometime soon to rip it up again. 'We've all died,' says Eddie Izzard. 'We've all scored big.' Jerry Sadowitz died tonight, but in this arena, nobody's ever scored quite as big as him. If there's any justice he'll do it again some day soon.

Dying is Easy, Comedy is Hard

Stan Nelson has a homemade video nasty hidden away in his sound booth. It's called The Tape of Shame, and it's a collection of lowlights from some of the worst open spots Stan has ever seen. Sadly, it only features those open spots who've played The Store since it moved to Piccadilly. Otherwise it would include many of the most famous names who've ever played here. 'Any comic who says they haven't died has never gone well,' says Terry Alderton. 'You have to die in this game.'

Unique acts with more potential usually take the most time to mature. 'In the first two years we didn't get a single laugh,' said Harry Hill, of his wilderness years in a duo called The Hall Brothers. 'If someone coughed we took it as a sign of encouragement. It really was that bad. After one of our shows a bloke came up to me and I assumed he was going to tell me how much he enjoyed it. But he looked me straight in the eye and said, "I'll be honest with you. I've seen some terrible comedians in my time, but you are shit. If you want my advice, give up now."'

'I got booed off once,' says American Dave Fulton. 'The English feel like it's a god-given right to heckle. I told them a joke they didn't get, so I explained to them why it was funny, why they were stupid for not understanding it, which is a big mistake with English crowds.' Especially this English crowd. 'Get off, get off, get off,' they yelled. Back in the dressing room, the other comics tried to cheer him up, but Fulton still felt worried when Don Ward walked in. 'Hey, Don,' said the compere, Mickey Hutton. 'Can we get a casket for Dave, because he fucking died.' That broke the ice and Fulton lived to fight another night. 'I didn't really care,' he says. 'If you take it too personally, it just eats you out.'

Fulton had a generous reception in the dressing room, according to Phil Davey. 'When you come offstage and you've had a really bad one, no one wants to talk to you. He's the unfunny guy. He's got the unfunny disease. It's like he's got the plague. That's the trouble with dying. It's like the loneliest place in the world to be back here amongst your peers after you've died because no one can say anything to you. Anything they say will make you feel worse.'

Davey remembers one comic with a unique approach to corpsing. When he dried during an open spot he fell over and played dead. At first it was hilarious but five minutes later he was still lying there. 'Get him off the stage,' Kinnie told the compere, Kevin Day. 'I can't,' protested Day. 'He hasn't finished his performance.' Eventually Day and Davey walked onstage to take him off, whereupon he ran into the dressing room, grabbed his bag, and ran off.

Even Mark Lamarr has died down here. 'There were nights when I started off really well and died on me arse,' he says. 'People can go on in the first show and encore, and get booed off in the second one.' It isn't the comic that's changed, merely the mood around the room. 'I love to watch comics die,' admits Sean Lock. 'Everybody does. Because of that sheer panic. The look in their eyes. The dry mouth. I remember I died once and Bob Mills walked on as compere with loads of tissue paper in his mouth. There is also that sense of camaraderie. Everyone's died and you can all have a laugh about it afterwards.' And if the act before you dies, you're almost certain to storm it. 'I always imagine they're making me a nice cake,' says Lock. 'They're icing it. Now they're putting the candles on.' And then he strolls on stage and eats it.

'I can't think of a single top act today who was at The Store who didn't die,' says Bob Mills, 'but it didn't really matter.' Often the audience was too drunk, or a comic was trying some new material. 'I like films,' Mills remembers Paul Merton saying. 'I'm a bit of a film buff. What is a buff, exactly? If you like classic cars, are you a classic car buff? If you like powder puffs, are you a powder puff buff? Am I the only person who

Jim Tavare and his double bass

thinks that's funny?' He was. 'He did it for another ten minutes and died on his arse but it didn't matter.'

In fact, it doesn't matter how many times you die, you can still find success in the end, if you have the talent, and the tenacity. For the first few years of his comic career, Jim Tavare was universally acknowledged, even by himself, as the worst comic on the entire circuit. That he's now one of the best is a tribute to his stubborn self-belief and sheer staying power. Malcolm Hardee's Tunnel Club had a Get Jim Tavare Off In Under Thirty Seconds spot every Sunday night. When Tavare finally lasted thirty-one seconds, he wasn't invited back. 'When you die a death, it's terrible,' he says. 'You can't hear. Your ears go numb and you have an out-of-body experience.'

Yet Tavare harbours no hard feelings about the hecklers who made his life a misery. 'It was a very creative art form,' he says, and to prove it, he rattles off a few of his old favourites. 'I'm a schizophrenic,' began one of his one-liners. 'Why don't you both fuck off?' shouted a heckler. His *Star Trek* routine didn't fare much better. 'It's comedy, Jim, but not as we know it,' yelled a Trekkie in the stalls.

Even though Tavare didn't have much of an act, he had the hide of a rhino. 'I realised you had to keep trying until it no longer hurt,' he explains. 'I always compare it to a game of golf. If you have one good shot, that's enough to make you play next week.' 'What are you still doing this for?' asked other comics. 'When are you going to give up?' But their put-downs simply spurred him on.

His act started to turn the corner after his wife told him to ignore the hecklers, rather than trying to take them on, but it was his double bass that really made the difference. It was hard work lugging it around on tubes and night buses, and it didn't stop the heckles. 'Midget with a violin,' shouted one punter. However most punters liked it. 'They used to appreciate the fact that I'd gone all that way with a huge double bass for one joke.' It also allowed him some welcome anonymity offstage. 'That bloke with the cello was shit, wasn't he?' a drunken punter once told him at the bar. 'Yes,' agreed Tavare. 'He was fucking useless.'

Happy Birthday

Tonight, Monday 17 May, 1999, The Comedy Store is twenty years old. Well, sort of. In fact, the actual anniversary isn't until Wednesday, but Wednesday is a Players night, and Tuesday is reserved for The Cutting Edge, so tonight's the night that Don Ward is celebrating The Store's twentieth birthday, with a special gala show featuring many of the top stand-ups who've played this place during the Nineties, and even a few Eighties veterans from the Leicester Square Store as well. Rising stars like Ed Byrne and Rhona Cameron, older hands like Jeff Green and Mickey Hutton, visiting Americans like Maria Falzone, even trad turns like Phil Cool. However, the Soho Store pioneers are the Banquos at this feast. Where are The Comic Strip when you really need them? Hattie Hayridge and Jenny Eclair are the closest we get to the old guard. More representative of today's Store are post-Alternative comics such as former Butlins Redcoat and Southend footballer Terry Alderton, plus East Ender Ricky Grover.

'When you're an Alternative comedian, there's pressure on you,' pants Ricky Grover, still recovering from his shadow boxing entrance. 'There's certain material you can't do. Nothing sexist, which is a shame, because my wife's a lazy bastard. Every time I go to the sink, it's full of washing up. I can't even have a piss.' Grover is nothing like a normal Alternative comic, and his billing at this landmark bash shows how far The Store's compass has shifted with these changing times. 'I'm not one of those clever political comedians,' admits this heavyweight contender run to fat. 'I wish I was one of them clever ones who come on here and use words like irony. The irony of that is I don't know what it means. Now you don't know whether I'm clever or not, do you? Might be. Might not. It's up to me, innit?'

Paul Tonkinson, Ricky Grover and Malcolm Hardee at The Comedy Store's twentieth Birthday Party

'I've been doing this for sixteen years and I'm still a bit shit sometimes,' says Jenny Eclair, but tonight she's on fine form. 'I got into stand-up comedy because I thought, "Loads of blokes involved in the business." But I have to say now, all stand-up comics – crap shags. That Lee Evans? It's like trying to fuck a fish on a skateboard. The trouble with male stand-up comics is, they don't know when to stop being funny and start being a beast. I don't want jokes. I want to be slapped and shaved. Last thing I want in bed is a good laugh. If I want to laugh and come at the same time, I'll toss myself off with a glove puppet.'

'Jenny is available for children's parties,' announces the compere, Kevin Day.

The Store has come a long way since that frenetic opening night, but tonight, fittingly, the atmosphere isn't all that different. There's no free champagne, and the show starts at seven, not midnight, but the stalls are packed with freeloading broadsheet hacks, TV luvvies and other media liggers. 'This is a benefit for Romanian orphans,' says Kevin Day, 'although there's so many fucking journalists on the guest list, I think the orphans owe us money at the moment, so few people have paid to get in.' They're outshouted if not outnumbered by the gossiping comics at the bar, but even these hardened stand-up professionals shut up for tonight's star turn, Lee Evans.

There was always something about Lee Evans. 'I've seen this kid from Southend,' Mickey Hutton told Jeff Green, after he first saw Evans, over a decade ago. 'He's fucking brilliant. He just does noises. He's fantastic.' 'I've never seen anyone like this before,' thought Steve Punt, the first time he saw Evans at The Store. Yet it could all have been very different. For three years Evans had been trying, and failing, to make it on the mainstream circuit. Punters stole his piano, and even threw a fire extinguisher at him, and when he finally found The Store, he was about to pack it in. 'It blew me right away,' he said. 'I couldn't believe what I was seeing and hearing. This was really creative. What the comics were doing was often off the wall but it came from deep down in the heart and gut as well. It was like discovering a new country.'[1] Like all the best comics, he still had some sticky gigs early on. 'I remember seeing Lee Evans do a try out and more or less die on his arse,' recalls Jenny Eclair. Since then, he's conquered British comedy, but it wasn't until he came into the dressing room and took off his shirt to reveal a musclebound West Coast torso that she realised what a big star he'd become.

Lee Evans performing at The Comedy Store's twentieth birthday celebrations

'When Lee comes down, he sets the place on fire,' says Don Ward. 'The room just erupts.' And tonight it's an inferno. 'I love you!' shouts a female punter. 'Thanks, Mum,' says Evans. He's reading from notes, but these new gags still bring the house down. 'I've written it,' he says. 'I just can't fucking remember it.' You've got to be pretty confident to use a night like this to work in fresh material. 'Shit joke,' he confesses, after one untried one-liner receives a little less than rapturous applause. 'I'll never use it again.' Yet most comics would settle for the sort of laugh he gets, even off this relative dud, and his audacity wins a second wave of laughter. No wonder Jo Brand calls Evans the perfect Store comic.

'He must have been shit,' says Day, as Evans leaves on an ecstatic tide of applause. 'I've never seen an audience so pleased to see the compere again.' Everyone laughs even louder. 'Once again, ladies and gentlemen,' booms the disembodied voice of Stan Nelson. 'Please take your plates back to the diner and your glasses back to the bar.'

Afterwards, a gaggle of comics, staff, hacks and liggers stagger through Chinatown to Teatro's, Lee Chapman's fashionable bar on Shaftesbury Avenue. 'Within five minutes of coming in here, I met three comedians who said, "Fuck me, it's taken me twenty years to get a free drink out of Don Ward,'" says Jim Barclay, looking a bit incongruous propping up the designer bar. 'It was just like a school reunion,' says Donna McPhail. 'No one talked about work.' At Teatro's, she realised how fond she really was of all these people, and what a mark they'd made on her life. 'You were so encouraging to me when I was just starting,' she told Kim Kinnie. 'Whatever,' he replied, like she was taking the piss. 'No,' insisted McPhail. 'Honest to God.' Eventually, after five minutes' persuasion, he finally accepted her compliment. And maybe, just maybe, he believed her.

But although it was a party, the mood backstage was still uptight. 'I didn't take any chances,' says Jenny Eclair. 'The Store is one of those places you play in front of your peers. You couldn't trust who was going to see you, and who was going to say what about you behind your back.' 'Is it going to be awkward?' wondered Dave Cohen, on his way there. 'Are there going to be fights?' But when he arrived, he soon changed his mind. 'There were so many people there, and we hadn't seen each other for so long, and there was so much to catch up on, that at the end of three and a half hours, I still hadn't spoken to everybody I wanted to speak to, and we were being kicked out, and that's got to be the sign of a good party,' he says. 'We've all seen each other be brilliant and we've all seen each other be crap, so you can never have a situation where you're in a room with someone who's going to lord it over you.' Even if that someone is Lee Evans. 'Chatting away to him, it was like we were at The Store and we'd just been on the bill together,' says Cohen. 'We've all sat in that scuzzy dressing room in Leicester Square.'

As they chatted about old times, the same question kept cropping up. Do you miss it? Each time Cohen said he didn't, he remembered something else he missed, like the way Kim Kinnie always bucked him up when he had a bad gig. 'After I'd stopped doing stand-up, I couldn't help but feel that because I hadn't succeeded at it, that in some way it was a kind of failure,' he says. Yet that night Tim Clark complimented him about the writing he's done since, and Cohen realised there is a world elsewhere. 'I'd defined my career as not being successful by looking at people like them,' he says. 'For them to then say to me, "How do you do it?" That made me feel yes, stand-up was a valid thing that I did for a long time. It wasn't something I failed at. It was something I did and was good at when I was doing it. When I was no longer capable of doing it, I moved on to something else.' Yet whenever he writes a new gag, he still wishes he could test drive it that night, at The Store. 'For all that people say it's got too commercial and it's not as political as it used to be, The Store is actually one place you can genuinely go and be guaranteed to get some politics. You can't guarantee that at Jongleurs.'

Which is why it was a shame more genuine originals weren't at this show. 'I was slightly disappointed a lot more of the old performers didn't turn up,' says Ainsley Harriott. 'I was incredibly surprised, when I went on to the party afterwards, that so many of the performers didn't realise there was something happening. All they knew about was the party. They knew nothing about what was happening down at The

Store.' The press picked up on this omission, and the bill which tilted heavily towards newer names, and away from old timers.

'We found a bunch of nice, but rather complacent white, mostly straight men, just back from touring in Australia, America or Hong Kong,' wrote Alexander Games in the *Standard*. 'Radicalism mellows with age,' wrote Brian Logan in the *Guardian*. 'Righteous anger was in chronically short supply.' The headline writers had a field day. 'It's a fangless business being funny today,' said the *Standard*. It was the *Daily Mail*, that bastion of Conservative Middle England, that put aside what The Store once was, and focused instead on what it had become. 'Cracking a joke is better than making a point,' wrote the *Mail*'s Michael Coveney. 'We felt that the future of British stand-up was in very safe hands.' *Private Eye* captured the mood in a cartoon by Heath. 'We didn't watch television in the Eighties,' rues a queuing punter. 'We went to The Comedy Store to see Rik Mayall, Nigel Planer, French & Saunders, Alexei Sayle. Now you have to stay in and watch television if you want to see them.' 'They really are Alternative,' says another. 'Now they're very rich.' Make that very rich indeed. Last year, Mr & Mrs Monsoon, the production company Saunders owns with her husband Adrian Edmondson, was one of Britain's fifty richest broadcasters, worth £10 million. That's more than half a million £15 appearance fees at the old Soho Store. It was Charles Spencer who best summed up the mood of the press. 'The anger, the urgency and the bracing unpredictability of the early days of Alternative Comedy have long gone, and I miss them badly,' he wrote in the *Telegraph*. 'But perhaps it is just my own lost youth I'm mourning.'

However, the press helped to chase away the anger and unpredictability he mourned. 'The atmosphere back here was quite tense, because there were so many journalists in,' says Ed Byrne, backstage, the afternoon after the night before. 'Having only been doing comedy for five years, only been playing The Store for three, I was quite surprised to be asked to be on the twentieth anniversary show and it was quite an honour.' But he couldn't help but wonder where old Store stars like Alexei Sayle had got to. Well, they were all out in force the following night, on the Soho side of Shaftesbury Avenue, as pioneers like Clive Anderson, Nigel Planer, Peter Richardson and Sayle himself, all so conspicuous by their absence at Ward's show, congregated at The Ivy for Peter Rosengard's rival birthday bash.

'Birthdays are often emotionally difficult, as Peter Rosengard can testify,' reports the *Evening Standard*, the next day. 'He wasn't invited to The Comedy Store's twentieth birthday party at Teatro last night, despite having co-founded the Soho club with Don Ward. So he's throwing his own alternative bash at the Ivy tonight.'

Like Her Majesty The Queen, The Comedy Store has two birthdays. And the atmosphere at The Ivy could scarcely be more different from Ward's celebration the night before. In a private room above one of London's most fashionable restaurants, waiters glide silently across deep carpets, bearing trays of canapés and bubbly. Beside the free bar, a young female pianist warbles cruise ship standards. Teatro is only a few minutes' walk away, but upstairs at The Ivy is another world. When The Store was still a twinkle in his eye, Peter Rosengard used to purr along Oxford Street in his Rolls-Royce convertible, and twenty years later, he still hasn't lost his taste for the high life, or his flair for putting on a sophisticated show.

Even after all this time, it's difficult to find a neutral bystander in Ward and Rosengard's feud. Jim Barclay, Ronnie Golden and Nick Revell are among the few comics who've turned up to both events. Clive Anderson, Nigel Planer, Peter Richardson, and Alexei Sayle are here, as well as David Dein, vice chairman of Arsenal Football Club, plus future BBC Director General Greg Dyke. But among old hands like Tony Allen, Arnold Brown and Andrew 'mad as a bucket of prawns' Bailey, I can spot only one stand-up from The Store's younger generation, Adam Bloom. As the pianist belts out her saloon bar classics, a little louder with every verse, and the commotion builds from tipsy murmur to boozy, booming hubbub, Peter Rosengard steps onto the makeshift stage.

'You know when you're a kid, you always think there's a better party on a Saturday night wherever you are?' asks Rosengard. 'Well, for two and a half years, 1979 to 1981, The Comedy Store was that place to be. It was exciting, it was dangerous, and tonight we have a lot of people who were there on the opening night. I'd like to thank people like Alexei Sayle, without whom we would never have had a Comedy Store. I want to thank Clive Anderson, who appeared on the opening night. Let's hear it for these people. Arnold Brown, Jim Barclay, Tom Tickell.'

Last night, Don Ward's party gathered together the best of modern stand-up, but at tonight's rival birthday bash, Rosengard has assembled a Who's Who of vintage Alternative Comedy. Yet he can't resist a little artistic licence, and these comics won't let him get away with it. 'This gong hasn't been seen in public in eighteen years,' he declares, grandly, regarding the mammoth instrument which has pride of place on this tiny podium. 'It's not even the right gong,' protests Malcolm Hardee from the audience. 'The right gong's in his house.' Hardee points at Roger Pomphrey, who's stood nearby. 'I'm being heckled by my own comedians,' says Rosengard, but he carries on regardless. 'Keith Allen tried to kill me. Alexei Sayle tried to strangle me. And these are some of the better nights.' Tonight, he'll recreate that chaos. 'Frustrated dentists, frustrated accountants,' continues Rosengard, despite the din, all the old slogans still pouring out of him, twenty years on.

'I've always enthusiastically encouraged Peter in all his endeavours,' says tonight's compere Clive Anderson, as he takes Rosengard's place behind the mike. 'Anything to take him away from life insurance. But I never imagined twenty years ago, standing in front of a load of drunks, not interested in me and having no material, I never thought in twenty years' time I'd still be here in front of a load of drunks with no material.'

'Peter Rosengard's an extraordinary person,' says Clive Anderson, a few months later. 'He's a salesman par excellence.' Anderson's participation in this bizarre anniversary revue demonstrated Rosengard's extraordinary powers of persuasion. 'Will you get up and introduce people?' Rosengard asked Anderson. 'No, absolutely not, Peter, I don't want to do that,' replied Anderson, but even as he said so, he knew his protests were in vain. And in the end, it wasn't so bad after all. 'I'm never very comfortable in those "in" kind of audiences because I don't think you can do an ordinary performance, but in terms of just standing up and saying, "Hello, here's the next act," it was all right. It was nice to see some of the people, personally, who I hadn't seen for years, and I remember standing in the wings with Tony Allen and Jim Barclay and all those quite committed comedians with their politics and stuff. Not just the politics. That makes them sound just like activists. But their commitment to the rules of comedy and things you can do and you can't do.' And the comedy they still do today.

'Shit, I know your face from somewhere,' thought Tom Tickell, when he saw Clive Anderson that night. 'I was just about to go up and say so, until someone pointed out who he was.' Another comic he can't recall thanked Tickell for a joke he had told him twenty years before. The comic had used it ever since, but Tickell had long since forgotten it, so the comic refreshed Tickell's memory. 'A wet Sunday in the middle of the Yorkshire Moors, spacecraft comes down, out comes a little Martian, desperate to meet an earthling. It's raining, everyone's gone in, half the world is watching television, and he wanders off down the road. Twenty minutes later, fuck all has happened. Forty minutes later, he's still walking. An hour later he finally comes to a deserted filling station. So he goes up to a petrol pump and says, "Take me to your leader." The petrol pump, knowing its place, remains mute. "Right," said the Martian. "Take me to your leader." Still no reply. Finally, the Martian says, "Take me to your leader. And what's more, take your cock out of your ear when you're talking to me."'

'Can I have some audience participation?' an unwary apprentice stand-up asks this audience from hell. 'No,' shouts someone in the crowd. 'You're supposed to be doing fucking jokes,' yells another. Comics are the worst kind of punters. This apprentice stand-up doesn't stand a chance. 'We used to have a gong in the old days,' shouts someone else. 'You don't get out much, do you, mate?' responds this rookie comic, taking arms against a sea of troubles. 'Things have changed in twenty years.' But not that much. 'Gong,' shout several hecklers, at once, and this game wannabe gets off before he's gonged off. 'I've got magnificent breasts,' declares the next act. 'Get them out,' yells an unreconstructed punter. 'You've ruined my finale now, you cunt,' replies this young comedienne. 'Nice comedy,' says her heckler. 'Shame about the breasts.' While Rosengard has certainly recreated the chaos of the old Soho Store, with this kind of material, it's like Alternative Comedy never happened. 'How long have we got to put up with this?' asks a heckler. The gong provides the answer.

'Because the evening's getting so exciting, I'm going to hand over to a more experienced compere,' says Clive Anderson. 'A man who's making a rare appearance with his clothes on. Malcolm Hardee.' 'Knob out,' shout the crowd, but unusually, Hardee does not disrobe. 'You play at The Ivy twice in your career,' says Hardee. 'Once on the way up. Once on the way down. It's good to be back.' The gags that follow are some of the oldest known to man, but Hardee doesn't give a damn if he dies, and this indifference inspires confidence, as the house laughs at groaners it'd boo from either of the younger stand-ups who preceded him. 'Some advice to people who want to be comedians,' says Hardee, charitably. 'What you should never do is lose your temper with anyone onstage. I've done it once and that was in Glasgow. This bloke hated me. He said, "You fuck off, you sassenach bastard, or I'll fucking hit you."' 'That was me,' shouts a Scotsman in this crowd.

'This is one of the worst gigs I've ever done,' declares Hardee. 'I'll gong myself off.' But that magic word jogs his memory. 'That isn't the original gong,' he says. 'That's a fraud. The man who's got the original gong is standing right there. The original gong was nicked by a brilliant bloke called Keith Allen on the last night but fair play to that bloke there. He nicked it off Keith Allen. It's round his house.' 'That's true,' says Roger Pomphrey. 'It wasn't even a gong, was it?' Hardee asks him. 'No,' says Pomphrey. 'It was an oyster fucking tray.' 'It was an oyster tray,' repeats Hardee. 'There's a bit of history for you.' And with that, Hardee hands the mike back to Clive Anderson. 'He used to be a barrister,' says Hardee. 'Unfortunately, he did one of my cases.'

Anderson brings on the next act, yet this is no newcomer, but the oldest alternative comedian in the universe. 'Peter Rosengard has changed a lot of peoples' lives,' says Arnold Brown. 'Twenty years ago I was an accountant living comfortably in Hampstead. Today I'm living on the nineteenth floor of a crack estate in Harlesden.' But at least during the two decades in between, he's supported Frank Sinatra. 'We must give tribute to the one person who changed the face of British comedy,' adds Brown. 'But enough about Alexei.' Yet there's no doubt who he's really talking about. 'Peter, you have raised shyness to an art form. Your very initials are PR.' It's a backhanded compliment, but a compliment nonetheless. 'Despite public demand, Peter keeps on coming up with the ideas. What can one say about Peter that he hasn't said himself?' But Brown says a few things even Rosengard has never said before. 'He's a meshuggeneh. A madman with vision. Other people's vision. But I'd like to toast this man because, despite everything, The Comedy Store changed everything and we've got to give Peter credit for that.'

'What a bizarre evening,' says Clive Anderson, taking Brown's place on this makeshift stage. But it's about to get stranger still. Brian Fester bounds into the room, looking like an enormous insect. He plays a manic mouth organ solo, then shouts, 'Give us a G!' 'G!' yells the audience. 'Give us an O!' 'O!' we all yell. 'Give us an N!' 'N!' 'Give us a G!' 'G!' 'What have you got?' 'Gong!' And with that, Mr Fester scuttles away again. To anyone under forty, it's completely incomprehensible. Only Soho Store veterans know Fester is merely one of the many alter egos of weird performance artist Andrew Bailey, and that this weird performance is a precise replica of the Soho Store turn he did nearly twenty years ago.

'Why am I doing this job?' asks Clive Anderson. 'I just came along for a free drink. Well done, Andrew Bailey. Now we're going to go on with somebody I'm told is a star of the future if not the present, or possibly the past.' 'Has anyone got any coke?' asks the next apprentice act. 'Does anyone want to see my new tattoo?' He dies, but tonight, nobody who wasn't at the Soho Store has any chance of survival. 'I'm appalled,' says Nick Revell, who's on immediately afterwards. 'In the old days of The Comedy Store we were politically conscious. We were doing comedy about what was happening in the world. We were protesting. We were trying to build a better world. And in that spirit I'd like to do a small poem.' Suitably chastened, this audience shuts up and listens up. 'Hey, Mrs Thatcher, you bastard,' recites Revell. 'We don't want your cruise missiles. Turn the task force back before it gets to the Falklands. Thank you very much. That's redressed the balance a bit.' It takes a few seconds for the penny to drop, but when everyone realises he's taking the piss, the laughter is deafening.

At its best, Alternative Comedy always poked fun at the Left as much as the Right, and tonight is no exception. 'I think we've recaptured the initial excitement of the opening night of The Comedy Store,' says Clive Anderson. 'This has been Peter Rosengard's barmitzvah.' And with that, he bids us all good night. Maybe in another twenty years, they'll do it all over again.

Manchester

When the first Comedy Store opened in May 1979, the initial budget was a thousand pounds. Tonight, twenty-one years later, as Ward opens his new Comedy Store in Manchester, it's already cost him almost two million. The start-up price isn't the only thing that's changed. The Soho Store had room for barely a hundred punters, with a tiny broom cupboard for a dressing room. This Manchester Store has five hundred seats, spread over two tiers of an imposing auditorium purpose-built for stand-up, plus a smart and spacious bar which holds a further four hundred, and a plush green room. Instead of scruffy photos in the stairwell, this staircase is decorated with hand prints of famous comics and Malcolm Hardee's dick print. *Fast Show* and *Cold Feet* star John Thomson provided the first set, a few weeks before tonight's opening night, as the club that started out rebelling against established showbiz ends up mimicking a Hollywood tradition.

'It's taken me twenty years to find the right home for a new Comedy Store,' says Don Ward. 'As soon as I came to Manchester and saw this development I knew it was the right time to open a second venue.' And tonight, you can see why. This state-of-the-art site occupies two newly renovated ex-railway arches in Deansgate Locks, Manchester's own Docklands, underneath a Victorian viaduct, all red brick and wrought iron, beside a spruced-up stretch of the Rochdale Canal. Chic café bars such as Loaf and Revolution occupy the neighbouring arches, and all around, the old relics of Manchester's Victorian pomp are being rapidly restored, transformed into trendy new restaurants and apartments. Ironically, one of the few local sites yet to be rebuilt is the derelict Hacienda, once Britain's trendiest night club, but it must surely be just a

matter of time before that handsome pile rejoins this rejuvenated panorama. As it was in Soho, The Store is a barometer of this revival. Soho was a run-down dump twenty years ago, when The Store set up shop in The Gargoyle. Maybe Deansgate's revamped waterfront will be the same sort of success story, another twenty years down the line. Outside this new Store, TV crews and provincial paparazzi hover, and security staff protect the visiting VIPs from the proper punters who pay their way. Less than a decade ago, at the old Leicester Square Store, comics were still using the dressing-room sink as their toilet. Now, just seven years later, only that grinning logo looks the same. Even the *Telegraph* found the atmosphere worryingly civilised.

An hour before tonight's show, Stan Nelson was pacing around this plush arena like an angry bear trying to fight his way out of a circus big top, but he needn't have felt so stressed. It's far too late to fret, and now the show's up and running, there's nothing left to worry about. This swish premier is going like a dream, although if any of those unreconstructed Alternative Comics from the old Soho Store had been here, it may have felt more like their worst nightmare. Paul Merton was the last onstage at the Leicester Square Store and the first onstage at the Piccadilly Circus Store, so it's apt that he's the first onstage here. And to mark this momentous occasion, he recycled some of his oldest one-liners. 'Paul Merton relayed a gag about a policeman on hallucinogenic drugs written in 1982, which bombed,' reported the *Telegraph*. 'Evidently at a loss as to what to do with his allotted ten minutes on stage, Merton didn't really make much impact,' wrote the *Manchester Evening News*. But apart from the press, nobody seemed too bothered about the age of Merton's material, least of all Merton himself. 'I learned French the hard way, from a Spaniard,' he drawls. 'I borrowed that joke from the Imperial War Museum.' 'Without The Comedy Store I wouldn't have a comedy career,' said Merton, afterwards. 'It's where I started. Tonight is really one of nostalgia for me. It's about coming back to my roots.'[1]

'This is like the Sultan of Brunei's comedy club,' announces local hero, John Thomson. But despite such sumptuous surroundings, the mike stand is playing up. 'It's like a fucking trombone,' he grunts, wrenching the mike back up to its proper height, before launching into a fast-forward medley of classic mimicry. Some of Thomson's impressions are ancient, but they're done with such panache that no one cares, and when this homecoming superstar turns around to reveal a pair of plastic buttocks, with a fake turd dangling between the cheeks, the whole house falls about. Scarcely the sort of joke to precipitate the downfall of capitalism, and bring an end to tyranny and injustice wherever it rears its ugly head.

'I'm the token homosexual,' explains Julian Clary, kicking off the second half. 'How lovely it is to be in Manchester, and I must say you look terrific, considering you don't eat properly. Just bread and dripping and maybe a bit of scrag at Christmas.' The comedian formerly known as The Joan Collins Fan Club has a flair for making even the most innocuous remarks sound obscene. 'You're peeling off a layer,' he says, as a man removes his jacket. 'It's not that kind of evening.' And there's nobody better at working the room. 'Are you in showbusiness?' he asks a bloke in the front row. 'No? Well get your drink off the stage. What's your name? Tarquin? That's a bit of a cry for attention. Is your hair naturally curly? Nature can be cruel. Watch out for me in the Sydney Olympics,' he says. 'I'm entering the synchronised rimming event.'

I nip out to the bar, and bump into Hattie Hayridge on the way back. She's not on tonight, but in Manchester, like London, The Store is one of the few clubs comics go to even when they're not working. When I get back to my seat, Dave Johns is onstage. 'I've got no jokes,' says Johns. 'I've never written a joke in my life.' But he can crack one-liners with the best of them. 'I phoned the Tourettes Syndrome Society and offered to do them a benefit gig,' he says. 'They told me to fuck off.' Big laugh. 'Fuck the comedy,' says Johns, surveying his palatial surroundings. 'Let's smash the place up.' Luckily, no one takes him at his word. 'You're frightened of me, aren't you?' this normally genial Newcastle comic asks a heckler who's foolish enough to interrupt. 'This isn't the telly. I can come offstage and kick your face in.' It's a high-risk strategy, but this heckler doesn't call his bluff. 'You can tell I'm working class,' he says. 'I've got bits of scratch cards under my fingernails.' Johns can read a room, and he can sense this crowd are growing tired. 'You've got about forty-six more acts,' he says, 'and then The Crankies to finish.'

Afterwards, in the ruck beside the designer bar, amid air-kissing hacks and free-loaders, small-screen celebs like Amanda Holden and a host of *Coronation Street* regulars mingle with local hangers-on. Meanwhile the comics swig free drinks upstairs, in the secluded splendour of the green room. 'If you see me standing at the bar and you want to come over and have a chat,' quips Boothby Graffoe onstage, 'leave me the fuck alone. It's an act.' Punters and stand-ups have always been very different people. 'I never understood it myself,' says Julian Clary, failing to fathom The Store's singular yet elusive attraction. 'It would never be my idea of a night out.' From the faded grandeur of The Gargoyle kitchen, via the sleazy glamour of The Subway back bar, in the end, the commercial imperatives of big business always beat the individuality out of even the most eccentric venture. The Manchester Store will be a good comedy club. It may even become a great club. But in another twenty years, will anybody want to write a book about it?

From Allen to Baddiel and Back Again

The last two people I interviewed for this book were Tony Allen and David Baddiel. I didn't plan it that way; in fact they were among the first people I contacted, yet it felt rather fitting when they ended up talking last of all. In a way, these contrasting comics are the first and last word in the story of The Store, the alpha and omega if you like. Allen, maybe more than anyone, was the epitome of what Alternative Comedy once was; Baddiel, maybe more than anyone, is the epitome of what it has become.

'Lenny Bruce finished his career out of his head on drugs, hassled by the police and dying on a toilet,' quips Tony Allen. 'That's how I started off.' 'The people who were around at the beginning of the circuit are all doing adverts now and living in Berkshire, which is sad,'[1] said Jo Brand. Well, Allen was around at the very beginning, before there even was a circuit, and he still lives in Ladbroke Grove. 'You can always recognise the drugs squad where I live, on Portobello Road,' he quipped. 'They're the only people in plain clothes.' And if he has done any adverts, I've certainly never seen them. But he does seem sad, about what club comedy could have been, and what it has become. Allen never sold out, but today he's a lone voice in the wilderness. 'I was just appalled by what was going on on Granada's *The Comedians*,' he says. 'When I actually took the time out in 'seventy-eight and early 'seventy-nine to go round and see traditional comedians working, I realised that what was on the television was a really watered-down version of what they were doing onstage, and what they were doing onstage was horrendous.' These comics had two different sets. One for the clubs and, hopefully, *The Comedians*, and another for the stag nights and the strippers. One routine still lingers in his mind's eye. 'A lot of comedians would put a black stocking on their head with holes for the eyes and mouth and they'd do a sort of West Indian stereotype,' he recalls. 'The horny black bloke who was over here, thieving and after white women.' Sometimes, there'd be black blokes in the audience, who'd grin and bear it, the purgatory of ethnic minorities the world over. But when Allen heckled, and walked out, other people would do the same, and he realised he wasn't the only one who was appalled.

There was another nascent circuit, comprising former folk singers like Glasgow's Billy Connolly, Birmingham's Jasper Carrott and Manchester's Mike Harding, whose comic introductions to their songs had eventually overwhelmed their music. These accidental comedians weren't remotely racist or sexist, but they weren't political either, and so they didn't have much influence on Allen. 'They were pretty important, but they weren't going far enough,' he says. 'They certainly didn't have a political agenda, and I was part of a very political sub-culture.' He was more interested in American comics like Lenny Bruce and Richard Pryor.

Allen lived in a commune, and performed in political theatre groups, and his fellow communards would come to plays and scrutinise his performance. One such play was a pub show Allen wrote in late '78. The central character was a stand-up comic, played by Jim Barclay. The play wasn't a big hit, but they both became fascinated by the stand-up genre. 'There was a whole ethos amongst the theatre groups of trying different art forms, the whole obsession with Brecht and what Brechtian theatre was, and using popular forms to try and express political ideas.' Allen was a man on a mission, to rid stand-up of its racism and sexism, and there wasn't any point in preaching to the converted. So Allen ventured into the trad clubs to try doing some stand-up for himself.

'They all did the same stuff,' he recalls. 'They all had the "coming home from the pub pissed with the wife in bed" sort of routine.' Allen did something completely different. 'I was talking about my squatting sub-culture and the political sub-culture,' he says. 'The stuff that I was doing which sent up my culture actually went down well.'

Allen's training ground was the stand-up free-for-all at Speaker's Corner. 'I learned a lot about how to deal with audiences and rather than just put them down, recognise what they were saying, where that came from and who they were by what they'd said and then start talking about them and what was informing their question, and start an argument with them.' He also introduced bands at benefit gigs on the squat circuit, where he saw how ranting poets handled the hubbub in a rabble-rousing, staccato style.

It was his playwriting partner, Ken Robinson, who told him about The Store. They'd written for The Royal Court Theatre and Theatre Royal Stratford East, and then Robinson showed him an advert in the *Evening Standard*, so Allen went along to The

Gargoyle, and auditioned for Peter Rosengard and Ashley Roy. 'You don't need me to do anymore of this,' Allen told them, after several minutes. 'You can see I can do it.' Allen became a regular. 'I was fascinated by it because it was the belly of the beast,' says Allen. 'It was the antithesis of everything I believed in.' But comedians are agitators. They work best when they go against the grain. 'Soho's done for love making what Russia's done for socialism,' he'd tell audiences at The Store.

Last time he played The Store was in Piccadilly Circus seven years ago. He died a death. 'It's a tourist audience,' he says. 'It's an audience that's in London for the night to see a football match or a show or a rock gig and then they go to The Comedy Store for a late-night drink because they've never been there before.' But it wasn't all for nothing. 'We stopped what was quite clearly incitement to racial hatred,' he says. 'The most scary thing you can imagine. Having your house fire bombed with your kids in bed, which is what racism at the roots is all about.' It was Alternative Comedy which drove racist gags out of the mainstream, and Allen's gags defined Alternative Comedy.

'The entertainer gives the audience what it wants,' says Allen. 'The artist gives the audience what it didn't know it wanted.' For a while, he did both. 'If you didn't go in hard and you weren't on a mission it may not have happened,' he says. 'The people I was with would come into the dressing room and start taking comedians apart.' 'What are you doing that fucking shit for?' they'd ask the other acts. 'Fucking tell them!' Allen would say. 'You keep out of it!' they'd reply. 'I was a real puritan,' he says. 'I must have snubbed a lot of people and behaved very badly to a lot of people that were actually doing quite interesting stuff and finding their way.' Allen would argue with other acts, especially if he thought their act was racist or sexist in any way. 'I must have made a lot of enemies,' he says. 'But fuck it. The way I look at it, politically it had to be done. I was on one. I still am.'

David Baddiel saw Tony Allen on his first visit to The Store, but his own background could scarcely be more different. A double first from Cambridge and a blue-chip Light Ent apprenticeship in the Footlights, then starring roles in two of TV's most successful comedy shows, *The Mary Whitehouse Experience* and *Fantasy Football League*. With Robert Newman, he played the first comedy gig at Wembley Arena, and with Frank Skinner and The Lightning Seeds, he had a platinum number one with 'Three Lions', English football's unofficial national anthem.

Baddiel first went to the Leicester Square Store when he was still a student. He was surprised how close the acts were to the audience. He thought The Store would be more like a theatre. The evening made a big impact on him, and when he went back to Cambridge, he did his best to drag Footlights into the Eighties, by insisting they didn't just do character monologues and sketches, but stand-up too. 'I have no ability really to do what a lot of people there had done, which was kind of character monologues,' he says. 'My abilities were purely and simply being able to get up onstage and talk about myself. And I didn't particularly know how to do that then, although funnily enough, the other person who really influenced me at the time, who then became

one of the regulars at The Store, but who preceded me at Footlights, was Nick Hancock.' Like Baddiel, Hancock did straight stand-up in Footlights, which was still a rarity at that time.

John Hegley became a particular inspiration, especially his hard-edged, aggressive delivery, without the wink and smile that characterised the mainstream comics of the day. 'I can do that,' thought Baddiel.

In 1986, he phoned The Store for an open spot. 'What have you done?' asked Kim Kinnie. 'Cambridge Footlights,' replied Baddiel. 'He practically put the phone down,' says Baddiel. It was only five years since the famous Footlights team featuring Stephen Fry, Hugh Laurie, Tony Slattery and Emma Thompson had won the first Perrier Award, but since 1981, Alternative Comedy, and The Comedy Store, had altered the comic agenda. 'It changed really radically, from being like a golden key to being an absolute millstone.' It didn't matter that Clive Anderson and Nick Hancock had both been in Footlights. The Store was keeping up its proletarian appearances, and by the time his debut came around, he'd learned to keep quiet about his guilty secret.

'It was three o'clock in the morning and there were six open spots, and I was the third on, and there was a fight in the audience,' he says. 'Steve Frost had made a joke about canaries being gassed, which is what used to happen in the mines, and someone shouted something about yids and Steve Frost got really upset.' A big fight broke out, and by the time it had been broken up, the crowd had peaked, the energy had evaporated, and instead of drunken heckles, Baddiel encountered total silence. 'It was like playing to dead people,' he says. 'Nothing. No response at all. I thought, "Am I alone in here?"' He might as well have been. He didn't return for a year.

He went back as one half of a double act, Black & Baddiel, and just about broke even, eventually making the breakthrough in 1988. By then, Kim Kinnie had seen him elsewhere and gave him a half-spot at the end of the first half, which was a lot easier. He got a booking, and remained a regular here until he stopped playing the circuit in 1991. 'It really was one of my favourite gigs,' he says. 'It was also the only place that I really died at after I was well established.' He'd done a gig in Ipswich the night before with Patrick Marber. They'd stayed in a bed and breakfast, and Baddiel, an insomniac, couldn't sleep. 'I was completely knackered,' he explains. 'There was some heckling, which I normally would have been able to deal with, but I just wasn't up for it.' Next thing he knew, he'd lost control. 'I'd seen it happen to other people, but I wasn't used to it myself.' It was quite a shock. 'The walls are closing in,' shouted a heckler. 'That's true,' thought Baddiel. 'That's definitely true. The voice of god.' And so he left. The next act on was Jack Dee, and he stormed it, as comics tend to do when the act before them has died. 'Where are you going?' Jim Tavare asked Baddiel, as he headed back up the stairs, to the sound of raucous laughter. 'I think you're really great. You'll be back tomorrow.' He had to be, and he had a stormer. That was the last time he ever died.

Baddiel didn't just fit in at The Store. He also helped to change it. 'I don't want to do stuff about politics,' he decided. 'I don't really want to do stuff about topical satire. I just want to do stuff about me.' Sex, football and pop music were the sort of things Baddiel could be funny about, but there was a bit more to it than that. 'I just didn't want to be seen as what I felt was a passing thing, which was the very anti-Thatcherite Alternative Comedy thing.' Baddiel was right about the way this new wind was blowing. The comics he gigged with at The Store who became big stars were all pretty apolitical: Jack Dee, Sean Hughes, Eddie Izzard, and his future comic partner and flatmate, Frank Skinner.

The first time Baddiel ever saw Skinner was at The Store, onstage, when he was still gigging under his real name, Chris Collins. 'I know you from medical school,' yelled a punter. It was a nonsensical heckle. Skinner had never been to medical school, but he wasn't phased. 'Oh yeah,' said Skinner. 'You were the one in the jar.' Baddiel realised almost any spontaneous riposte is better than a pre-prepared put-down. 'It's better from behind,' yelled a heckler, apropos of nothing. 'Rather like your face,' replied Baddiel. It wasn't the world's wittiest response, but it was spontaneous, and it got a big laugh. Baddiel was on his way.

Not all the fun came from watching rising stars. Baddiel also saw some spectacular disasters. 'As soon as he stepped onstage you thought, "Who on earth has told you to do this?"' says Baddiel, recalling one especially unsuccessful open spot, who stood behind the mike like someone who was waiting to be punched. 'Within about a second of him going onstage the audience started heckling, and then after a minute this bloke in the back said the best heckle I've ever heard, which is, "Everybody hates you, everybody hates you, you must know from school."'

Baddiel was bound for far bigger, if not funnier things, but he was still thrilled when Kim Kinnie asked him to compere The Store. 'It was one of my proudest moments,' he says. He'd always worried about being a bit of an outsider on this mockney circuit. Cambridge. Jewish. Middle Class. 'Am I really one of the lads?' he wondered. Compering The Store was as close as it came to knowing he really belonged. And it was an especially magnanimous gesture, since Baddiel and Kinnie didn't always see eye to eye. 'If Bernard Manning came down here now, he'd storm it,' said Kim, after Baddiel had done a great set. 'None of my stuff was ever at all sexist, racist or whatever,' says Baddiel. 'It just wasn't particularly left wing.' They patched up their differences in the gents.

Now he's happier doing solo shows, but sharing a bill at The Store did teach him to be Funny with a capital F. Some comedians said they weren't interested in making an audience laugh, so much as making them think. 'You really couldn't get away with that bullshit at The Comedy Store,' he says. 'You have to get laughs, otherwise you're dead, and that suited me, because I wasn't about making the audience think. I was about making the audience laugh. What I was interested in was making them laugh in new ways, at new things that maybe were on the edge of their consciousness, that they hadn't thought about or hadn't heard anyone else talk about before, but that's it. I'm not interested in putting forward a kind of moral argument. That doesn't seem to me to be the comedian's job, and it seems to me The Comedy Store is the best arena for that.'

He's proud his photo is on the wall, but if he feels any nostalgia, it's not for being onstage, but backstage. If there's anything he misses about the circuit, it's sitting in that seedy dressing room. 'There was nowhere else that you felt "we're all in the same boat",' he says. 'We were all together and the night was resting on all our shoulders.' And what a set of shoulders. 'I'd be on a bill with Jack Dee and Jo Brand and Eddie Izzard and Frank, and they're all famous now and that's extraordinary.' And while The Comic Strip became famous as a team, Baddiel's colleagues became famous doing very different things. 'They kind of fed off each other, whereas the generation I was in was mainly people who were to become famous doing their own thing.' Doing your own thing is more creative, but it's bound to be more solitary. To be a rising star is a shared experience. To be a star is to be utterly alone.

He's been back to other comedy clubs, but never back to The Store. 'The audience go mental because they hate to see people they've never heard of, so they think they've got a bargain,' he explains. 'You can't recapture that experience of winning them over, which, once you've done it, is very fulfilling, but I can also live without it. Every night, thinking, "I've got to win them over, every night I have to win them over, and at some point I'm not going to win them over."' Yet although he doesn't have to do that anymore, that anonymity was important. 'The contract with the audience is the same for everyone.'

He's not so sure he could do it now. 'I just thought, "Right, I'll go and do The Comedy Store and I'll end up doing it regularly, and then I'll become a compere." I was pleased and surprised when it happened. At the same time, part of me thought, "This is what my destiny is," and now I can't imagine it. In the same way as when I was eighteen I hitch-hiked round Europe, and now I think, "What the fuck was I doing hitch-hiking round Europe? I could have got killed."'

The End

'Comedy naturally wears itself out, destroys the very food on which it lives, and by constantly and successfully exposing the follies and weaknesses of mankind to ridicule, in the end leaves itself nothing worth laughing at.'

William Hazlitt, **On Modern Comedy**, 1817

'Anyone can be famous for fifteen minutes,' boasts that big neon billboard above the corner of Coventry Street and Haymarket. 'The Comedy Store. Celebrating Twenty Years Of Laughter.' For sure, The Store is famous now. Has been for a while. But what exactly is it famous for? Revolution? Hardly. Anarchy? Not really. Experiment? Not any more. Fame and influence often move in opposite directions. Once upon a time, The Store was a badly kept secret. No rave reviews, merely word of mouth. Now it's closer to being the brand leader of a booming business sector. Inside, amid a display of tourist souvenirs – sweatshirts, baseball caps, badges, posters – an autographed Manchester United football sits in pride of place behind locked plate glass. 'This is the Man United of comedy,' says comedienne Jo Jo Smith, and that football is a perfect symbol for the way The Store has changed. It's the icon that best sums up The Store's steady shift from underground attraction to blue-chip high-street brand.

During two decades, The London Store has only travelled a few hundred yards, from Soho via Leicester Square to Piccadilly Circus, but really it's come a very long way indeed. Its first and final premises are worlds, even centuries apart. Its old neighbours were clip joints and blue bookshops. Like a fish and chip shop on a high street full of fast food burger bars, Ward's Gargoyle Club sold fairly honest, if not entirely wholesome fayre. Strip, plus some stand-up after hours.

Today The Store rubs shoulderpads with TGI Fridays, The Fashion Café, His Master's Voice, Sega World, even Planet Hollywood. Today, *Live Bed Show* is the title of a West End play by Arthur Smith. And who's complaining? Not the acts. Not the audience. Not the management. Not me. Well, not much. It's neither trend-setting nor romantic, yet you needn't run a gauntlet of working girls, or squeeze into a tiny lift. The early show ends before last orders, so you don't have to traipse around town hunting for a night bus or a minicab. There are always at least four reliable comedians on the bill, plus a seasoned compere. At worst, the comics are competent. At best, they're first rate. You've usually seen most of them on telly. Some even have their own series. Sometimes, there are real stars on show. A-list celebs, people your parents, even your grandparents, have heard of, who pack out nationwide tours of proper theatres.

There are far fewer surprises now, but many more laughs per minute. 'Most of the acts that were allowed to make a living then wouldn't get three minutes now,' says Jenny Eclair. 'It's miles more professional,' says Arthur Smith. 'In the early days, Keith Allen would come on with no clothes on, and there'd be fights. Now you're going to get four or five really good acts, you know they're good acts, and they're going to get a laugh every ten seconds.'

And so we're willing to pay West End prices to sit and watch. 'Everyone gets a much more sensible wage now,' says Bob Mills. 'I'm sure punters find it much more enjoyable. The Store audience today will never see the likes of Tony Allen again, having his occasional ten minutes of brilliance. They'll never see Bob Boyton again, doing twenty minutes of absolute shit, but three minutes of genius at the end, because nobody's going to book that now. But then again, an audience now will never have to sit through some of the shit they sat through at The Store.' Yet most of the time, those punters didn't mind. Like some demented stand-up Tardis, even on a bad night, a night out at The Store seemed greater than the sum of its parts. Now that equation is reversed, and if today's best Store bills seem to punch a bit below their weight, it's because today's Store punters prefer a more consistent quality of stand-up to more hit-and-miss home-baked humour. 'They don't want anything slightly off the wall that you have to think about too much,' says Jo Brand. 'A few jokes about ginger people and a few jokes about fat people, something about what's on telly, something about Vanessa Feltz, and good night.' And you can't blame the up-and-coming comics for playing safe. The Store used to be the only place to play. Now it's somewhere to aspire to.

As the alternative invades the mainstream, so The Store becomes more conventional. Store comics now do corporate functions, even entertain the troops, previously the preserve of trad turns. Tim Clark has entertained companies like British Telecom, Volkswagen, Saatchi & Saatchi, Dixons, Pepsi, Guinness and Whirlpool. 'I had to burst in, in the middle of a conference, with a washing machine on a trolley, pretending to be a dissatisfied customer.' He's written speeches for Gordon Brown and Graham

Taylor. He played The Grim Reaper in an ad for Virgin Atlantic. He spent a month amusing British holidaymakers in Spanish hotels, and played the Middle East, as a last-minute stand-in for Chas & Dave.

'The commercial end of the market catches on real fast,' says Simon McBurney. 'People honed their comedy to go onto TV, then the comedy became less interesting. Every time something becomes established, something dies.'

The comedy boom seems inevitable now, a natural fusion of high- and lowbrow, middle and working class, Culture and Light Ent, performance art and fast food. Yet like every success story, there was a time when nobody would bet on it. Well, nobody apart from Rosengard and Ward. 'I watched the Fringe circuit die and I thought The Store and the rest of the comedy clubs would go the same way,' says Steve Steen. Yet as the circuit grows, the old sense of a small community withers, and veterans like Arnold Brown don't come here anymore. 'The Store for me had lost its excitement,' he explains. 'The whole point about comedy is unexpectedness.' Brown blames commercial pressure, particularly from TV. 'A TV producer is in, and you want to give them five minutes of your best material,' he says. 'If you don't, you don't land that series.'

'People can calculate, "If I can do a really good twenty-five minutes tonight, and I do it six nights in a row, in that time, statistically, I'm bound to be seen by a thrusting young Channel 4 producer or somebody who's just back from the Edinburgh Fringe," and then it becomes just a step in a career,' explains Clive Anderson. 'The trouble is it's all turned into a clearing house for going into telly.' Comics like Anderson miss the Soho Store's shambolic ambience, but maybe what they miss most of all is their reckless youth. 'We were all in the same boat together when The Store started,' says Anderson. 'They certainly weren't there to see me. They weren't really there to see anybody. They were just there to see what happened, and that is a good atmosphere and probably a very creative atmosphere in its way, but you can't preserve that in aspic.'

'It is a poignant experience to recall those early beginnings of comedy anarchy at The Store where there was many an unpredictable evening of dangerous, electrifying brilliance where no subject was taboo and fights would break out among audiences disagreeing about what was being said onstage,' recalled Arnold Brown. 'We simply made up the rules as we went along.'[1] 'There was a bit more colour, a bit more light and shade,' agrees Alan Davies. 'It wasn't a career move,' says Julian Clary. 'It was a self-contained little world. It wasn't a stepping stone to anything and so inevitably once it becomes that, you get all sorts of Oxbridge people saying, "I'll just do the circuit for six months and then I'll be ready for my series."' And even Don Ward misses those giddy days when few comics ever expected to make much money, and some of them didn't even want paying. 'Now everybody knows the quality required to become a star,' he says. 'In those days, it really was for the love and fun of it.'

'Paul Merton would go on under an assumed name,' recalls Hattie Hayridge. 'He'd do his act really badly, deliberately, just to get heckled off. He'd get punchlines wrong and all the comics would be killing themselves laughing, and the audience would be going "fuck off!" He'd do heckle put downs very badly. People would tell him "you shouldn't do that. They're going to think you're really shit." He'd say "I don't care. They won't know its me." Now no one would get up at The Store under an assumed name and deliberately do it shit just for the fun of it. Everyone's much more self-conscious about their career.'

'There's an old school who say, "It's gone too commercial now, it's the McDonalds of comedy,"' says Sean Meo, who's somewhere in between. 'There's always the opportunity to do the lowest common denominator.' Yet Meo doesn't see it that way. 'Don's as fair as anyone, really. He has a responsibility, when they're paying that kind of money, to give them a good show, and people just care less. That revolutionary attitude that comics had then has gone.' Style follows content, and a lot of older acts lose out both ways. 'It's inevitably got tighter and quicker and pacier, and the fact that they've fallen by the wayside and don't get booked seems to be a cue for them to moan about it now,' adds Meo. 'It's a very honest profession, and you're either funny or you're not. A good comic can adapt.'

'They ain't good enough,' says John Connor, of those old hands who say The Store isn't anarchic anymore. 'They haven't been good enough for years. Weren't good enough when they were going. If they were any good, they'd be doing The Store. An audience should be entertained. That's what you're doing. It's comedy. I do a show where you entertain. You have to entertain the audience first, but then you can take them down other routes. But it's comedy first and it's being funny first. Then you can be risky, but its aim is to entertain the audience. There's no point in doing something unless an audience wants to go and see it. This is not subsidised theatre.' And skills that take so long to nurture can quickly disappear. 'It's like jogging, you can't just go out when you haven't run for six months and try and run six miles,' says Tim Clark. 'Don's always saying he occasionally gets people from the old days coming back who were big time in the old days and haven't done it for years and can't do it now.'

Recently, for the first time in a long time, Jim Barclay went back to The Store to do a ten-minute try out, to see if he still had what it takes. He hadn't done stand-up for ages, and felt terribly nervous all over again. 'I was good then,' he thought, in an attempt to calm his nerves. 'Why shouldn't I be good now?' But while he'd been away, his old club had altered beyond all recognition. 'I was rubbish,' he admits. 'What I had to say wasn't what they wanted to hear. All the acts that go on there now are very good at picking up whatever's going on in the front row and building a relationship with the audience.' Working a room was never Barclay's style, and it never will be. 'I don't want to be arsed to remark on that person's funny hat or where they're from,' he says. 'I haven't got time. I've got my own agenda. I've always had my own agenda.' But although his old radical consensus has long since been swept away, he still believes the Light Ent revolt he helped to instigate was worthwhile. 'The Bernard Mannings, the

Jim Davidsons are now seen as jokes in themselves, and for that single achievement it was worth all the effort,' he says. 'I don't take much of the credit for that, but I was glad I was part of that movement that actually did undermine all that. What I'm sad about is that it was never carried through from there. We cleared away one agenda and never replaced it with anything.' His business nouse gave the club an accidental sort of purity, an artistic and political neutrality that subsidised spaces always lack. That's why it could accommodate acts as diverse as Tony Allen and Terry Alderton.

'Don had a lot of bottle to try what he did, when he did,' explains Paul Zenon. 'Doing something that was largely experimental took some bottle. He set it up as a business. He didn't set it up with an agenda of changing the world.'

But Don Ward isn't only a good businessman. *The Stage* also called him 'arguably the finest scout of new comic talent in Britain', and one of Ward's finest scouting skills is that he lets new comics come to him. If The Store hadn't moved with the times, this book would be an obituary for a club that went bust years ago, and those acts would have one less place to go. To keep the paying punters coming through the door, you need lots of laughs, and laughter, unlike applause, is a gut reaction. Like a belch or a fart, it's involuntary and amoral. Laughter, not creativity, is the ultimate commercial imperative. And so there are far fewer eccentrics nowadays. 'I saw the Iceman at Tooting Lido, not that long ago,' says Arthur Smith. 'He looked a bit sort of down and out.' We shall not see his like again. Well, not down here, at any rate.

An even bigger casualty has been the subversive humour that made The Store so famous in the first place. 'It's exhausting trying to perform stuff which, for want of a better phrase, precipitates the downfall of capitalism,' explains Jim Barclay. 'Audiences don't want it. They feel threatened by it, and the performers don't know why they should bother.' 'Do you think comedy can change things?' Kim Kinnie once asked Paul Merton. 'No,' replied Merton. 'Otherwise Laurel and Hardy would have ruled the world.' Today's wannabes see that most radical comics tend not to end up on telly, and adapt accordingly to survive. 'There are far fewer comics who choose the topical political route,' says Kevin Day. 'There are various routes to fame and fortune, and radicalism isn't one of them. The more Irish storytellers who win the Perrier Award, the more Irish storytellers you'll see at The Store.' But it's ultimately audiences who decide who works and who doesn't, and today's punters seem less interested in politics too. 'The British public are much more interested in laughing about sex and drugs than they are about some insight into New Labour,' explains up and coming comic Andy Parsons. 'If there was an audience for anarchic comedy, people would seek it out, and there'd be other places that put it on,' agrees Simon Clayton. 'It's gone more mainstream because society's gone more mainstream, and there's less to rebel about, so that's reflected in our entertainment.'

Nowadays, most comedians don't take risks. 'Now you have to stick rigidly to your script because you can't afford to try things out,' says Jim Tavare. But did they ever? 'It's possible for a comic to look anarchic, but in fact to have rehearsed every second, and only a raving maniac would go onstage in front of a paying audience if they didn't feel what they were doing was funny,' says Steve Punt. 'I don't think the circuit was radical or anarchic at all,' says Mickey Hutton. 'It never was. You had the odd comic who'd try and be as anarchic and radical as possible, but they didn't get laughs. You can't just play to people who are like you. My mum and dad come down here and they love it.' 'People say it's not like the old days,' says Jeff Green, 'but I know about the old days as much as they do, and I think it's better value for money.'

'I don't know if this golden age of radical comedy ever existed,' says Bob Boyton. 'I never saw it. When I started out there was very little politics. I hadn't seen very much Alternative Comedy, and it might have been I wouldn't have gone into it if I had. The Store was never the Leicester Square branch of the SWP. It was clearly a money-making business, and Don's a very good businessman. And while I might have a macro political analysis of what's wrong with that, and what's wrong with exploitative labour, at least there was an honesty to it.'

But above all it's the punters who've changed. In the Eighties, stand-up was a recessionary art form, a cheerful protest and a cheap night out. In the Nineties, it became an aspirational leisure activity. 'They broke down a huge amount of barriers,' says Alistair McGowan, 'but there was more to complain about then.' Most crowds and most comics simply aren't so broke or angry anymore. 'At the end of the day, all it is, is laughs,' says Donna McPhail. 'You can't moan about the lack of creative freedom when you're getting huge handfuls of dosh.'

Today, a smart casual crowd files down a narrow staircase, into an air-conditioned cellar, past the fast-fading monochrome mugshots of comics, many of whom are becoming more anonymous with each passing year. Most of these punters know little about the old days and care a whole lot less. They take The Store entirely for granted, as if it had always been there. And that, more than anything, is a surefire sign that it really has arrived. Yet when these comics start sparking and this show starts buzzing, and that explosive stand-up chemistry bubbles up, and begins to fizz, you could be back in The Gargoyle Club, watching Keith Allen, Clive Anderson or Alexei Sayle. 'There is still a relationship,' says Kim Kinnie, of the unique atmosphere you find down here and in no other comedy club on earth. 'I don't think it has lost sight of what it was at all.'

However much The Store alters, the main event never varies. 'I still think, in the right hands, stand-up comedy is one of the best art forms there is,' says Kevin Day. 'It still retains its capacity to surprise and it still retains its immediacy.' 'Little tingles go down the back of your spine,' agrees Don Ward, describing the thrill of seeing a worldwide star like Lee Evans storm the club he built up over two decades, from a five hundred pound hobby into a multi-million pound business. 'After twenty years, it's still exciting.'

Tonight, deep underground, behind a black fire door with a red sign on it that says Keep Out, as if anyone without a comic death wish would ever dare to venture inside, let alone onto the spotlit stage beyond, a handful of stand-ups huddle in a cramped and spartan dressing room, waiting for their final call. Meanwhile, out front, a disembodied voice booms over the house tannoy around the fast filling auditorium, as Stan Nelson calls time from his tiny stageside booth, just like he's called it a few thousand times before. 'Five minutes to the show, ladies and gentlemen,' drawls Stan, as the lights go down and the music goes up, not quite drowning the excited hubbub of tipsy expectation, as four hundred punters take their seats in stand-up subterranea. 'Five minutes to tonight's show.'

Acknowledgements

You can skip this bit, unless you think you deserve a name check, and can be bothered to look for it in the list below. For the benefit of anyone who still wants to read on, everyone in this book deserves my thanks. My agent, Julian Alexander, at Lucas Alexander Whitley, who patiently helped me make a start and gently persuaded a publisher to pay me for my efforts. My editor, Antonia Hodgson at Little, Brown, who made sense of my research and gave this material a shape and structure, without ever acting like my boss. Basil Comely, series editor of *Omnibus* at the BBC, without whose support I wouldn't have dared take any time out to write this in the first place. Ben Olins, and latterly Tim Lusher, editors of the *Guardian Guide*, without whom my advance would have run out even sooner. Lufthansa German Airlines (0845 7737 747; www.lufthansa.co.uk) for helping me get to Hamburg. And many thanks to the staff of The Store, who kindly let me hang around while they were trying to run this comedy club. In particular, thanks to Wendy Frediani and to Barbara Herbin, the Store's archivist, who provided invaluable help during my research. There's no way I could have spent so much time in the club without feeling some affinity with the folk who work there, especially those unsung backstage heroes, from bar staff to bouncers, whose unrequited love of the place is echoed in every thankless task they perform. These folk know far more about The Store than any past, present or future star, and their selfless contribution to this book was immense. Yet true to form, they'd mostly rather remain anonymous, answering my quibbles and keeping their patience, while dealing with all the daily tasks that keep this club up and running, from celebs to sewers, and all points inbetween.

I've listed the books I've used elsewhere, but several broadcast recordings proved equally useful, especially the BBC's *History Of Alternative Comedy*, their *Nationwide* report of the opening night, and their radio documentary about The Comedy Store Players, plus LWT's *South Bank Show* about Paul Merton on ITV. And thanks to Open Mike for letting me get in the way while they recorded their Comedy Store show for Channel 5, and for making a series that actually conveys some of the thrill of live comedy. On TV, that's no mean feat.

But most of all, thanks to all the interviewees who gave up their time to answer my questions. This is their book. Without them, there'd be nothing in it. If you found any of this remotely funny, or even vaguely interesting, it's down to them, not me. Stars who had nothing to gain, and a little to lose, from this enterprise. Acts who agreed to talk, despite things I wrote in the past that had displeased them. And comics who hadn't a clue who I was, or what I was up to, but talked to me anyway. It's a long list, but it could have been longer. If you've ever played The Store and I missed you out, and you're peeved rather than relieved, I'll see you in the second edition, if there ever is one. And whether you wanted to talk about it or not, thanks for finding the courage to stand up and play this place. I've had lots of fun watching, I really have, and I'm only one of many faceless punters grateful to share the reflected fun of someone else's sense of humour. John Lahr called the critic's work a life without risk, and he's right. The names on this list belong to the folk who took the risks. After all, if nobody had answered those small ads, all those years ago, The Store would still be a strip club, and we would all be watching *The Comedians* on TV. So my thanks to all the following, for saving us from a trad diet of trite one-liners. Never in the field of Light Entertainment was so much owed by so many to so few.

Terry Alderton; Tony Allen; Stephen K. Amos; Clive Anderson; Mark Arden; Bennett Arron; David Baddiel; Andrew Bailey; Bill Bailey; Robin Banks; Eddie Bannon; Jim Barclay; Arj Barker; Chris Barrie; Mark Billingham; Richard Blackwood; Simon Bligh; Adam Bloom; Bob Boyton; Jo Brand; Eddie Brill; Arnold Brown; Tony Burgess; Ed Byrne; Glazz Campbell; Rhona Cameron; Otiz Canneloni; Scott Capurro; Tim Clark; Julian Clary; Simon Clayton; Dave Cohen; John Connor; Phil Cool; Nick Coppin; Lee Cornes; Martin Coyote; Helen Da Silva; Phil Davey; Alan Davies; Ali Day; Kevin Day; Jack Dee; Hugh Dennis; Felix Dexter; Keith Dover; Debi Durst; Will Durst; Jenny Eclair; Simon Evans; Maria Falzone; Charles Fleischer; Charlotte Foley; John Fothergill; Stewart Francis; Wendy Frediani; Steve Frost; Dave Fulton; Emmy Gay; Kevin Gildea; Ronnie Golden; John Gordillo; Billy Green; Jeff Green; Steve Gribbin; Ricky Grover; Mike Gunn; Rich Hall; Nick Hancock; Malcolm Hardee; Ainsley Harriott; Kevin Hayes; Hattie Hayridge; John Hegley; Vic Henley; Philip Herbert; Barbara Herbin; Thomas Hermanns; Rainer Hersch; Dominic Holland; Pierre Hollins; Reginald D. Hunter; Lee Hurst; Mickey Hutton; Jeff Innocent; Eddie Izzard; Paul Jackson; Jane Janovic; Jocelyn Jee; Dave Johns; Milton Jones; Phill Jupitus; Peter Kay; Kim Kinnie; Daniel Kitson; Mandy Knight; Mark Lamarr; Burt Laurent; Jenny Lecoat;

Helen Lederer; John Lenahan; Rudi Lickwood; Sean Lock; Norman Lovett; Bruno Lucia; Chris Lynam; Lee Mack; Mark Maier; John Mann; Patrick Marber; Simon McBurney; Kevin McCarthy; Alistair McGowan; John McGrath; Oscar McLennan; Donna McPhail; Mike McShane; Sean Meo; Bob Mills; Jeff Mirza; John Moloney; Richard Morton; Neil Mullarkey; Henry Naylor; Stan Nelson; Owen O'Neill; Andy Parsons; Russell Peters; Roger Pomphrey; Martin Potter; Marcus Powell; Greg Proops; Steve Punt; Nick Revell; Andy Robinson; Peter Rosengard; Ashley Roy; Alexei Sayle; John Simmit; Marcus Simmons; Junior Simpson; Lee Simpson; Mark Skeete; Slim; Andy Smart; Michael Smiley; Arthur Smith; Jo Jo Smith; Martin Soan; Vivienne Soan; Jay Sodagar; Dave Spikey; Anvil Springstien; Steve Steen; Ian Stone; Jim Tavare; Paul Thorne; Tom Tickell; Toju; Paul Tonkinson; Richard Vranch; Curtis Walker; Don Ward; Nick Wilty; Gina Yashere; Paul Zenon.

Bibliography

Key among those books listed below are Michael Luke's elegant and literate *David Tennant And The Gargoyle Years*, which opens up the hidden history of The Store's first home; and the fascinating survey of The Store's salad days in Peter Wilmut's thorough, informative *Didn't You Kill My Mother-In-Law?* Both of these books have been invaluable. Mark Lewisohn's *Radio Times Guide To TV Comedy* is the bible of humour on the box. John Lahr's *Dame Edna Everage And The Rise Of Western Civilisation* proved it's possible to write a readable book about comedy onstage and backstage, as it happens. Some of the other books I've referred to don't have very much to do with comedy, but they still provide a useful backdrop to the wider world during the last twenty-two years. As for those that do, the best bits of the best ones are where the author lets comics speak for themselves, and for the most part, that's what I've tried my best to do here.

Chuck Anderson (Ed.), *Passport To Soho*, Random Thoughts, London, 1992

Jeffrey Bernard, *Low Life*, Duckworth, London, 1986

Jeffrey Bernard, *Reach For The Ground: The Downhill Struggle Of Jeffrey Bernard*, Duckworth, London, 1996

Oliver Bernard, *Getting Over It*, Peter Owen, London, 1992

Ian Bone, Alan Pullen & Tim Scargill (Eds), *Class War: A Decade Of Disorder*, Verso, London, 1991

Sean Bradley (Ed.), *Deliberately Thirsty*, Argyll Publishing, Argyll, 1999

Humphrey Carpenter, *That Was Satire That Was: The Satire Boom Of The 1960s*, Victor Gollancz, London, 2000

Raymond Chandler, *The Long Goodbye*, Hamish Hamilton, London, 1953

Peter Chippindale & Chris Horrie, *Stick It Up Your Punter! The Rise And Fall Of The Sun*, William Heinemann, London, 1990

Alan Clark, *The Tories: Conservatives And The Nation State 1922–1997*, Weidenfeld & Nicolson, London, 1998

John Cole, *As It Seemed To Me: Political Memoirs*, Weidenfeld & Nicolson, London, 1995

John Connor, *Comics: A Decade Of Comedy At The Assembly Rooms*, Papermac, London, 1990

William Cook, *Ha Bloody Ha: Comedians Talking*, Fourth Estate, London, 1994

Quentin Crisp, *The Naked Civil Servant*, Jonathan Cape, London, 1968

Quentin Crisp, *How To Become A Virgin*, William Collins, Glasgow, 1981

Hugh David, *Heroes, Mavericks And Bounders: The English Gentleman From Lord Curzon To James Bond*, Michael Joseph, London, 1991

Stephen Dixon & Deirdre Falvey, *Gift Of The Gag: The Explosion In Irish Comedy*, The Blackstaff Press, Belfast, 1999

Oliver Double, *Stand Up! On Being A Comedian*, Methuen, London, 1997

Daniel Farson, *Never A Normal Man: An Autobiography*, HarperCollins, London, 1997

John Fisher, *Funny Way To Be A Hero*, Frederick Muller, London, 1973

Bamber Gascoigne, *Bamber Gascoigne's Encyclopedia Of Britain*, Macmillan, Basingstoke, 1993

Trevor Griffiths, *Comedians*, Faber & Faber, London, 1976

Malcolm Hardee, *I Stole Freddie Mercury's Birthday Cake And Other Autobiographical Confessions*, Fourth Estate, London, 1996

Hattie Hayridge, *Random Abstract Memory: A Surreal Life Story*, Penguin, London, 1997

Nick Hornby, *Fever Pitch: A Fan's Life*, Victor Gollancz, London, 1992

David Housham & John Frank-Keyes, *Funny Business*, Boxtree, London, 1992

Derek Jarman, *Dancing Ledge*, Edited by Shaun Allen, Quartet, London, 1984

John Lahr, *Automatic Vaudeville: Essays On Star Turns*, William Heinemann, London, 1984

John Lahr, *Dame Edna Everage And The Rise Of Western Civilisation: Backstage With Barry Humphries*, Bloomsbury, London, 1991

John Lahr, *Light Fantastic*, Bloomsbury, London, 1996

Denis Leary, *No Cure For Cancer*, Anchor Books, Doubleday, New York, 1992

Jon E. Lewis & Penny Stempel, *Cult TV: The Essential Critical Guide*, Pavilion Books, London, 1993

Mark Lewisohn, *Radio Times Guide To TV Comedy*, BBC Worldwide, London, 1998

Graham Lord, *Just The One, The Wives And Times Of Jeffrey Bernard*, Sinclair Stevenson, London, 1992

Michael Luke, *David Tennant And The Gargoyle Years*, Weidenfeld & Nicolson, London, 1991

Patrick Marnham, *The Private Eye Story*, Andre Deutsch, London, 1982

Jon Savage, *England's Dreaming: Sex Pistols And Punk Rock*, Faber & Faber, London, 1991

Lord David Sutch with Peter Chippindale, *Life As Sutch: The Official Autobiography Of A Monster Raving Loony*, HarperCollins, London, 1991

Harry Thompson, *Peter Cook: A Biography*, Hodder & Stoughton, London, 1997

Harry Thompson, *Richard Ingrams: Lord Of The Gnomes*, William Heinemann, London, 1994

Tise Vahimagi, *British Television: An Illustrated Guide*, Oxford University Press, New York, 1994

Stephen Wagg (Ed.), *Because I Tell A Joke Or Two: Comedy, Politics And Social Difference*, Routledge, London, 1998

Roger Wilmut, *From Fringe To Flying Circus: Celebrating A Unique Generation Of Comedy 1960–1980*, Methuen, London, 1980

Roger Wilmut & Peter Rosengard, *Didn't You Kill My Mother-In-Law? The Story Of Alternative Comedy In Britain From The Comedy Store To Saturday Live*, Methuen, London, 1989

Peter York, *Style Wars*, Sidgwick & Jackson, London, 1980

Sources

Introduction

1 *Evening Standard*, 1999

Part One   The Story of the Club

Chapter One

1 *Comedy Review*, 1996
2 *Daily Telegraph*, 1999
3 Ibid.
4 *Evening Standard*, 1999
5 *Cartoons, Lampoons & Buffoons*, BBC Radio 4, 1998
6 *Guardian*, 2000
7 *City Limits*, 1988

Chapter Two

1 *Evening Standard*, 1999
2 *David Tennant and The Gargoyle Years*, 1991
3 *Didn't You Kill My Mother-In-Law?*, 1989
4 Ibid.
5 *Time Out*, 1988
6 *Radio Times Guide To TV Comedy*, 1998
7 *Mail on Sunday*, 1985
8 Ibid.
9 *Didn't You Kill My Mother-In-Law?*, op. cit.
10 *Time Out*, 1988

Chapter Three

1   *Daily Telegraph*, 1999
2   *Jewish Chronicle*, 1986
3   *Deliberately Thirsty*, 1999
4   *History of Alternative Comedy*, BBC2, 1999
5   *Didn't You Kill My Mother-In-Law?, op. cit.*
6   *History of Alternative Comedy, op. cit.*
7   *City Limits*, 1989
8   *Time Out*, 1988
9   *Evening Standard*, 1999
10 *History of Alternative Comedy, op. cit.*
11 *The Scotsman*, 1965
12 *Didn't You Kill My Mother-In-Law?, op. cit.*
13 *Time Out*, 1999

Chapter Four

1   *City Limits*, 1989
2   *History of Alternative Comedy, op. cit.*
3   *I Stole Freddie Mercury's Birthday Cake*, 1996
4   *Independent*, 1993
5   *Didn't You Kill My Mother-In-Law?, op. cit.*
6   Ibid.
7   *I Stole Freddie Mercury's Birthday Cake, op. cit.*
8   *Evening Standard*, 1999
9   *The Long Goodbye*, 1953
10 *Evening Standard*, 1999
11 *The Times*, 1995
12 *Evening Standard*, 1999
13 Ibid.
14 *New Musical Express*, 1985
15 *Didn't You Kill My Mother-In-Law?, op. cit.*
16 *History of Alternative Comedy, op. cit.*
17 *City Limits*, 1983
18 Ibid.
19 *Evening Standard*, 1995
20 *History of Alternative Comedy, op. cit.*
21 *Evening Standard*, 1993
22 *History of Alternative Comedy, op. cit.*
23 *Evening Standard*, 1984
24 *Didn't You Kill My Mother-In-Law?, op. cit.*
25 Ibid.
26 Ibid.
27 *History of Alternative Comedy*, BBC2, 1999
28 Ibid.
29 Ibid.
30 *Deliberately Thirsty*, 1999

Chapter Five

1 *Dancing Ledge*, 1984
2 *Today*, 1986
3 *Time Out*, 1999
4 *History of Alternative Comedy, op. cit.*
5 *Time Out*, 1993
6 *Comics*, 1990
7 *Radio Times*, 1986
8 *The Times*, 1985
9 *Independent*, 1993

Chapter Six

1 *Time Out*, 1999

Part Two   Nights Out at The Store

The Cutting Edge

1 *The Times*, 1991
2 *Time Out*, 1991

Jack Dee

1 *Evening Standard*, 1999

The Comedy Store Players

1 *Ten Years of The Comedy Store Players*, BBC Radio 4, 1995
2 *Ibid.*
3 *Ibid.*
4 *Ibid.*
5 *Time Out*, 1995
6 *Ten Years of The Comedy Store Players, op. cit.*
7 *Ibid.*

Comediennes

1 *Guardian*, 1999
2 *Ibid.*
3 *Ibid.*

Punters

1 *Random Abstract Memory*, 1997

The Management

1 *Guardian*, 1999

Luck of the Irish

1 *Gift Of The Gag*, 1999
2 *Ri Ra*, 1998
3 *Gift Of The Gag, op. cit.*

Americans

1 *Evening Standard*, 1999

In The House

1 *Vogue*, 1990
2 Ibid.

Punt & Dennis

1 *Ha Bloody Ha*, 1994

Television

1 *Scotland on Sunday*, 1994
2 *Didn't You Kill My Mother-In-Law?, op. cit.*
3 Ibid.

Happy Birthday

1 *Time Out*, 1992

Manchester

1 *Manchester Evening News*, 2000

From Allen to Baddiel and Back Again

1 *Big Issue*, 1993

The End

1 *Deliberately Thirsty*, 1999

Picture Credits

All reasonable effort has been made to trace the full copyright information for these photographs. Any relevant information on missing copyright data gratefully received. Numbers in brackets refer to page references.

(vi) Comedy Store Poster © The Comedy Store; (x) Alexei Sayle © Christopher Cormack; (xi) Ben Elton © Ian Dobbie; (xii) Richard Blackwood © UPPA; (xiii) Nick Hancock © The Comedy Store; (xiv) Jo Brand © UPPA; (6) Bouncers opening the doors for the night © Jez Coulson (8) Queues outside the Piccadilly Store © Jez Coulson/Insight; (12) Robin Williams © The Comedy Store; (14) Box office © Kev Dutton/Insight; (21) Peter Rosengard © Christopher Cormack, Don Ward © Christopher Cormack; (24) The Gargoyle Club © Christopher Cormack; (25) Barmaid at the Soho Store © Christopher Cormack; (30) Alexei Sayle © Christopher Cormack; (34) Clive Anderson © Ian Dobbie; (41) Arnold Brown © Christopher Cormack; (46) Andy de la Tour © Christopher Cormack; Jim Barclay © Christopher Cormack; (51) Rik Mayall and Adrian Edmondson © Christopher Cormack; (54) French & Saunders © Ian Dobbie; (56) Clive Anderson © Christopher Cormack; (61) Keith Allen © Christopher Cormack; (65)Tony Allen © Christopher Cormack; (68) Ben Elton © UPPA; (74) Chris Barrie © Ian Dobbie; (77) Peter Richardson © UPPA; (80) Rik Mayall © Christopher Cormack; (82) Mark Thomas © Jez Coulson/Insight; (86) Queues © Jez Coulson/Insight; (90) Paul Merton with Josie Lawrence © The Comedy Store; (91) Owen O'Neill *et al* © Jez Coulson/Insight; (93) Kevin Day with Mark Thomas © Jez Coulson/Insight; (95) Kim Kinnie © Jez Coulson/Insight; (97) Arthur

Smith © The Comedy Store; (100) Julian Clary © Peter Mountain; (109) Queues © Jez Coulson/Insight; (111) Comics including Rhona Cameron © Jez Coulson/Insight; (118) The original Cutting Edge team © Dominic Dibbs; (124) Steve Gribbin © Kev Dutton/Insight; (126) The Cutting Edge © The Comedy Store; (130) Jack Dee © The Comedy Store (136) The Comedy Store Players © Kev Dutton/Insight; (139) The founders of the Comedy Store Players © Ian Dobbie; (141) Richard Vranch © Kev Dutton/Insight; (142) The current core team © The Comedy Store; (148) Eddie Izzard © Jez Coulson/Insight; (154) Mandy Knight © International Artists; (158) Jo Brand © The Comedy Store; (160) Donna McPhail © Amanda Searle; (162) Jenny Éclair © UPPA; (164) Bill Bailey © The Comedy Store; (170) Tim Clark © Jez Coulson/Insight; (171) Tim Clark backstage © Jez Coulson/Insight; (177) Mark Lamarr © Jez Coulson/Insight; (178) Sean Lock © UPPA; (185) Daniel Kitson © Daniel Kitson; (190) Hattie Hayridge and Alan Davies © The Comedy Store; (201) Late-night audience © Jez Coulson/Insight; (210) At the box office © Jez Coulson/Insight; (212) Mark Skeete © Jez Coulson/Insight; (215) Stan Nelson © Jez Coulson/Insight; (218) Don Ward © Jez Coulson/Insight; (220) Jeff Green © DGPR; (223) Eccentric act... © Christopher Cormack; (224) Paul Zenon © DGPR; (236) Owen O'Neill © Jez Coulson/Insight; (239) Ed Byrne © The Comedy Store; (242) Phill Jupitus © UPPA; (249) Rich Hall © Off the Kerb; (255) Greg Proops © Kev Dutton/Insight; (265) Gina Yashere © Jez Coulson/Insight; (267) Richard Blackwood © UPPA; (276) Hancock and Mullarkey © The Comedy Store; (279) The Mary Whitehouse Experience © UPPA: (288) The Comic Strip © UPPA; (294) The Young Ones © BBC; (301) Jerry Sadowitz © The Comedy Store: (306) Jim Tavare © UPPA; (309) Paul Tonkinson *et al* © The Comedy Store; (310) Lee Evans © The Comedy Store: (318) The new Manchester Store © The Comedy Store: (324) Black & Baddiel © The Comedy Store.

'And yet it is every traveller's conceit that no one will see what he has seen: his trip displaces the landscape and his version of events is all that matters. He is certainly kidding himself in this, but if he didn't kid himself a little he would never go anywhere.'

Paul Theroux, **The Kingdom By The Sea**